DEPT.H™

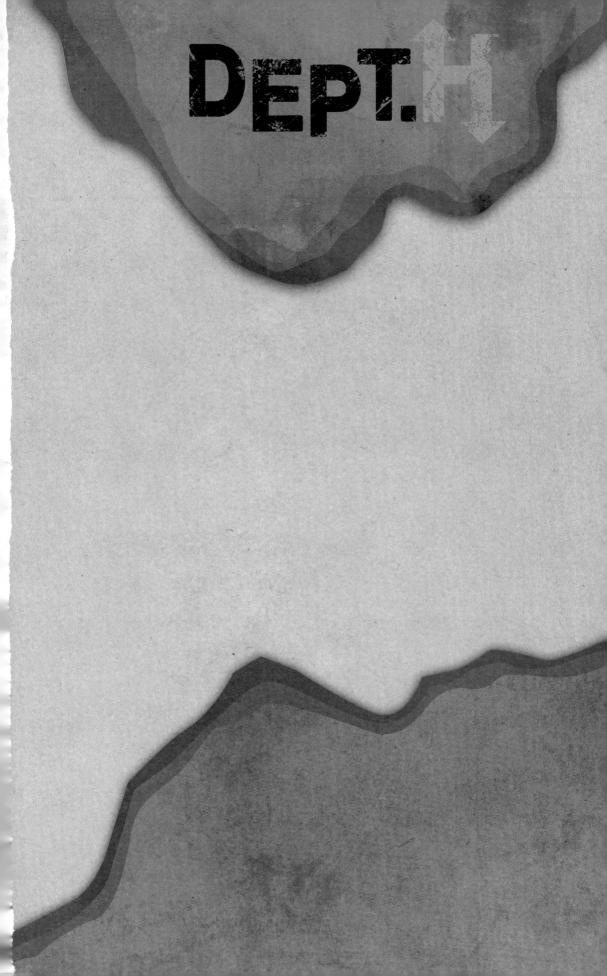

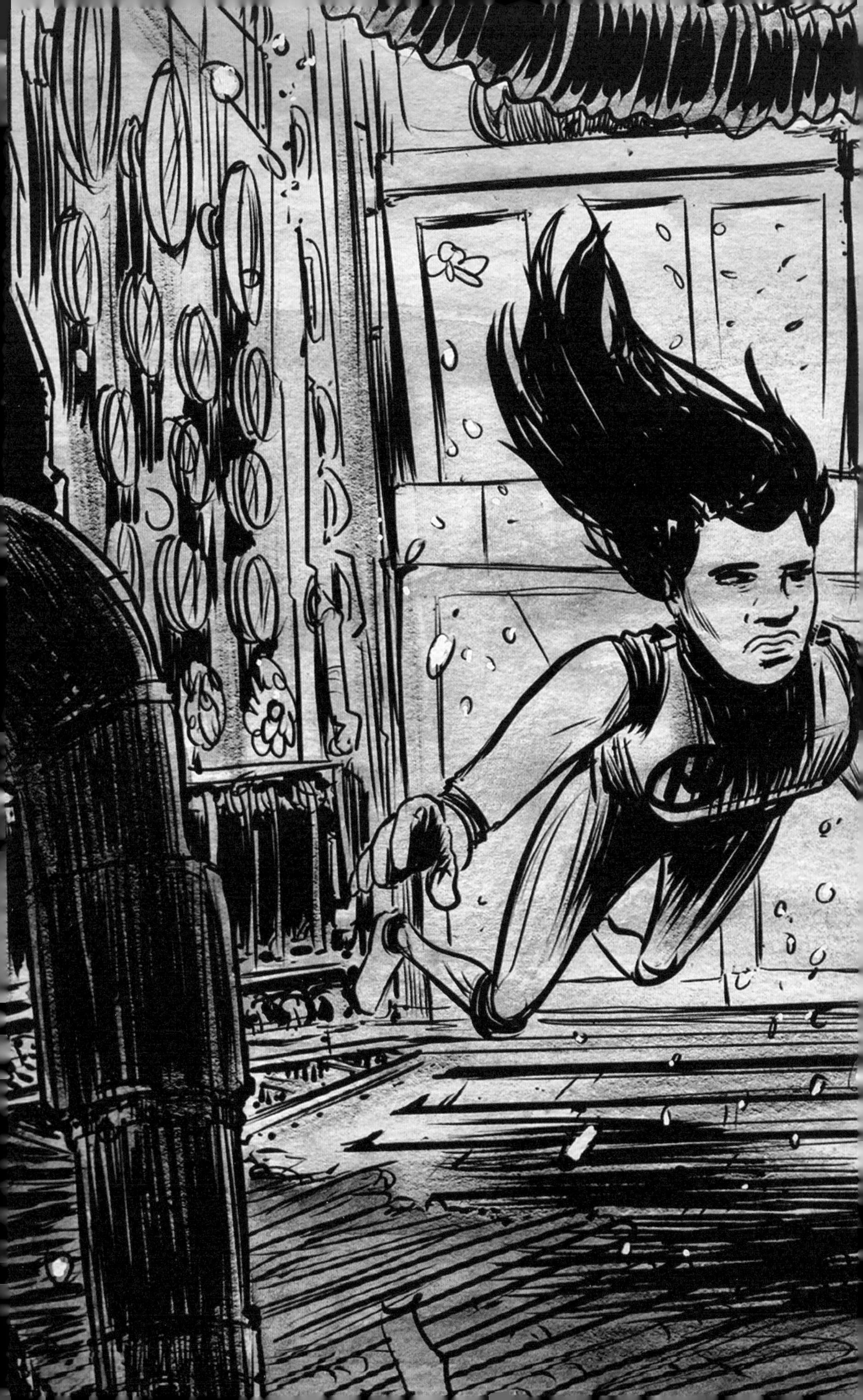

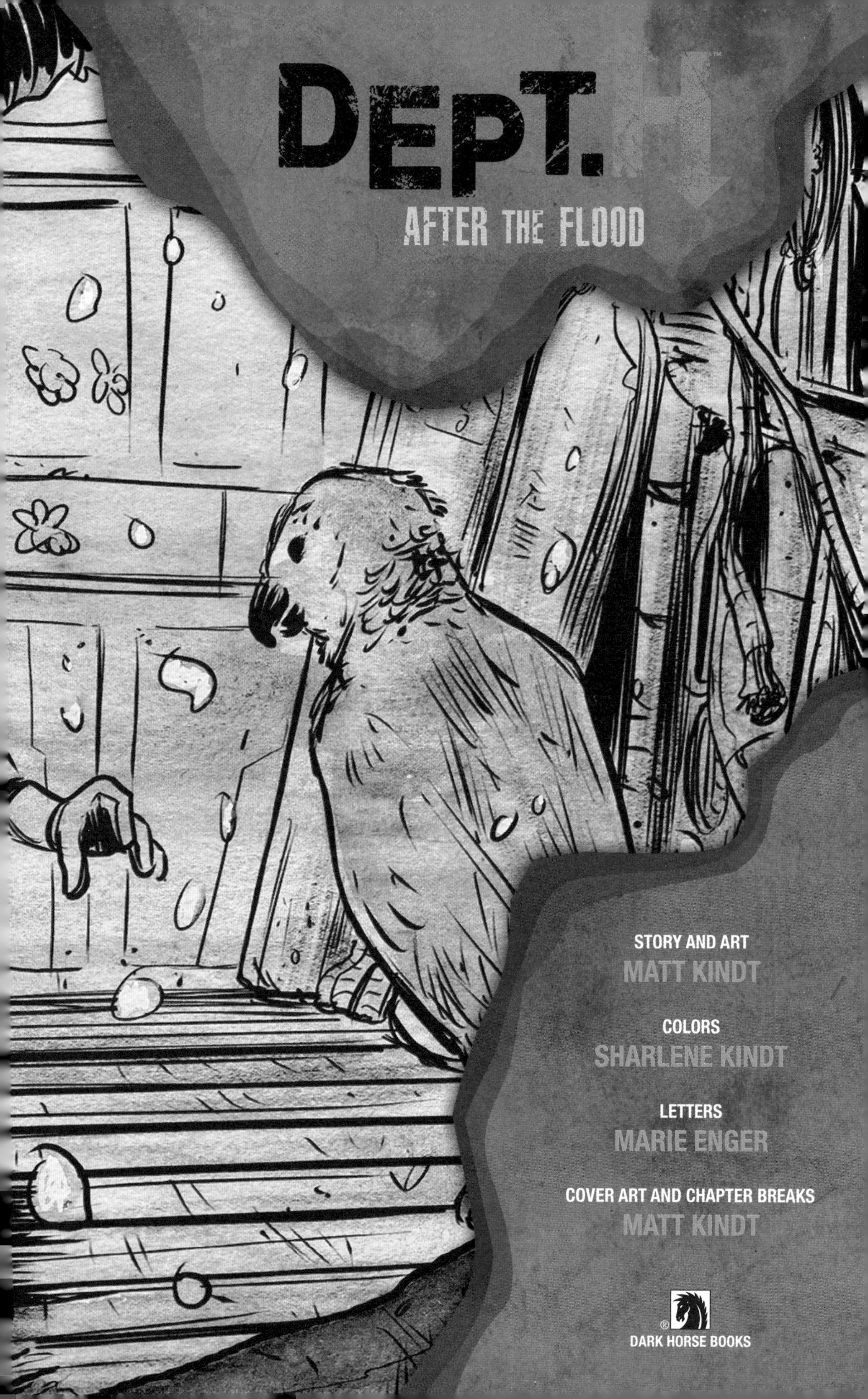

DEPT. H

AFTER THE FLOOD

STORY AND ART
MATT KINDT

COLORS
SHARLENE KINDT

LETTERS
MARIE ENGER

COVER ART AND CHAPTER BREAKS
MATT KINDT

DARK HORSE BOOKS

PRESIDENT AND PUBLISHER
MIKE RICHARDSON

EDITOR
DANIEL CHABON

ASSISTANT EDITOR
CARDNER CLARK

DESIGNER
ETHAN KIMBERLING

DIGITAL ART TECHNICIAN
ALLYSON HALLER

Neil Hankerson, Executive Vice President • Tom Weddle, Chief Financial Officer
Randy Stradley, Vice President of Publishing • Michael Martens, Vice President
of Book Trade Sales • Matt Parkinson, Vice President of Marketing • David
Scroggy, Vice President of Product Development • Dale LaFountain, Vice Pres-
ident of Information Technology • Cara Niece, Vice President of Production and
Scheduling • Nick McWhorter, Vice President of Media Licensing • Ken Lizzi,
General Counsel • Dave Marshall, Editor in Chief • Davey Estrada, Editorial
Director • Scott Allie, Executive Senior Editor • Chris Warner, Senior Books
Editor • Cary Grazzini, Director of Specialty Projects • Lia Ribacchi, Art Direc-
tor • Vanessa Todd, Director of Print Purchasing • Matt Dryer, Director of Dig-
ital Art and Prepress • Mark Bernardi, Director of Digital Publishing • Sarah
Robertson, Director of Product Sales • Michael Gombos, Director of Interna-
tional Publishing and Licensing

Published by Dark Horse Books
A division of Dark Horse Comics, Inc.
10956 SE Main Street
Milwaukie, OR 97222

First edition: July 2017
ISBN 978-1-61655-990-8

10 9 8 7 6 5 4 3 2 1
Printed in China

International Licensing: (503) 905-2377
Comic Shop Locator Service: (888) 266-4226

This volume collects the Dark Horse Comics series *Dept. H* issues #7–#12.

Names: Kindt, Matt, author, artist. i Kindt, Sharlene, colorist. l Enger,
   Marie, letterer.
Title: Dept. H / story and art, Matt Kindt ; colors, Sharlene Kindt ;
   letters, Marie Enger ; cover art and chapter breaks Matt Kindt.
Description: First edition. l Milwaukie, OR : Dark Horse Books, 2017-
   Contents: v. 2. After the flood.
Identifiers: LCCN 2016034697 l ISBN 9781616559908 (v. 2 : hardback)
Subjects: LCSH: Comic books, strips, etc. l BISAC: COMICS & GRAPHIC NOVELS /
   Crime & Mystery.
Classification: LCC PN6727.K54 D47 2017 l DDC 741.5/973--dc23
LC record available at https://lccn.loc.gov/2016034697

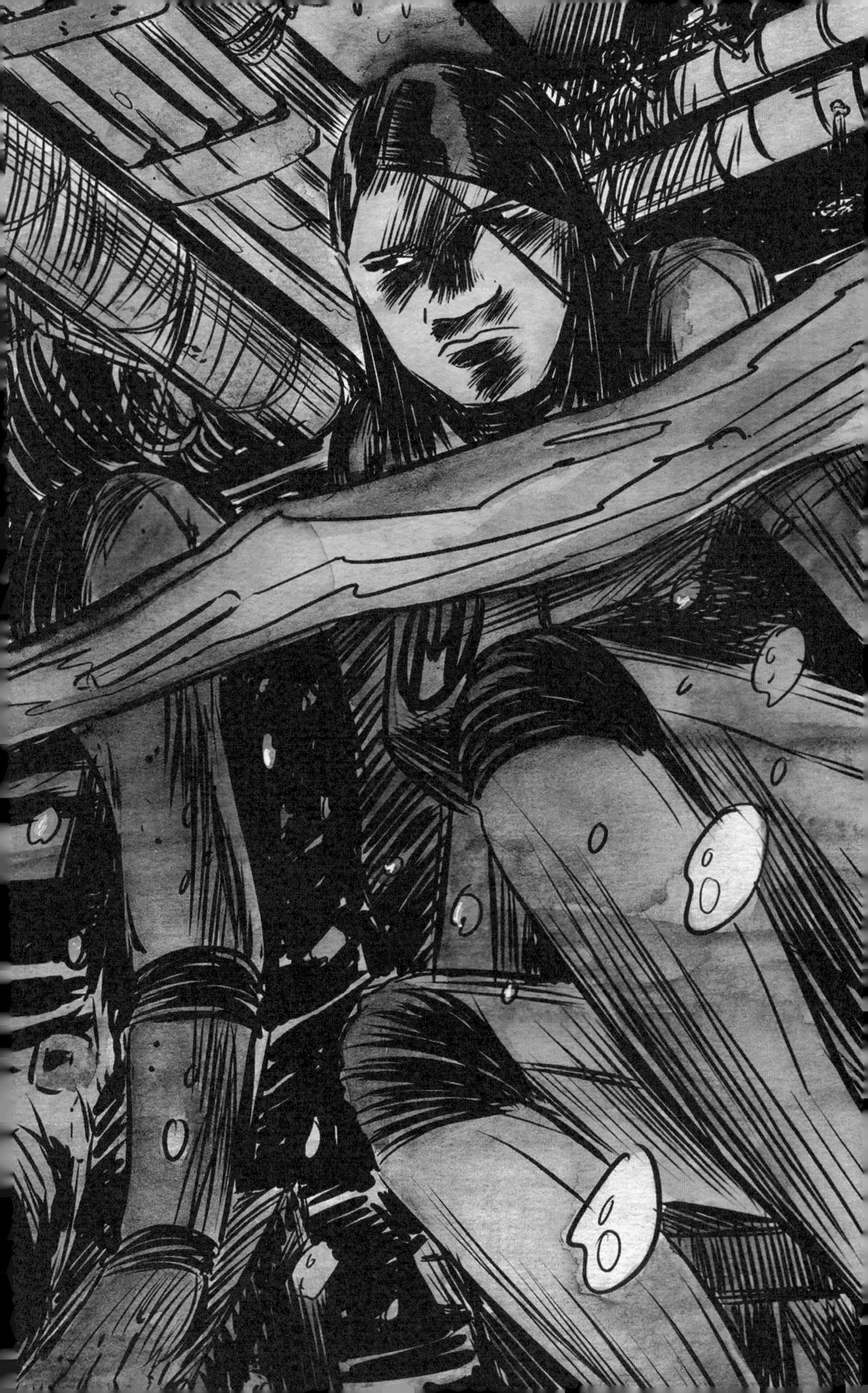

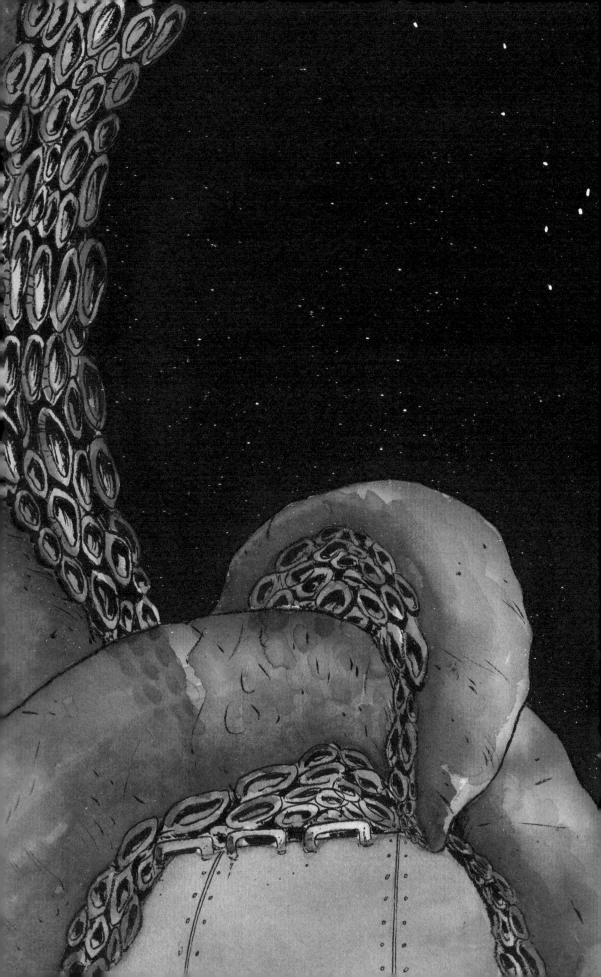

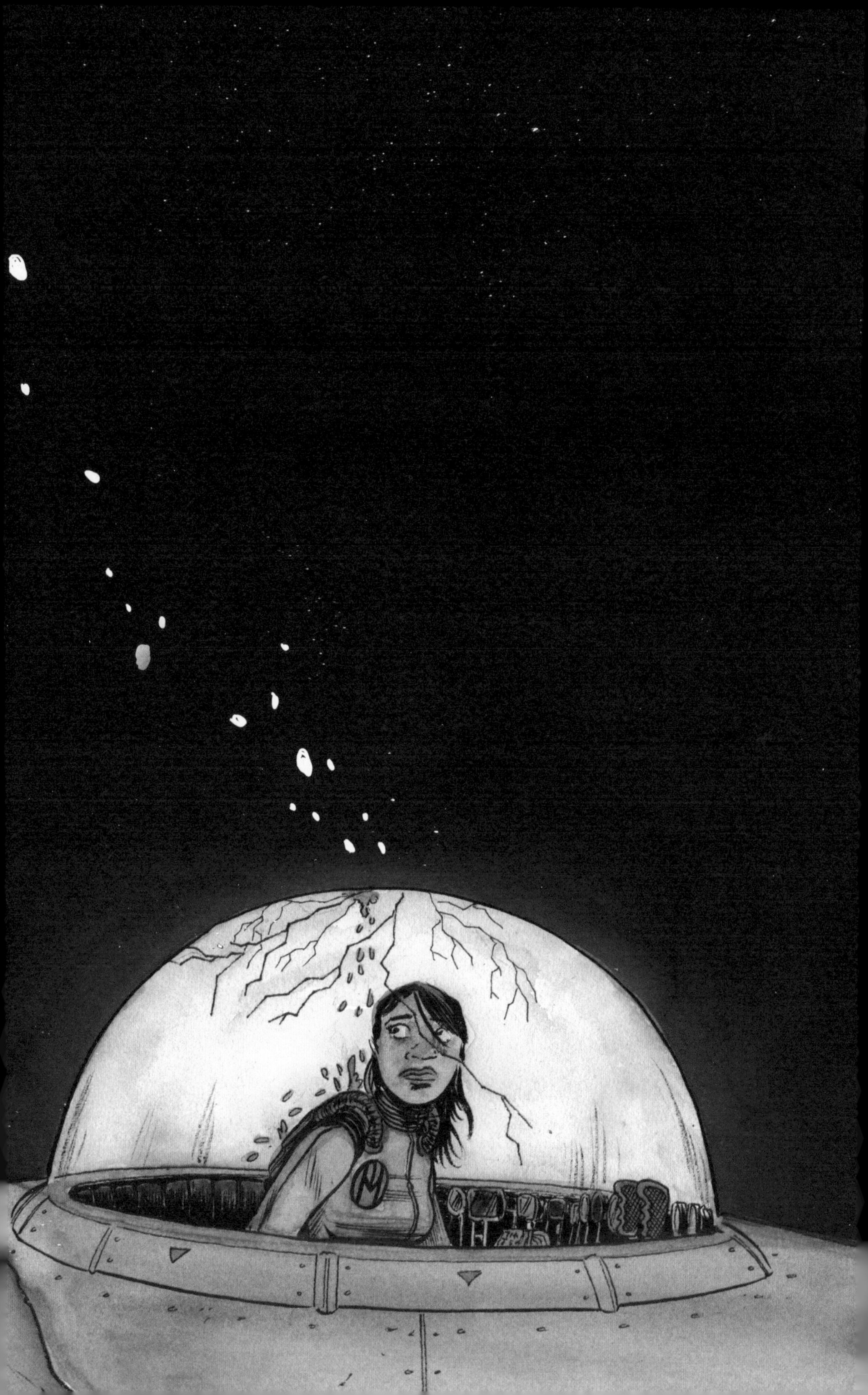

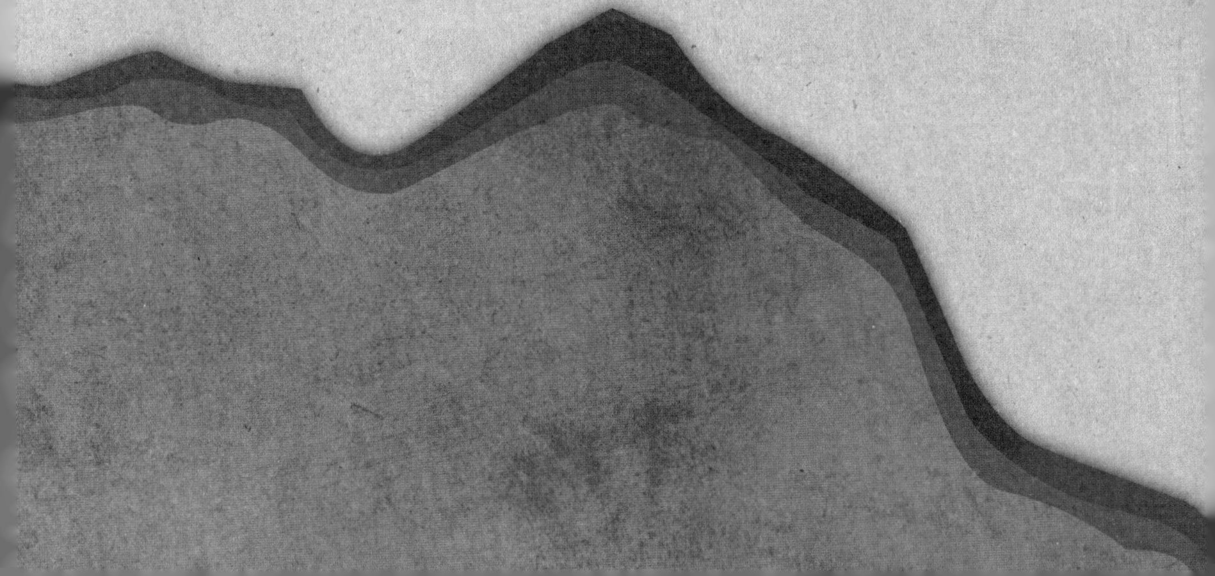

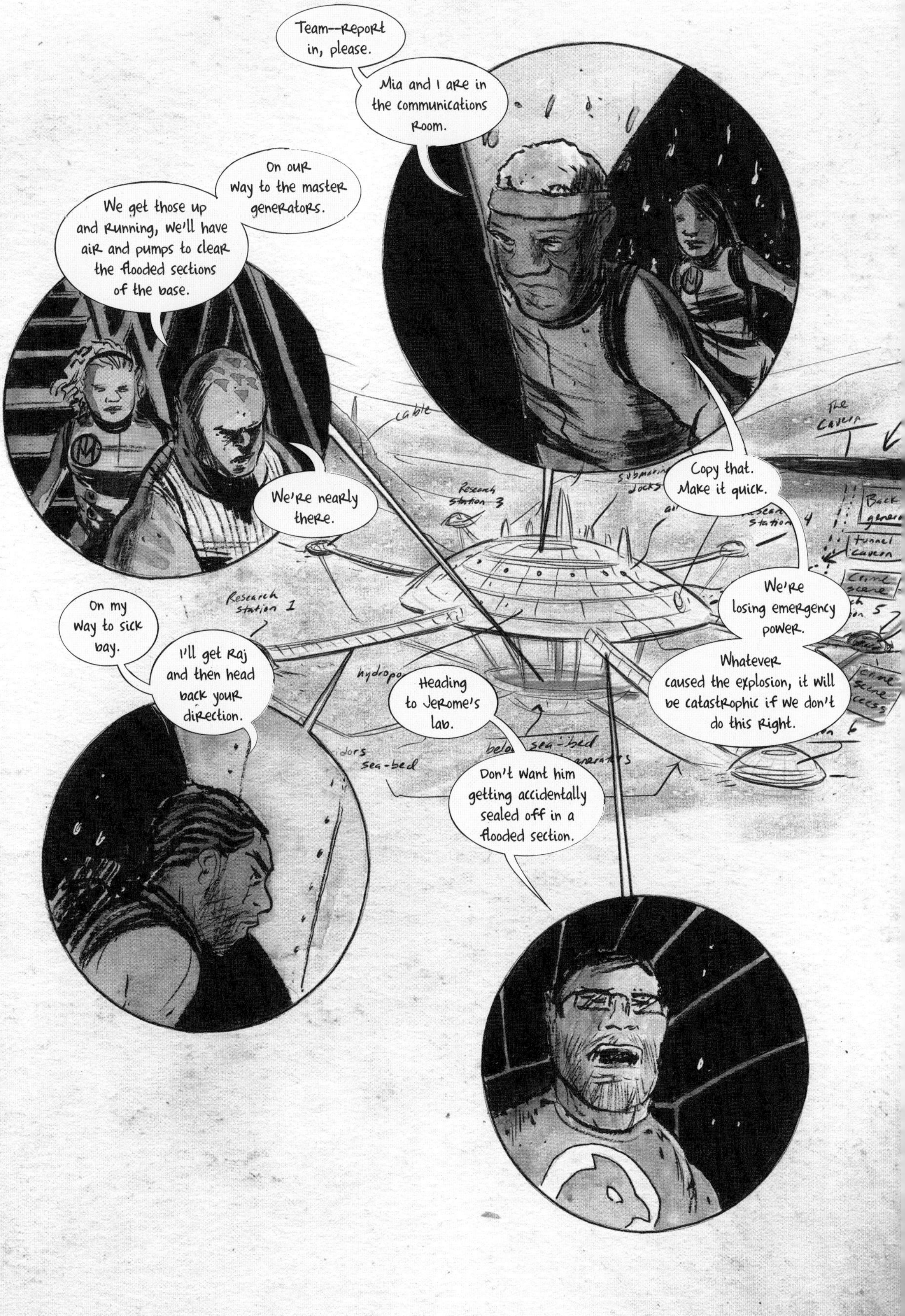

Team--Report in, please.
Mia and I are in the communications Room.
On our way to the master generators.
We get those up and Running, we'll have air and pumps to clear the flooded sections of the base.
We're nearly there.
Copy that. Make it quick.
We're losing emergency power.
Whatever caused the explosion, it will be catastrophic if we don't do this Right.
On my way to sick bay.
I'll get Raj and then head back your direction.
Heading to Jerome's lab.
Don't want him getting accidentally sealed off in a flooded section.

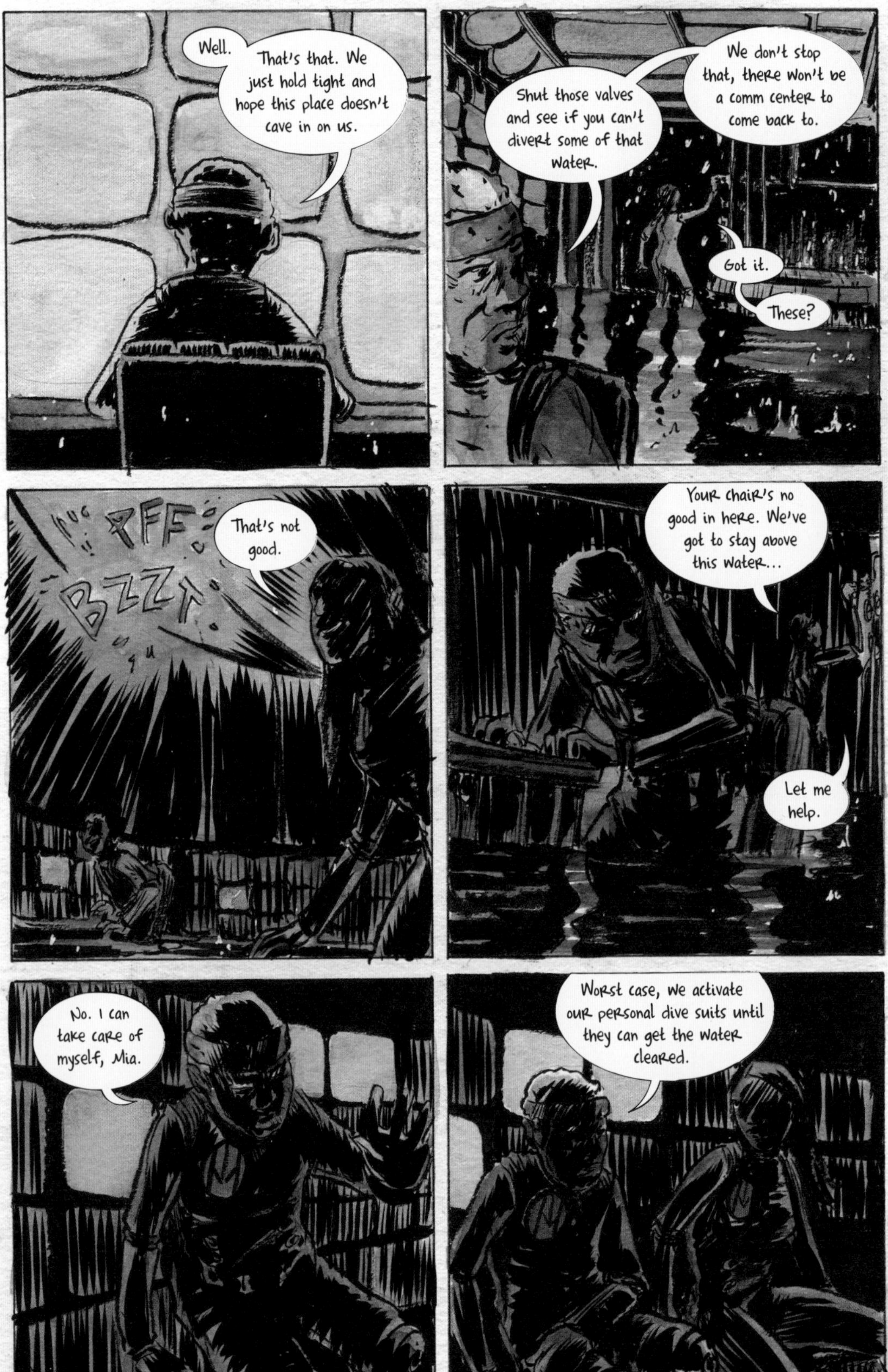
Well.
That's that. We just hold tight and hope this place doesn't cave in on us.
Shut those valves and see if you can't divert some of that water.
We don't stop that, there won't be a comm center to come back to.
Got it.
These?
PFF
BZZT
That's not good.
Your chair's no good in here. We've got to stay above this water...
Let me help.
No. I can take care of myself, Mia.
Worst case, we activate our personal dive suits until they can get the water cleared.

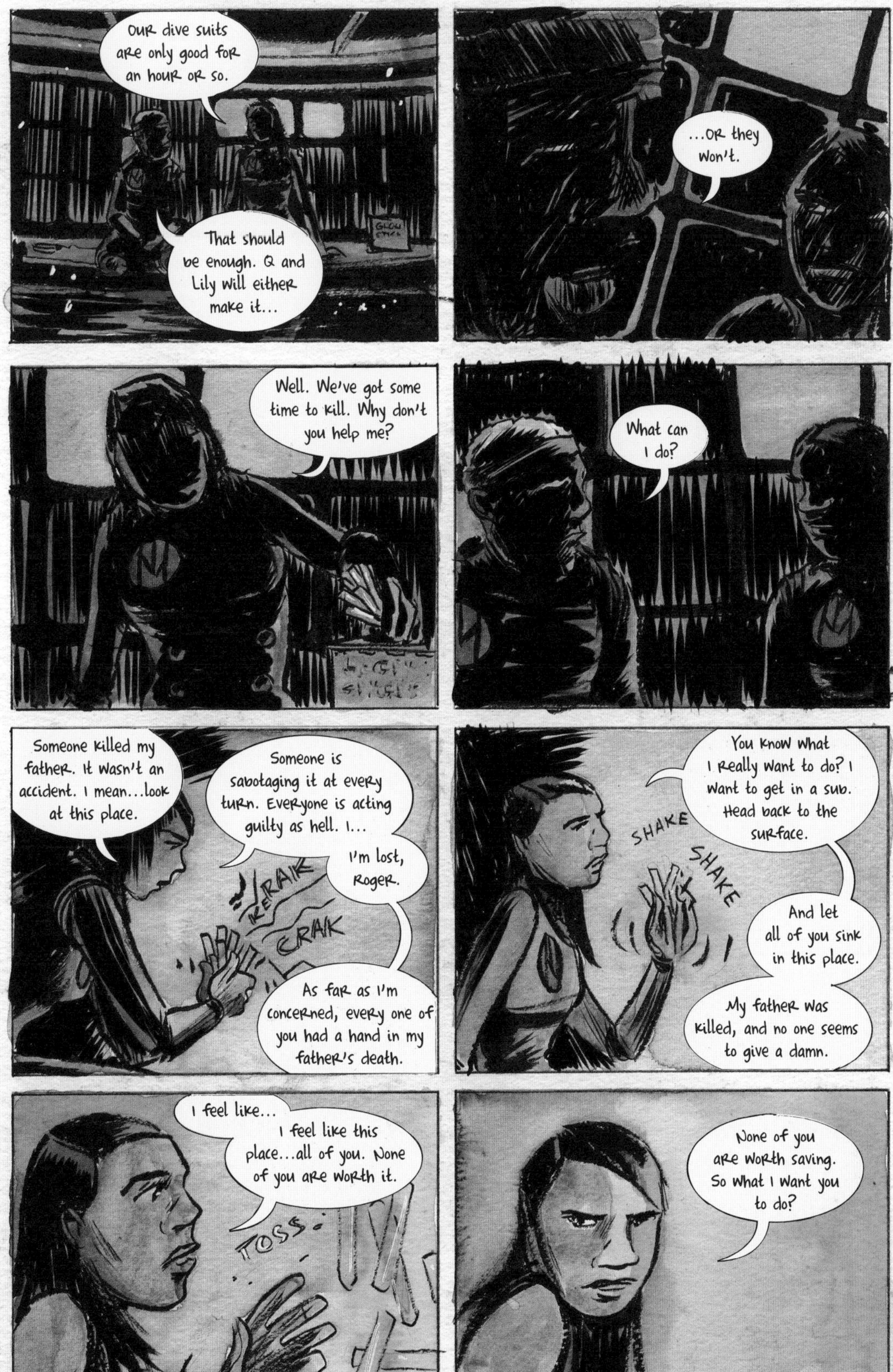
Our dive suits are only good for an hour or so.
That should be enough. Q and Lily will either make it...
...or they won't.
Well. We've got some time to kill. Why don't you help me?
What can I do?
Someone killed my father. It wasn't an accident. I mean...look at this place.
Someone is sabotaging it at every turn. Everyone is acting guilty as hell. I...
I'm lost, Roger.
KRAK
CRAK
As far as I'm concerned, every one of you had a hand in my father's death.
You know what I really want to do? I want to get in a sub. Head back to the surface.
SHAKE
SHAKE
And let all of you sink in this place.
My father was killed, and no one seems to give a damn.
I feel like...
I feel like this place...all of you. None of you are worth it.
TOSS
None of you are worth saving. So what I want you to do?

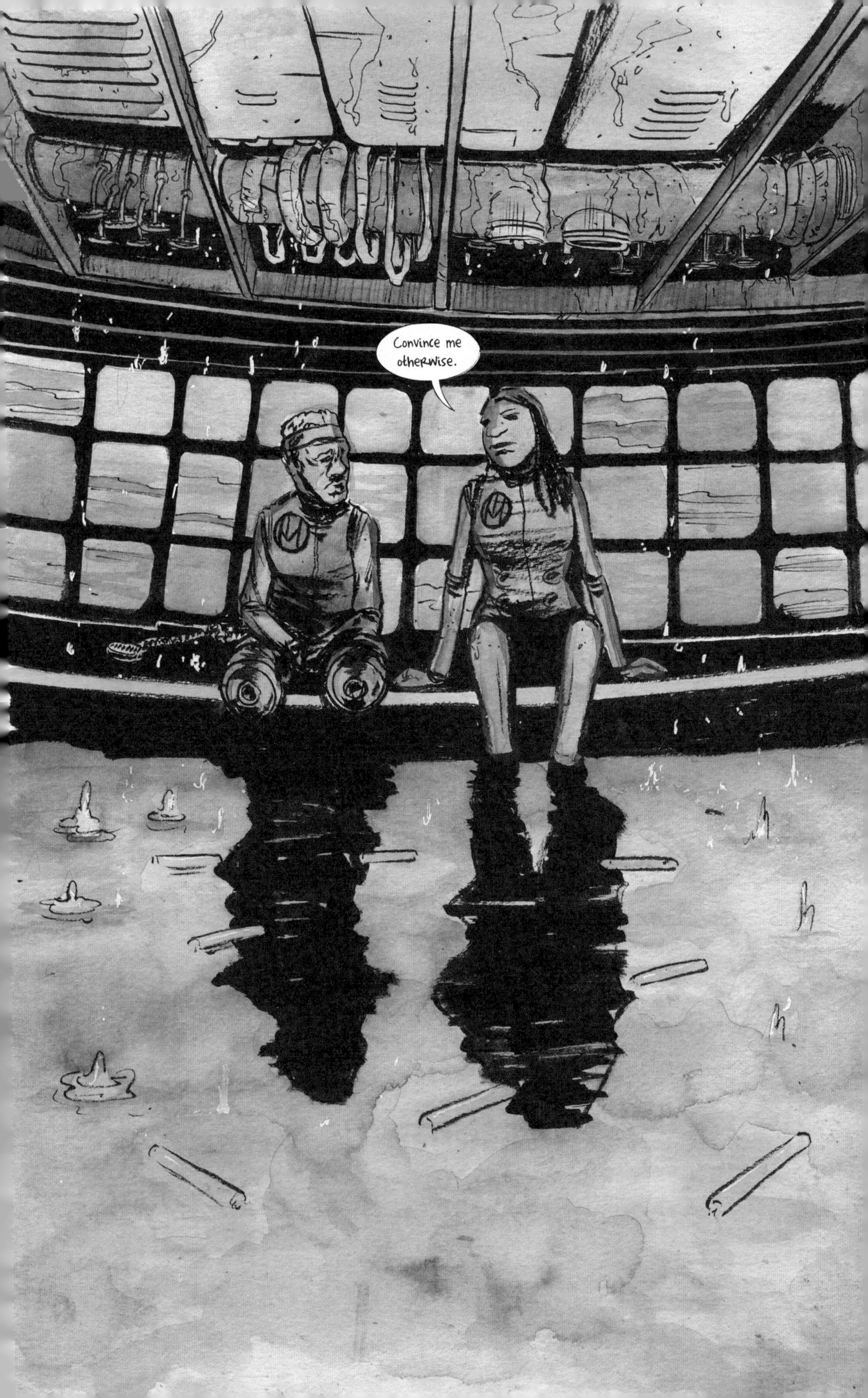
Convince me otherwise.

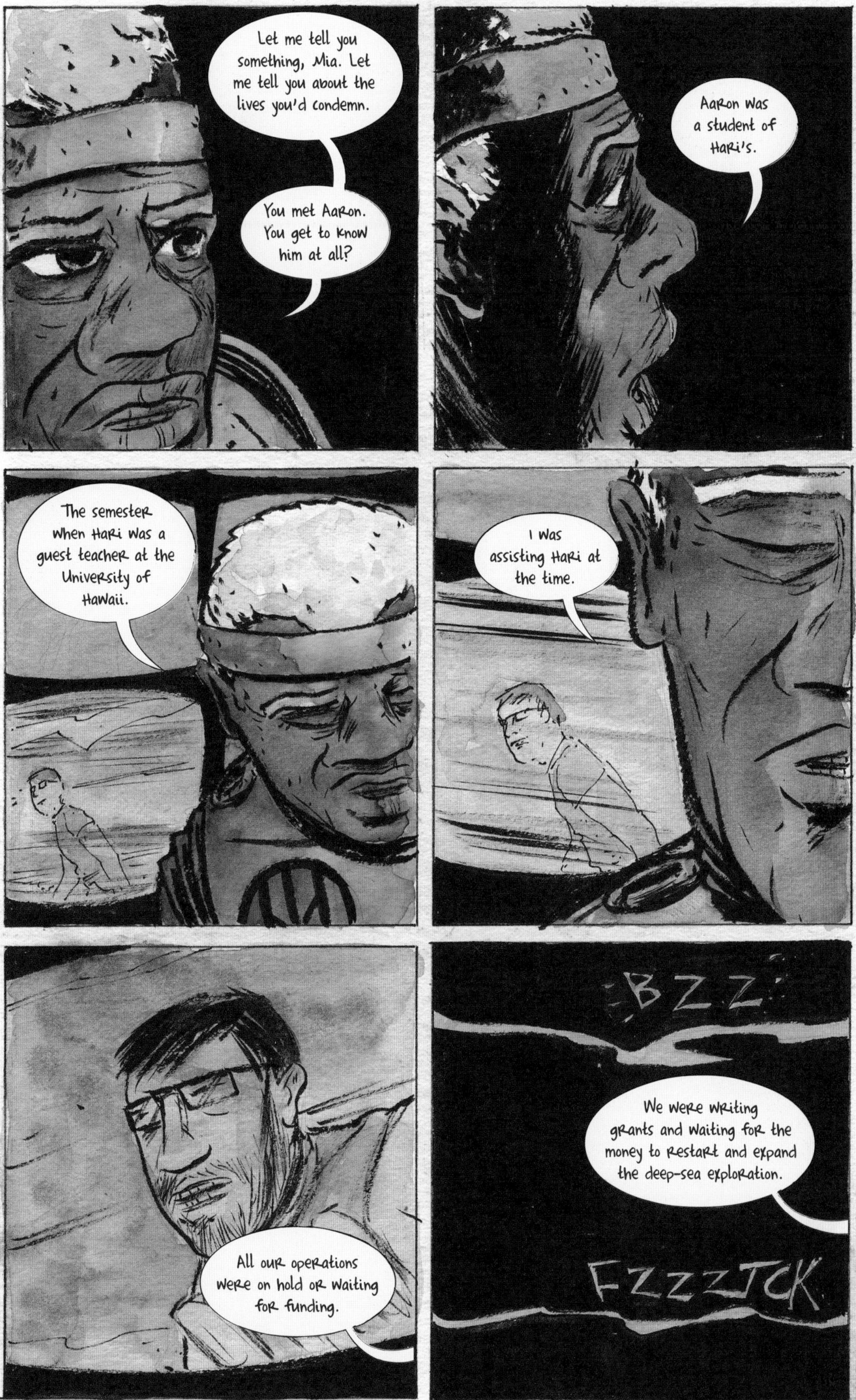
Let me tell you something, Mia. Let me tell you about the lives you'd condemn.
You met Aaron. You get to know him at all?
Aaron was a student of Hari's.
The semester when Hari was a guest teacher at the University of Hawaii.
I was assisting Hari at the time.
All our operations were on hold or waiting for funding.
BZZ
We were writing grants and waiting for the money to restart and expand the deep-sea exploration.
FZZZJCK

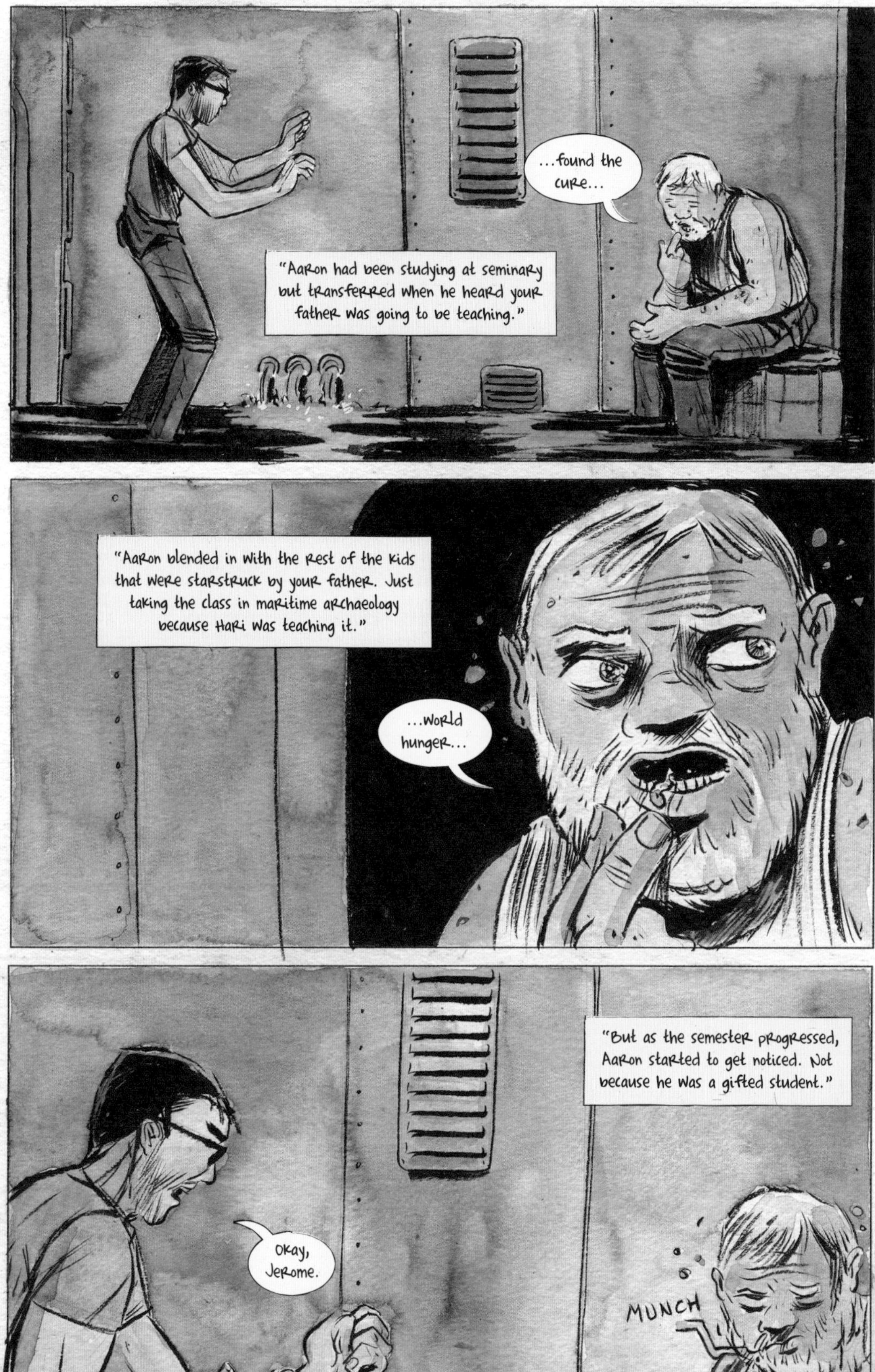
"Aaron had been studying at seminary but transferred when he heard your father was going to be teaching."
...found the cure...
"Aaron blended in with the rest of the kids that were starstruck by your father. Just taking the class in maritime archaeology because Hari was teaching it."
...world hunger...
Okay, Jerome.
"But as the semester progressed, Aaron started to get noticed. Not because he was a gifted student."
MUNCH

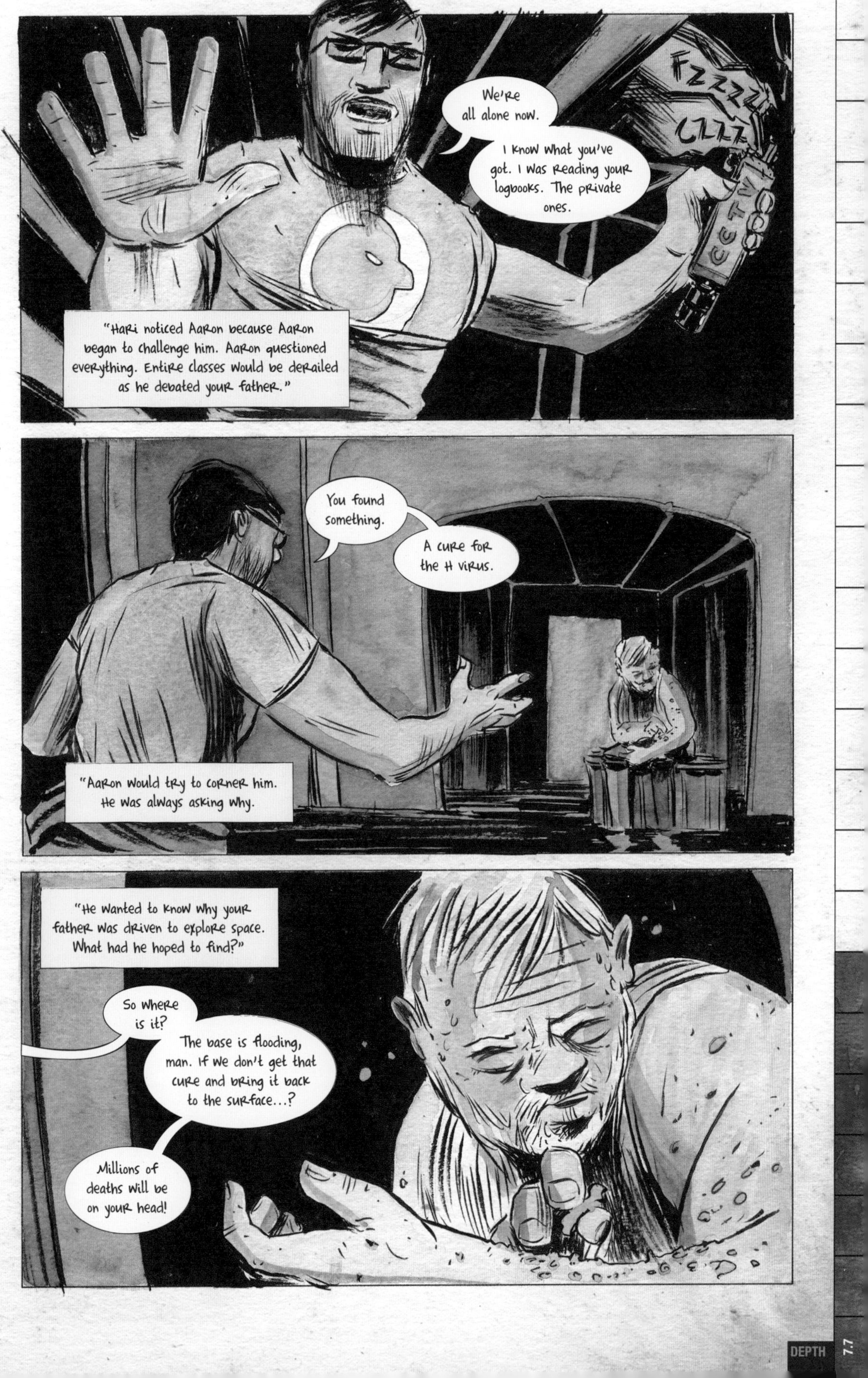
Fzzzz
czzz
We're all alone now.
I know what you've got. I was reading your logbooks. The private ones.
"Hari noticed Aaron because Aaron began to challenge him. Aaron questioned everything. Entire classes would be derailed as he debated your father."
You found something.
A cure for the H virus.
"Aaron would try to corner him. He was always asking why.
"He wanted to know why your father was driven to explore space. What had he hoped to find?"
So where is it?
The base is flooding, man. If we don't get that cure and bring it back to the surface...?
Millions of deaths will be on your head!

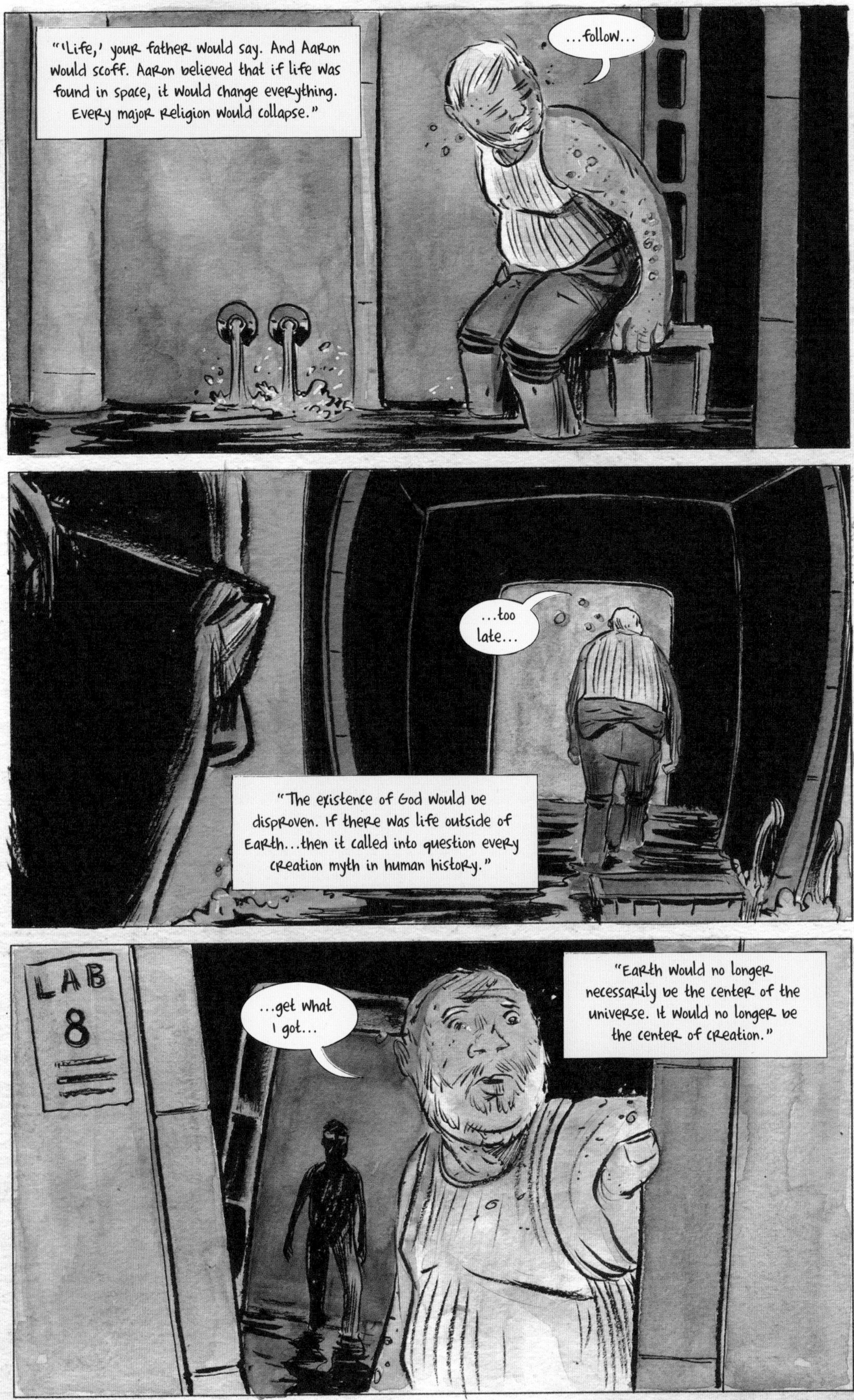
"'Life,' your father would say. And Aaron would scoff. Aaron believed that if life was found in space, it would change everything. Every major religion would collapse."
...follow...
...too late...
"The existence of God would be disproven. If there was life outside of Earth...then it called into question every creation myth in human history."
LAB 8
...get what I got...
"Earth would no longer necessarily be the center of the universe. It would no longer be the center of creation."

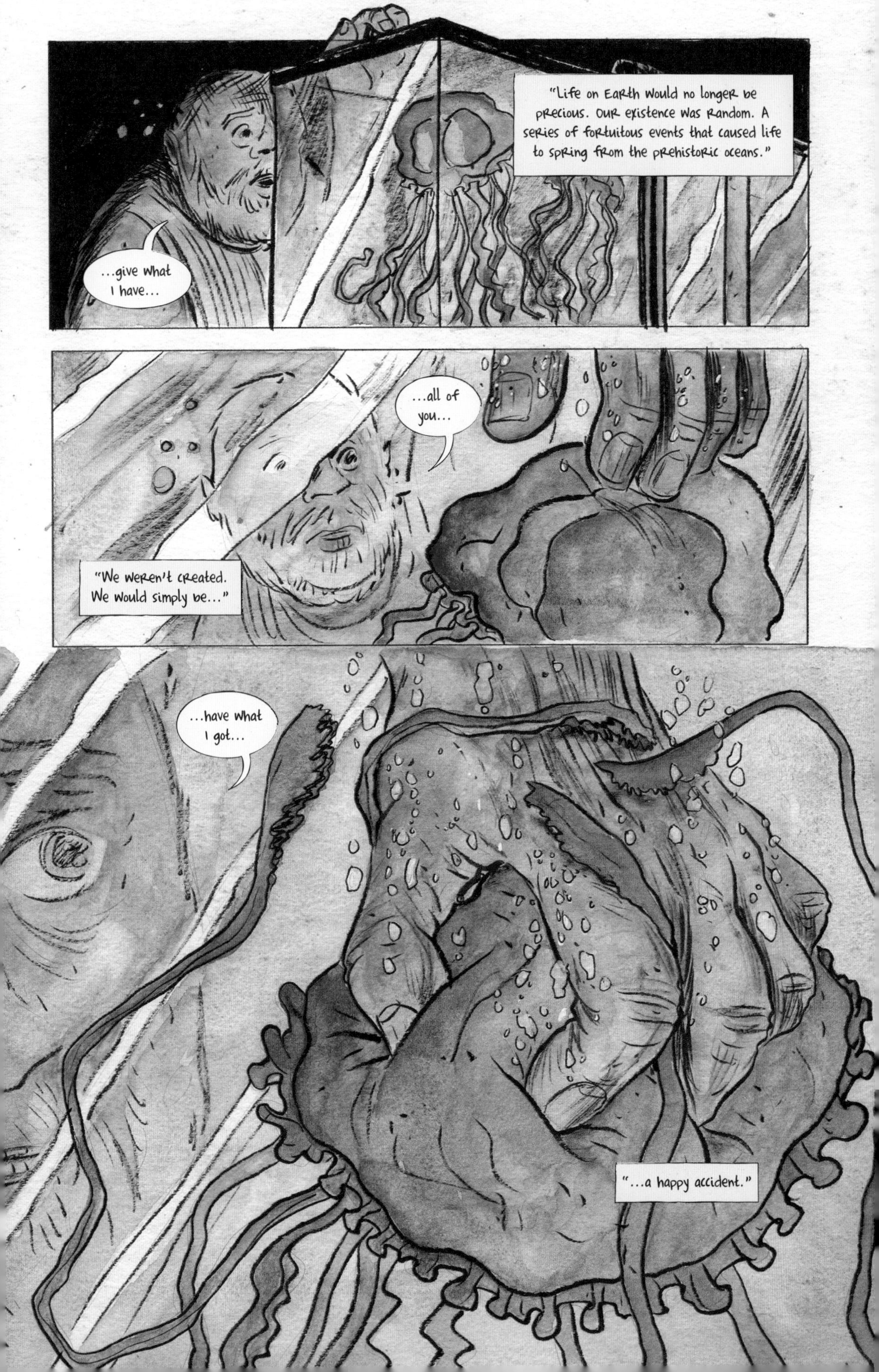
"Life on Earth would no longer be precious. Our existence was random. A series of fortuitous events that caused life to spring from the prehistoric oceans."
...give what I have...
...all of you...
"We weren't created. We would simply be..."
...have what I got...
"...a happy accident."

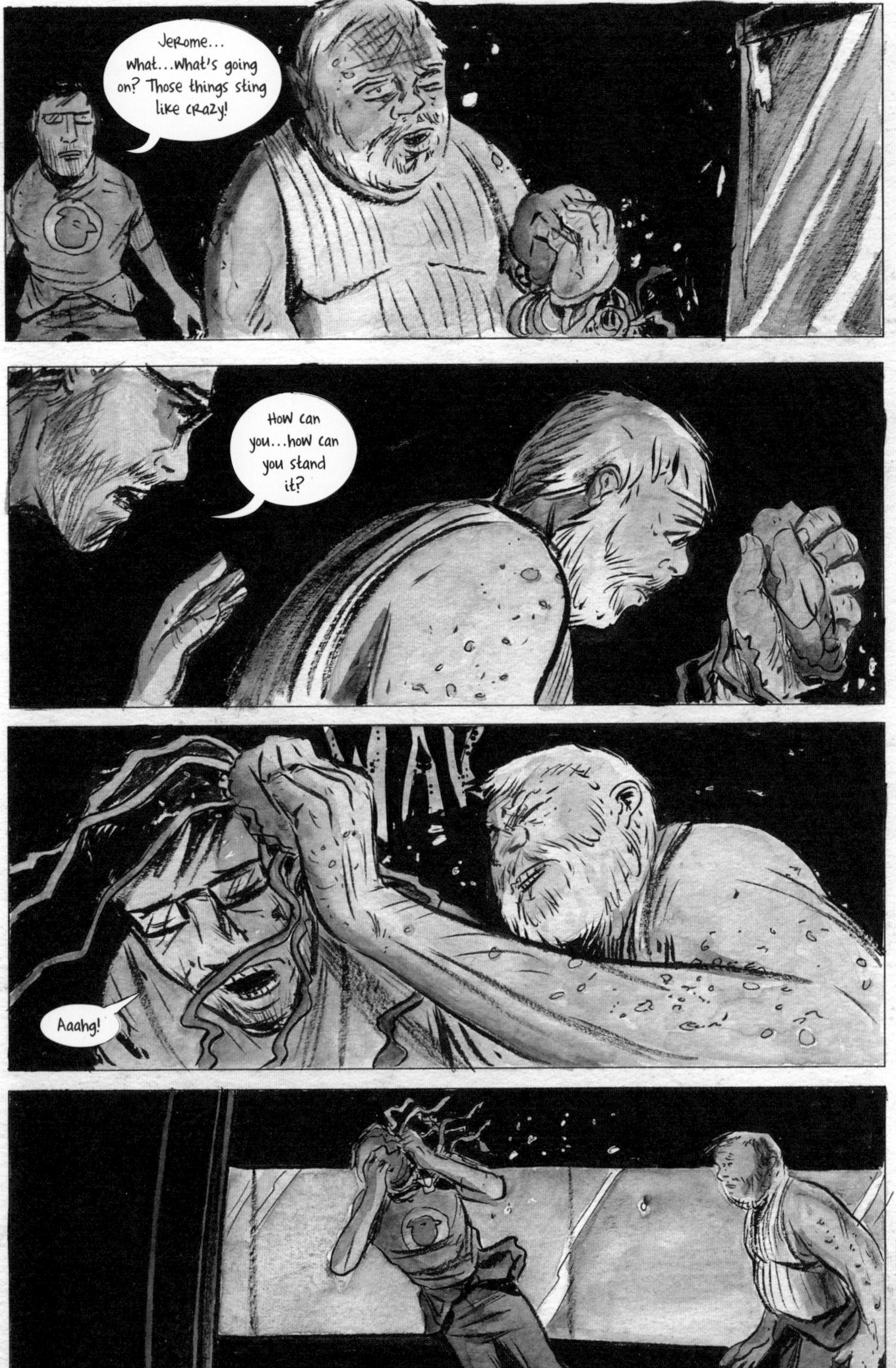
Jerome... what...what's going on? Those things sting like crazy!
How can you...how can you stand it?
Aaahg!

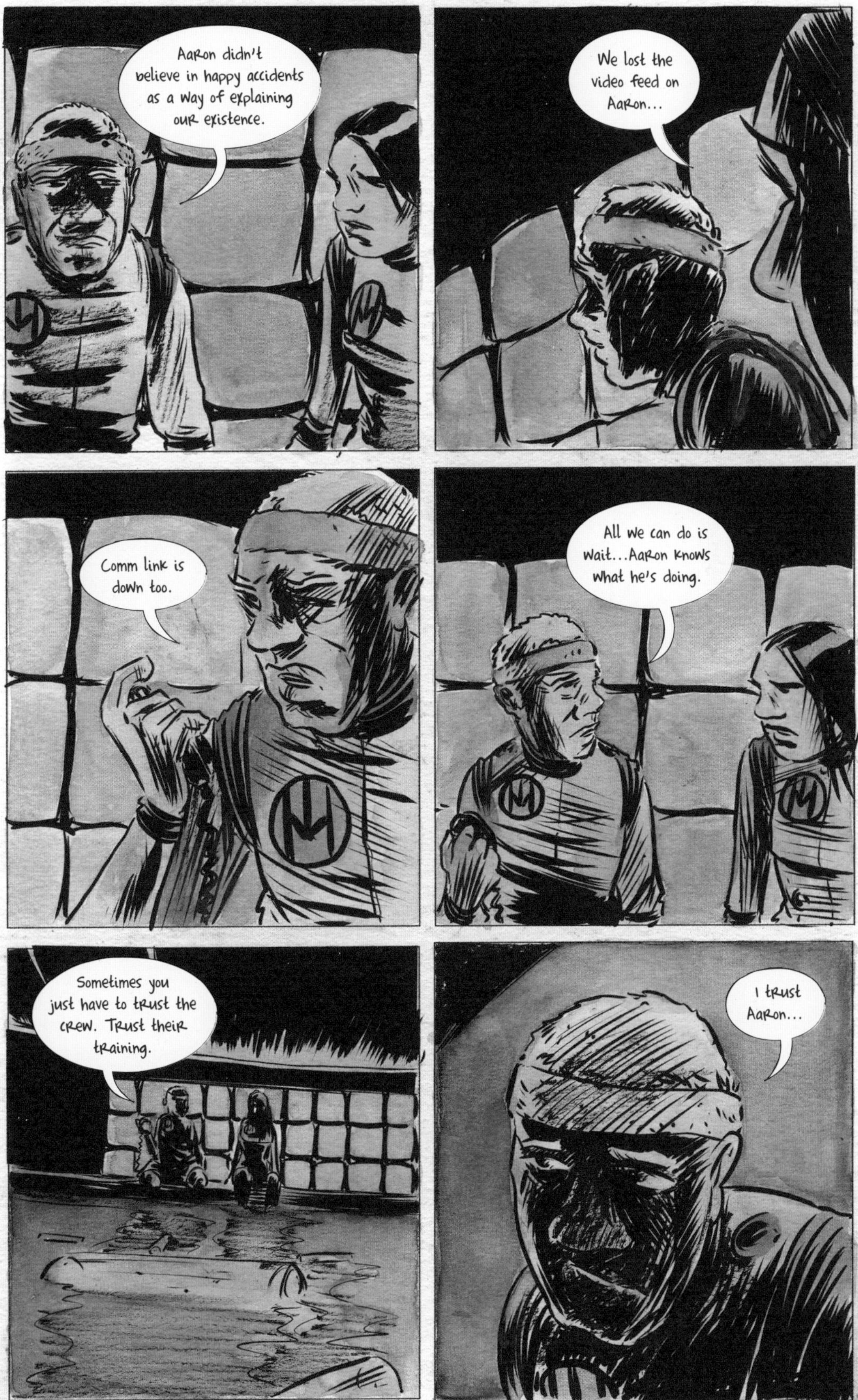
Aaron didn't believe in happy accidents as a way of explaining our existence.
We lost the video feed on Aaron...
Comm link is down too.
All we can do is wait...Aaron knows what he's doing.
Sometimes you just have to trust the crew. Trust their training.
I trust Aaron...

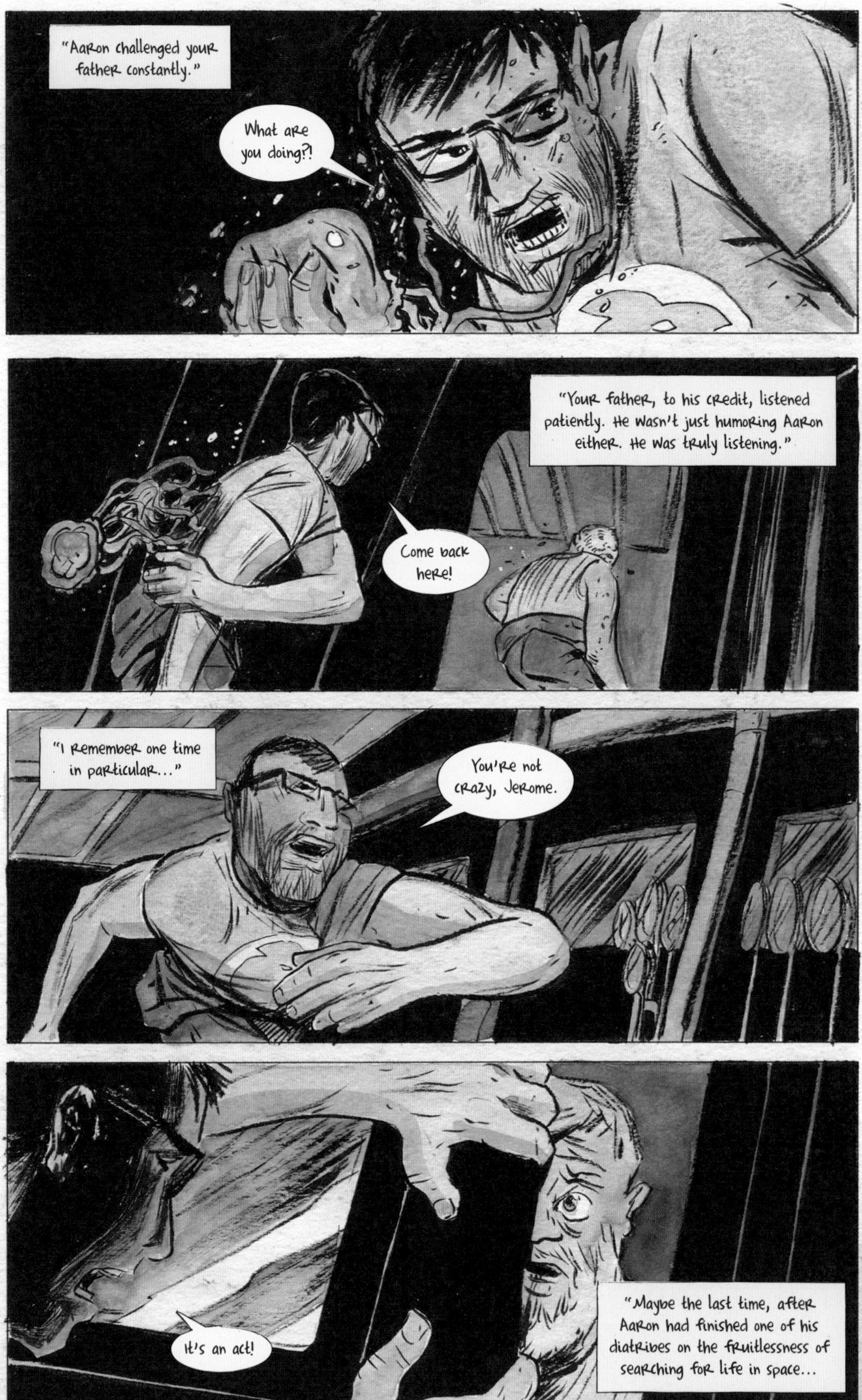
"Aaron challenged your father constantly."
What are you doing?!
"Your father, to his credit, listened patiently. He wasn't just humoring Aaron either. He was truly listening."
Come back here!
"I remember one time in particular..."
You're not crazy, Jerome.
It's an act!
"Maybe the last time, after Aaron had finished one of his diatribes on the fruitlessness of searching for life in space...

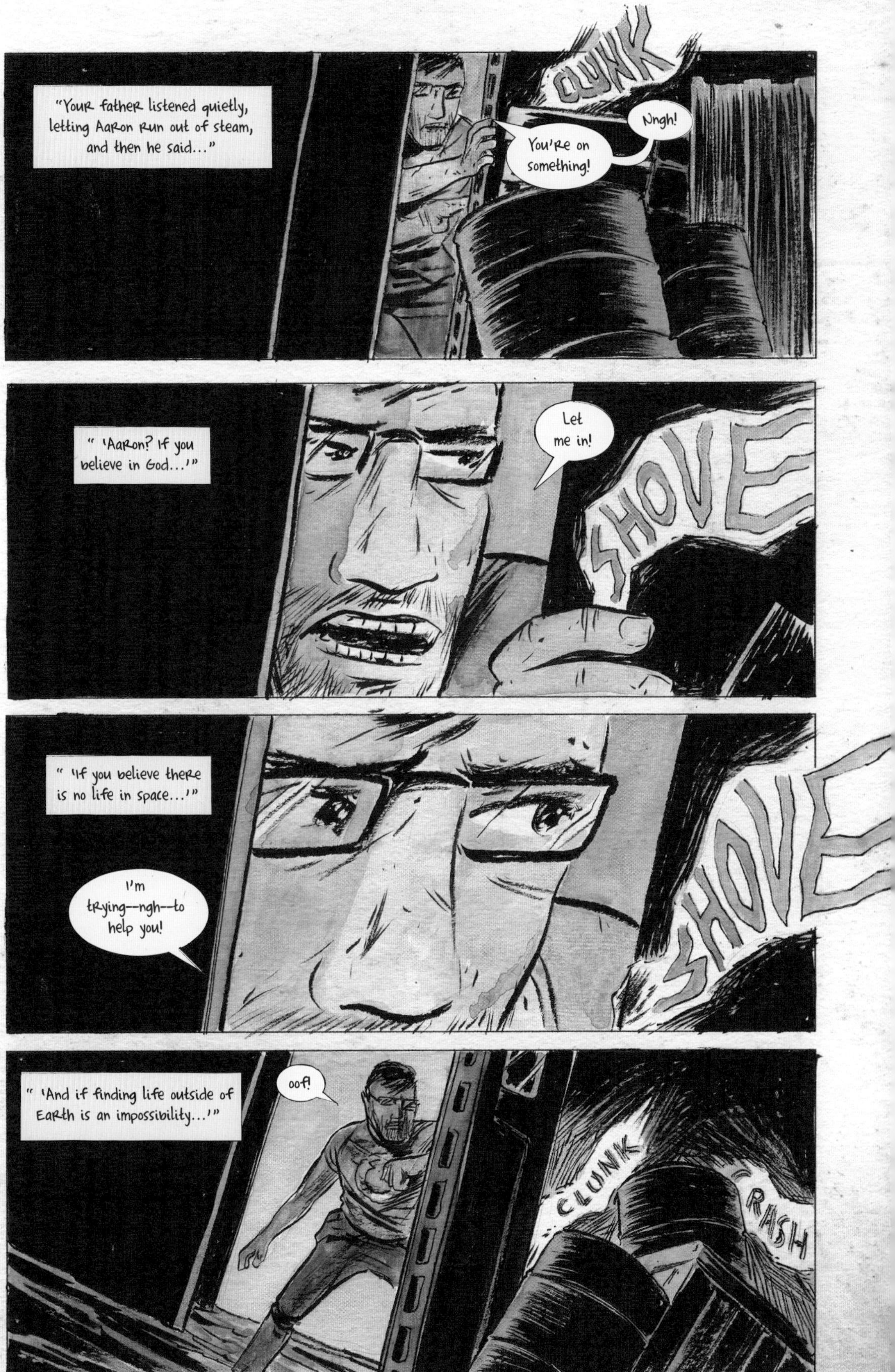
"Your father listened quietly, letting Aaron run out of steam, and then he said..."
You're on something!
Nngh!
CLUNK
" 'Aaron? If you believe in God...' "
Let me in!
SHOVE
" 'If you believe there is no life in space...' "
I'm trying--ngh--to help you!
SHOVE
" 'And if finding life outside of Earth is an impossibility...' "
oof!
CLUNK
CRASH

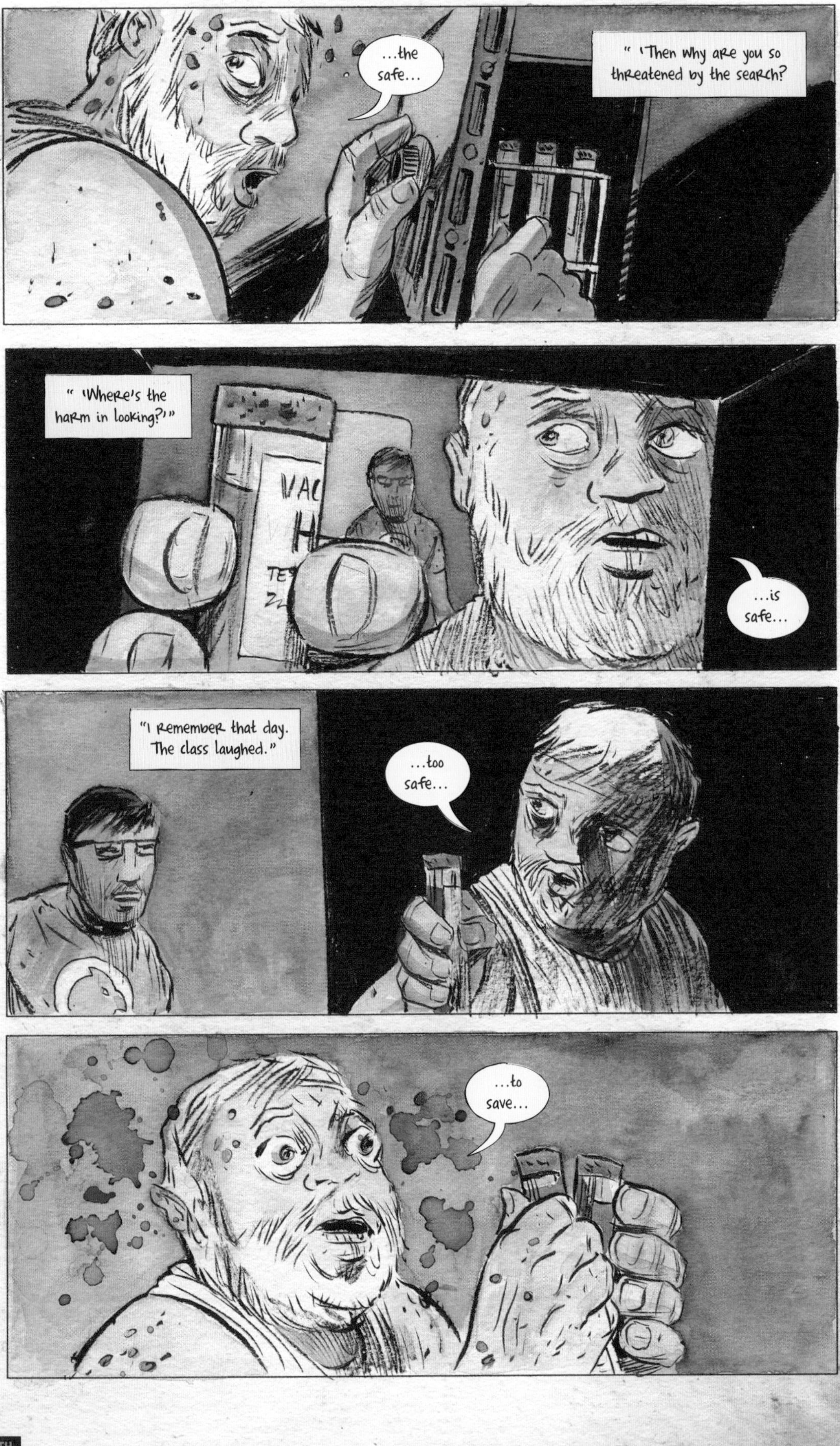
...the safe...
" 'Then why are you so threatened by the search?
" 'Where's the harm in looking?'"
...is safe...
"I remember that day. The class laughed."
...too safe...
...to save...

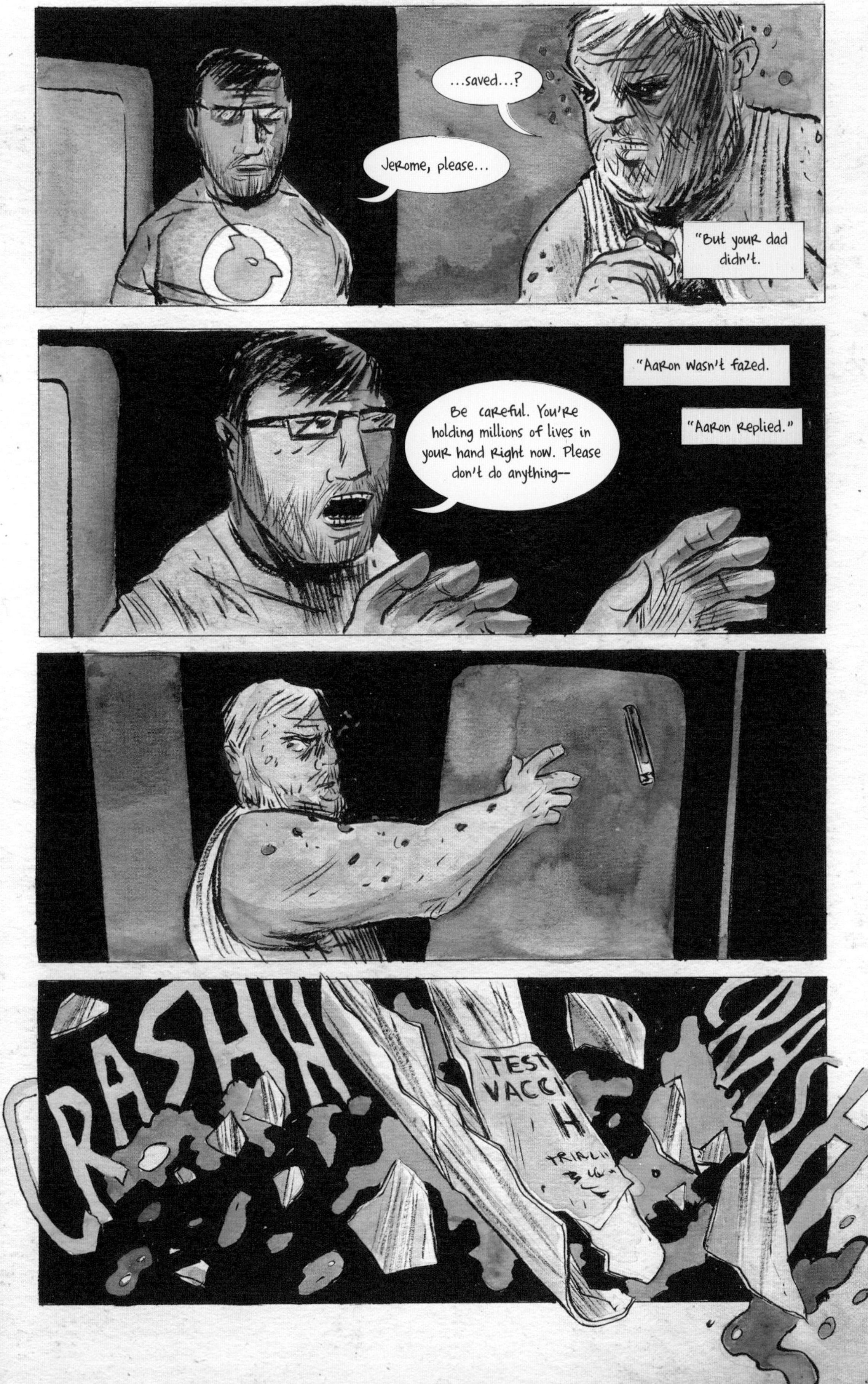
...saved...?
Jerome, please...
"But your dad didn't.
"Aaron wasn't fazed.
"Aaron replied."
Be careful. You're holding millions of lives in your hand right now. Please don't do anything--
CRASHH
TEST
VACCI
CRASH

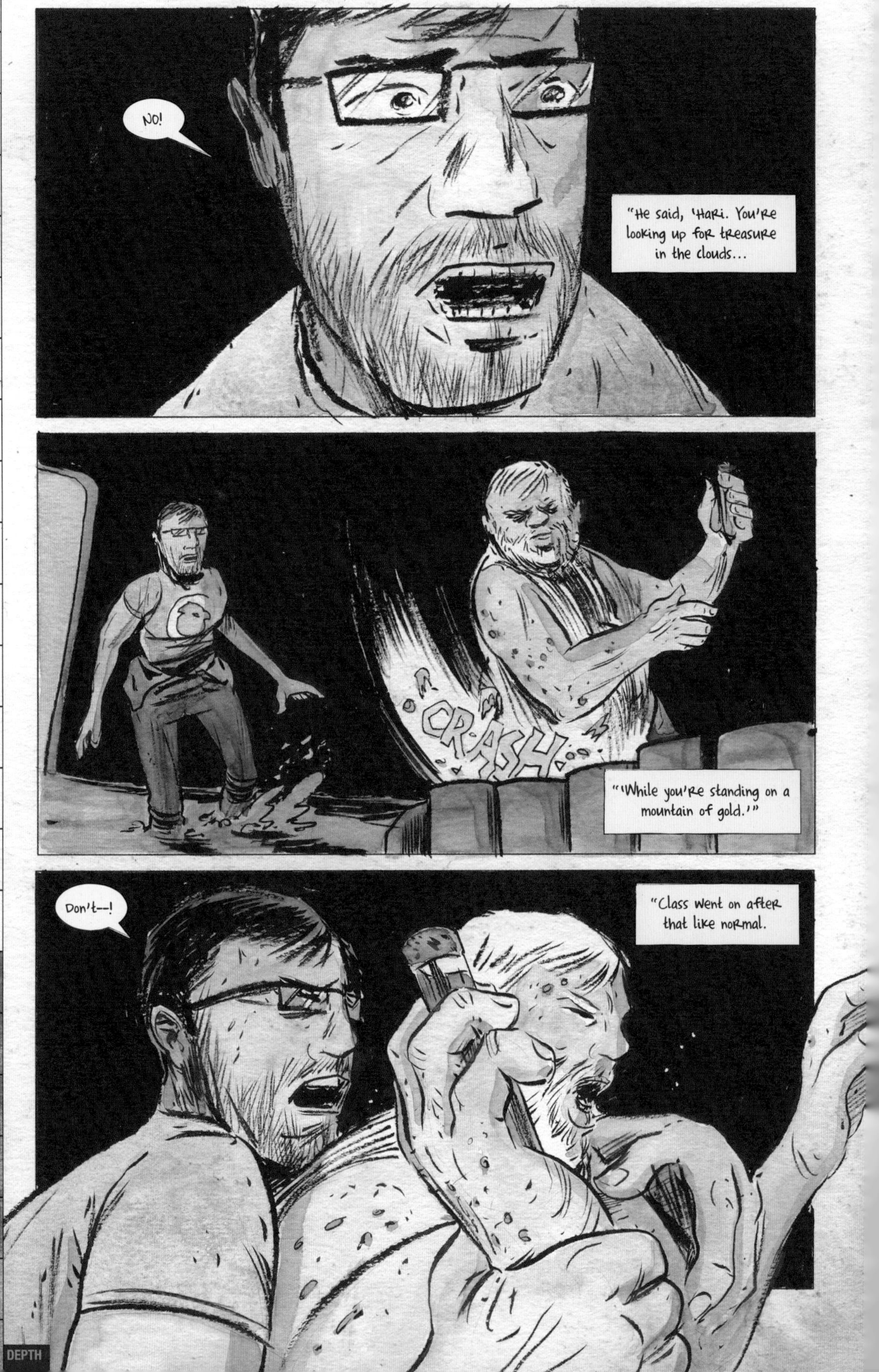
NO!
"He said, 'Hari. You're looking up for treasure in the clouds...
CR-ASH
"'While you're standing on a mountain of gold.'"
Don't--!
"Class went on after that like normal.

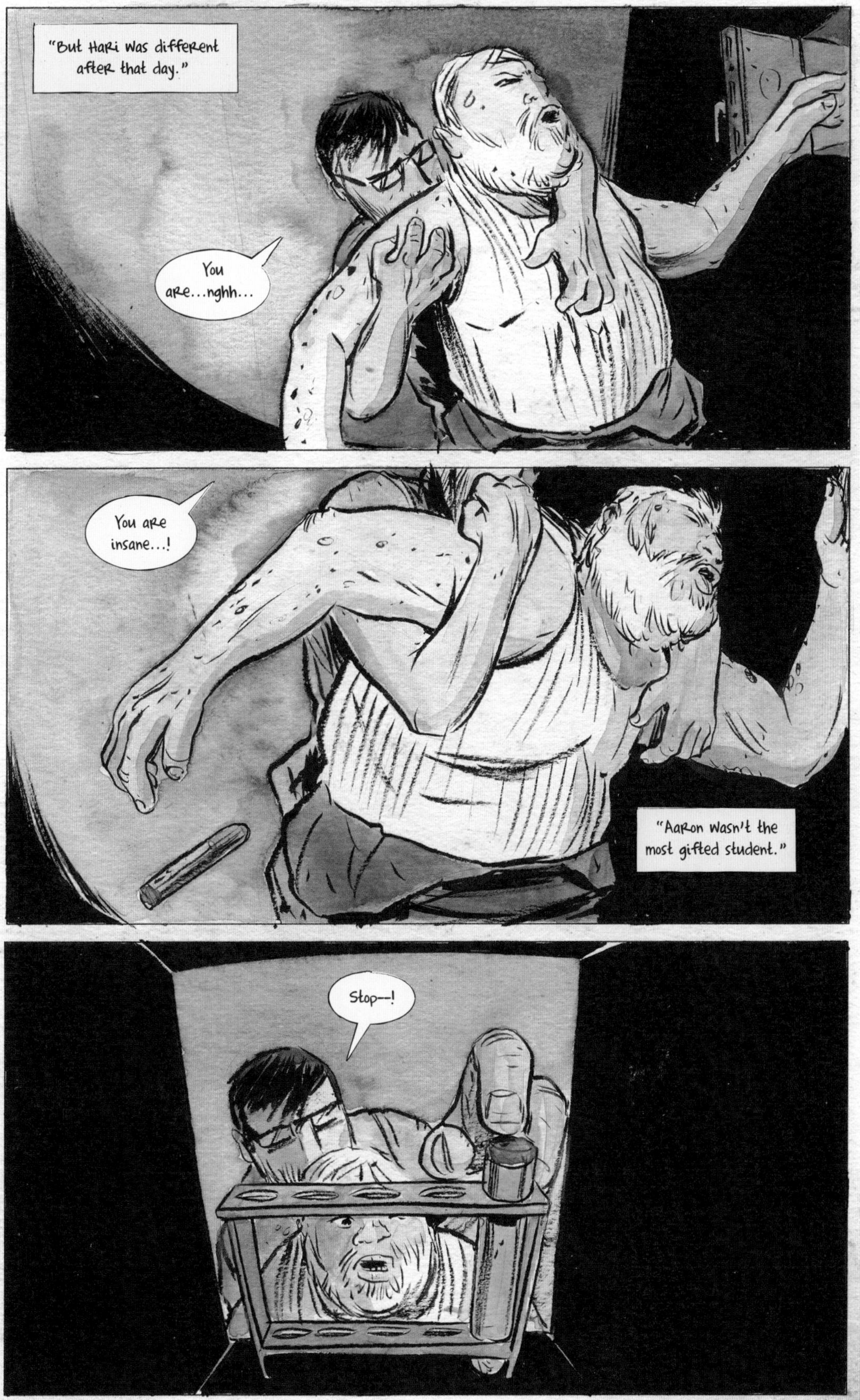
"But Hari was different after that day."
You are...nghh...
You are insane...!
"Aaron wasn't the most gifted student."
Stop--!

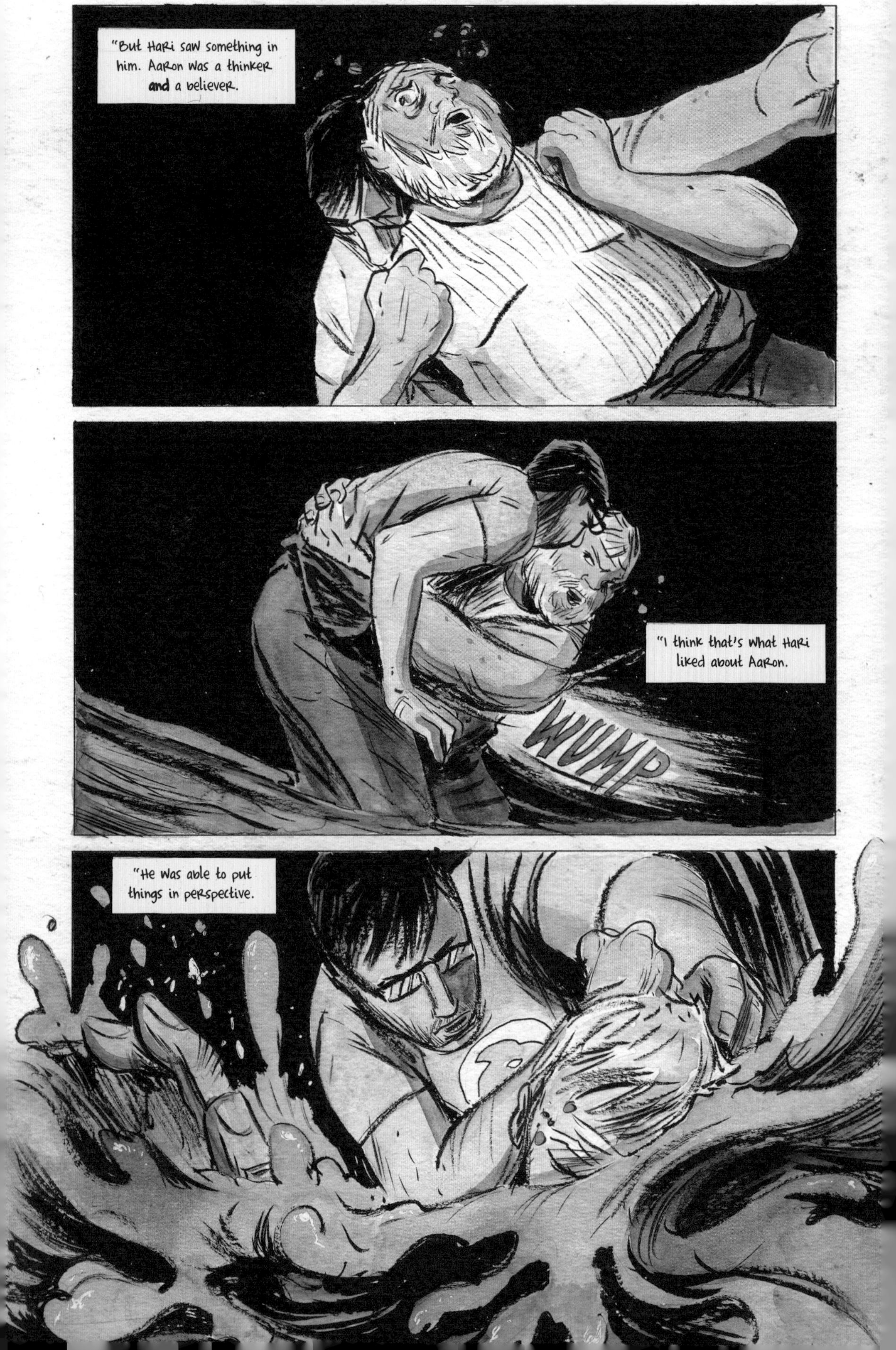
"But Hari saw something in him. Aaron was a thinker **and** a believer.
"I think that's what Hari liked about Aaron.
WUMP
"He was able to put things in perspective.

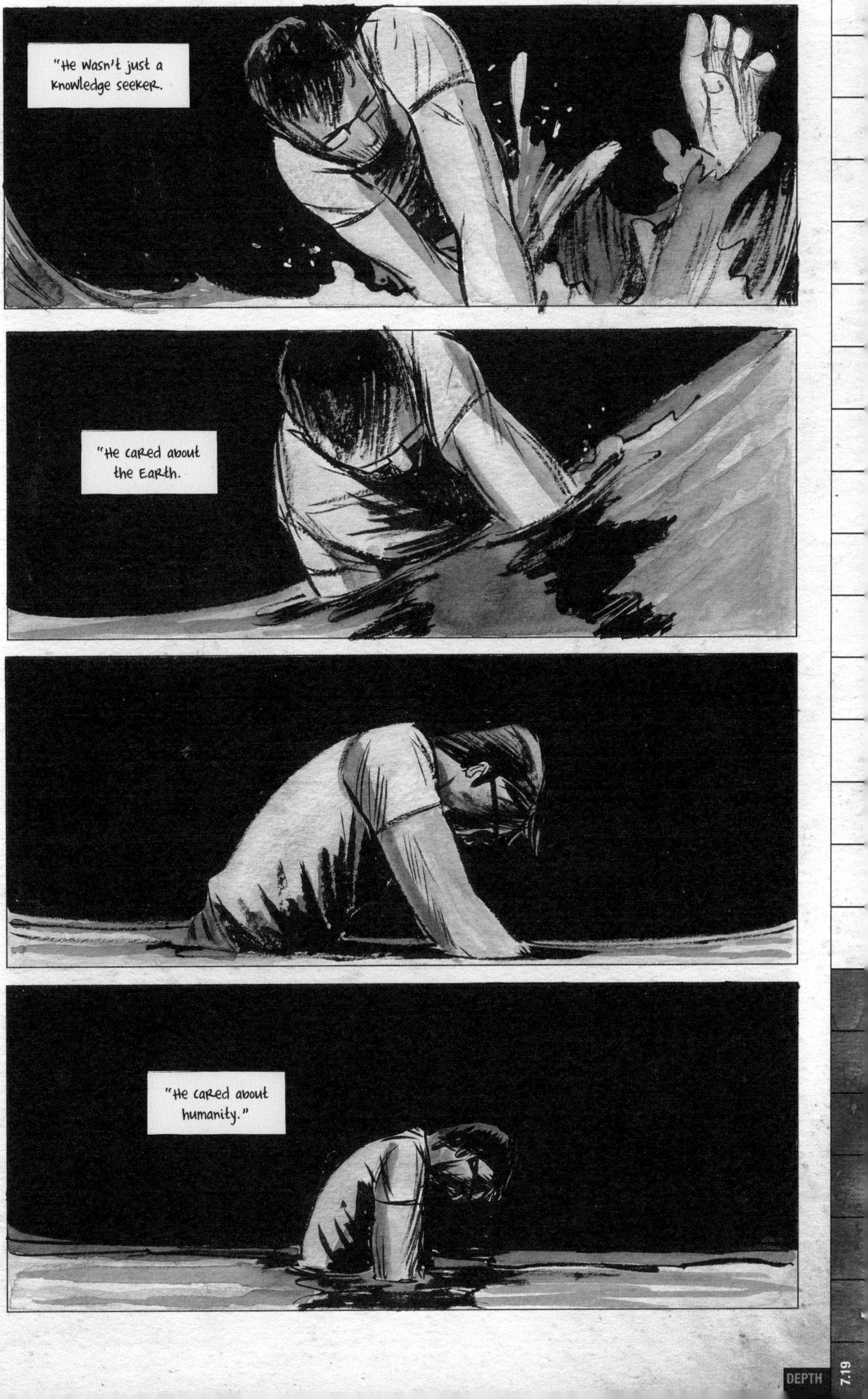
"He wasn't just a knowledge seeker.
"He cared about the Earth.
"He cared about humanity."

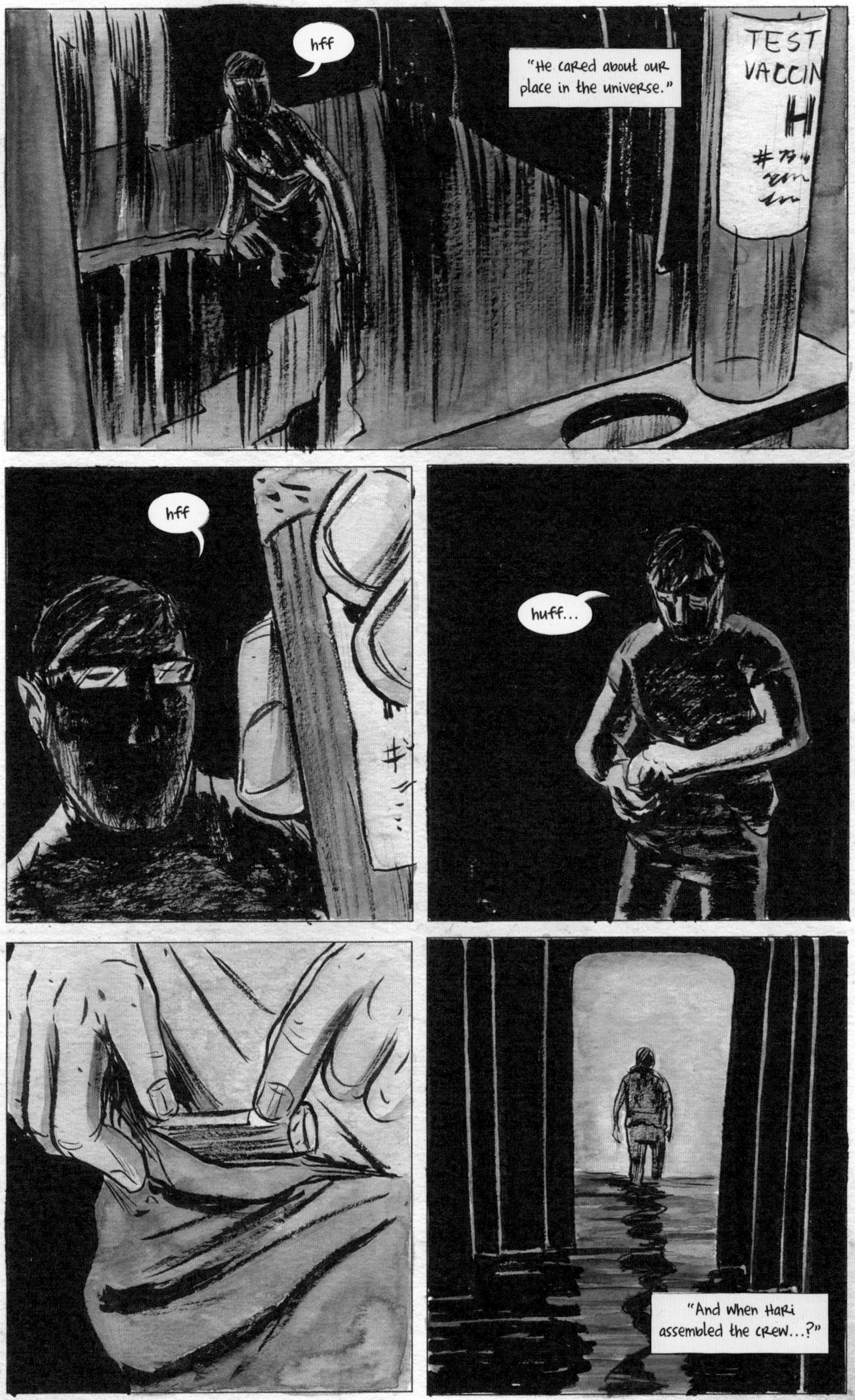
hff
"He cared about our place in the universe."
TEST
VACCIN
H
hff
huff...
"And when Hari assembled the crew...?"

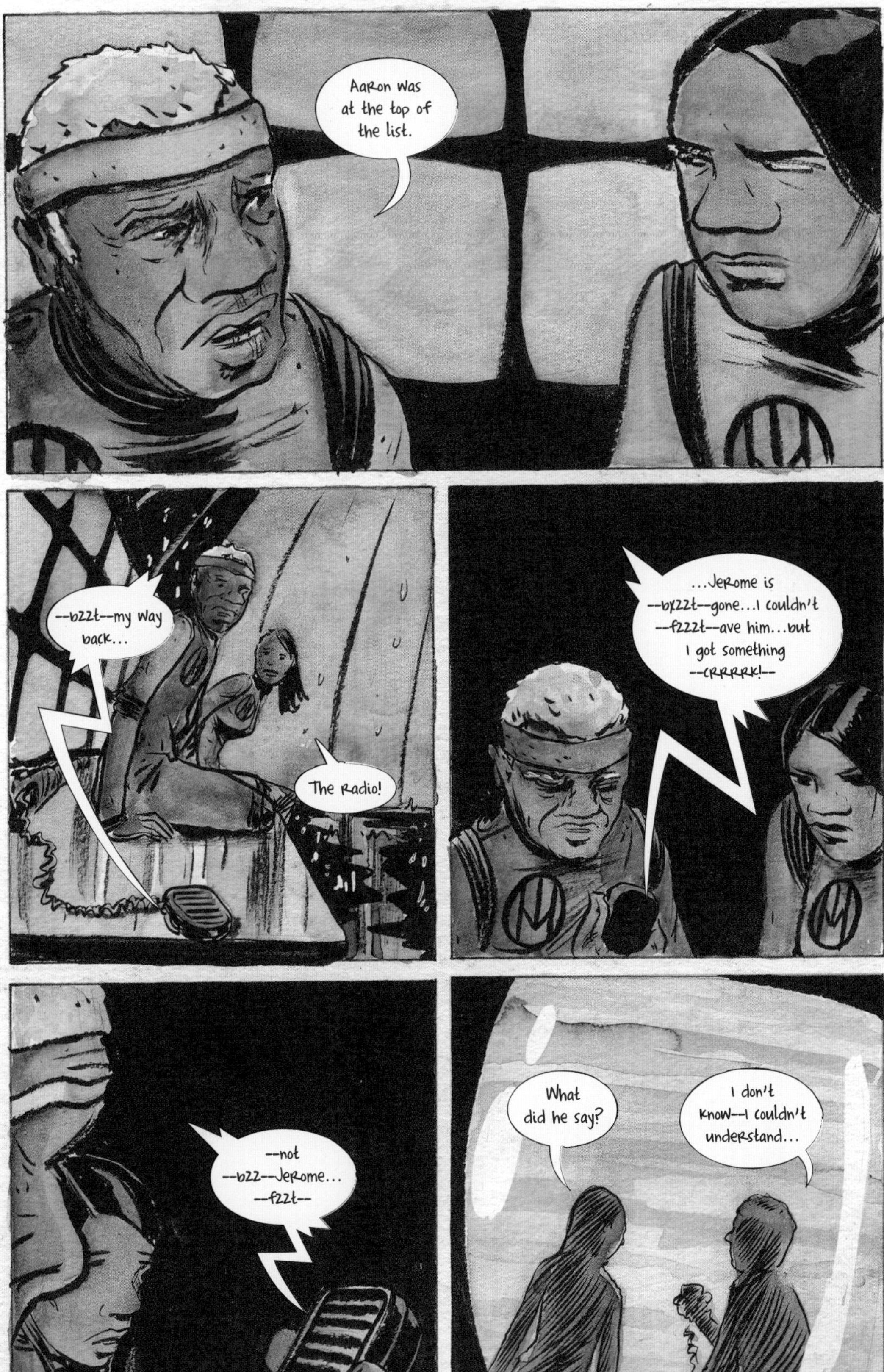
Aaron was at the top of the list.
--bzzt--my way back...
The radio!
...Jerome is --bxzzt--gone...I couldn't --fzzzt--ave him...but I got something --crrrrk!--
--not --bzz--Jerome... --fzzt--
What did he say?
I don't know--I couldn't understand...

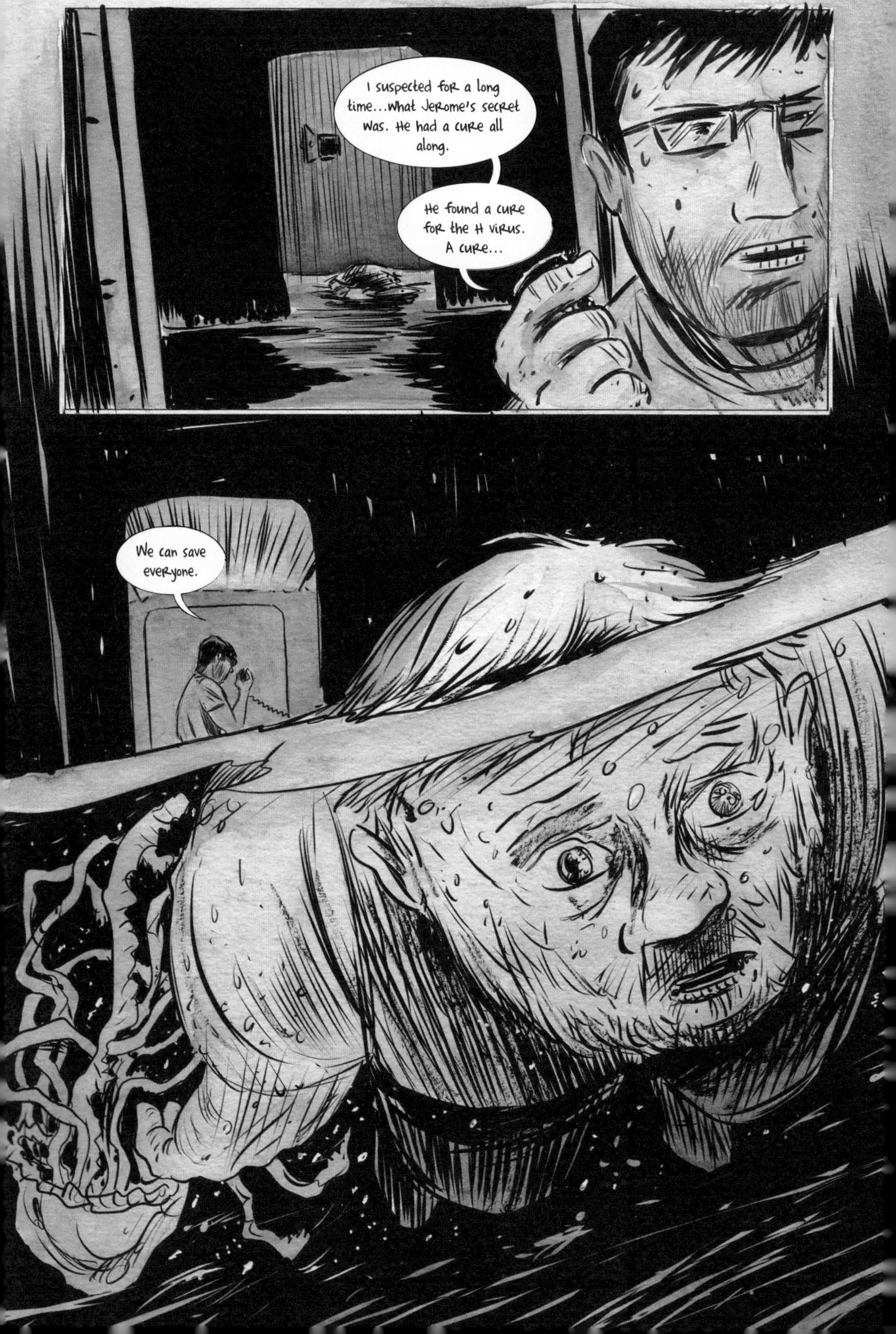
I suspected for a long time...what Jerome's secret was. He had a cure all along.
He found a cure for the H virus. A cure...
We can save everyone.

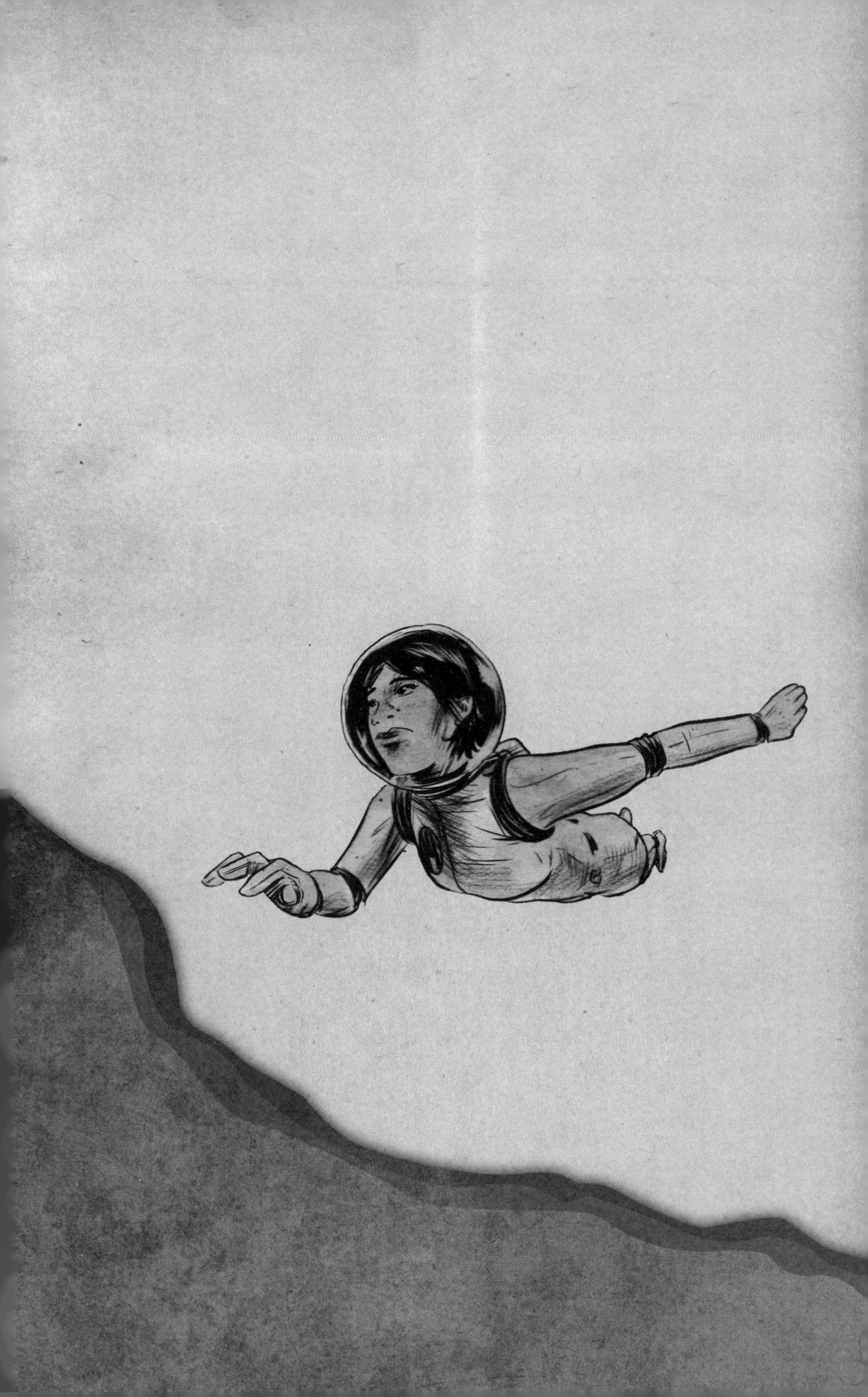

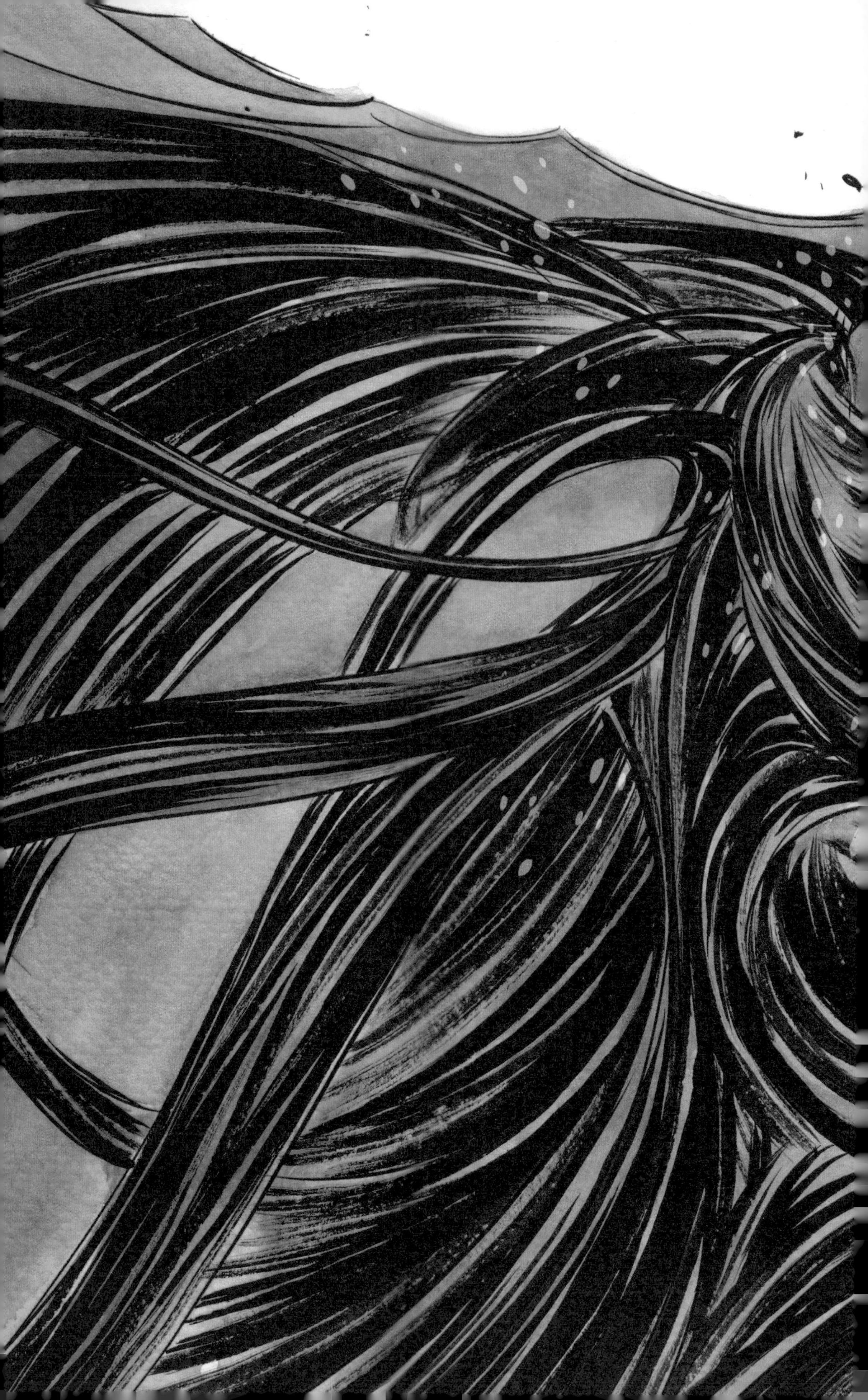

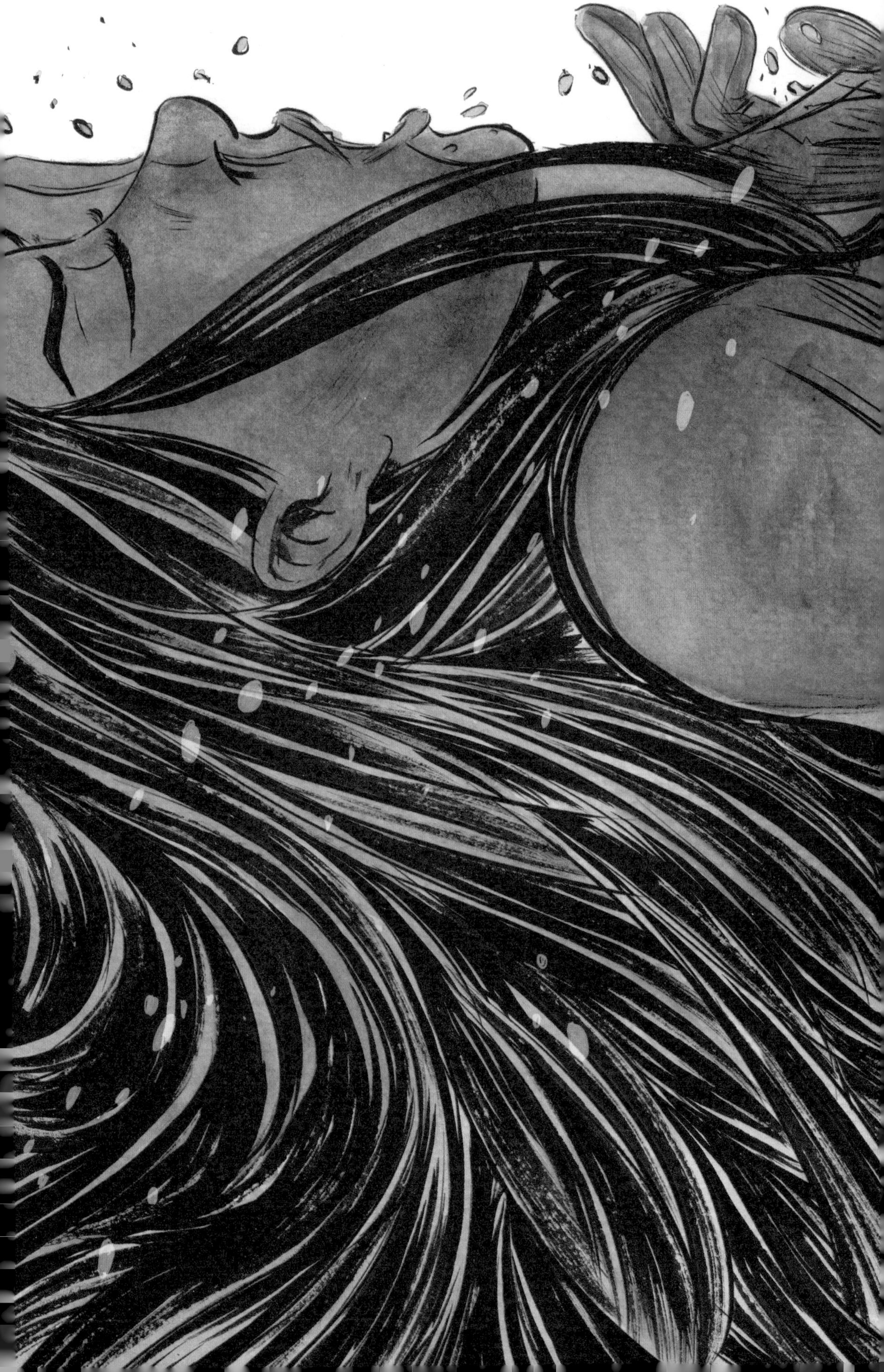

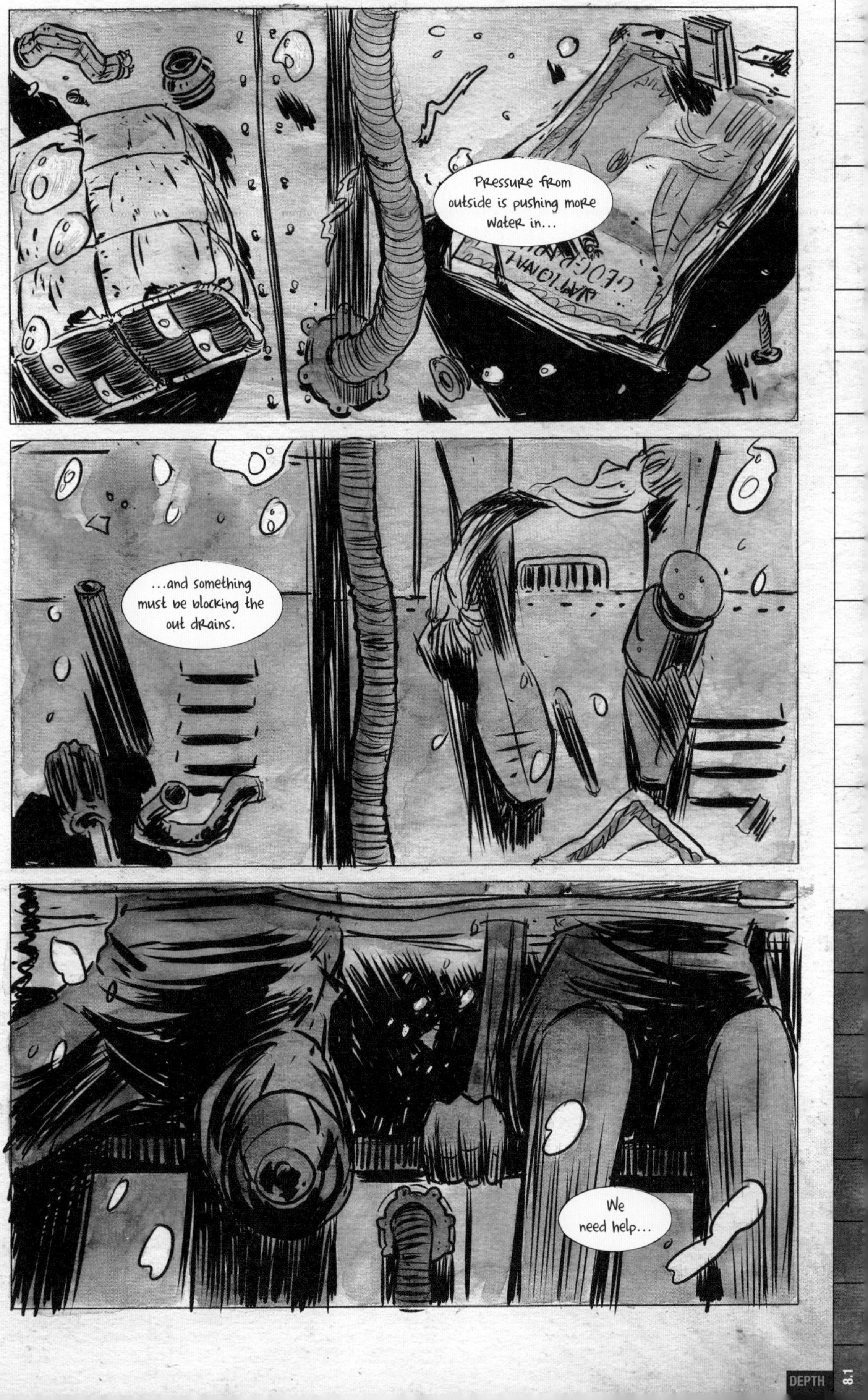
Pressure from outside is pushing more water in...
...and something must be blocking the out drains.
We need help...

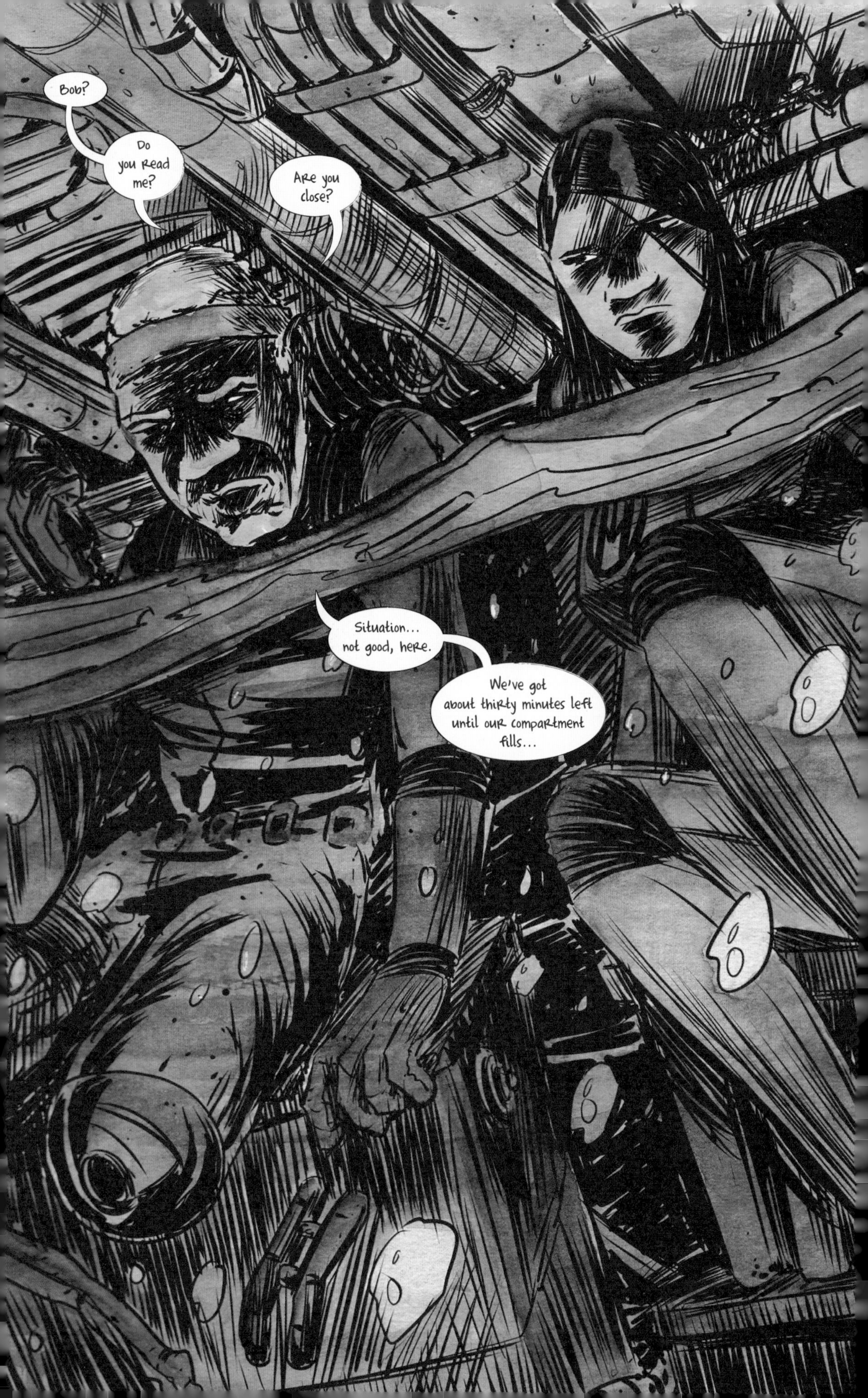
Bob?
Do you read me?
Are you close?
Situation... not good, here.
We've got about thirty minutes left until our compartment fills...

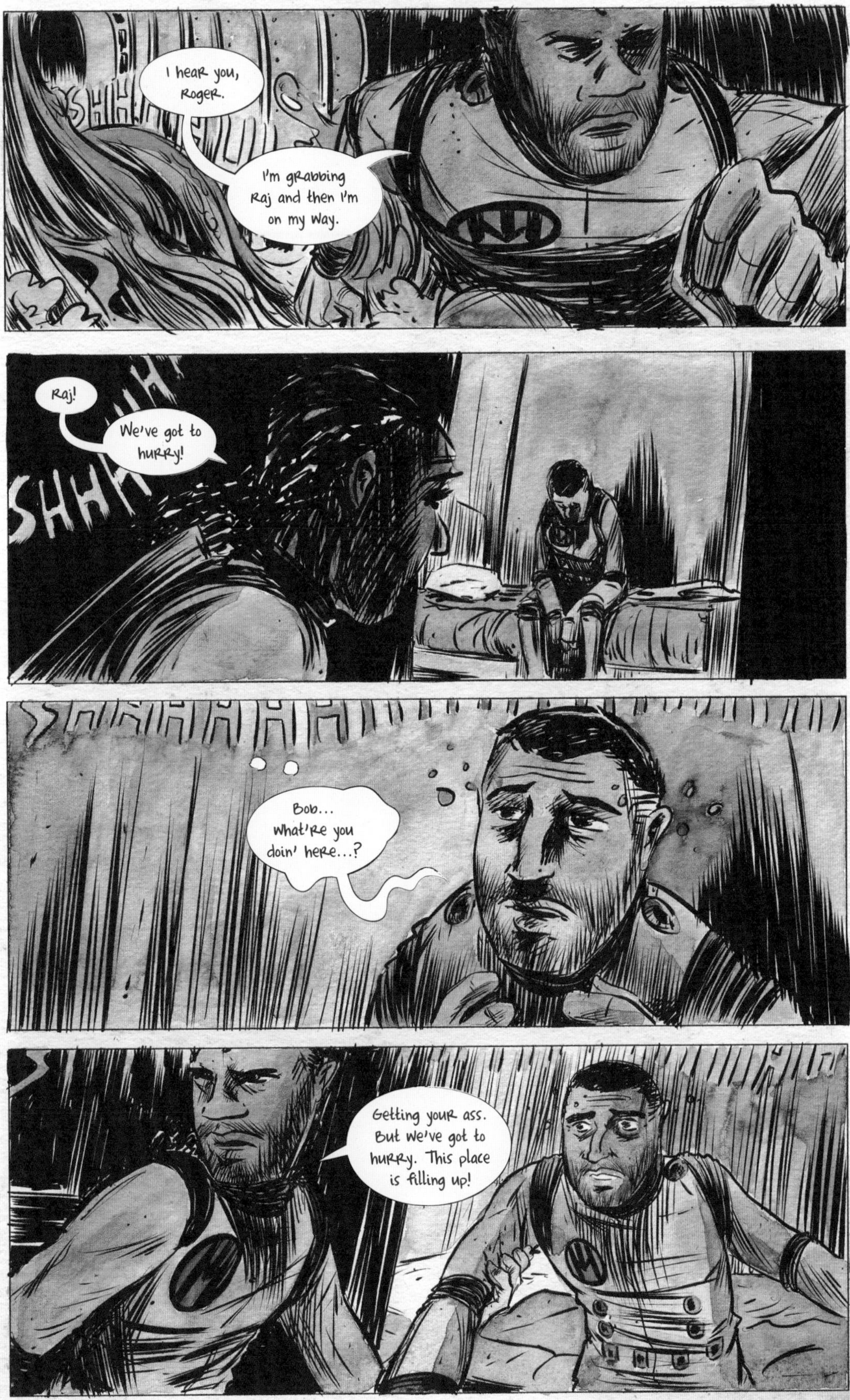
SHHHHHH
I hear you, Roger.
I'm grabbing Raj and then I'm on my way.
Raj!
We've got to hurry!
SHHH
SHHHHHHHHH
Bob... what're you doin' here...?
Getting your ass. But we've got to hurry. This place is filling up!

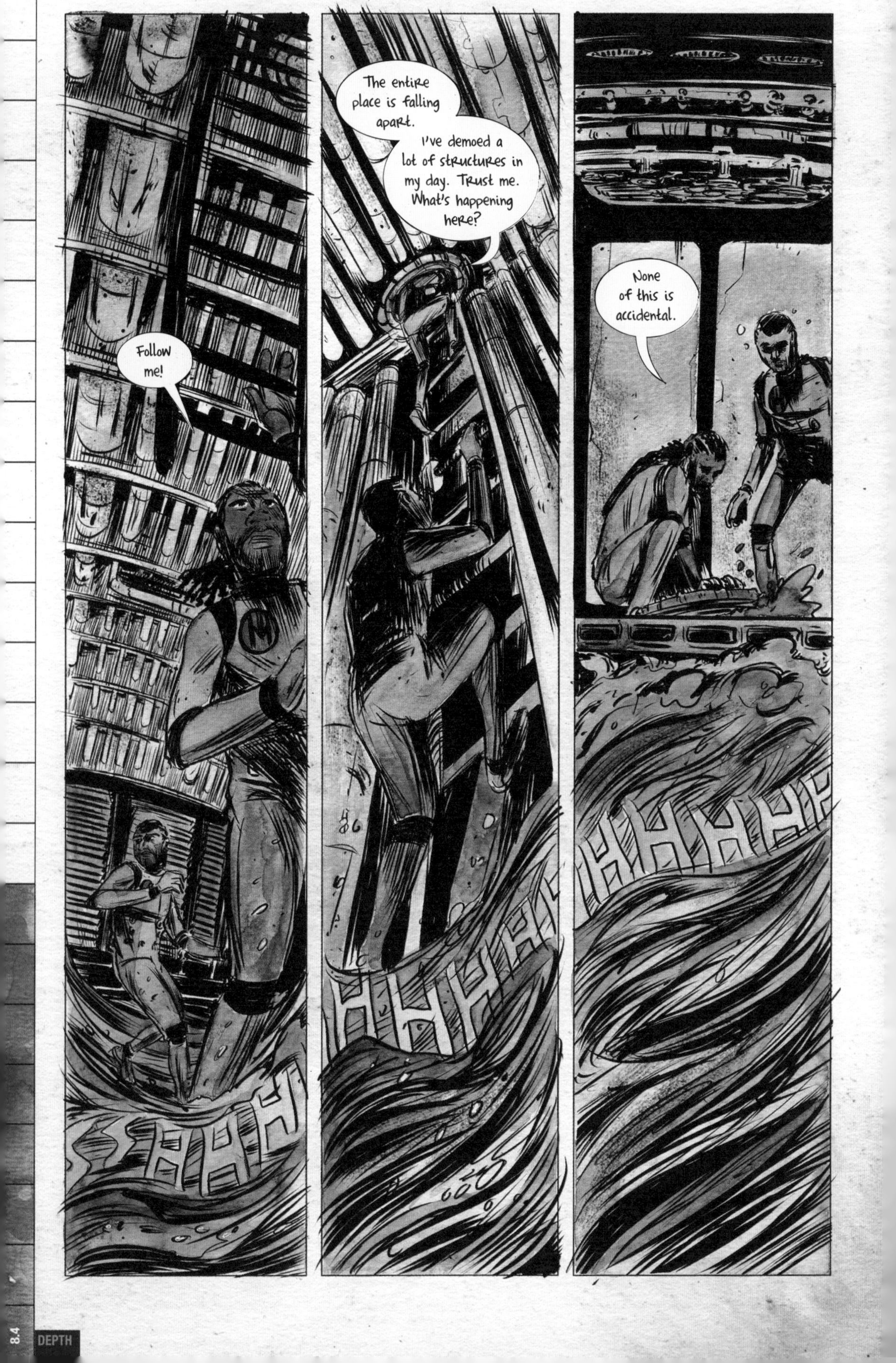
Follow me!
The entire place is falling apart.
I've demoed a lot of structures in my day. Trust me. What's happening here?
None of this is accidental.

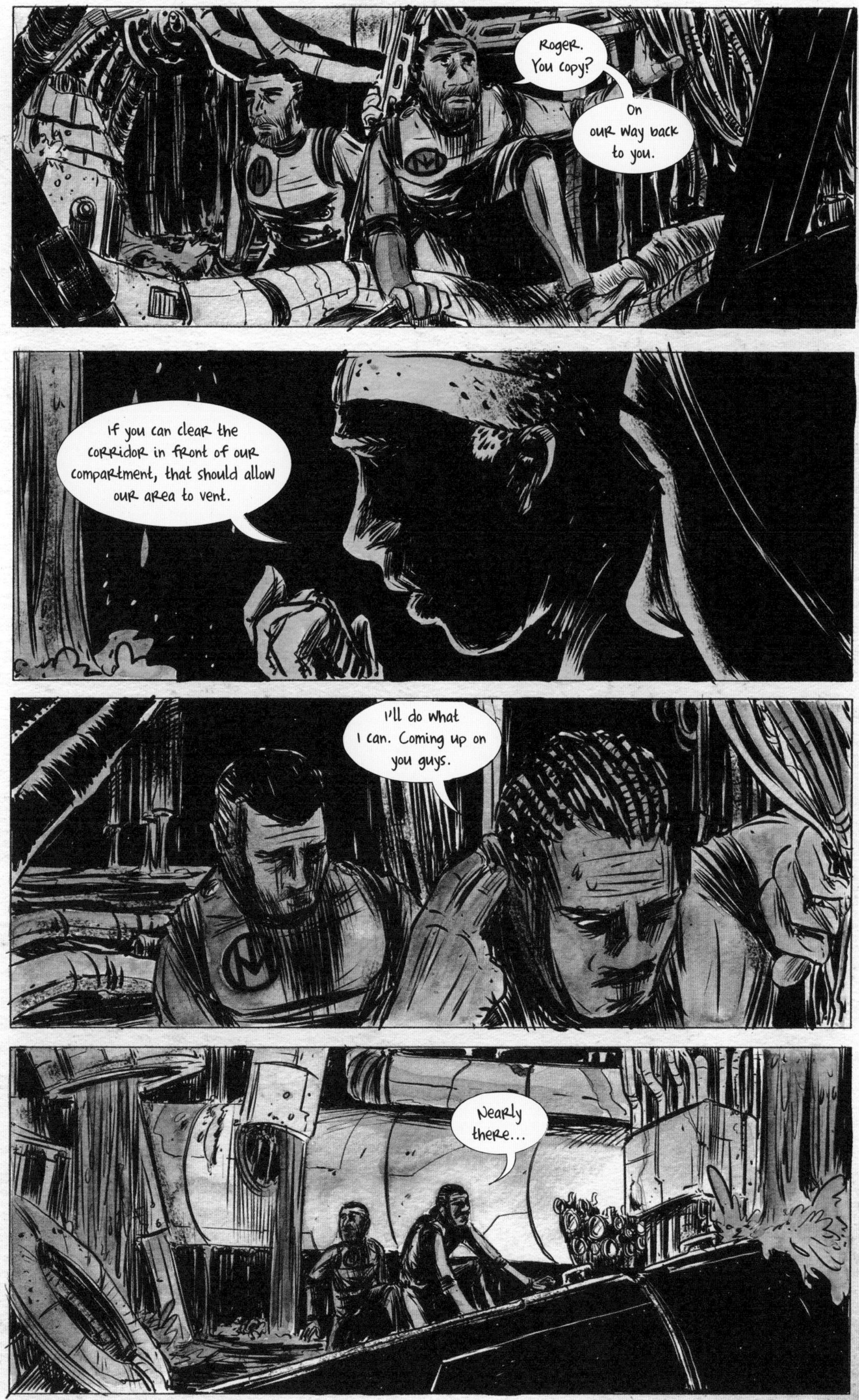
Roger. You copy?
On our way back to you.
If you can clear the corridor in front of our compartment, that should allow our area to vent.
I'll do what I can. Coming up on you guys.
Nearly there...

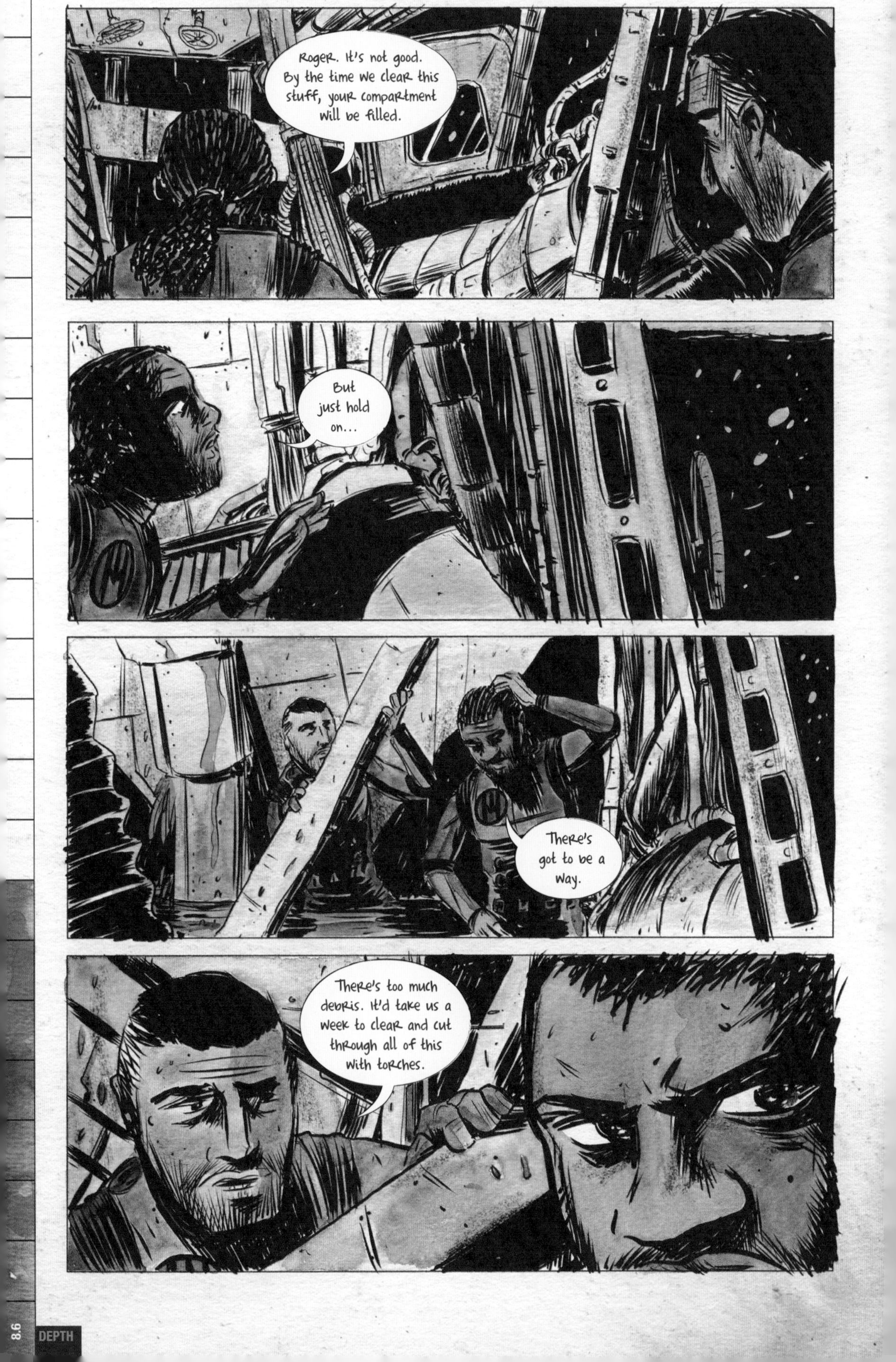
Roger. It's not good. By the time we clear this stuff, your compartment will be filled.
But just hold on...
There's got to be a way.
There's too much debris. It'd take us a week to clear and cut through all of this with torches.

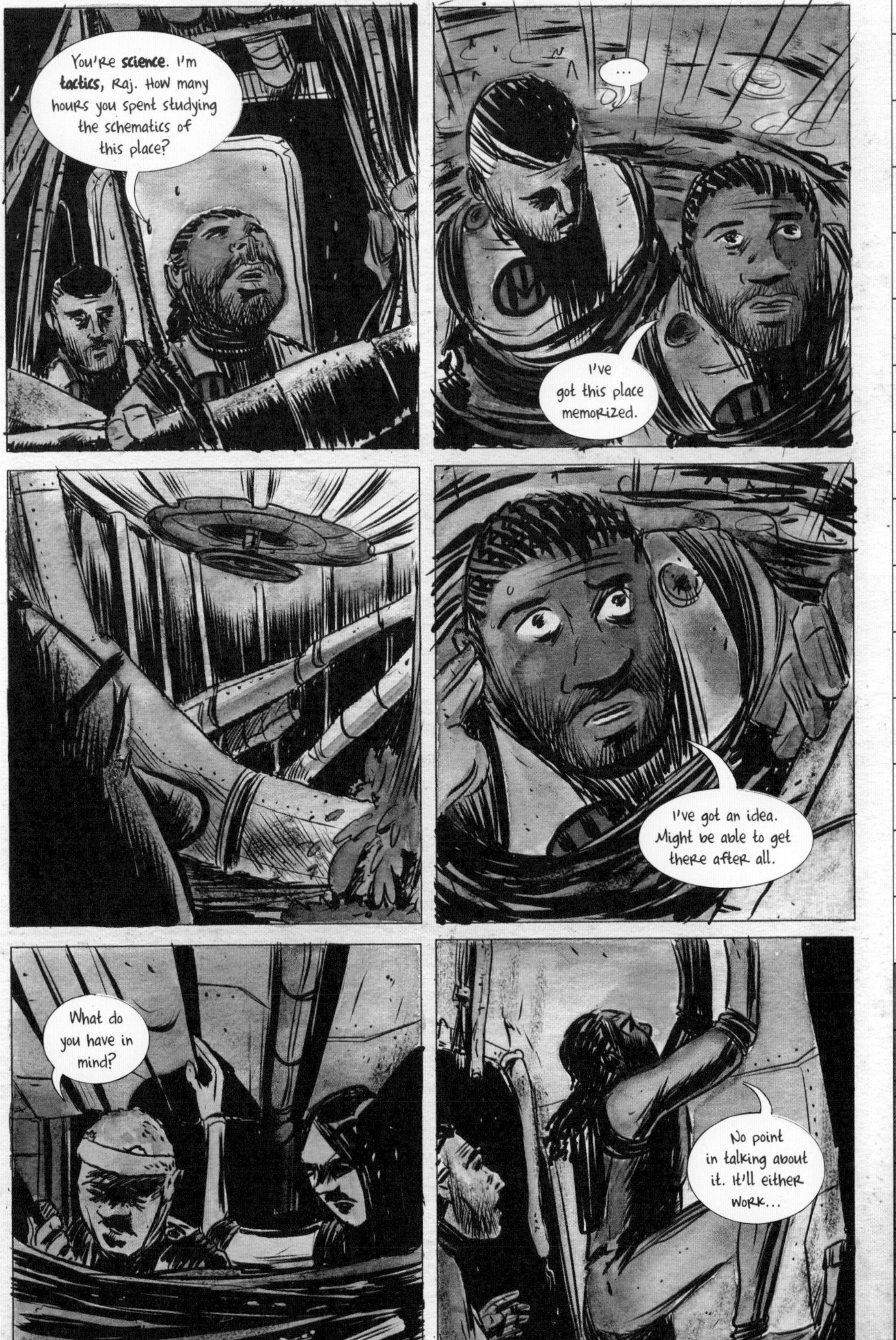
You're science. I'm tactics, Raj. How many hours you spent studying the schematics of this place?
...
I've got this place memorized.
I've got an idea. Might be able to get there after all.
What do you have in mind?
No point in talking about it. It'll either work...

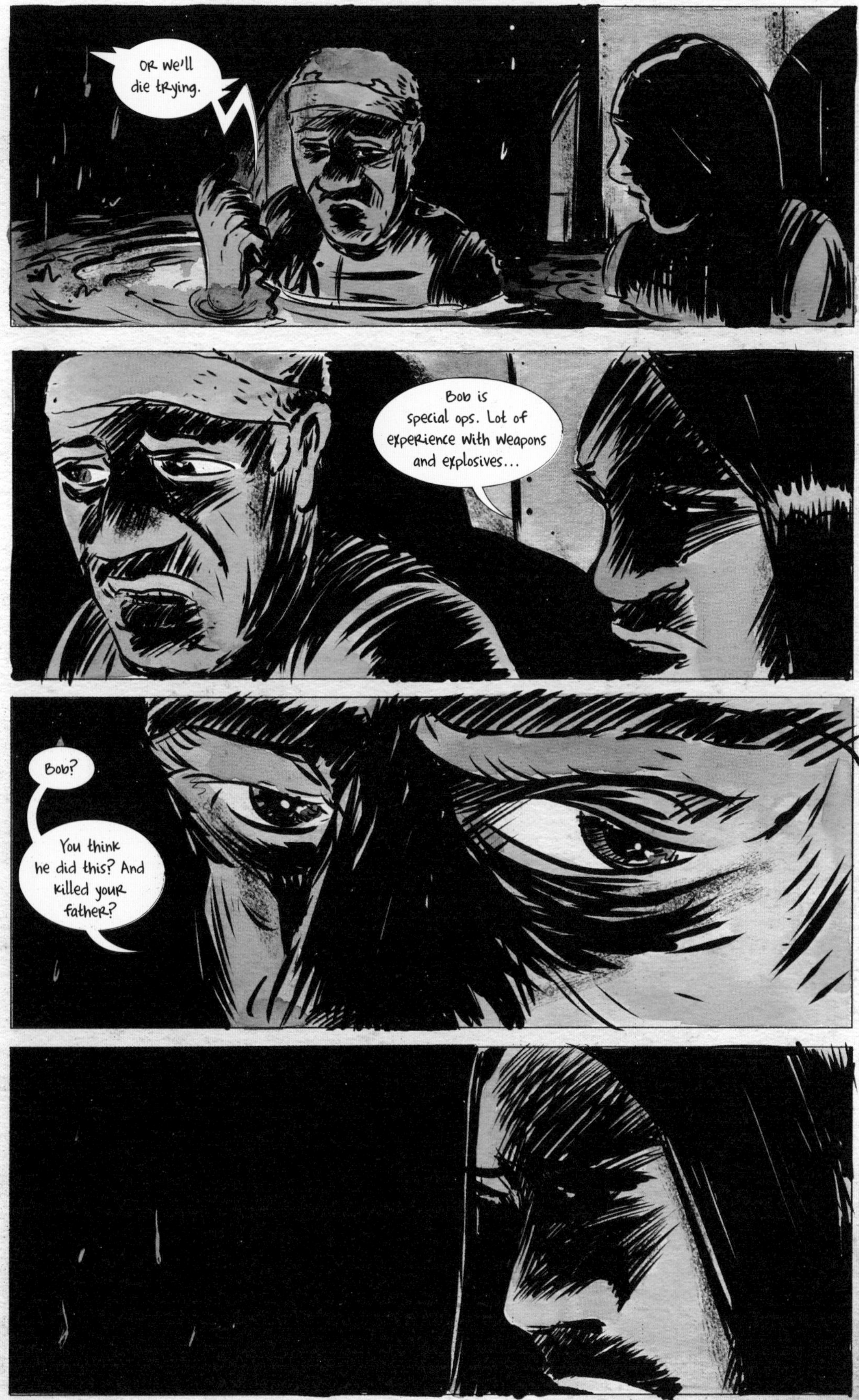
OR WE'LL die trying.
Bob is special ops. Lot of experience with weapons and explosives...
Bob?
You think he did this? And killed your father?

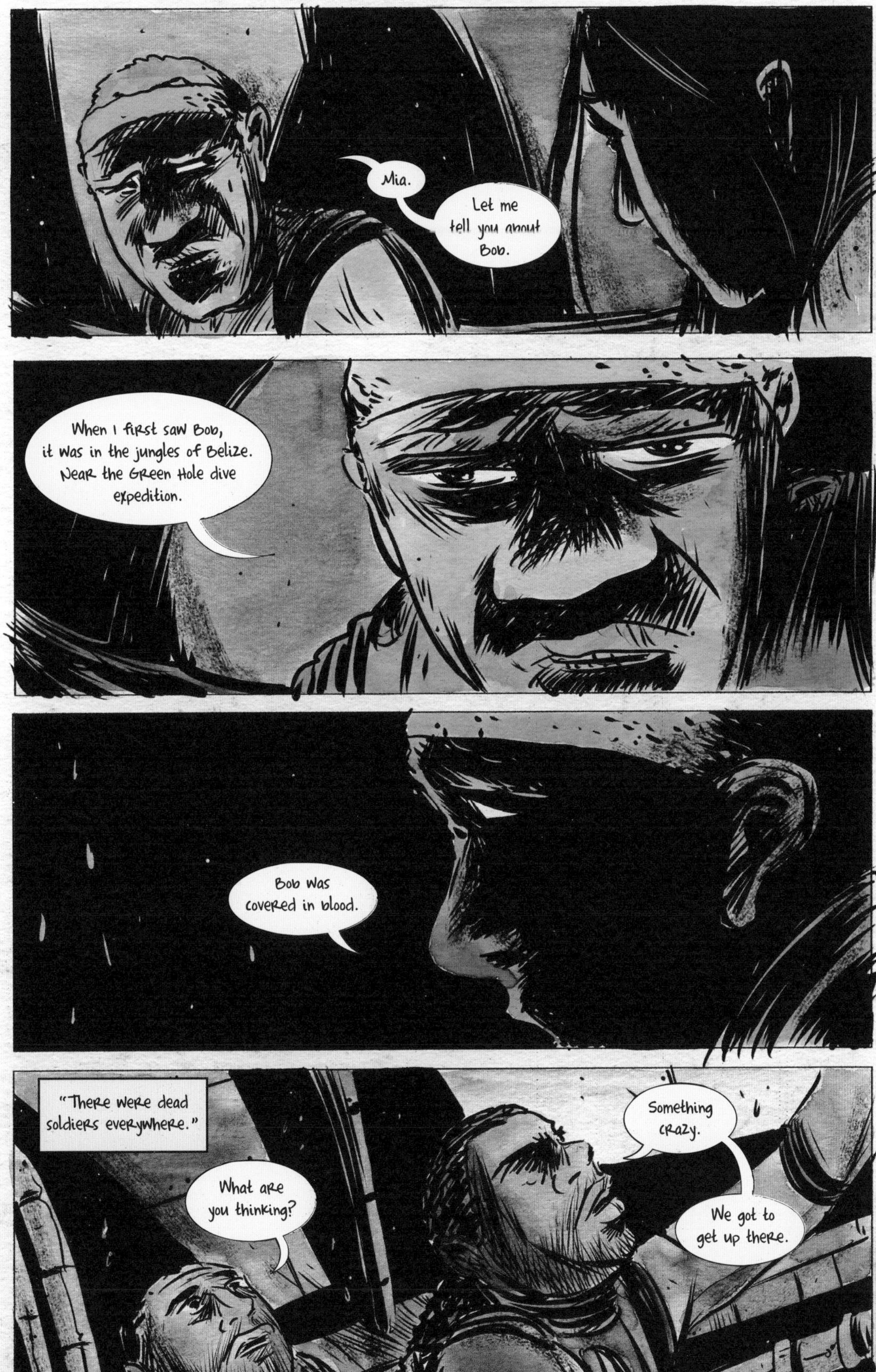
Mia.
Let me tell you about Bob.
When I first saw Bob, it was in the jungles of Belize. Near the Green Hole dive expedition.
Bob was covered in blood.
"There were dead soldiers everywhere."
Something crazy.
What are you thinking?
We got to get up there.

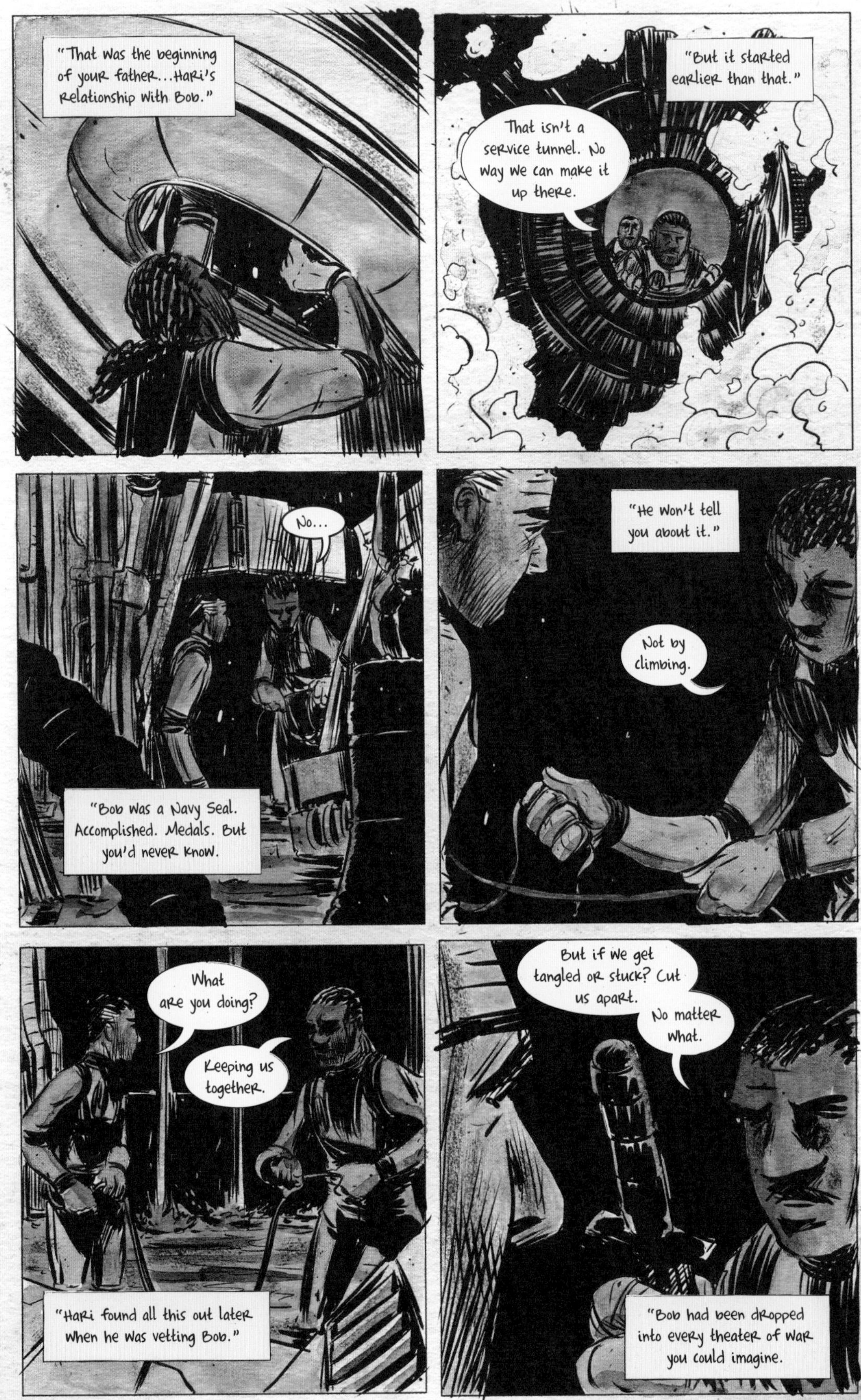
"That was the beginning of your father...Hari's relationship with Bob."
"But it started earlier than that."
That isn't a service tunnel. No way we can make it up there.
No...
"Bob was a Navy Seal. Accomplished. Medals. But you'd never know.
"He won't tell you about it."
Not by climbing.
What are you doing?
Keeping us together.
"Hari found all this out later when he was vetting Bob."
But if we get tangled or stuck? Cut us apart.
No matter what.
"Bob had been dropped into every theater of war you could imagine.

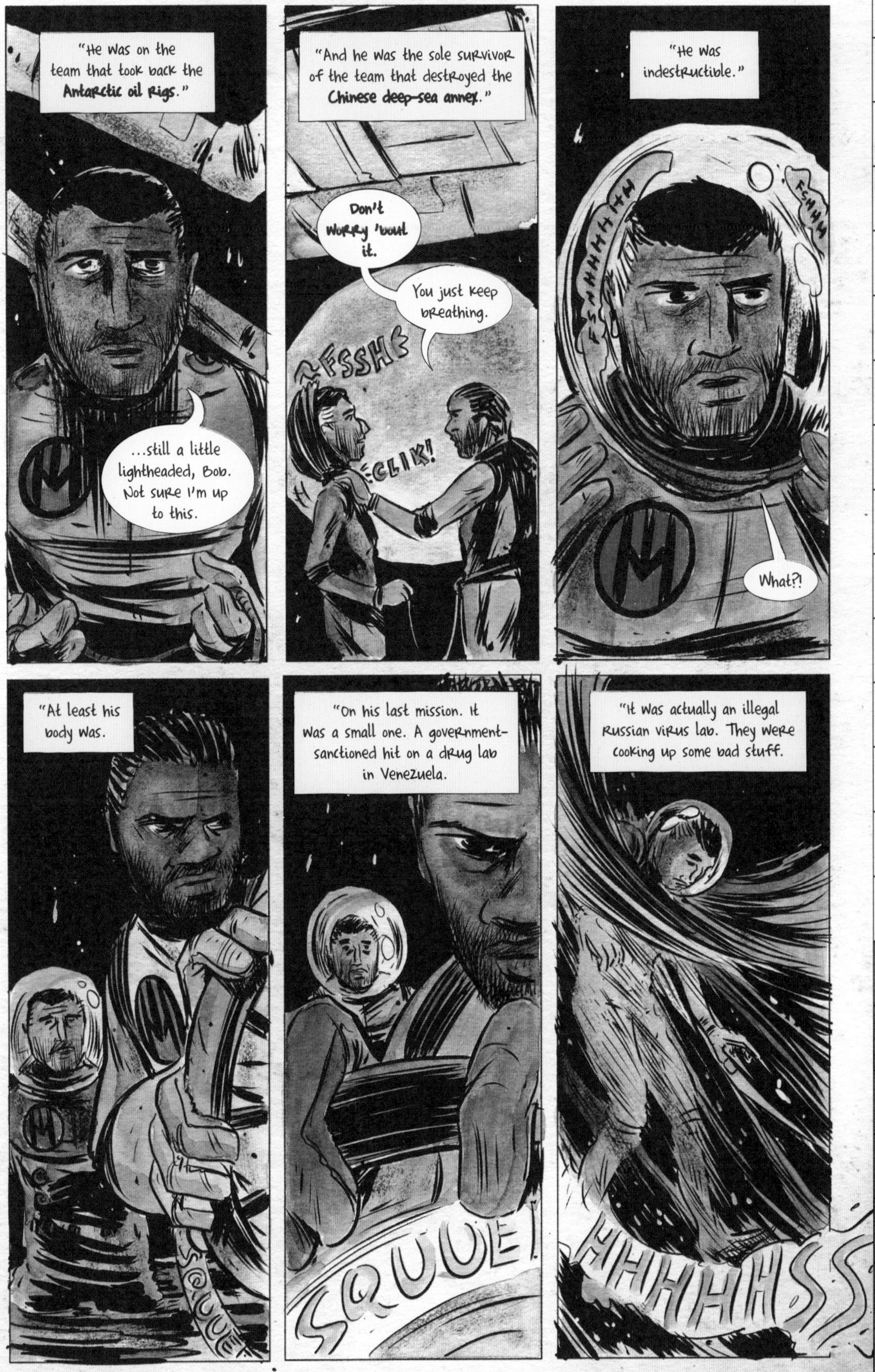
"He was on the team that took back the Antarctic oil rigs."
...still a little lightheaded, Bob. Not sure I'm up to this.
"And he was the sole survivor of the team that destroyed the Chinese deep-sea annex."
Don't worry 'bout it.
You just keep breathing.
FSSHE
CLIK!
"He was indestructible."
FSHHHHHHHH
FSHHHH
What?!
"At least his body was.
SQUUE
"On his last mission. It was a small one. A government-sanctioned hit on a drug lab in Venezuela.
SQUUEE
"It was actually an illegal Russian virus lab. They were cooking up some bad stuff.
HHHHHHSS

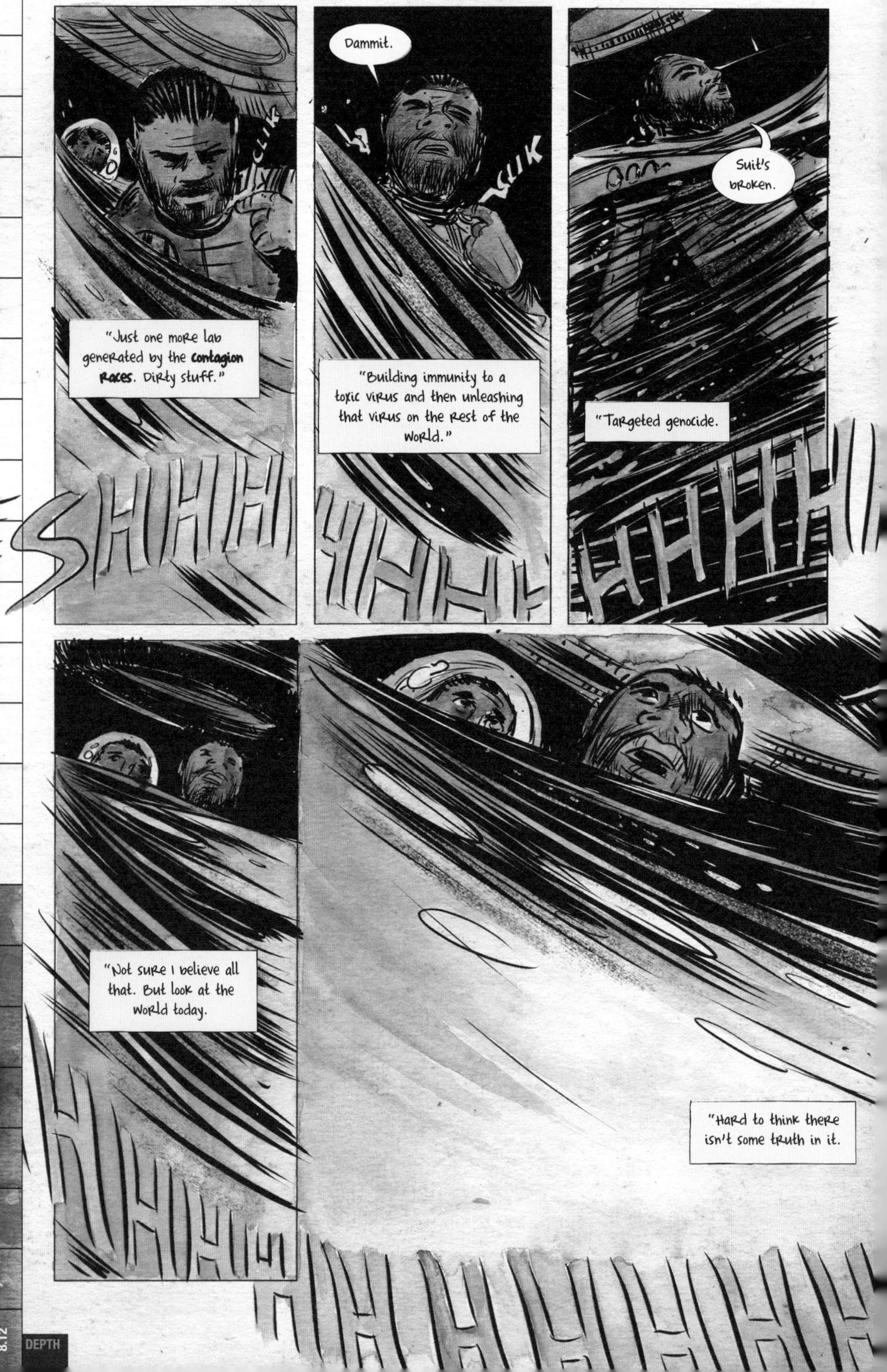
CLIK
"Just one more lab generated by the **contagion races**. Dirty stuff."
Dammit.
"Building immunity to a toxic virus and then unleashing that virus on the rest of the world."
Suit's broken.
"Targeted genocide.
"Not sure I believe all that. But look at the world today.
"Hard to think there isn't some truth in it.

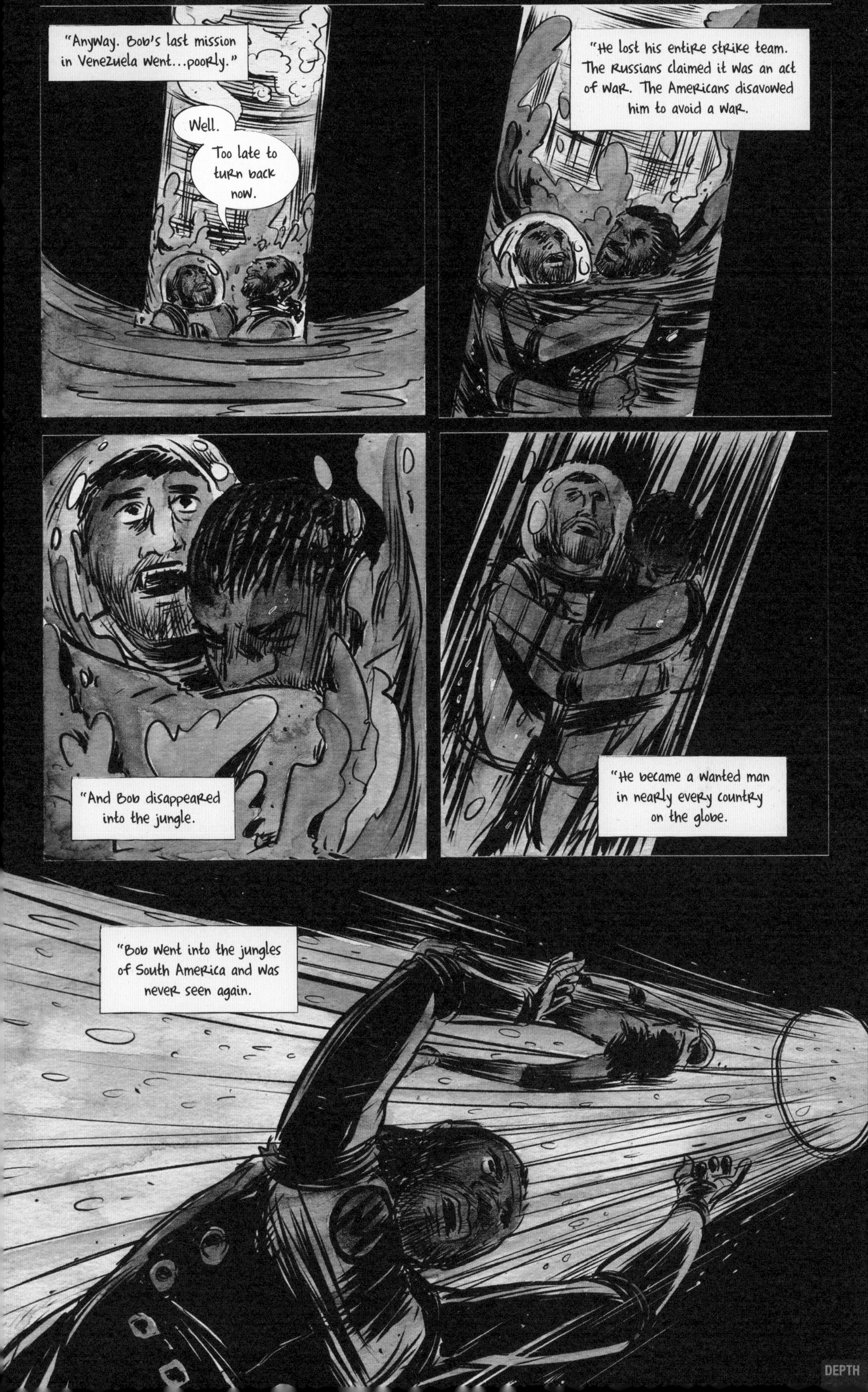
"Anyway. Bob's last mission in Venezuela went...poorly."
Well.
Too late to turn back now.
"He lost his entire strike team. The Russians claimed it was an act of war. The Americans disavowed him to avoid a war.
"And Bob disappeared into the jungle.
"He became a wanted man in nearly every country on the globe.
"Bob went into the jungles of South America and was never seen again.

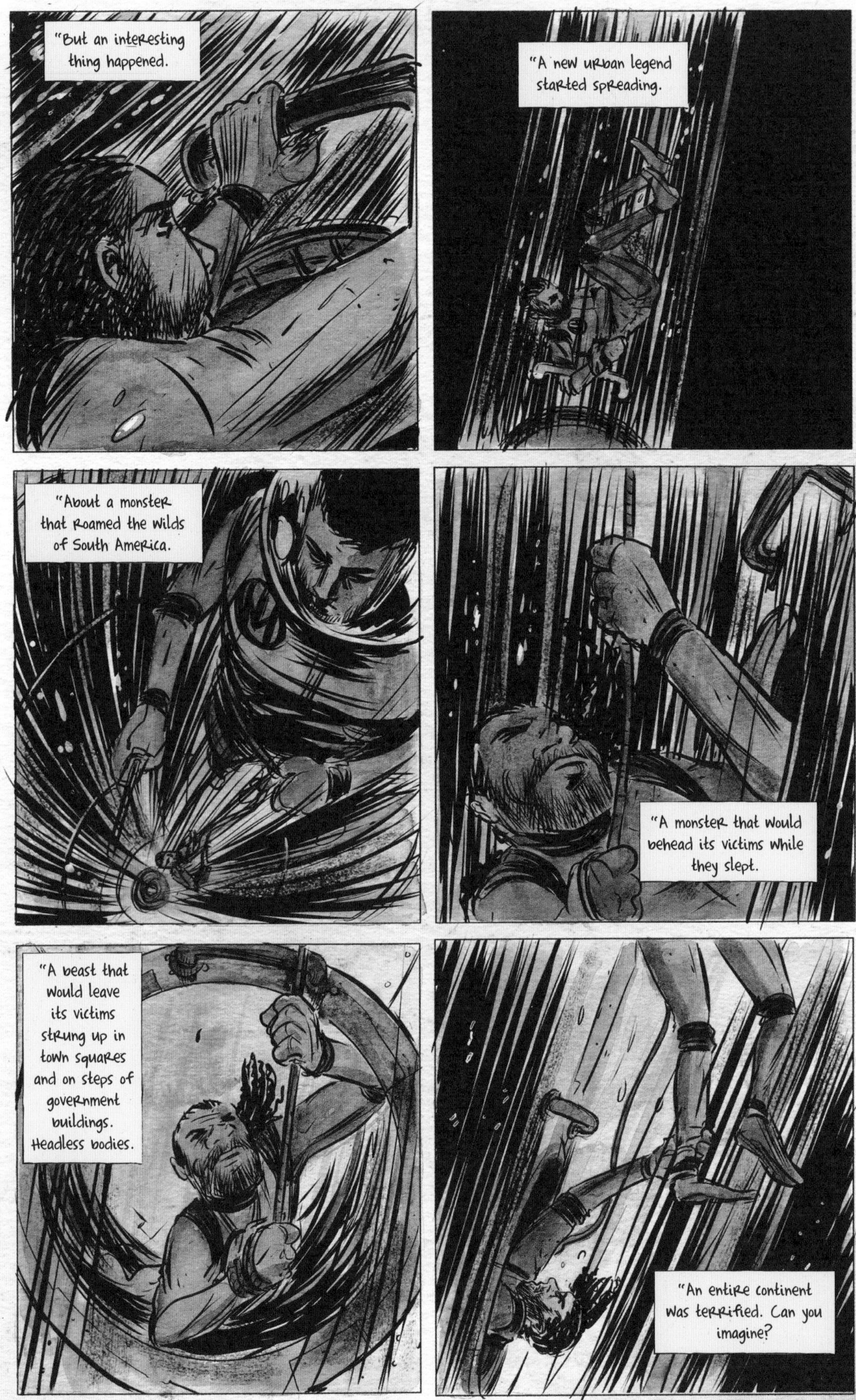
"But an interesting thing happened.
"A new urban legend started spreading.
"About a monster that roamed the wilds of South America.
"A monster that would behead its victims while they slept.
"A beast that would leave its victims strung up in town squares and on steps of government buildings. Headless bodies.
"An entire continent was terrified. Can you imagine?

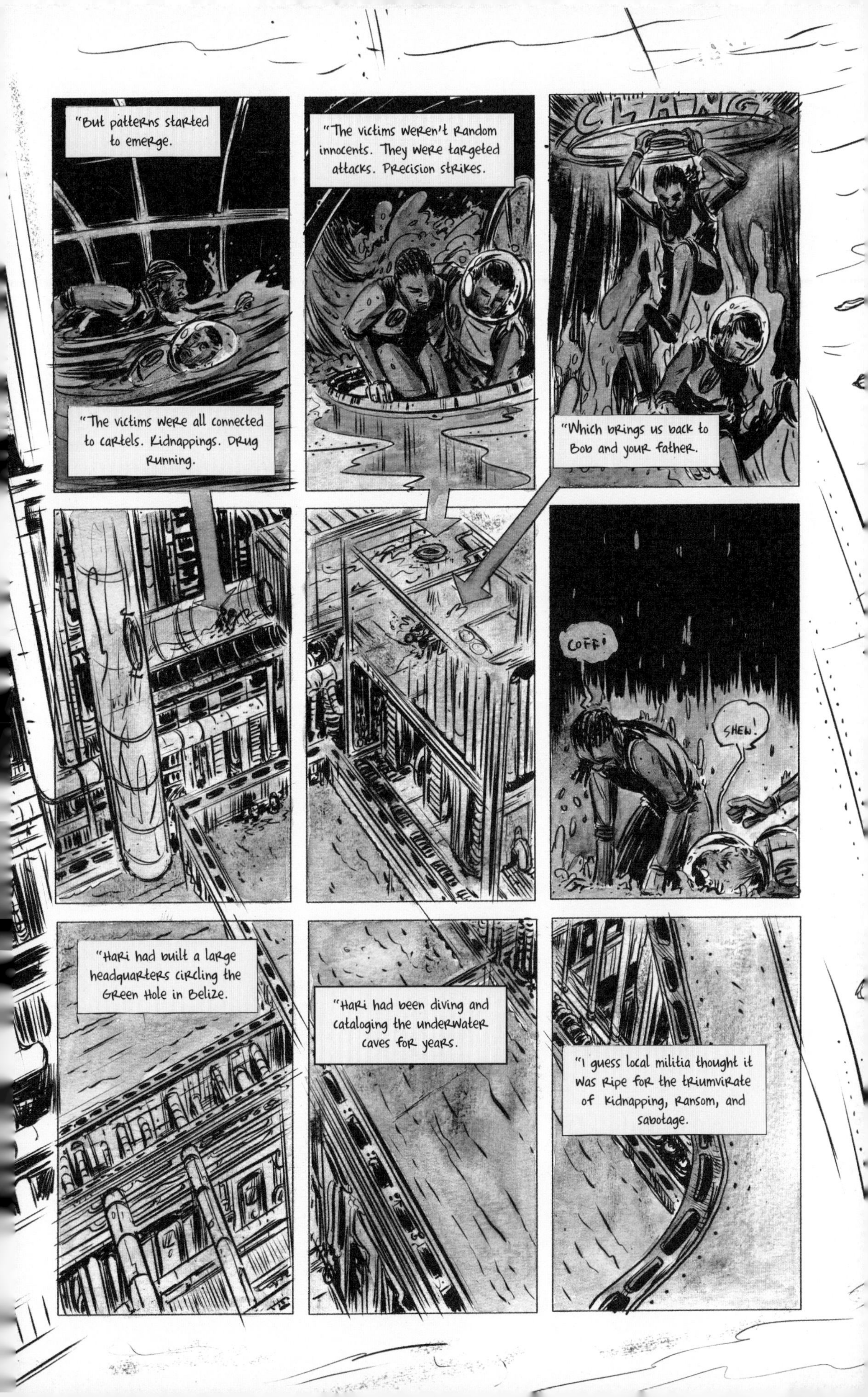

"But patterns started to emerge.
"The victims were all connected to cartels. Kidnappings. Drug Running.
"The victims weren't Random innocents. They were targeted attacks. Precision strikes.
CLANG
"Which brings us back to Bob and your father.
COFF!
SHEW!
"Hari had built a large headquarters circling the Green Hole in Belize.
"Hari had been diving and cataloging the underwater caves for years.
"I guess local militia thought it was ripe for the triumvirate of kidnapping, ransom, and sabotage.

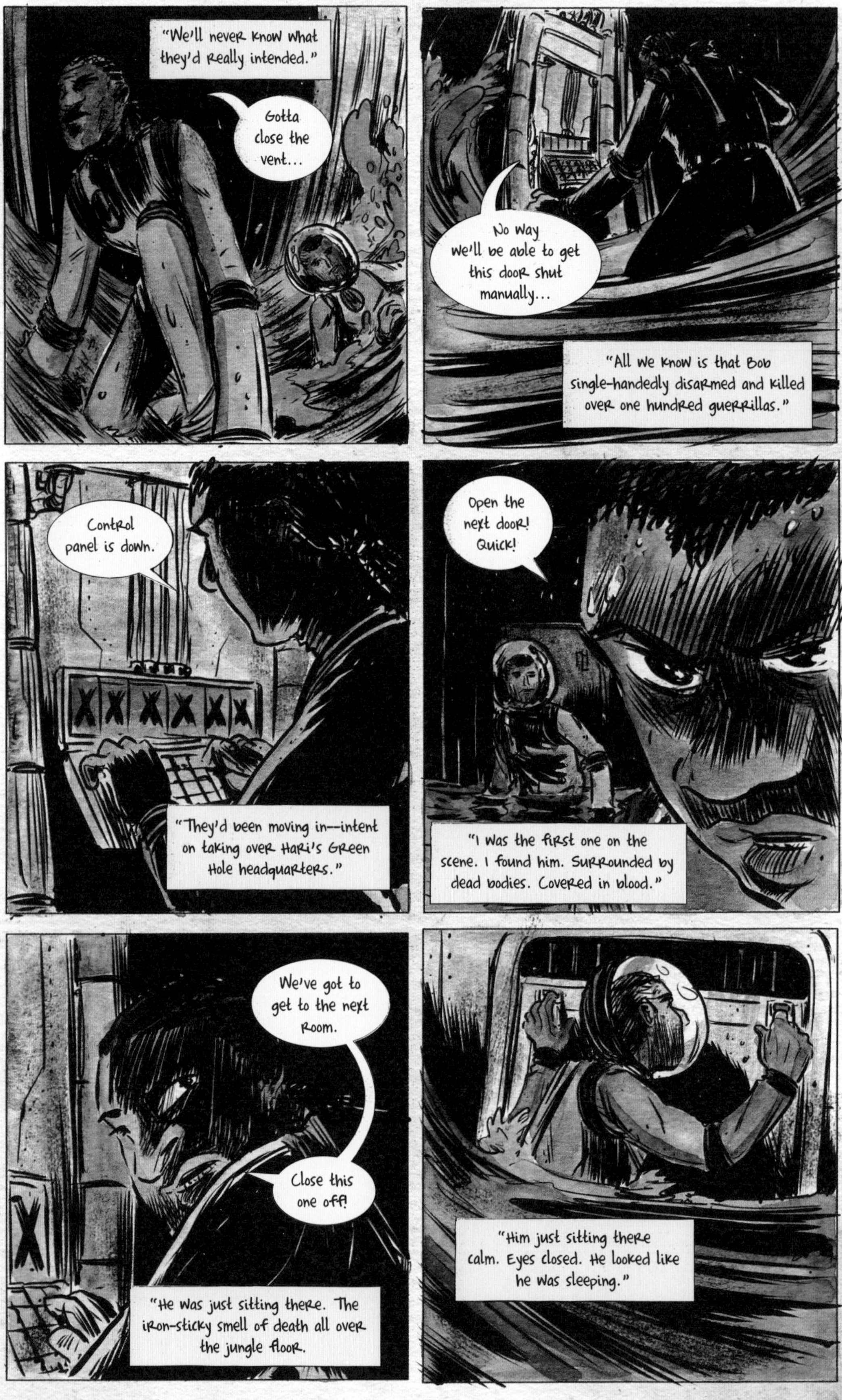
"We'll never know what they'd really intended."
Gotta close the vent...
No way we'll be able to get this door shut manually...
"All we know is that Bob single-handedly disarmed and killed over one hundred guerrillas."
Control panel is down.
"They'd been moving in--intent on taking over Hari's Green Hole headquarters."
Open the next door! Quick!
"I was the first one on the scene. I found him. Surrounded by dead bodies. Covered in blood."
We've got to get to the next room.
Close this one off!
"He was just sitting there. The iron-sticky smell of death all over the jungle floor.
"Him just sitting there calm. Eyes closed. He looked like he was sleeping."

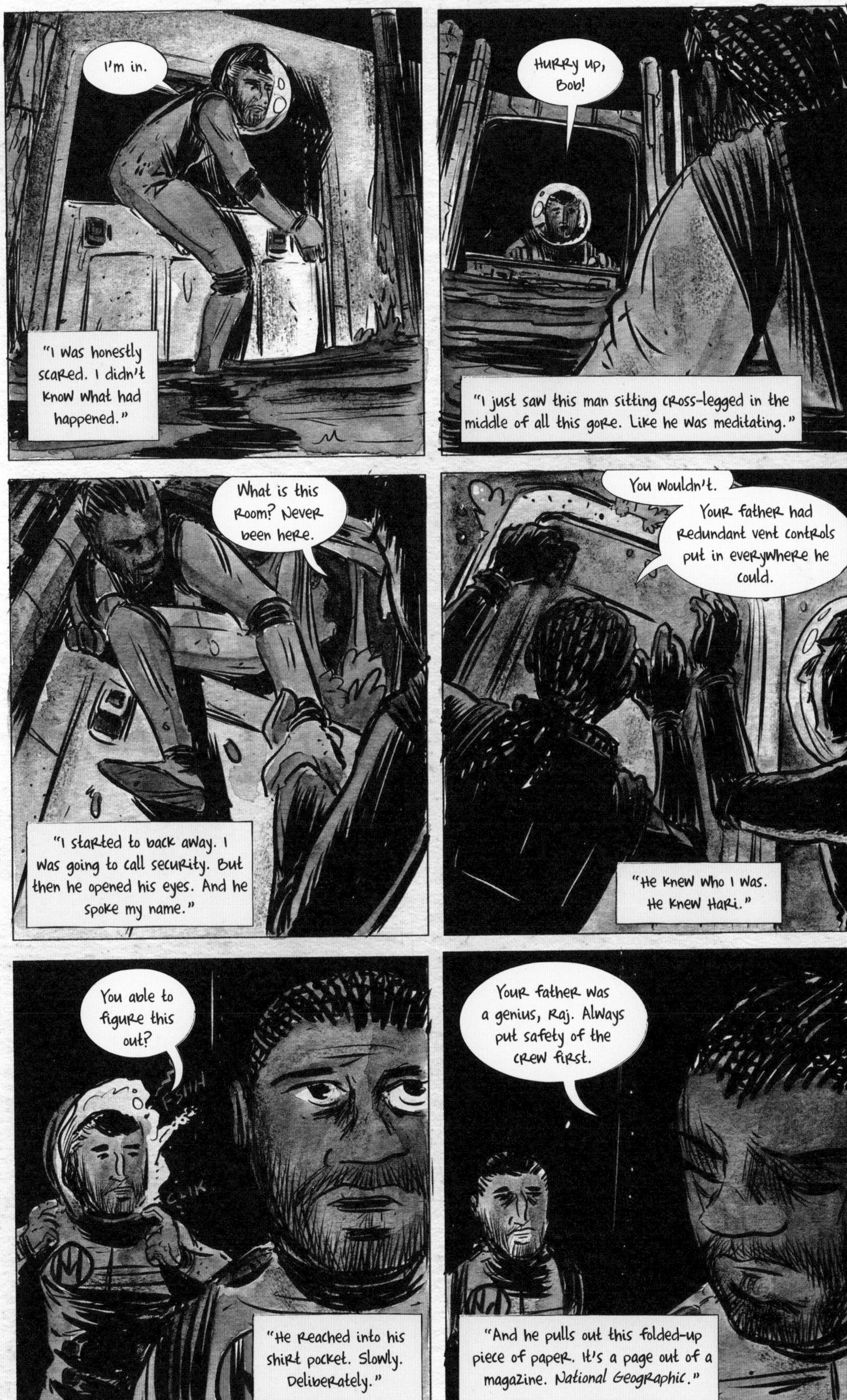
I'm in.
"I was honestly scared. I didn't know what had happened."
Hurry up, Bob!
"I just saw this man sitting cross-legged in the middle of all this gore. Like he was meditating."
What is this room? Never been here.
"I started to back away. I was going to call security. But then he opened his eyes. And he spoke my name."
You wouldn't.
Your father had redundant vent controls put in everywhere he could.
"He knew who I was. He knew Hari."
You able to figure this out?
FSHH
CLIK
"He reached into his shirt pocket. Slowly. Deliberately."
Your father was a genius, Raj. Always put safety of the crew first.
"And he pulls out this folded-up piece of paper. It's a page out of a magazine. National Geographic."

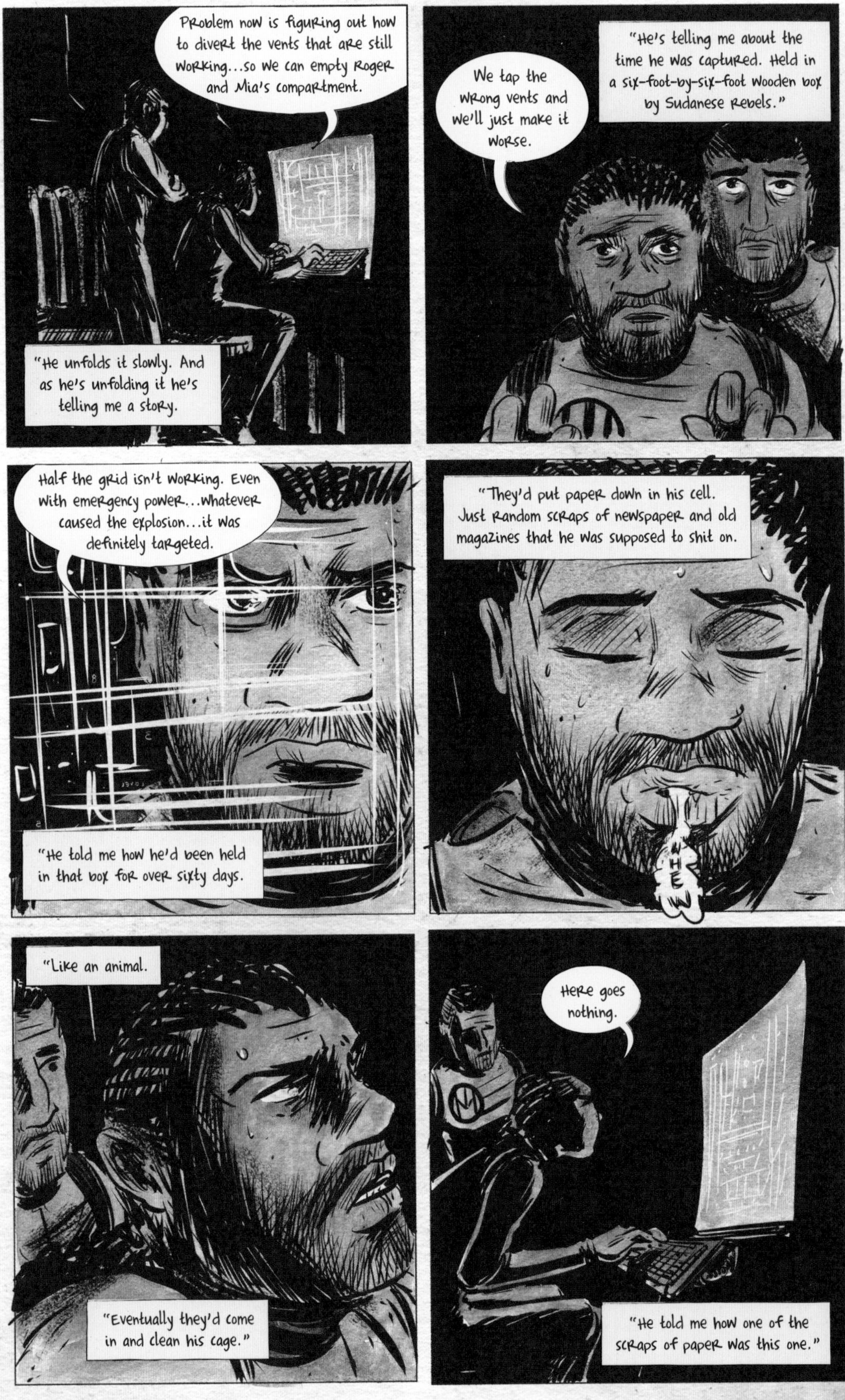
Problem now is figuring out how to divert the vents that are still working...so we can empty Roger and Mia's compartment.
"He unfolds it slowly. And as he's unfolding it he's telling me a story.
We tap the wrong vents and we'll just make it worse.
"He's telling me about the time he was captured. Held in a six-foot-by-six-foot wooden box by Sudanese rebels."
Half the grid isn't working. Even with emergency power...whatever caused the explosion...it was definitely targeted.
"He told me how he'd been held in that box for over sixty days.
"They'd put paper down in his cell. Just random scraps of newspaper and old magazines that he was supposed to shit on.
"Like an animal.
"Eventually they'd come in and clean his cage."
Here goes nothing.
"He told me how one of the scraps of paper was this one."

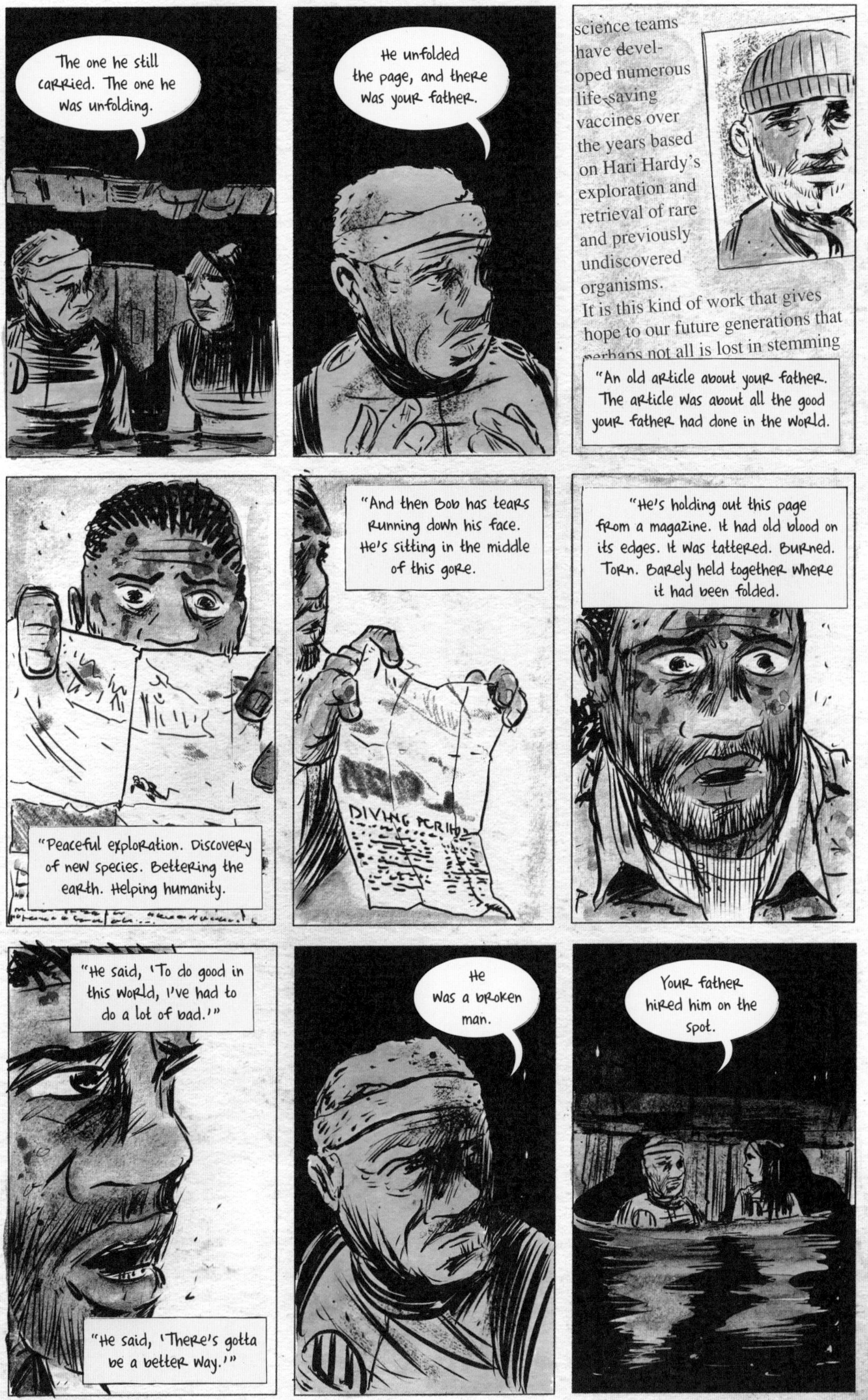
The one he still carried. The one he was unfolding.
He unfolded the page, and there was your father.
science teams have developed numerous life-saving vaccines over the years based on Hari Hardy's exploration and retrieval of rare and previously undiscovered organisms.
It is this kind of work that gives hope to our future generations that perhaps not all is lost in stemming
"An old article about your father. The article was about all the good your father had done in the world.
"Peaceful exploration. Discovery of new species. Bettering the earth. Helping humanity.
"And then Bob has tears running down his face. He's sitting in the middle of this gore.
"He's holding out this page from a magazine. It had old blood on its edges. It was tattered. Burned. Torn. Barely held together where it had been folded.
"He said, 'To do good in this world, I've had to do a lot of bad.'"
"He said, 'There's gotta be a better way.'"
He was a broken man.
Your father hired him on the spot.

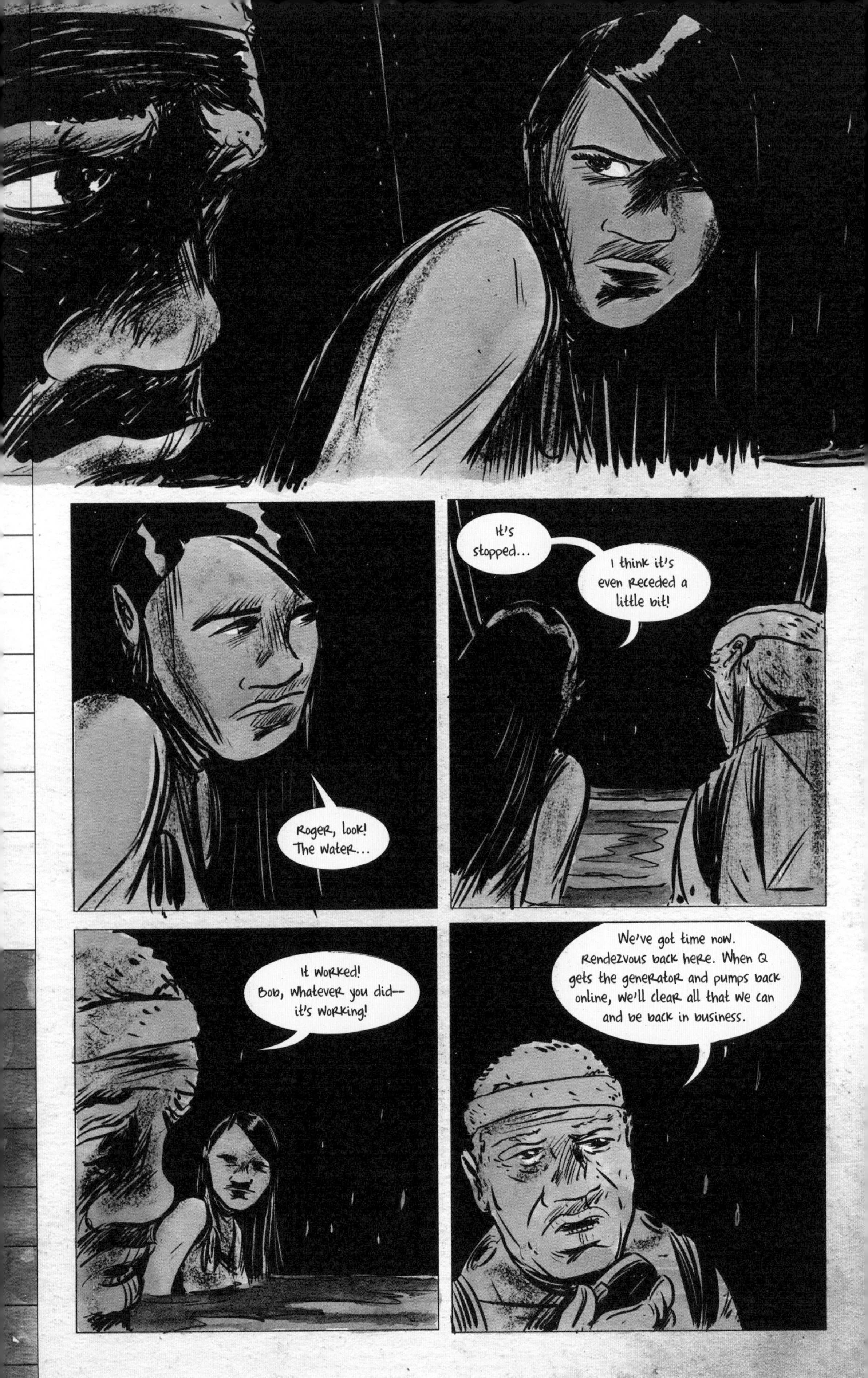
Roger, look! The water...
It's stopped...
I think it's even receded a little bit!
It worked! Bob, whatever you did-- it's working!
We've got time now. Rendezvous back here. When Q gets the generator and pumps back online, we'll clear all that we can and be back in business.

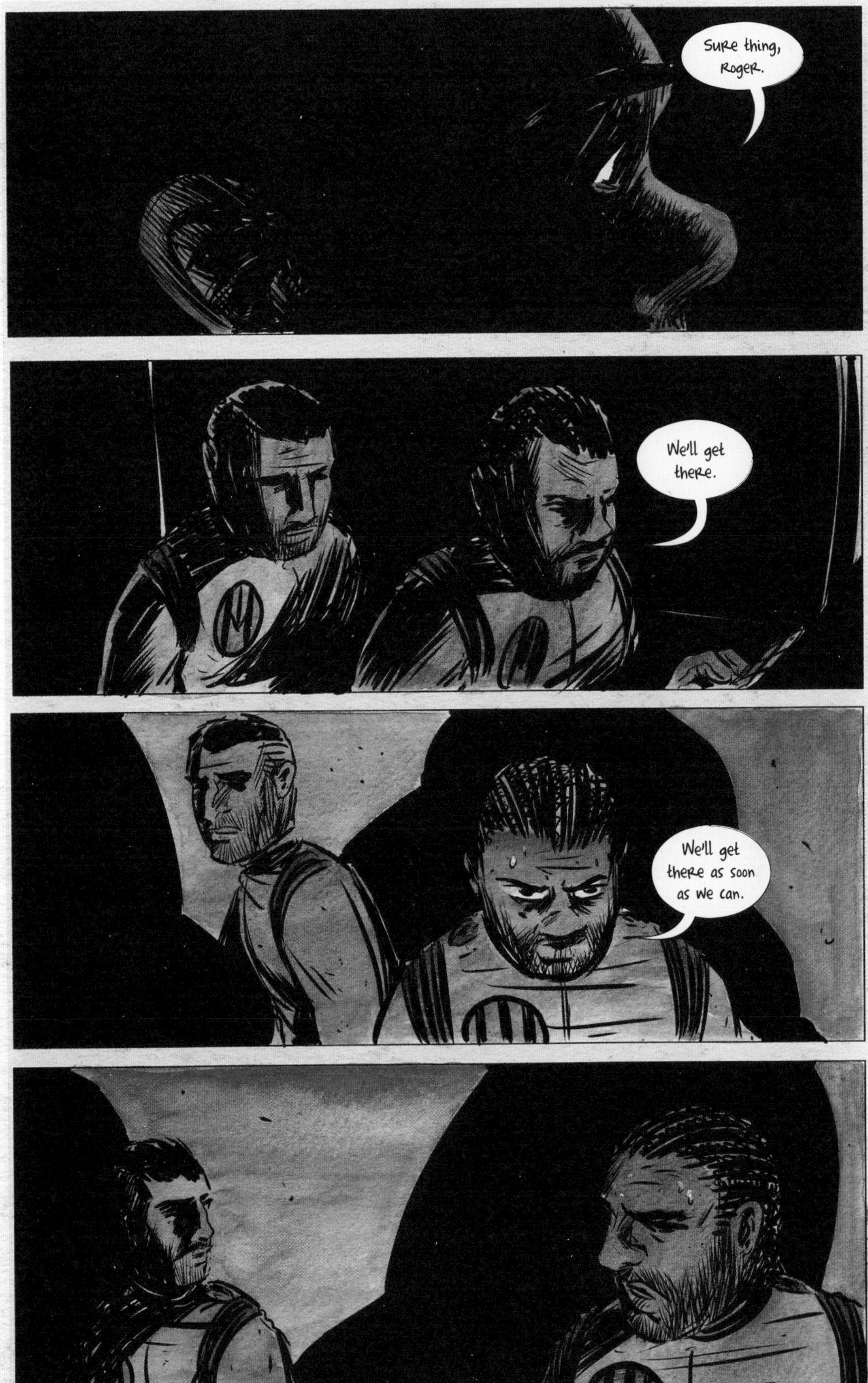
Sure thing, Roger.
We'll get there.
We'll get there as soon as we can.

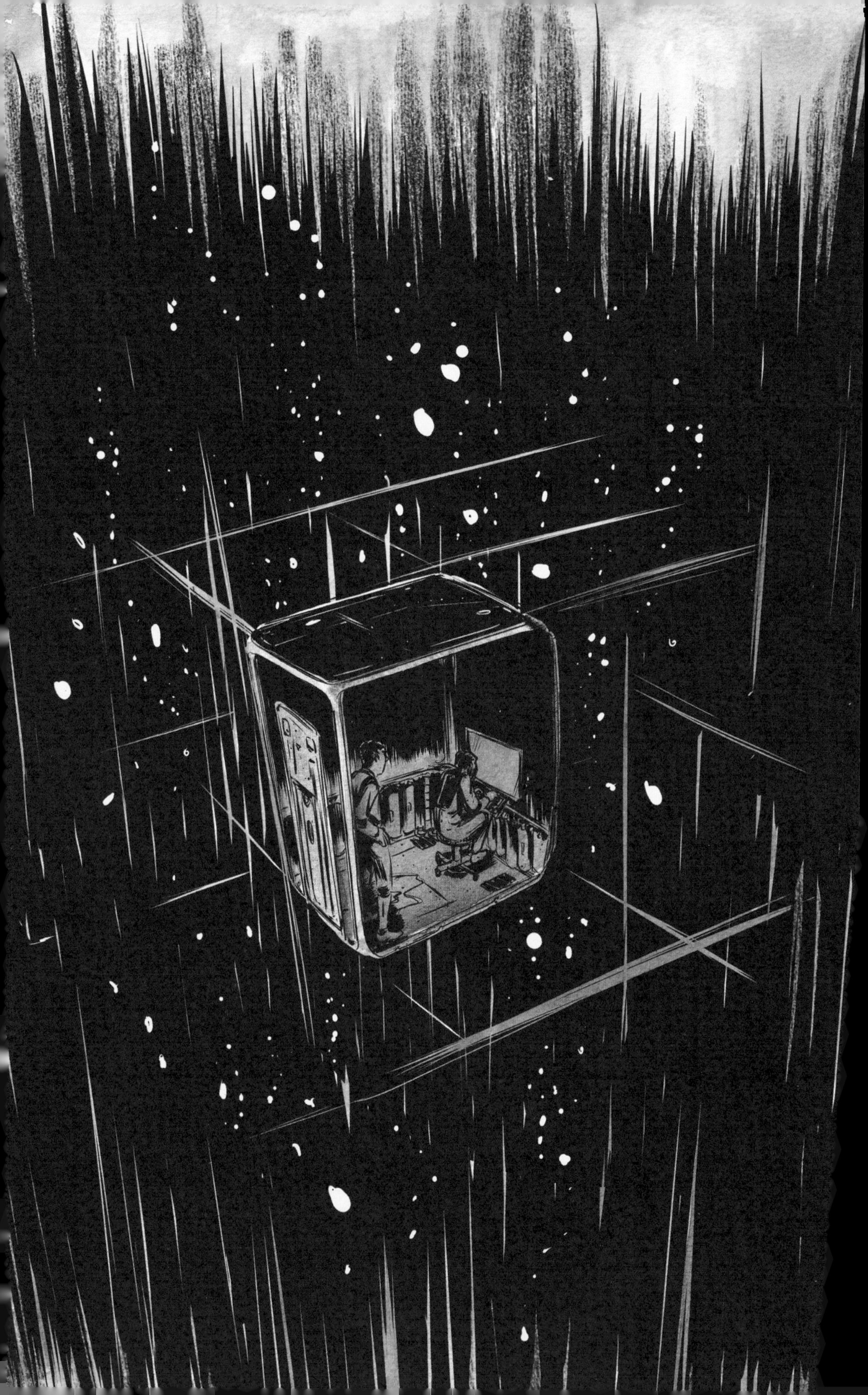

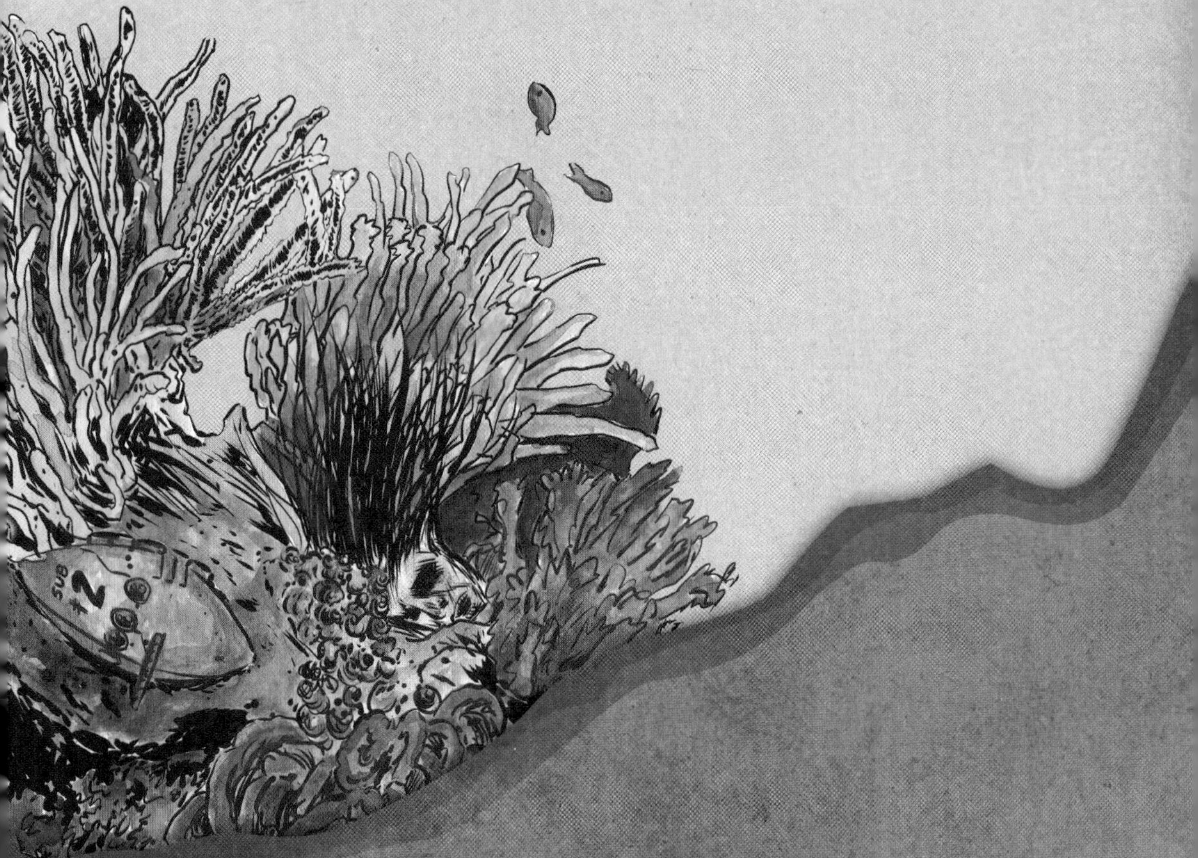
SUB
*2

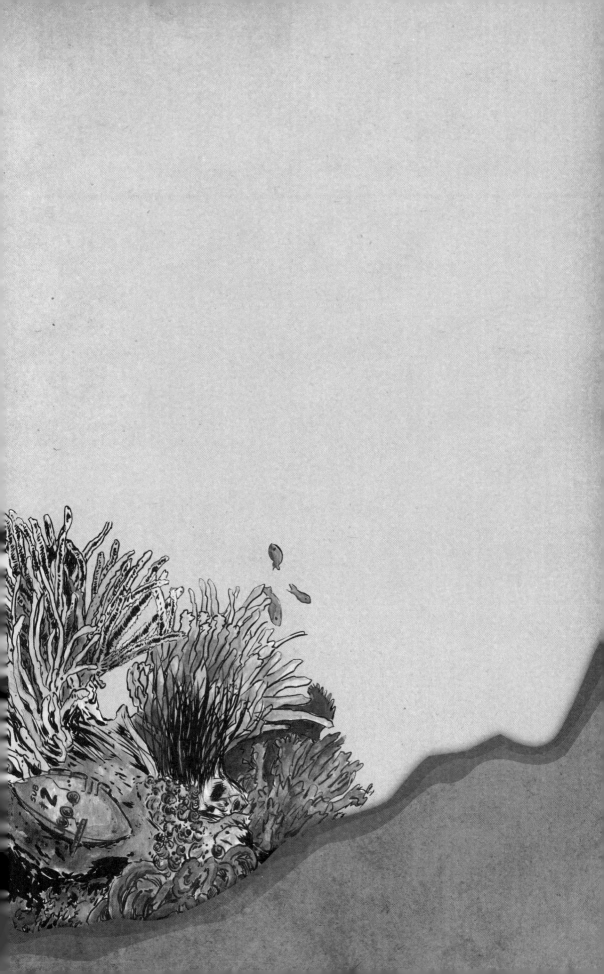

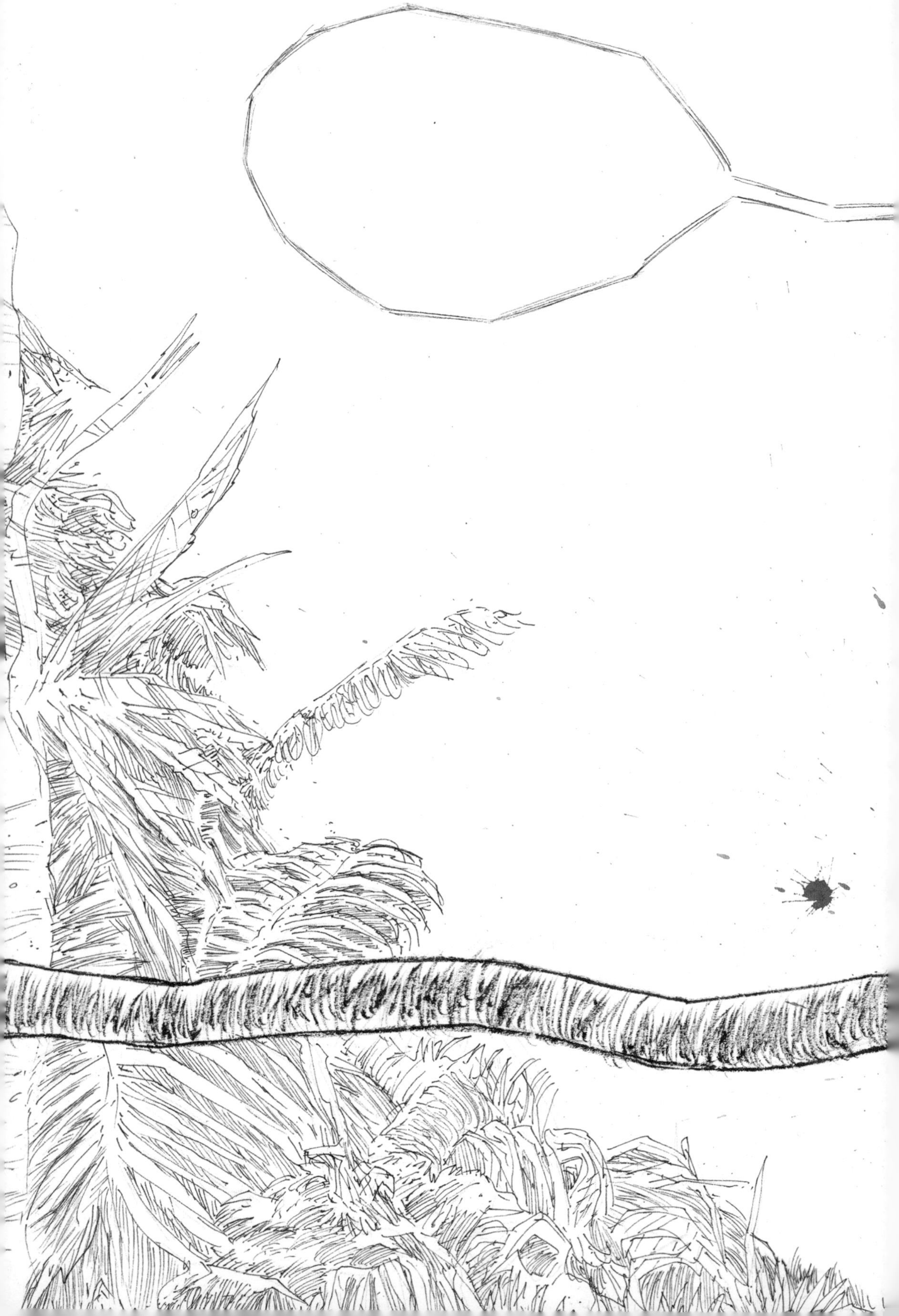

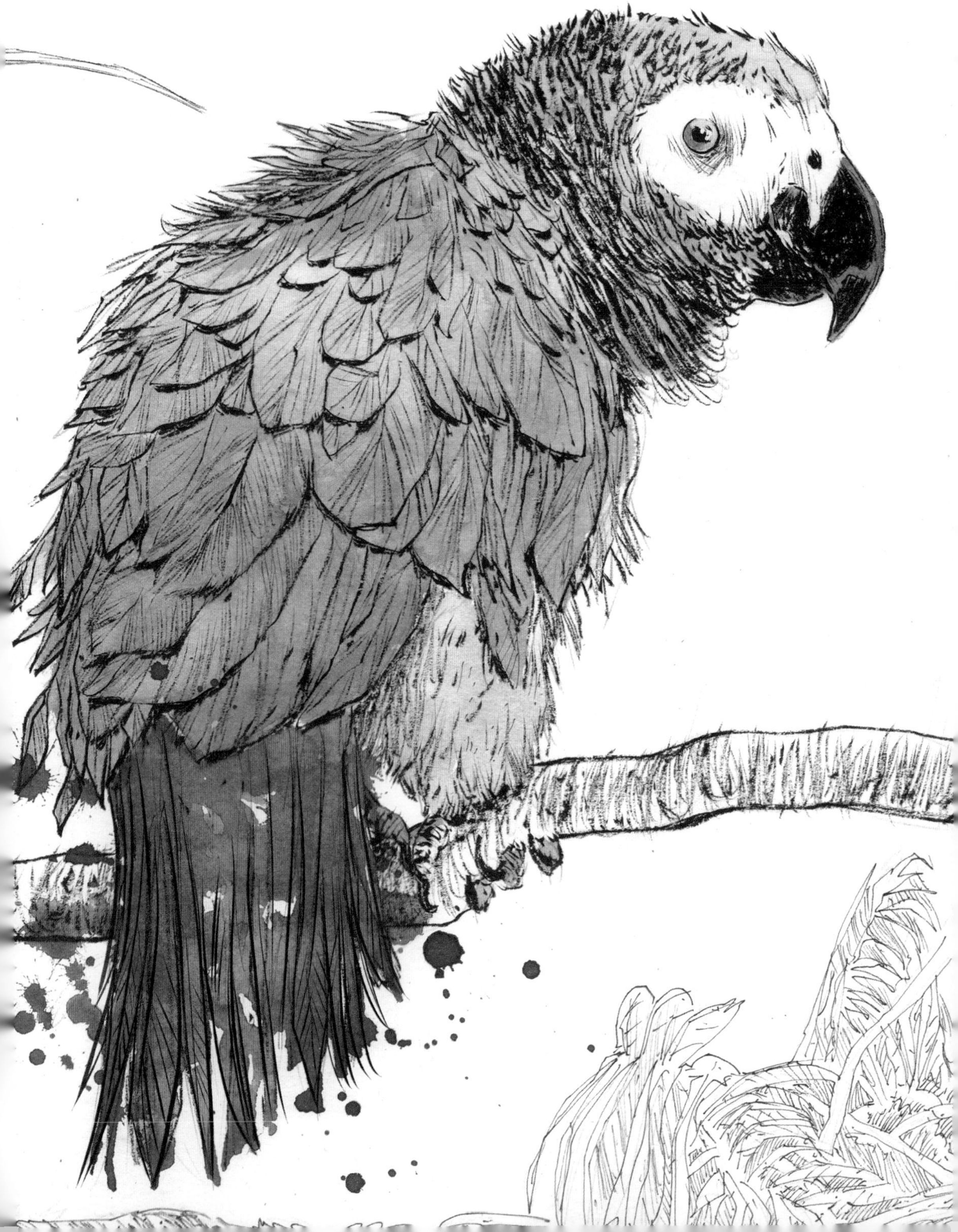

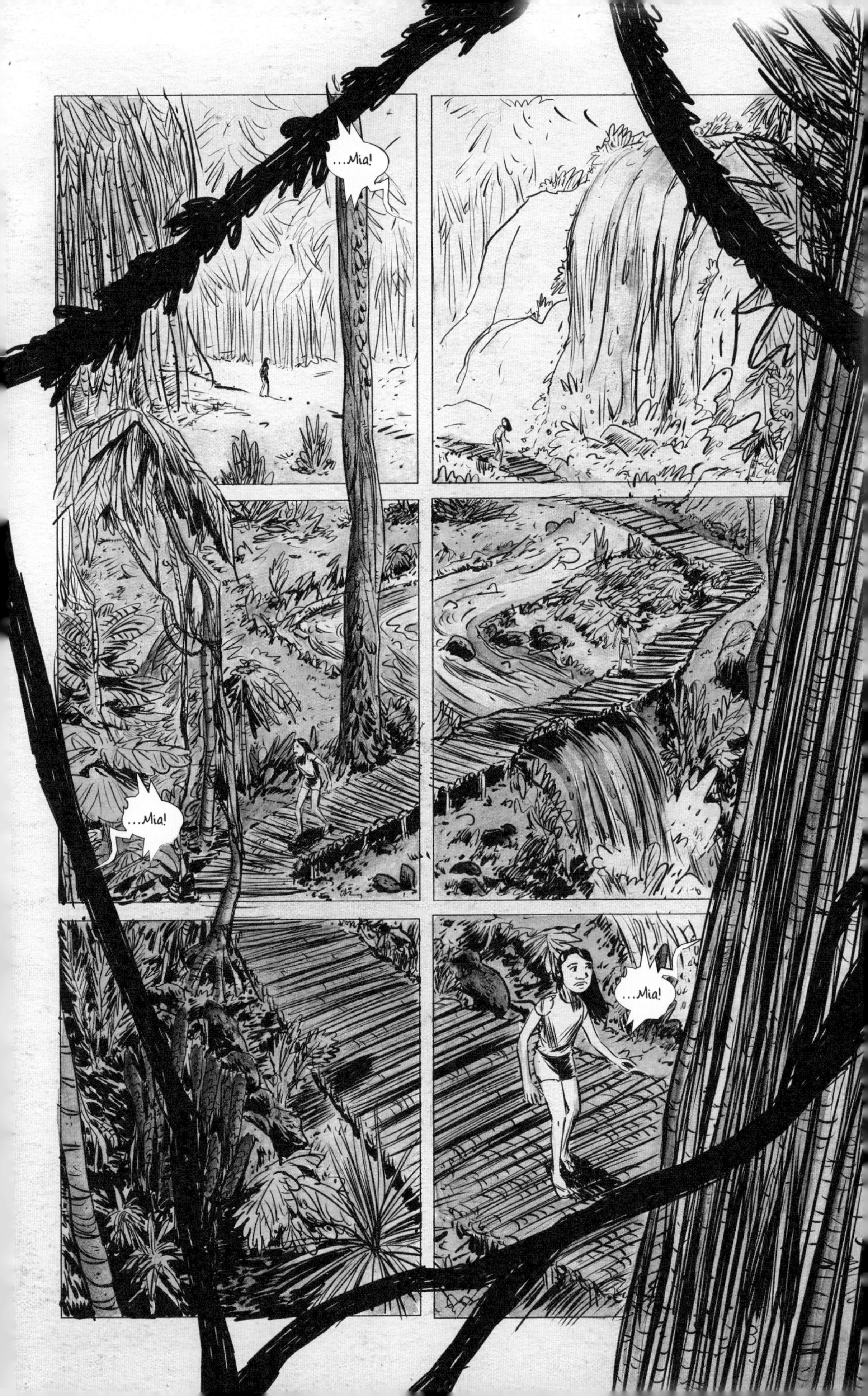
…Mia!
…Mia!
…Mia!

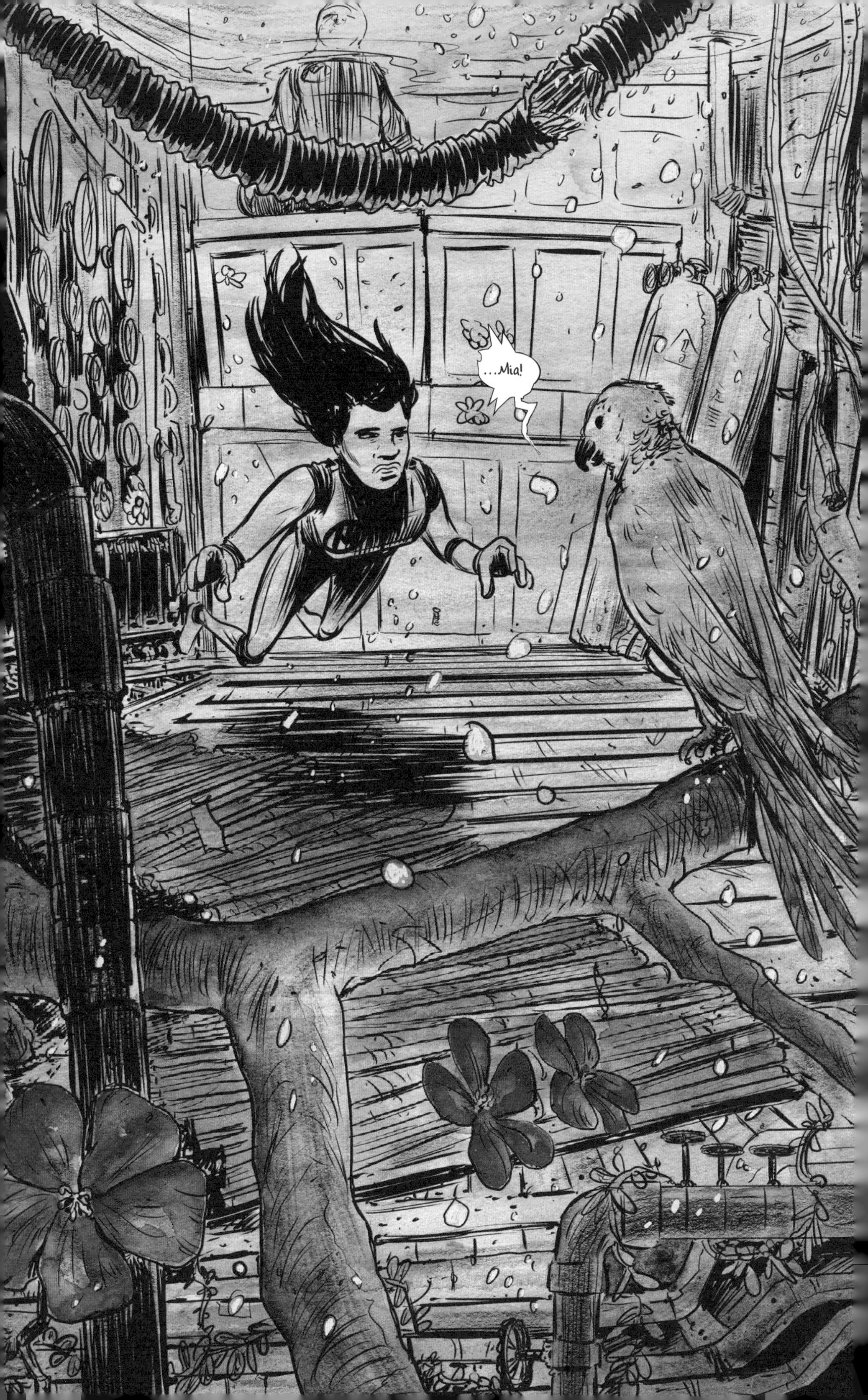
...Mia!

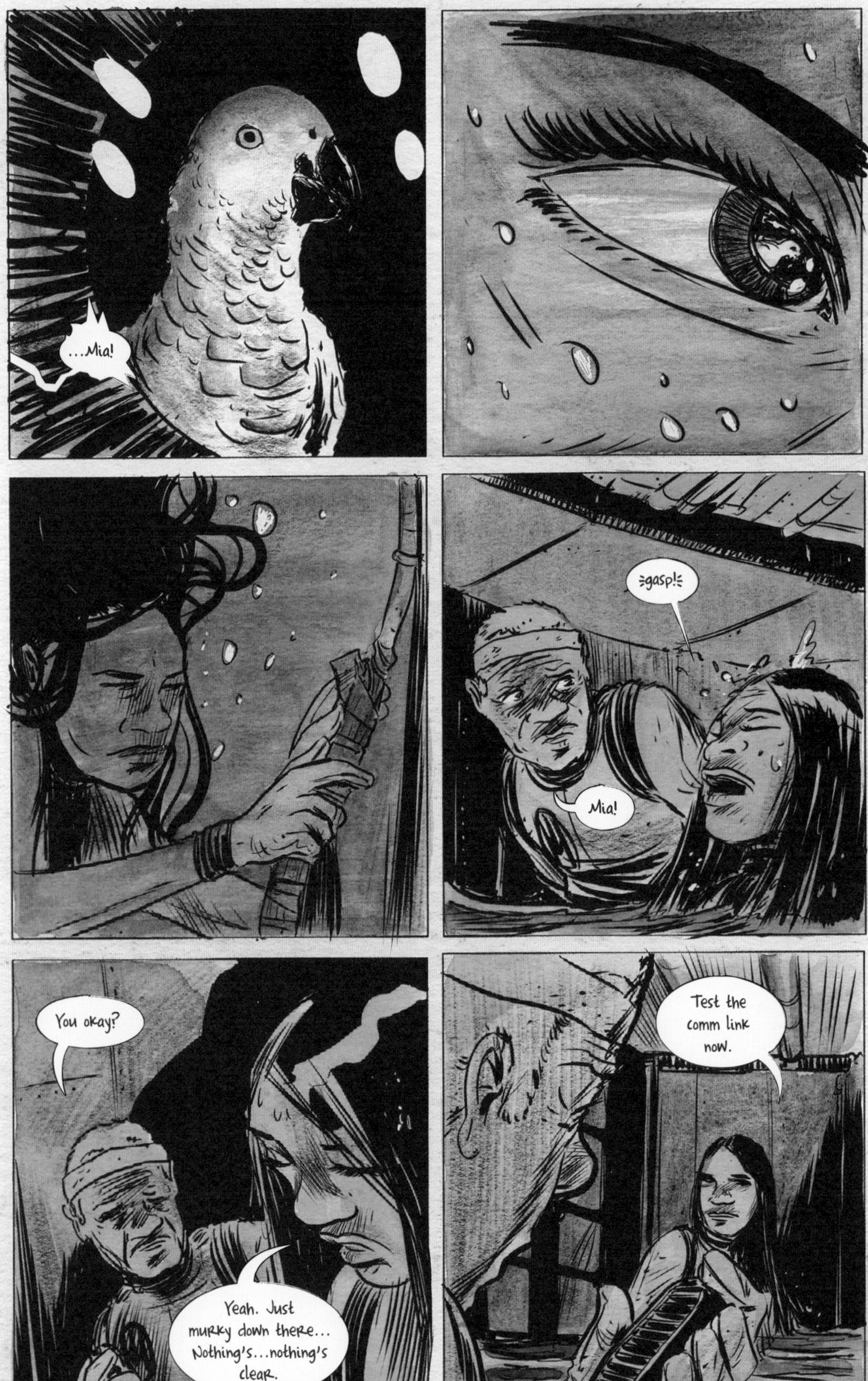
...Mia!
≈gasp!≈
Mia!
You okay?
Yeah. Just murky down there... Nothing's...nothing's clear.
Test the comm link now.

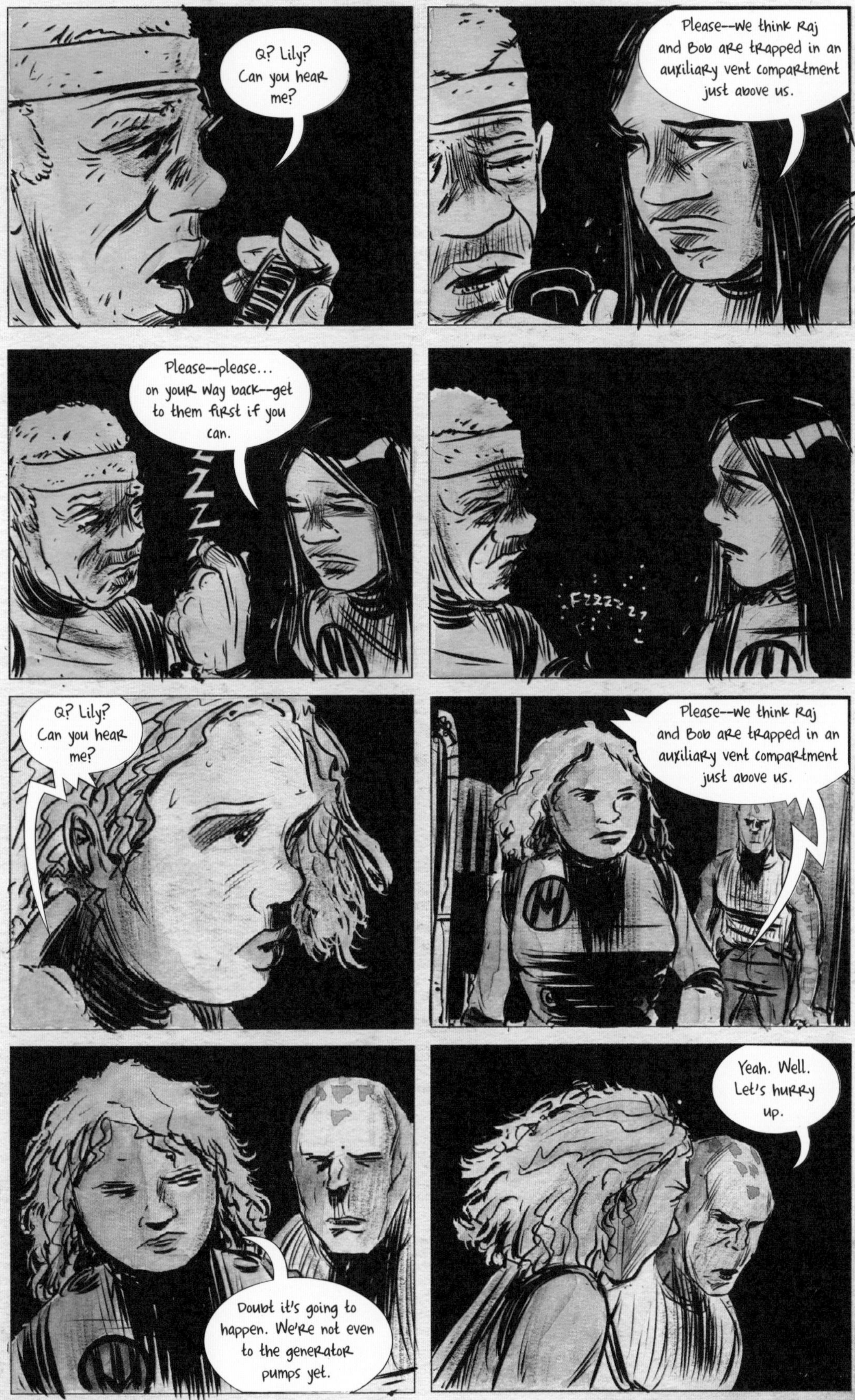
Q? Lily? Can you hear me?
Please--we think Raj and Bob are trapped in an auxiliary vent compartment just above us.
Please--please... on your way back--get to them first if you can.
ZZZZ
FZZZZZZ
Q? Lily? Can you hear me?
Please--we think Raj and Bob are trapped in an auxiliary vent compartment just above us.
Doubt it's going to happen. We're not even to the generator pumps yet.
Yeah. Well. Let's hurry up.

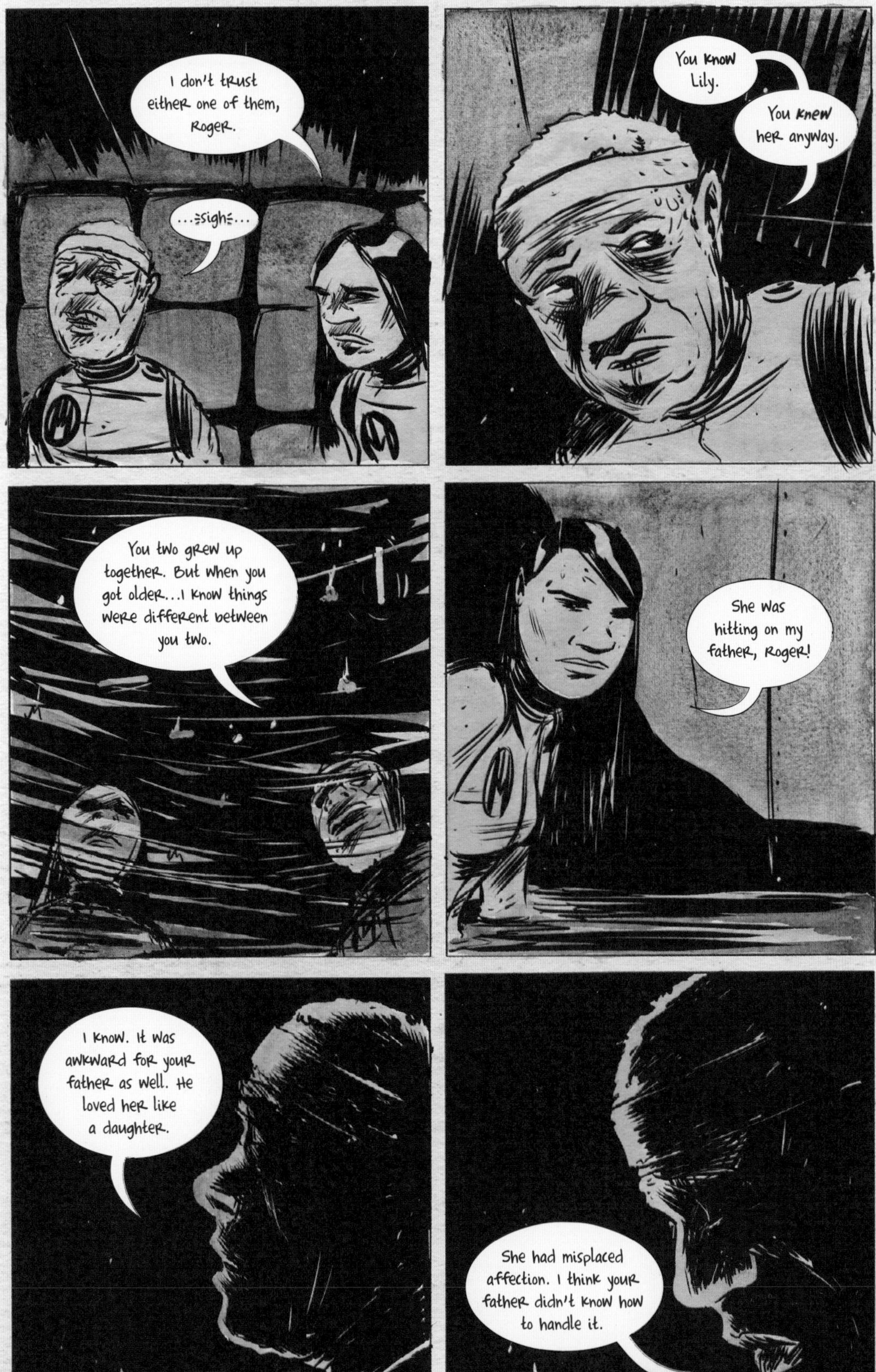
I don't trust either one of them, Roger.
...sigh...
You know Lily.
You knew her anyway.
You two grew up together. But when you got older...I know things were different between you two.
She was hitting on my father, Roger!
I know. It was awkward for your father as well. He loved her like a daughter.
She had misplaced affection. I think your father didn't know how to handle it.

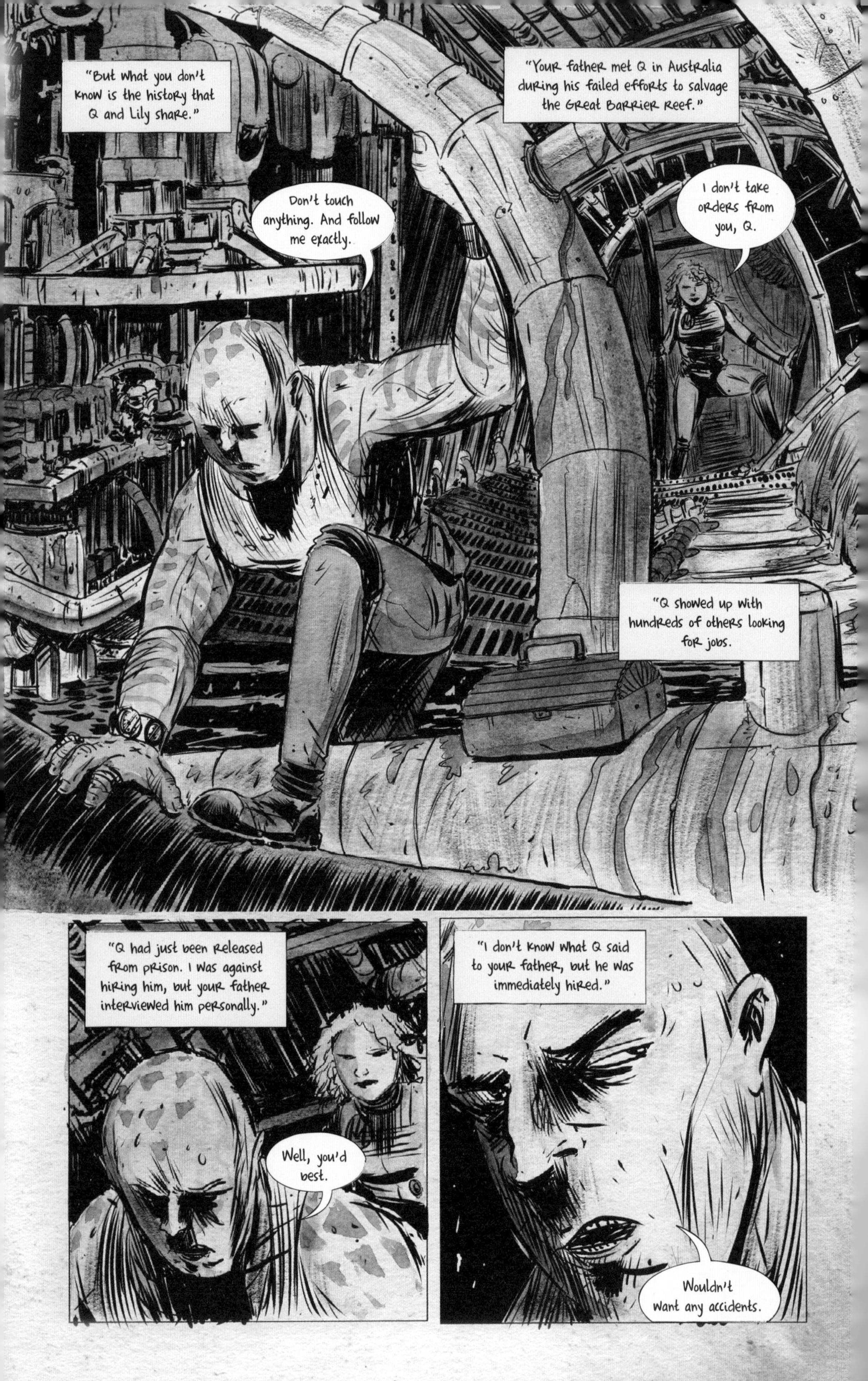
"But what you don't know is the history that Q and Lily share."
"Your father met Q in Australia during his failed efforts to salvage the Great Barrier Reef."
Don't touch anything. And follow me exactly.
I don't take orders from you, Q.
"Q showed up with hundreds of others looking for jobs.
"Q had just been released from prison. I was against hiring him, but your father interviewed him personally."
Well, you'd best.
"I don't know what Q said to your father, but he was immediately hired."
Wouldn't want any accidents.

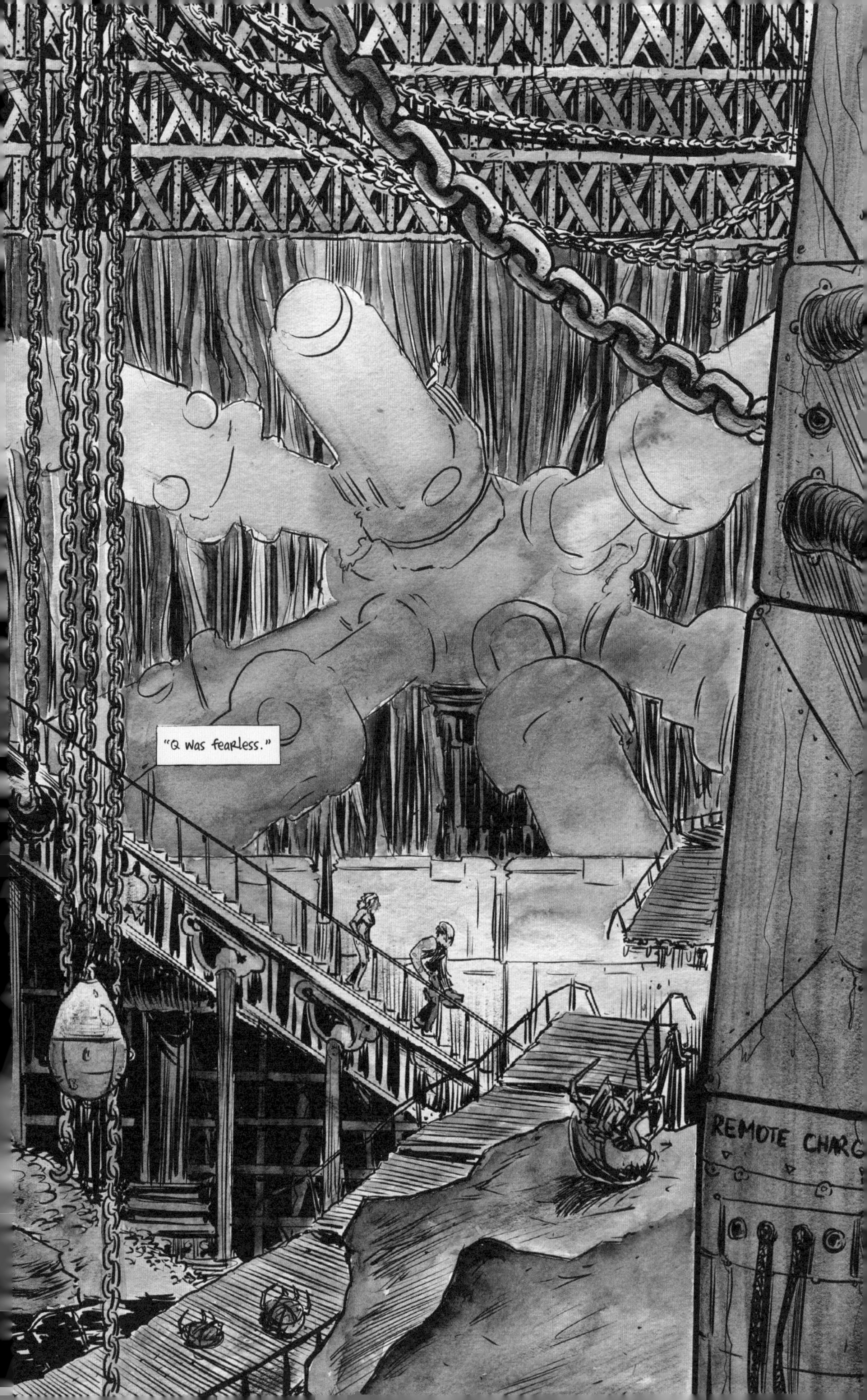
"Q was fearless."
REMOTE CHARG

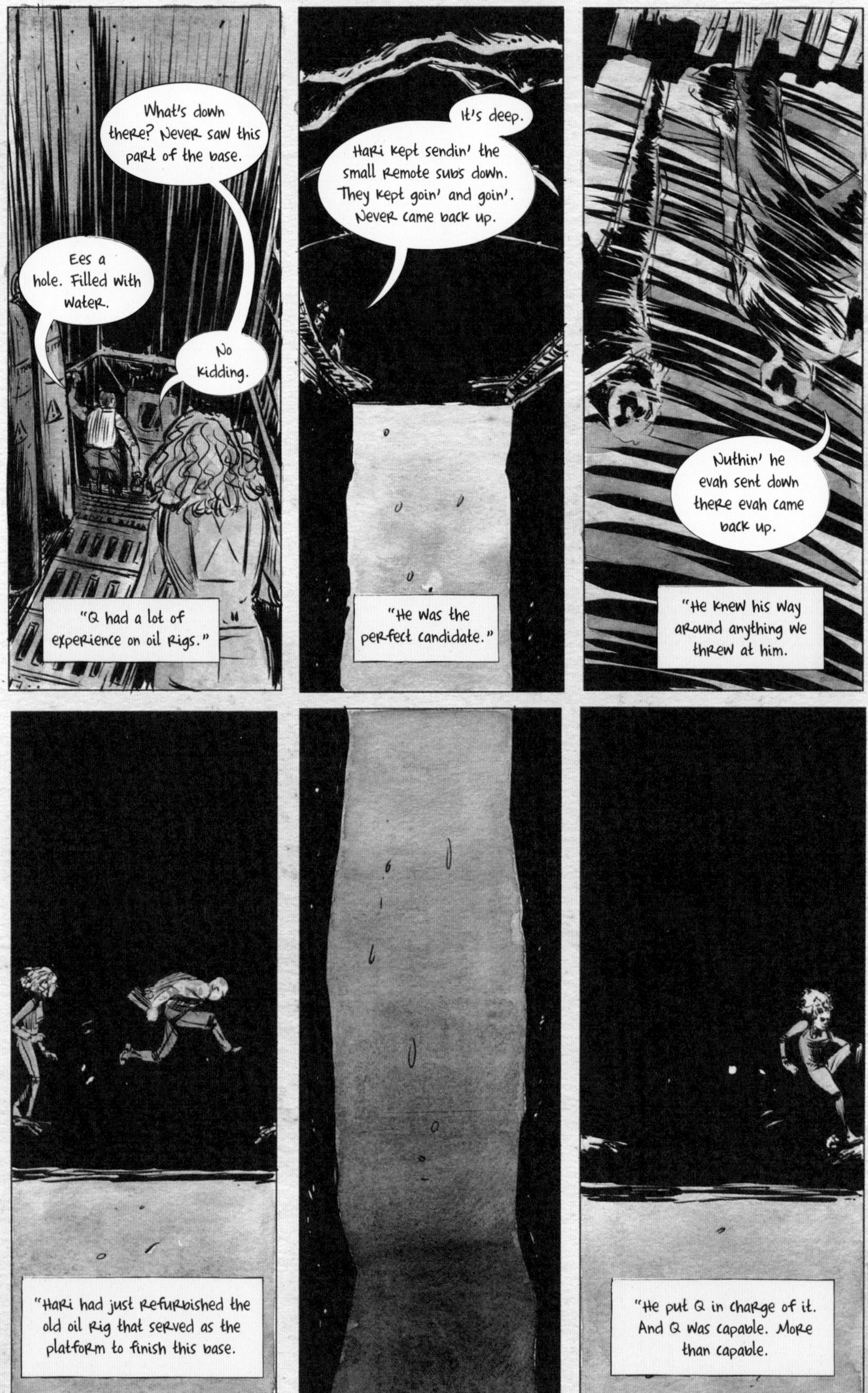
What's down there? Never saw this part of the base.
Ees a hole. Filled with water.
No kidding.
"Q had a lot of experience on oil rigs."
It's deep.
Hari kept sendin' the small remote subs down. They kept goin' and goin'. Never came back up.
"He was the perfect candidate."
Nuthin' he evah sent down there evah came back up.
"He knew his way around anything we threw at him.
"Hari had just refurbished the old oil rig that served as the platform to finish this base.
"He put Q in charge of it. And Q was capable. More than capable.

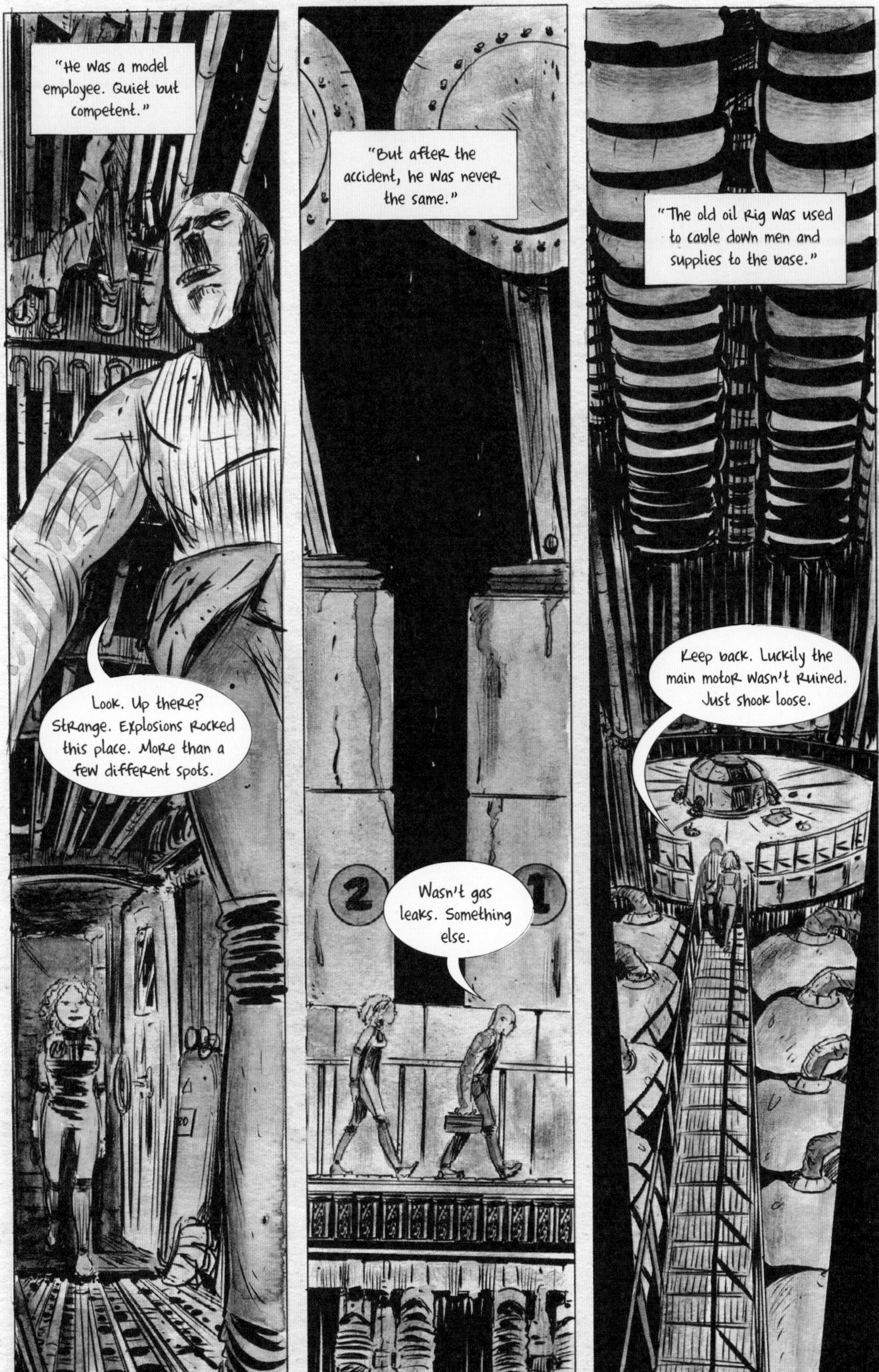
"He was a model employee. Quiet but competent."
Look. Up there? Strange. Explosions rocked this place. More than a few different spots.
"But after the accident, he was never the same."
2
1
Wasn't gas leaks. Something else.
"The old oil rig was used to cable down men and supplies to the base."
Keep back. Luckily the main motor wasn't ruined. Just shook loose.

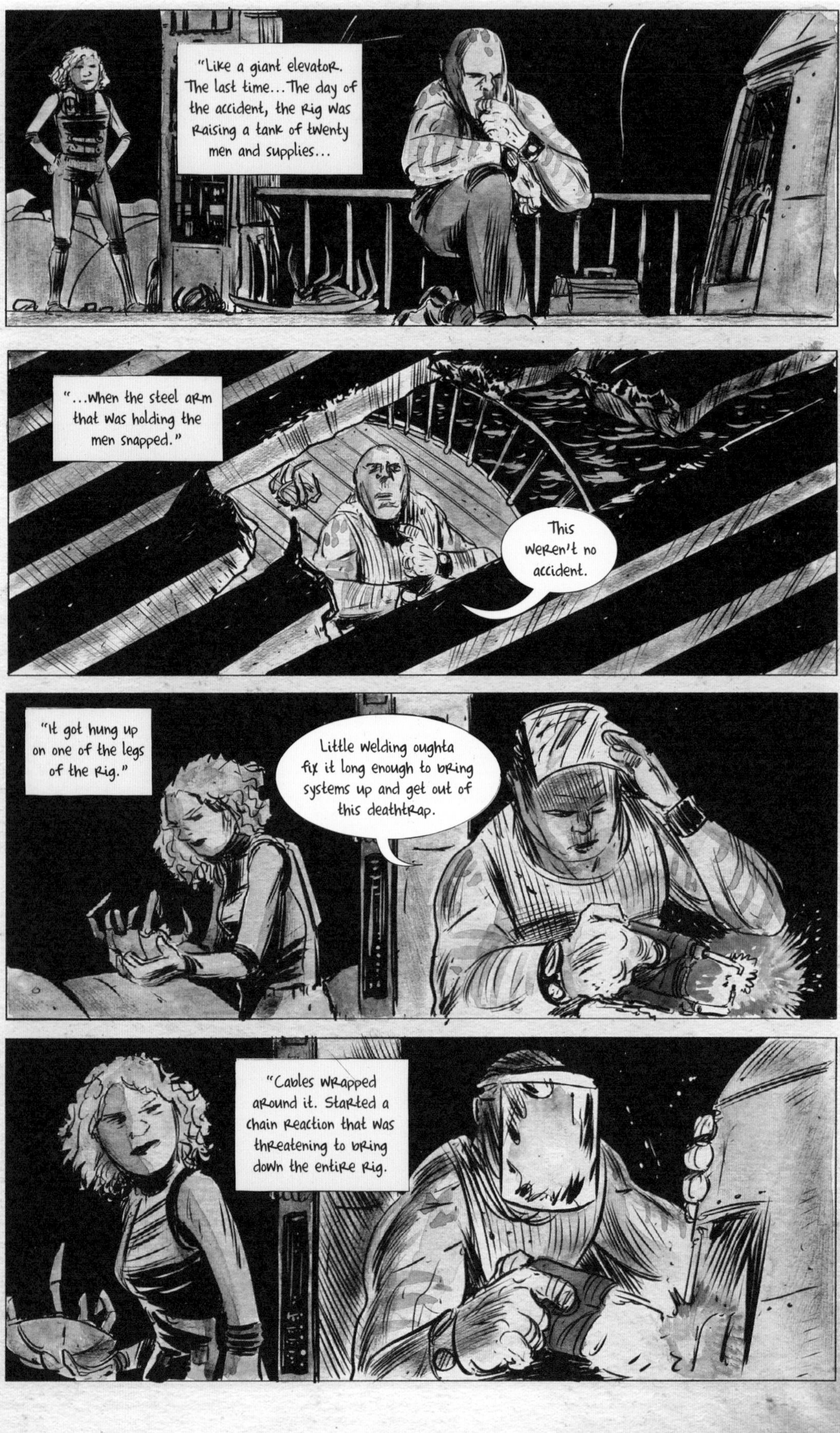
"Like a giant elevator. The last time... The day of the accident, the Rig was raising a tank of twenty men and supplies...
"...When the steel arm that was holding the men snapped."
This weren't no accident.
"It got hung up on one of the legs of the Rig."
Little welding oughta fix it long enough to bring systems up and get out of this deathtrap.
"Cables wrapped around it. Started a chain reaction that was threatening to bring down the entire Rig.

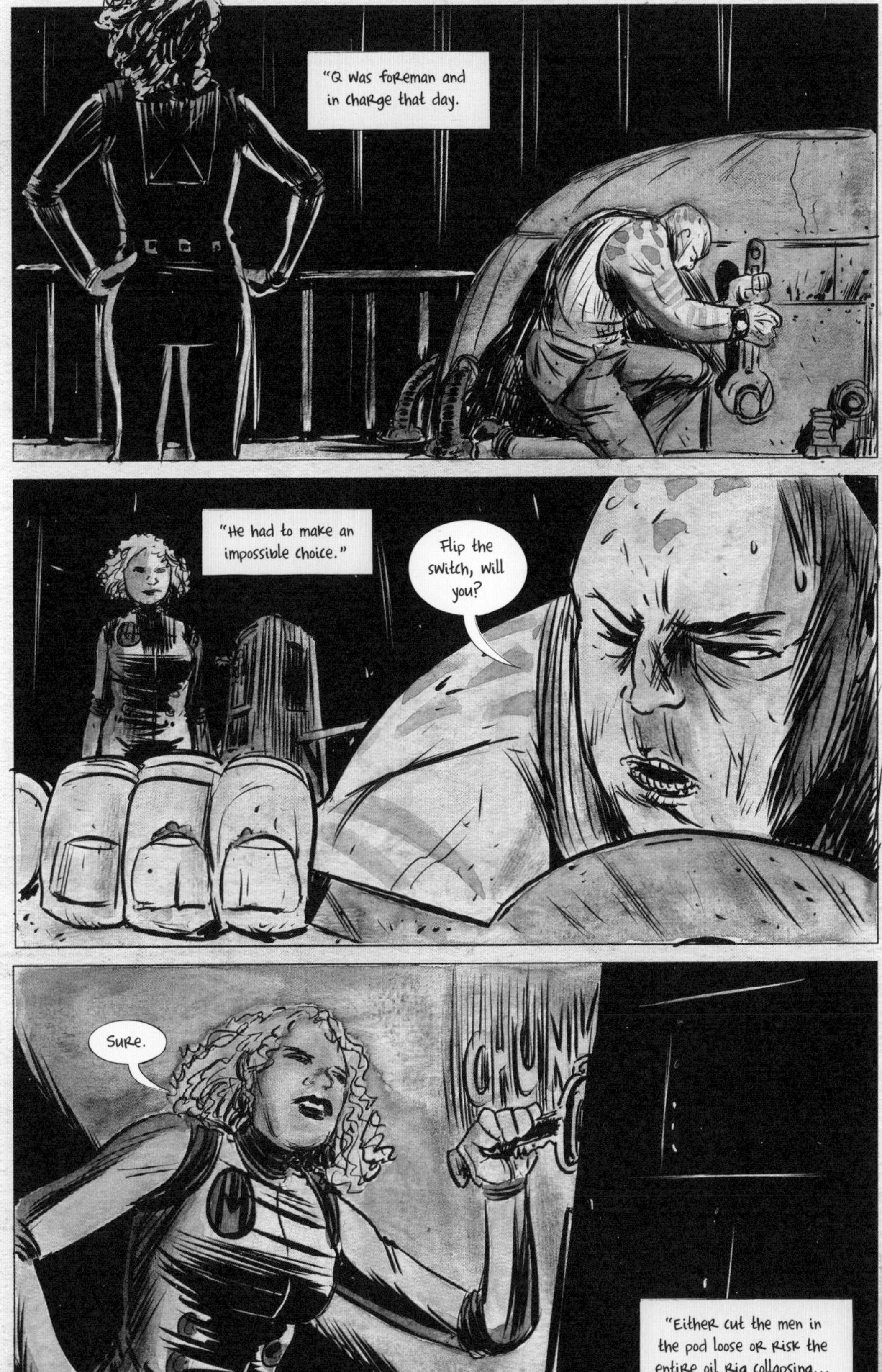
"Q was foreman and in charge that day.
"He had to make an impossible choice."
Flip the switch, will you?
Sure.
CHUNK
"Either cut the men in the pod loose or risk the entire oil rig collapsing...

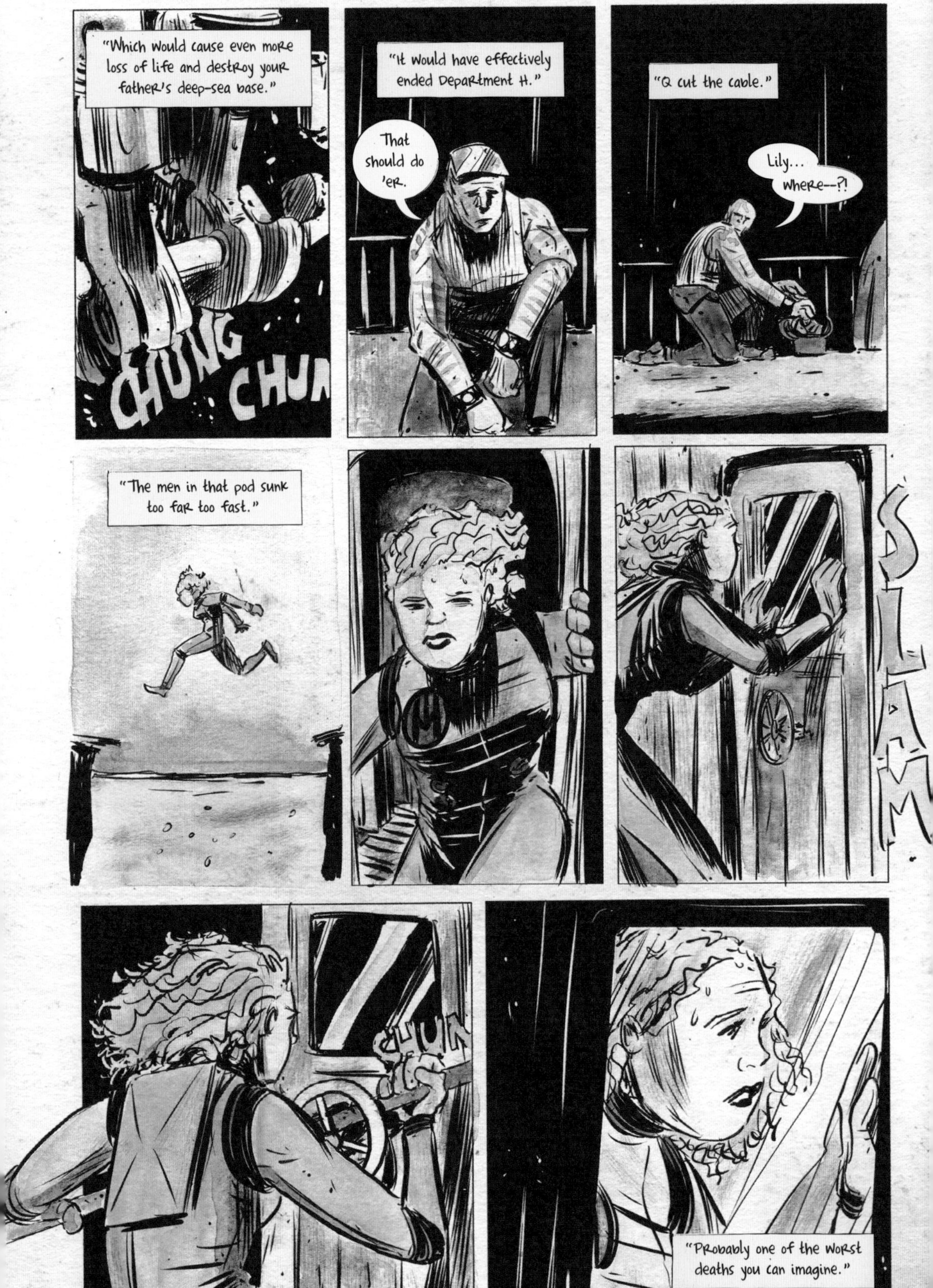
"Which would cause even more loss of life and destroy your father's deep-sea base."
CHUNG CHUN
"It would have effectively ended Department H."
That should do 'er.
"Q cut the cable."
Lily... where--?!
"The men in that pod sunk too far too fast."
SLAM
CHUN
"Probably one of the worst deaths you can imagine."

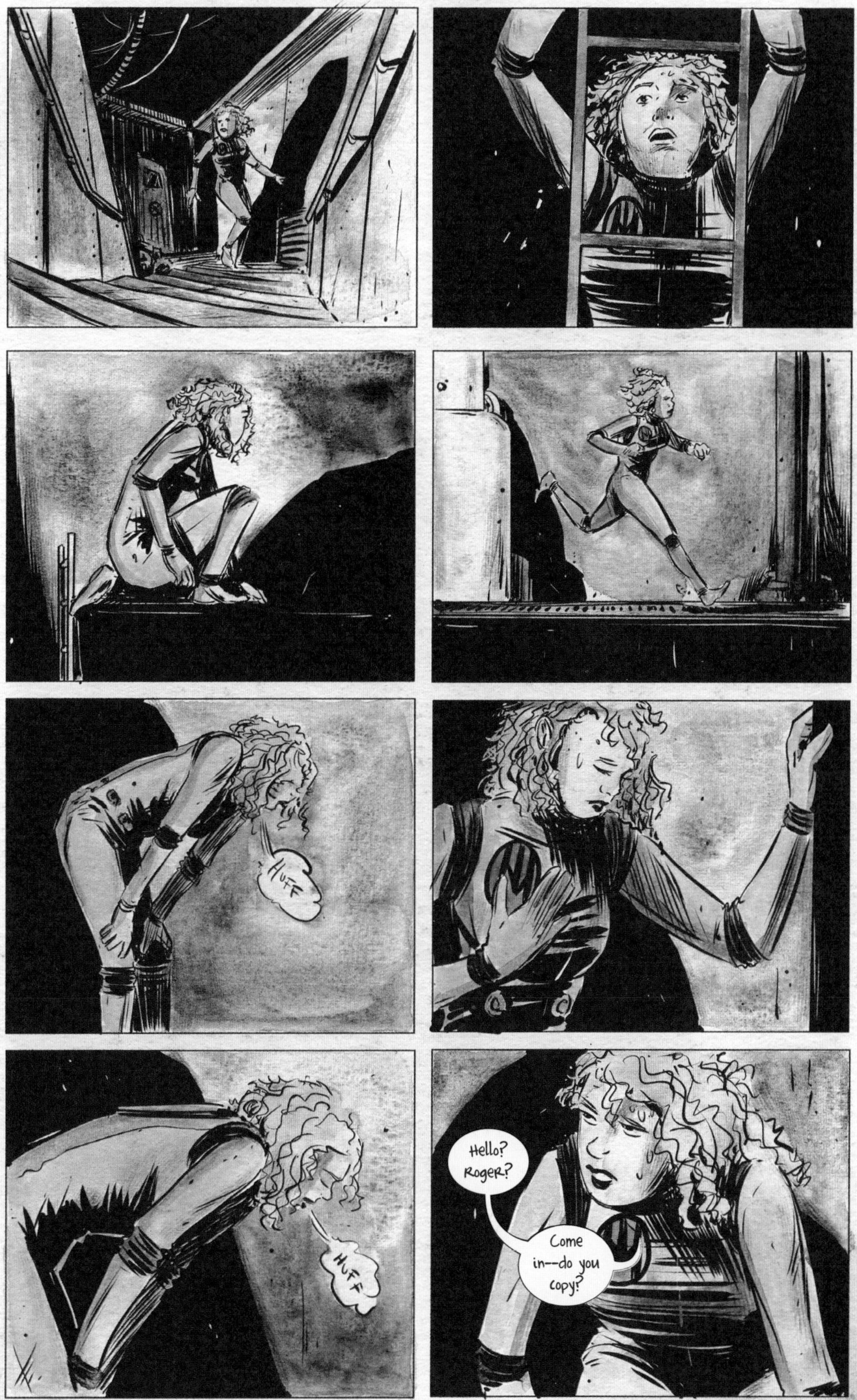
HUFF
HUFF
Hello? Roger?
Come in--do you copy?

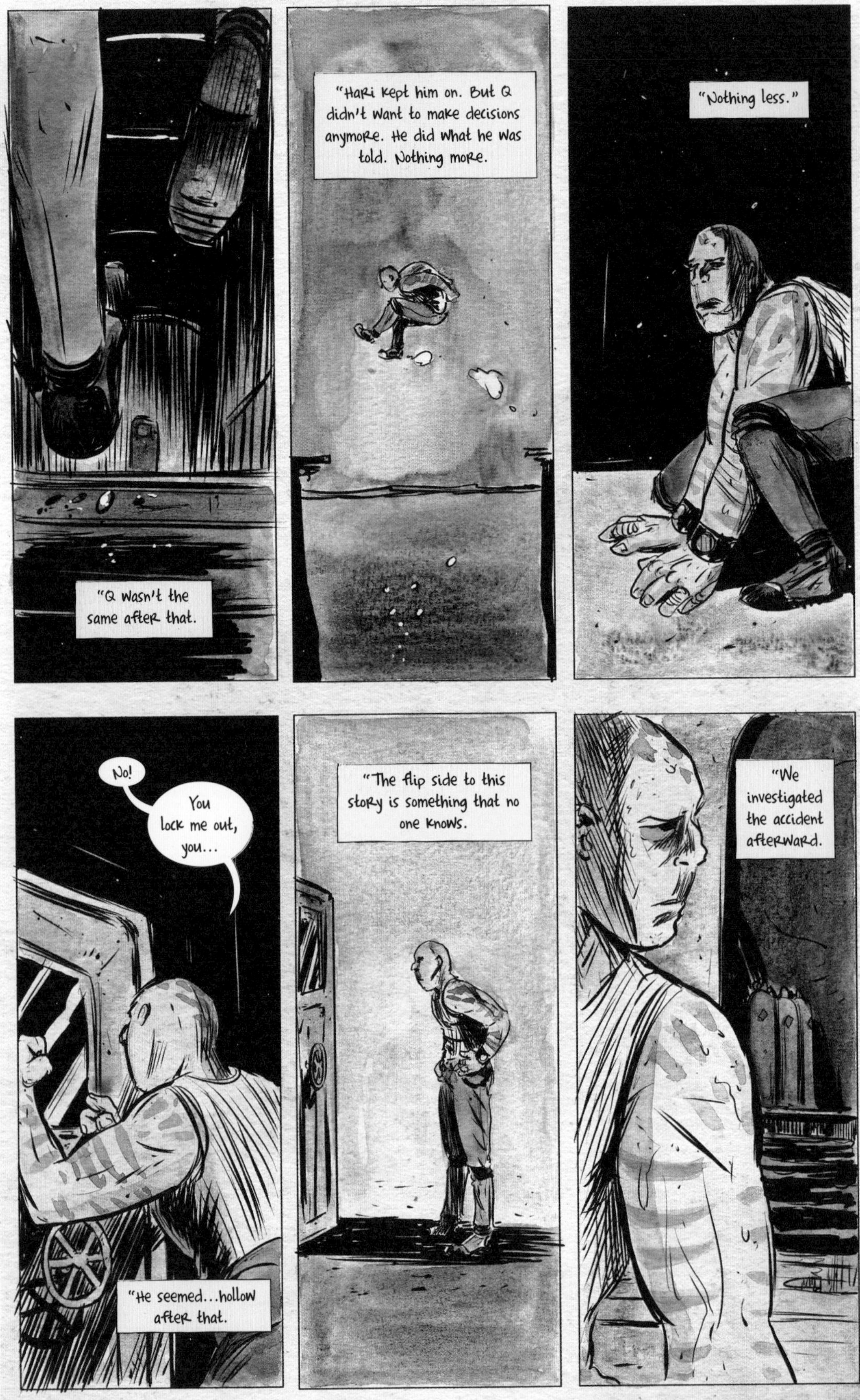
"Q wasn't the same after that.
"Hari kept him on. But Q didn't want to make decisions anymore. He did what he was told. Nothing more.
"Nothing less."
No!
You lock me out, you...
"He seemed...hollow after that.
"The flip side to this story is something that no one knows.
"We investigated the accident afterward.

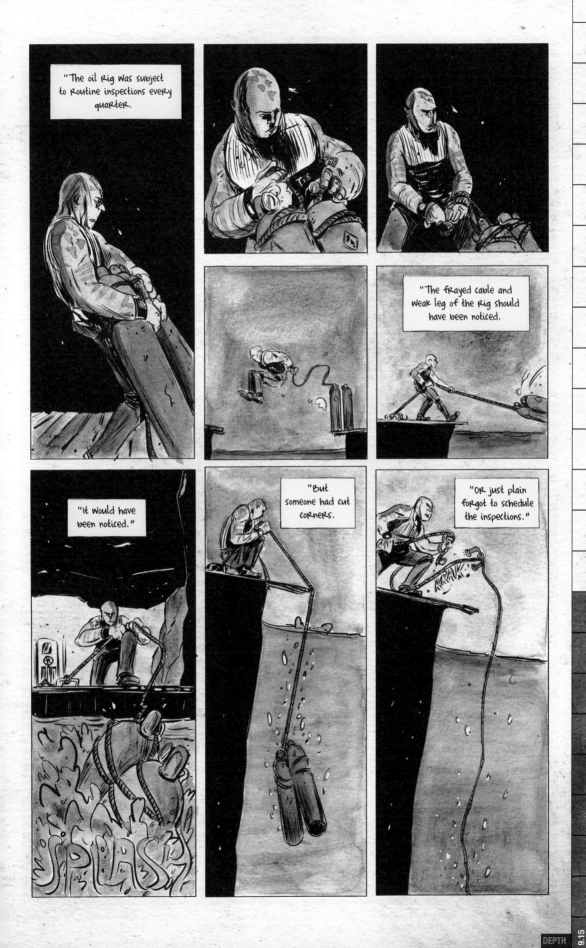

"The oil rig was subject to routine inspections every quarter.

"The frayed cable and weak leg of the rig should have been noticed.

"It would have been noticed."

"But someone had cut corners.

"Or just plain forgot to schedule the inspections."

SPLASH

KRAK

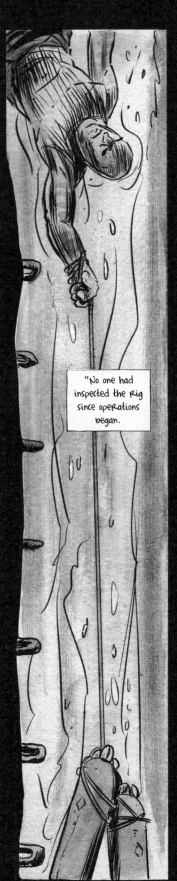

"Q was obsessed. Convinced that there was blame to be laid.

"No one had inspected the Rig since operations began.

"Q was sure that it was more than an accident.

"He became paranoid.

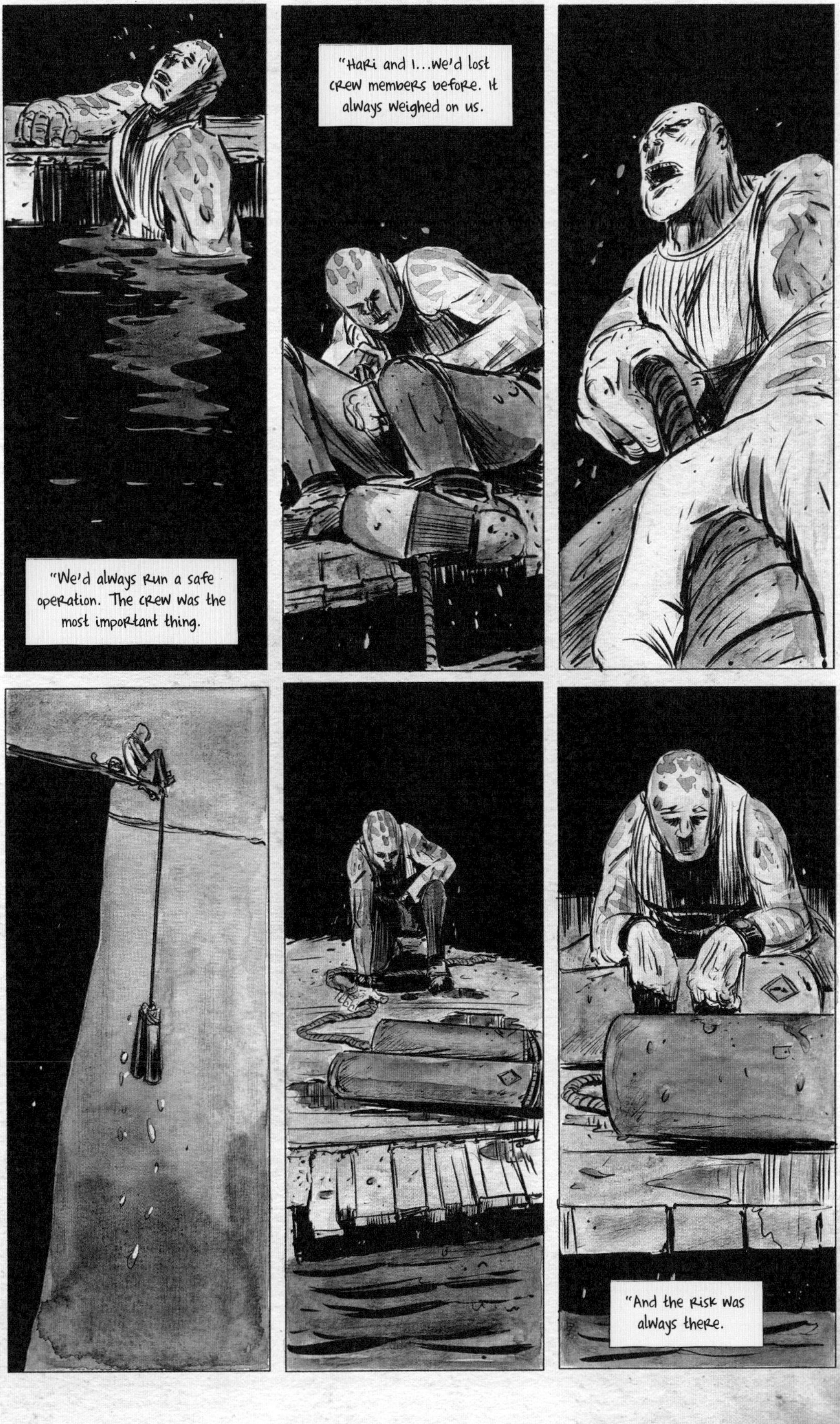
"We'd always run a safe operation. The crew was the most important thing.
"Hari and I...we'd lost crew members before. It always weighed on us.
"And the risk was always there.

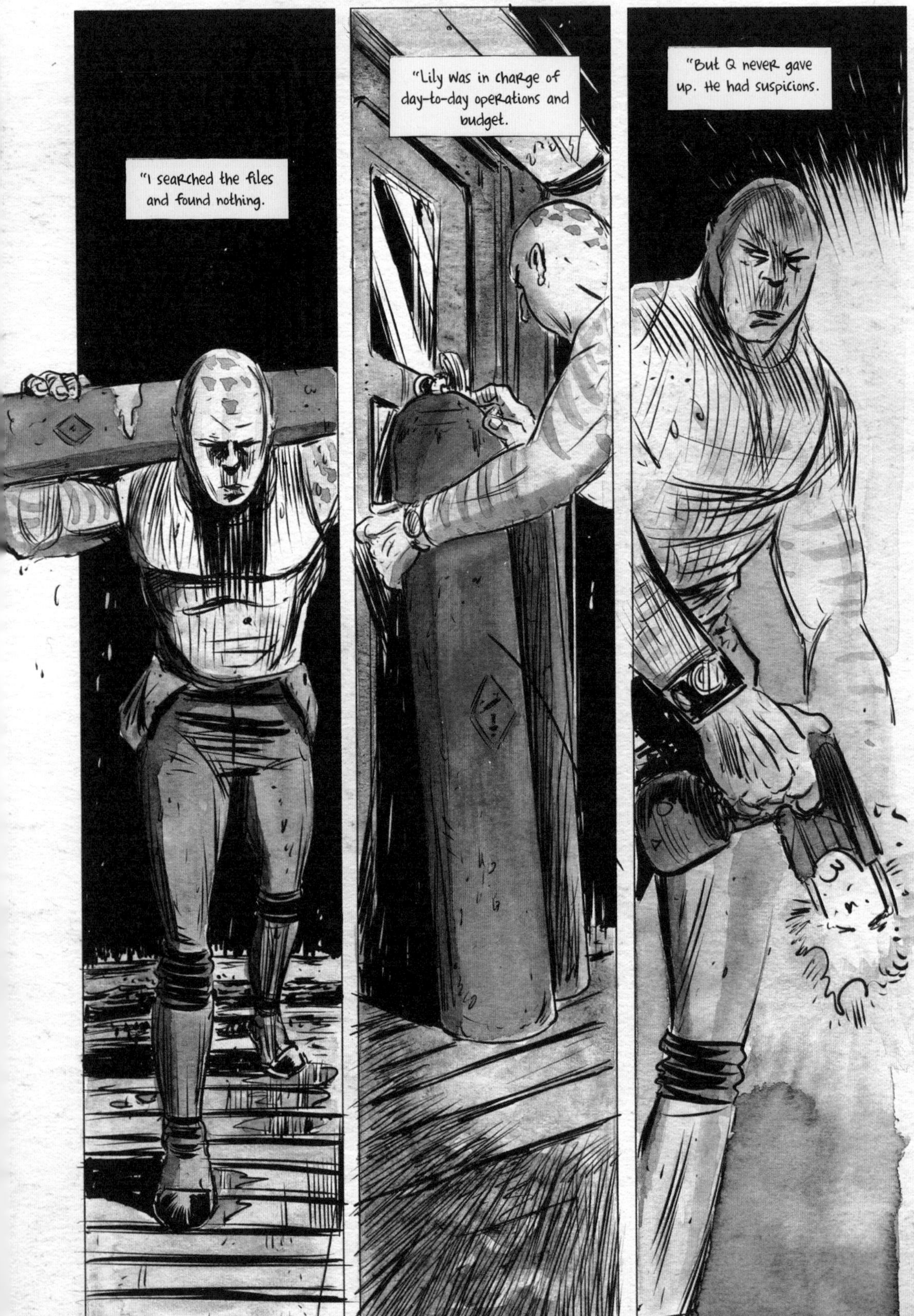
"I searched the files and found nothing.
"Lily was in charge of day-to-day operations and budget.
"But Q never gave up. He had suspicions.

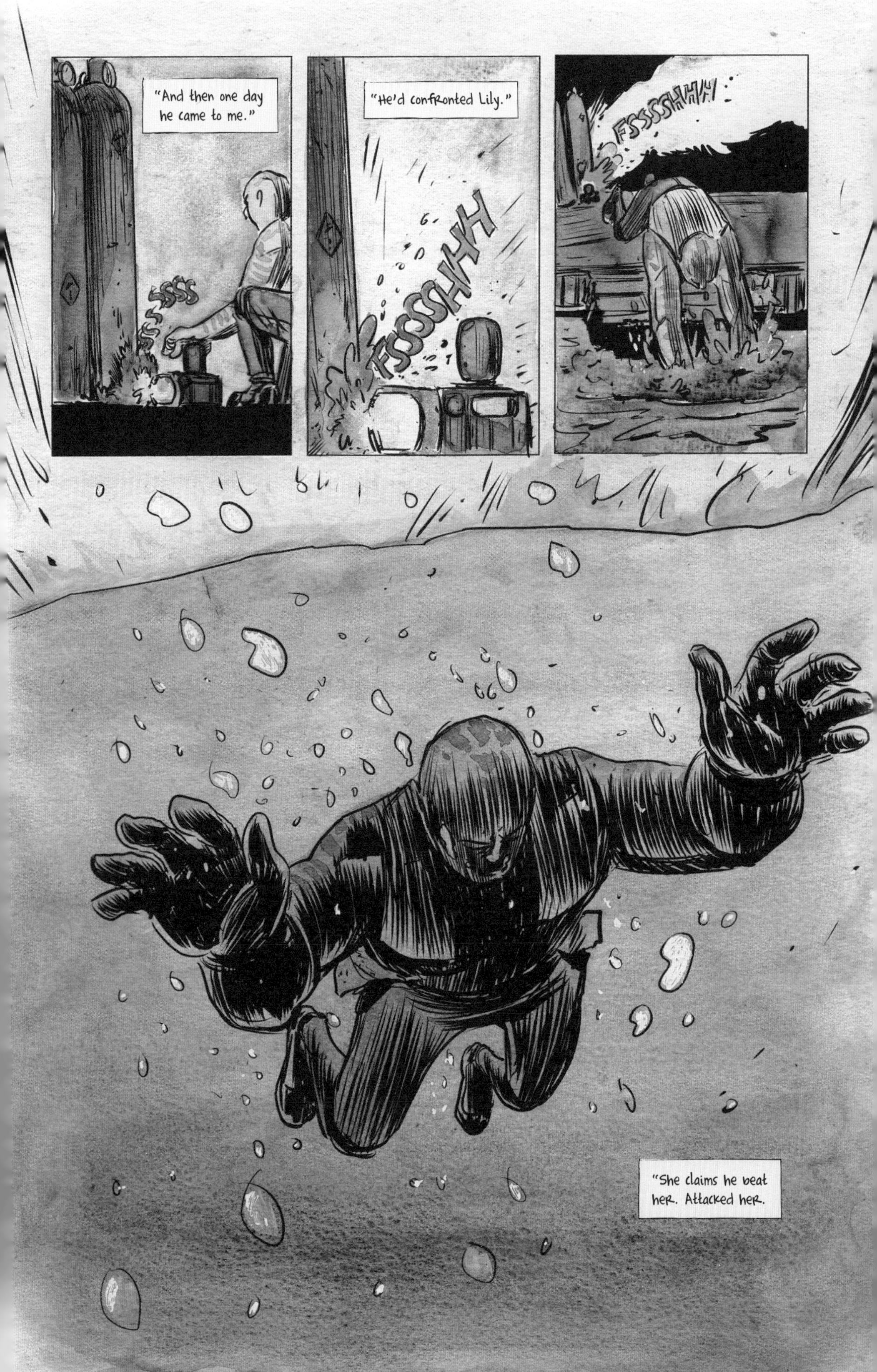
"And then one day he came to me."
SSSS
"He'd confronted Lily."
FSSSSHHH
FSSSSHHHH
"She claims he beat her. Attacked her.

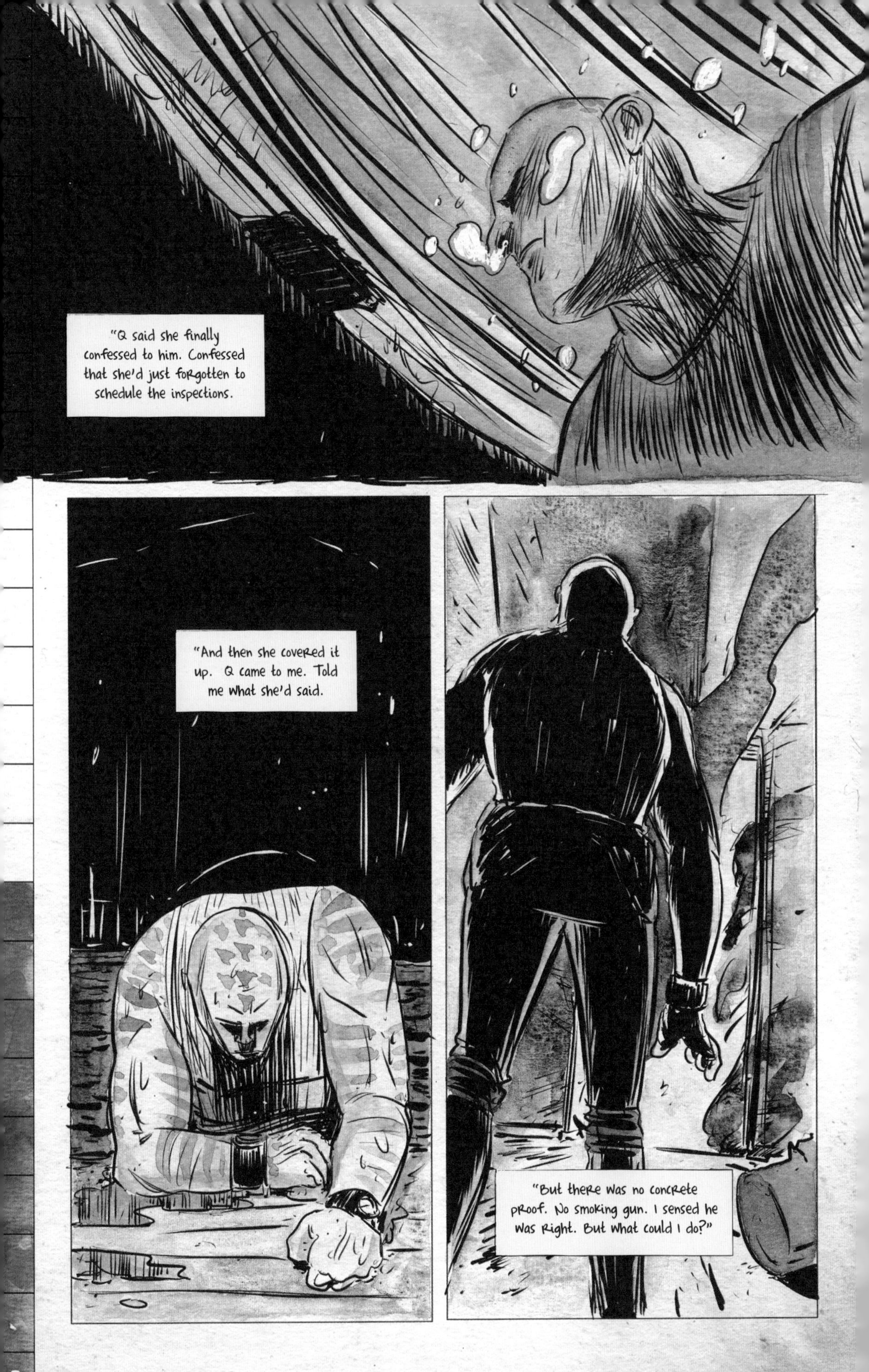
"Q said she finally confessed to him. Confessed that she'd just forgotten to schedule the inspections.
"And then she covered it up. Q came to me. Told me what she'd said.
"But there was no concrete proof. No smoking gun. I sensed he was right. But what could I do?"

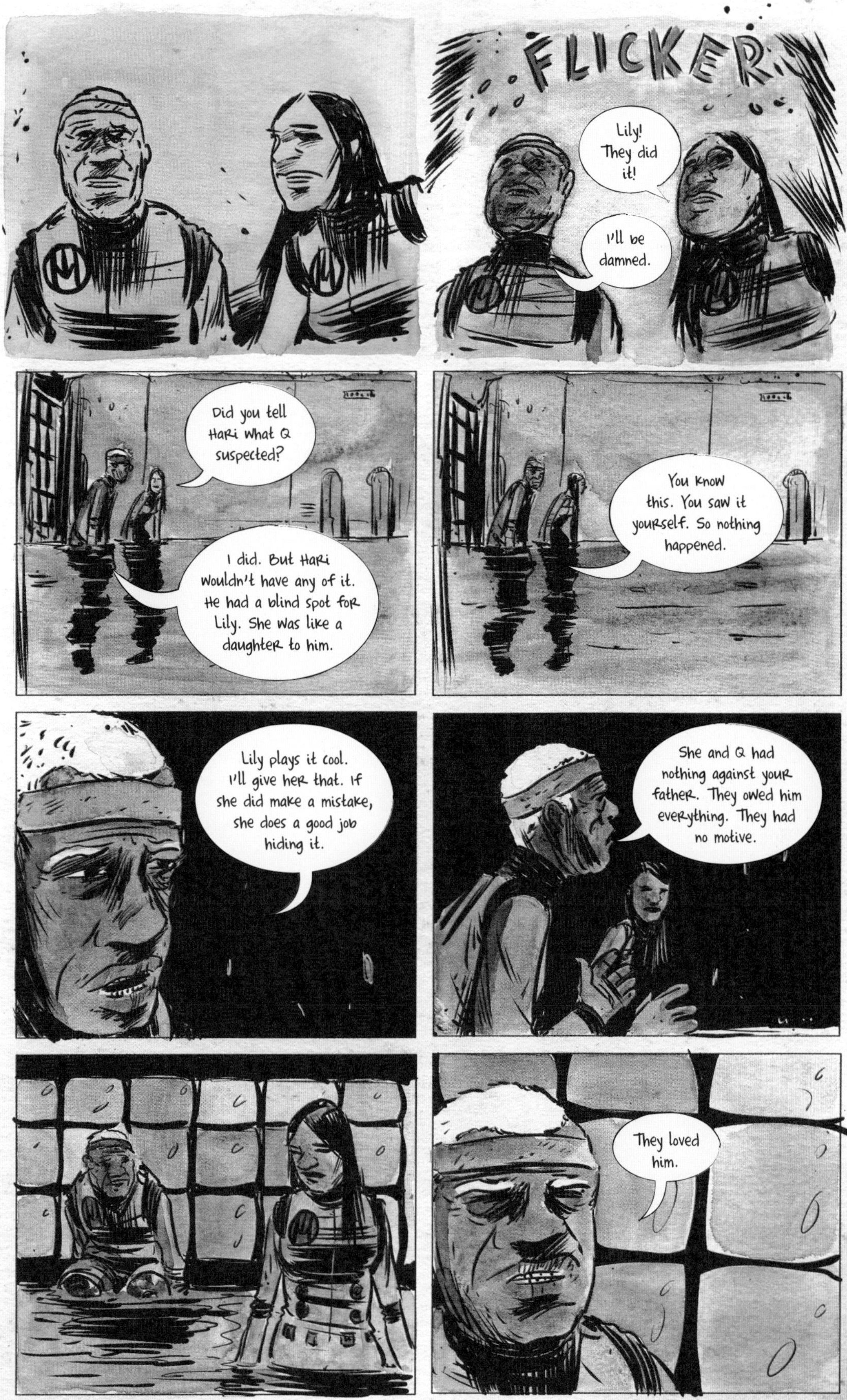

FLICKER
Lily! They did it!
I'll be damned.
Did you tell Hari what Q suspected?
I did. But Hari wouldn't have any of it. He had a blind spot for Lily. She was like a daughter to him.
You know this. You saw it yourself. So nothing happened.
Lily plays it cool. I'll give her that. If she did make a mistake, she does a good job hiding it.
She and Q had nothing against your father. They owed him everything. They had no motive.
They loved him.

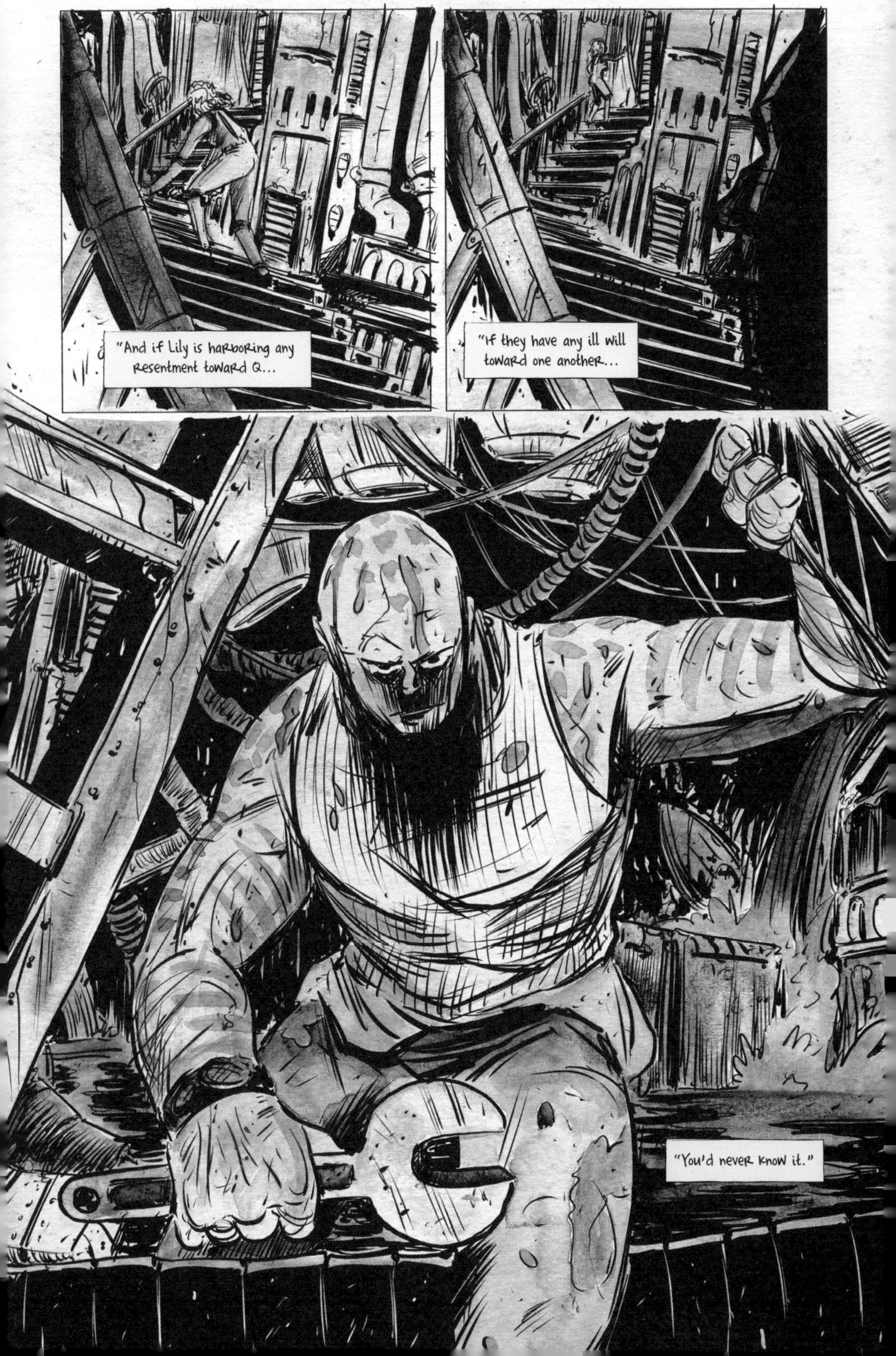
"And if Lily is harboring any resentment toward Q...
"If they have any ill will toward one another...
"You'd never know it."

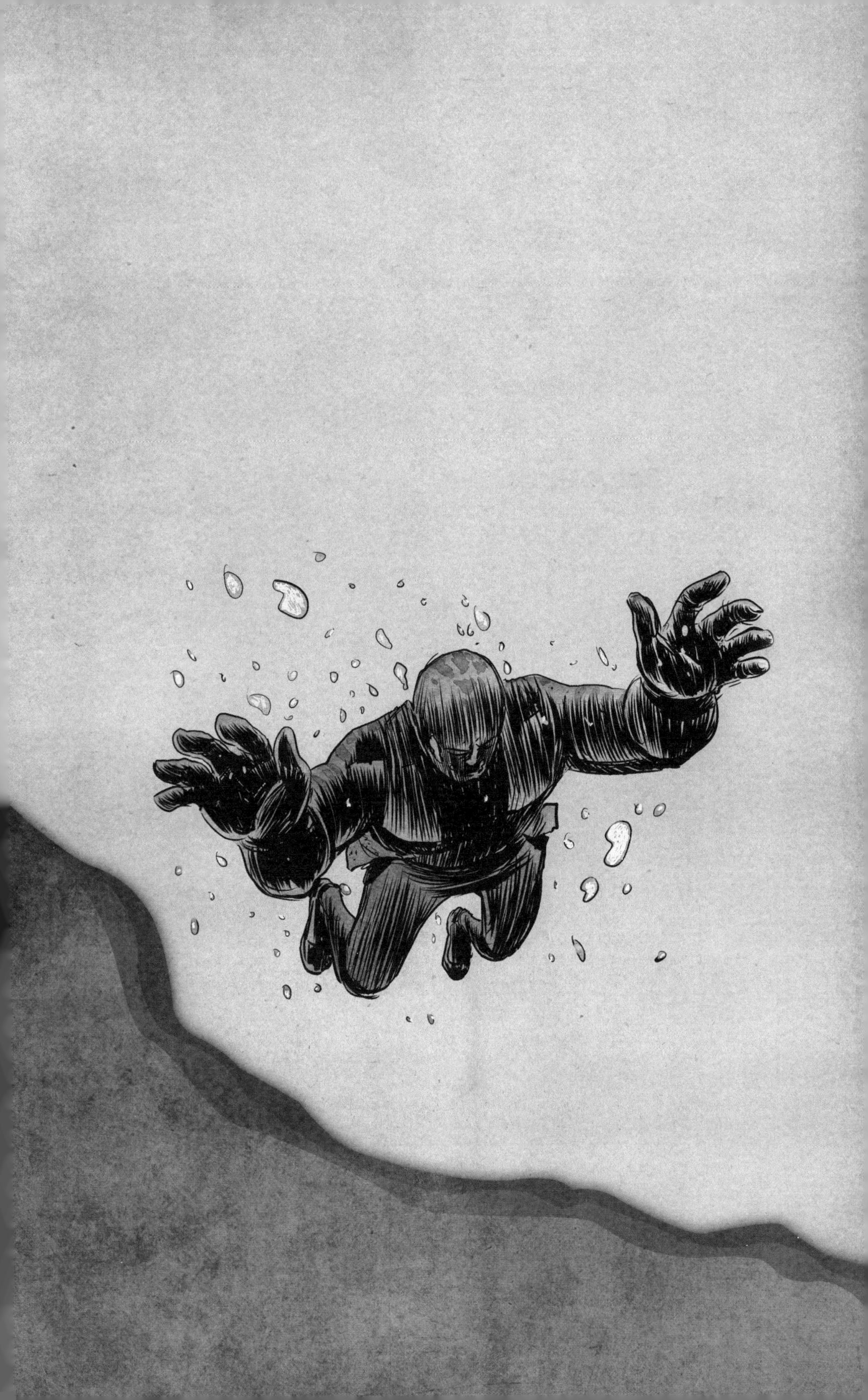

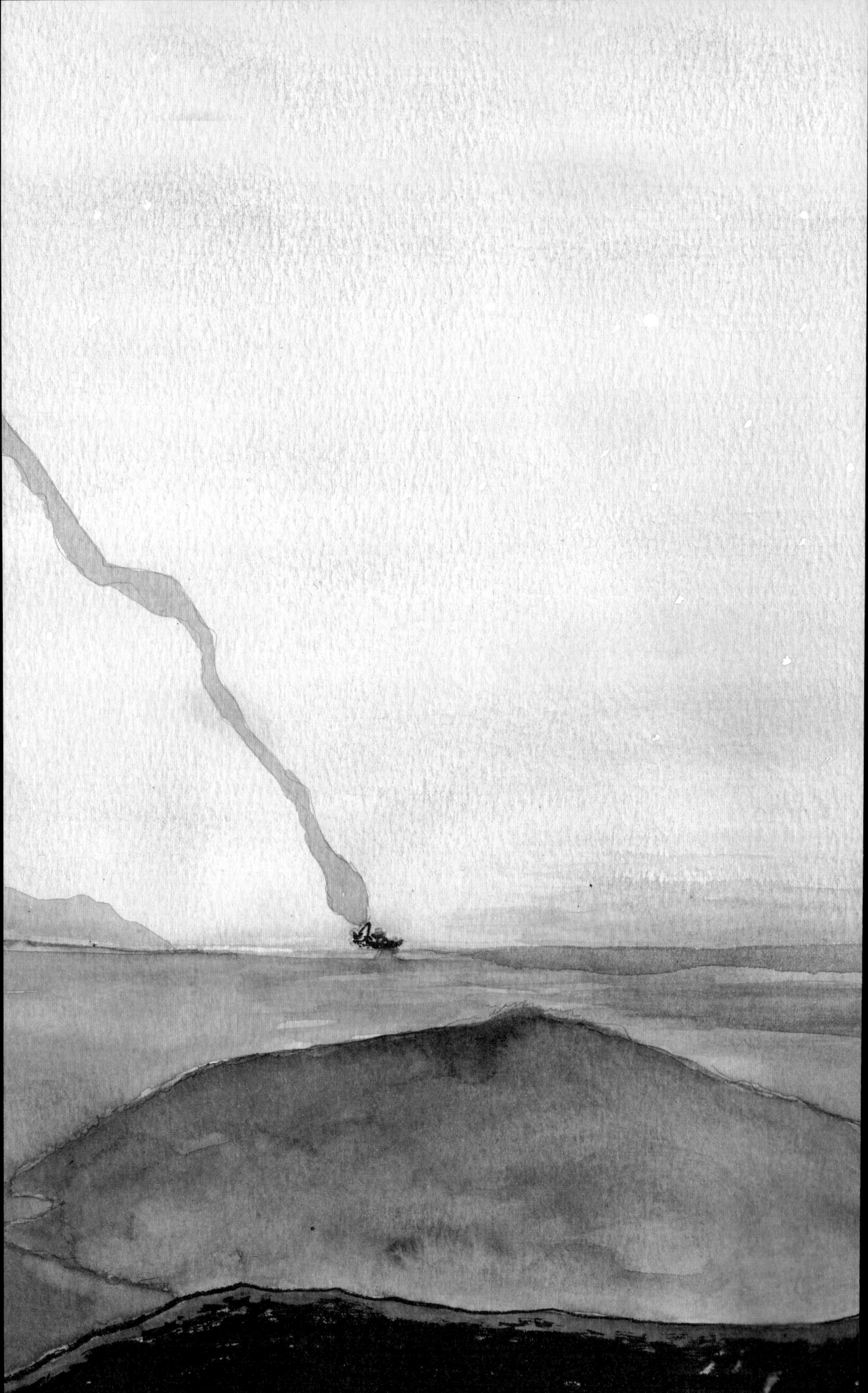

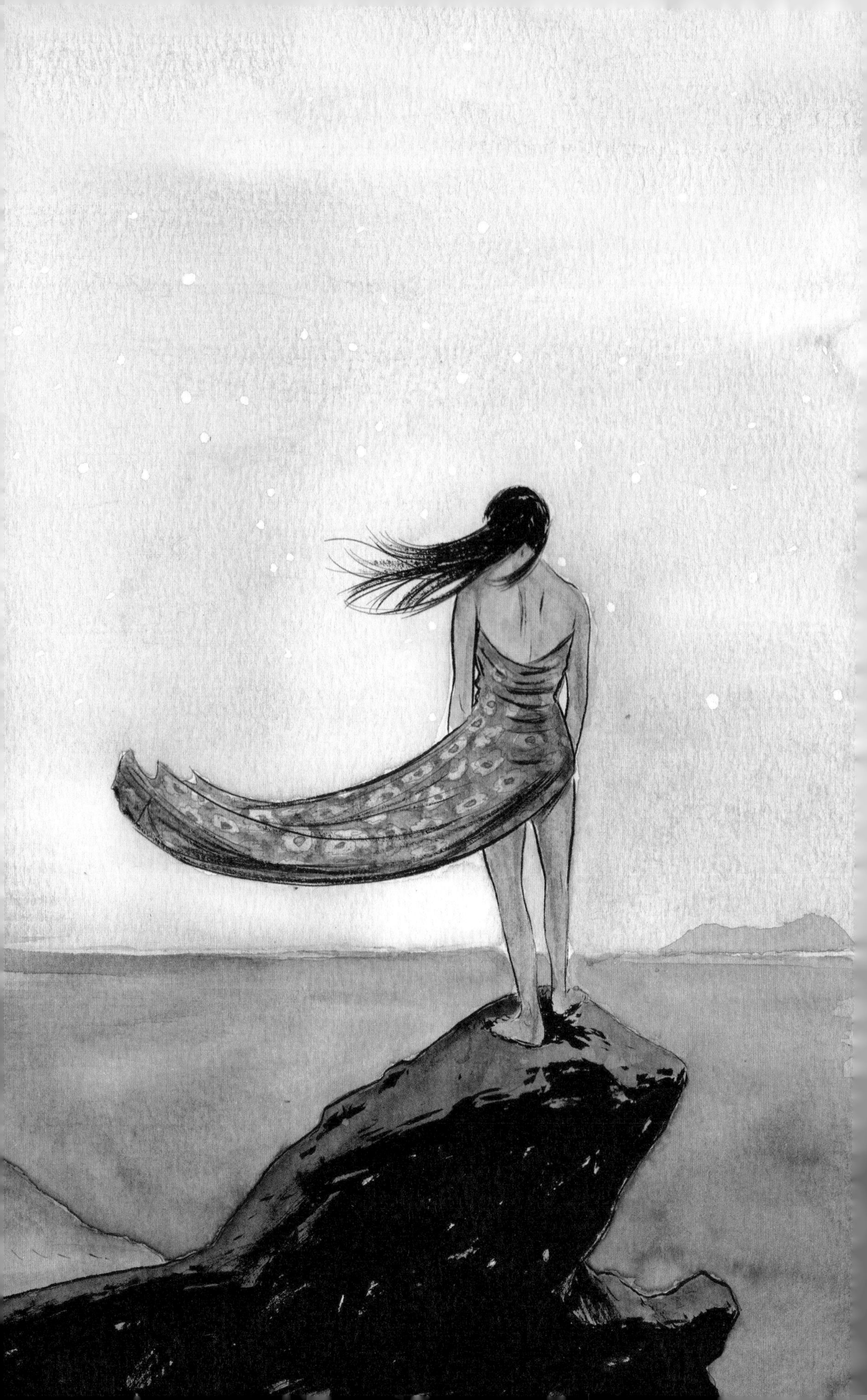

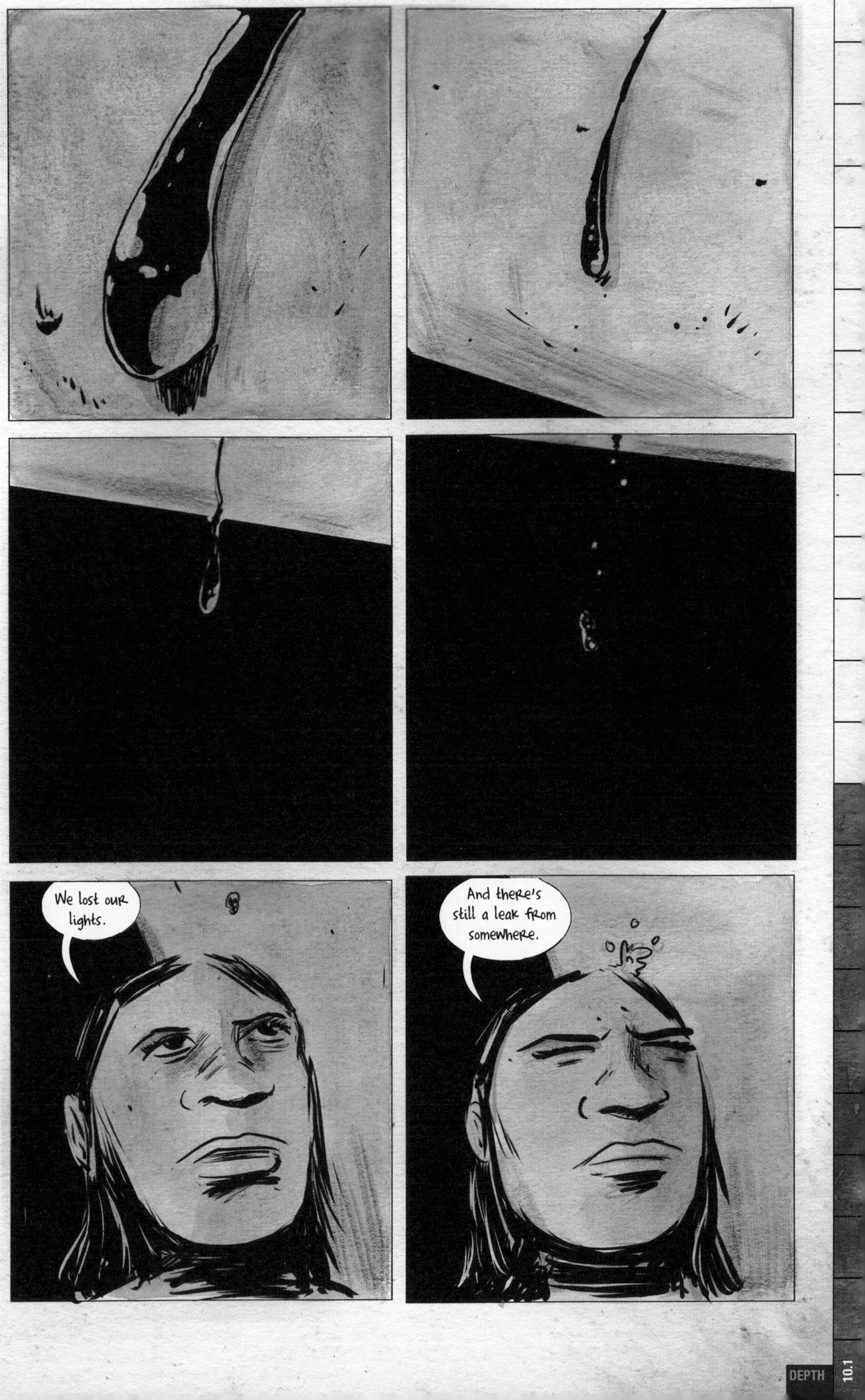
We lost our lights.
And there's still a leak from somewhere.

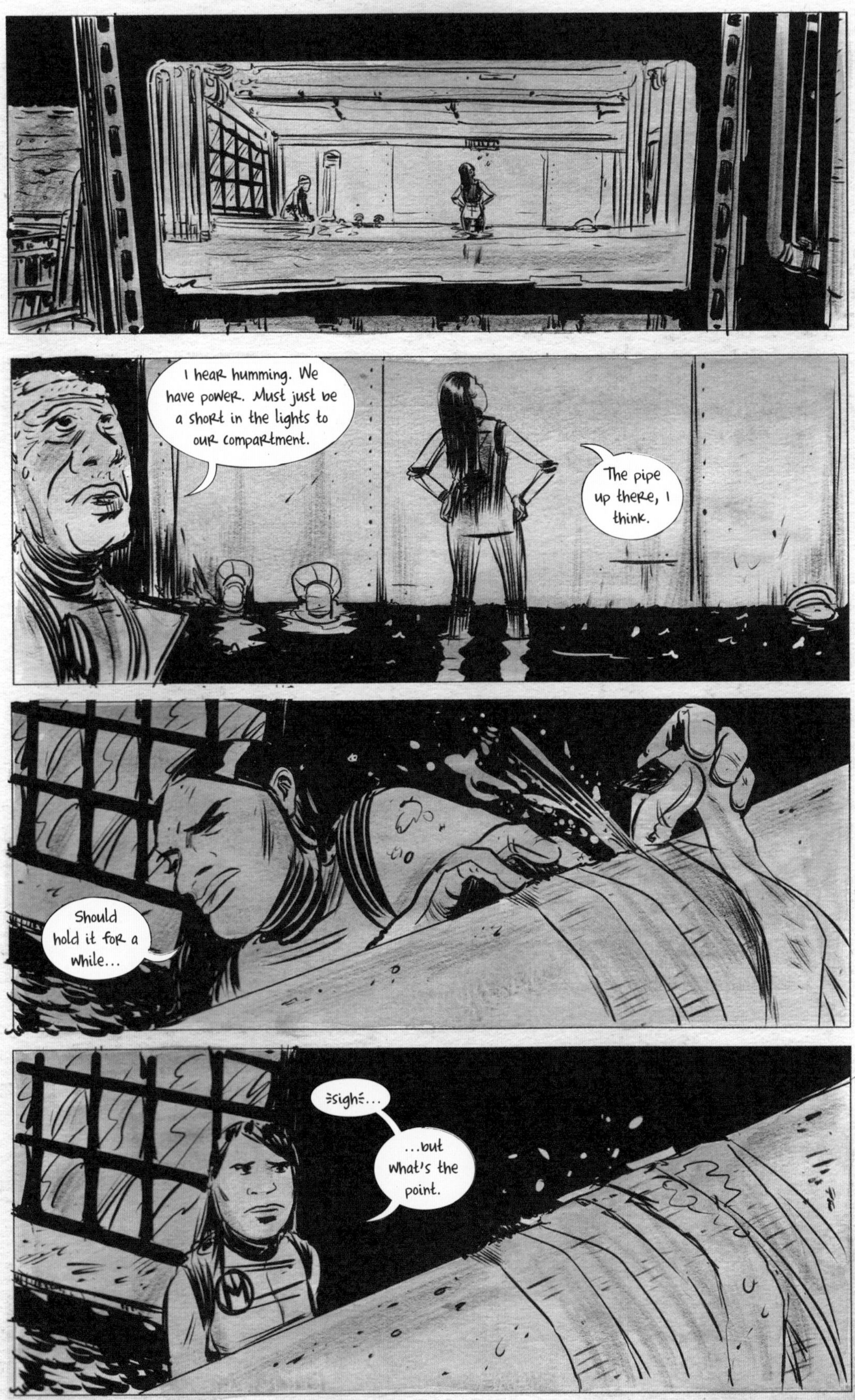
I hear humming. We have power. Must just be a short in the lights to our compartment.
The pipe up there, I think.
Should hold it for a while...
≡sigh≡...
...but what's the point.

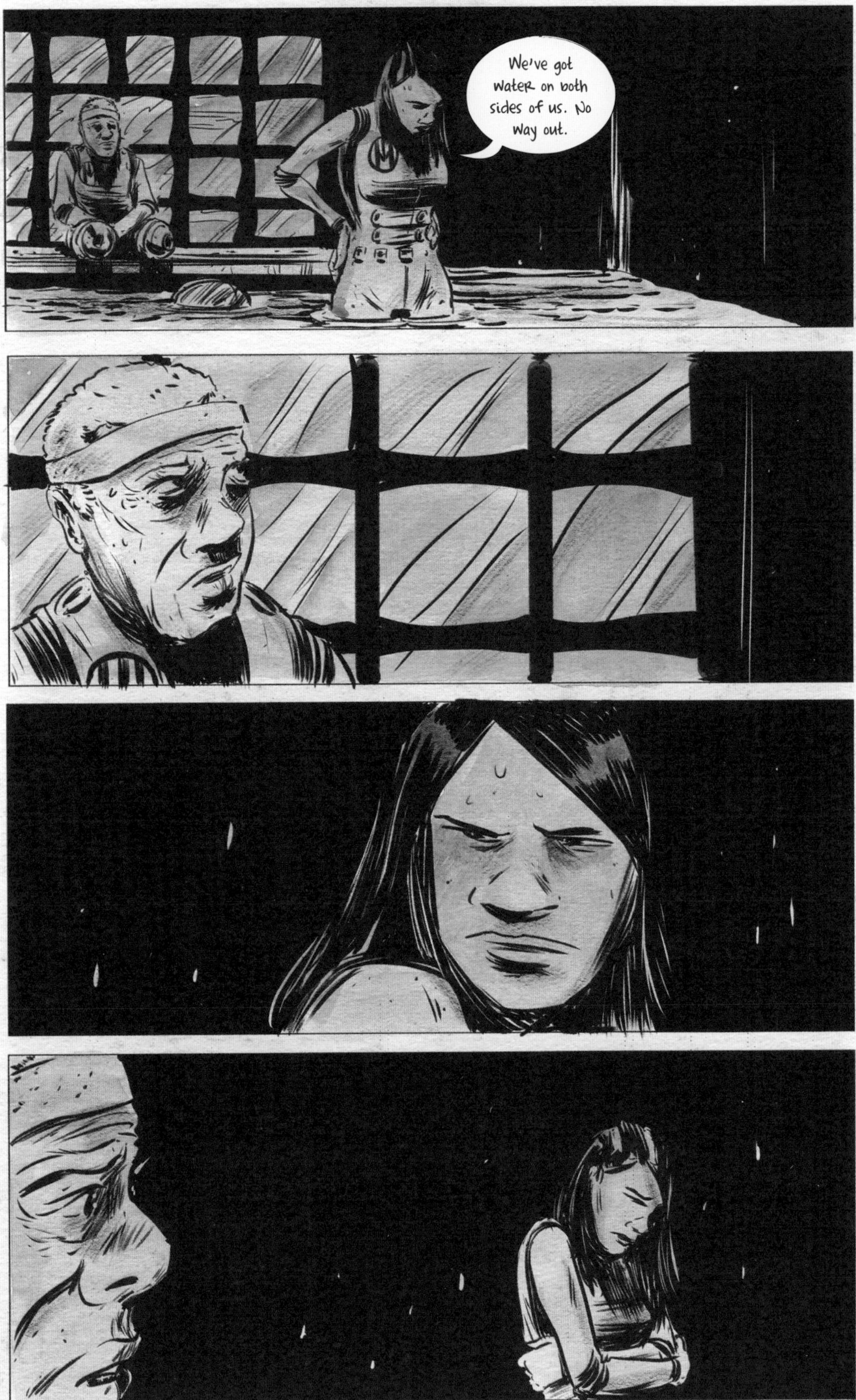
We've got water on both sides of us. No way out.

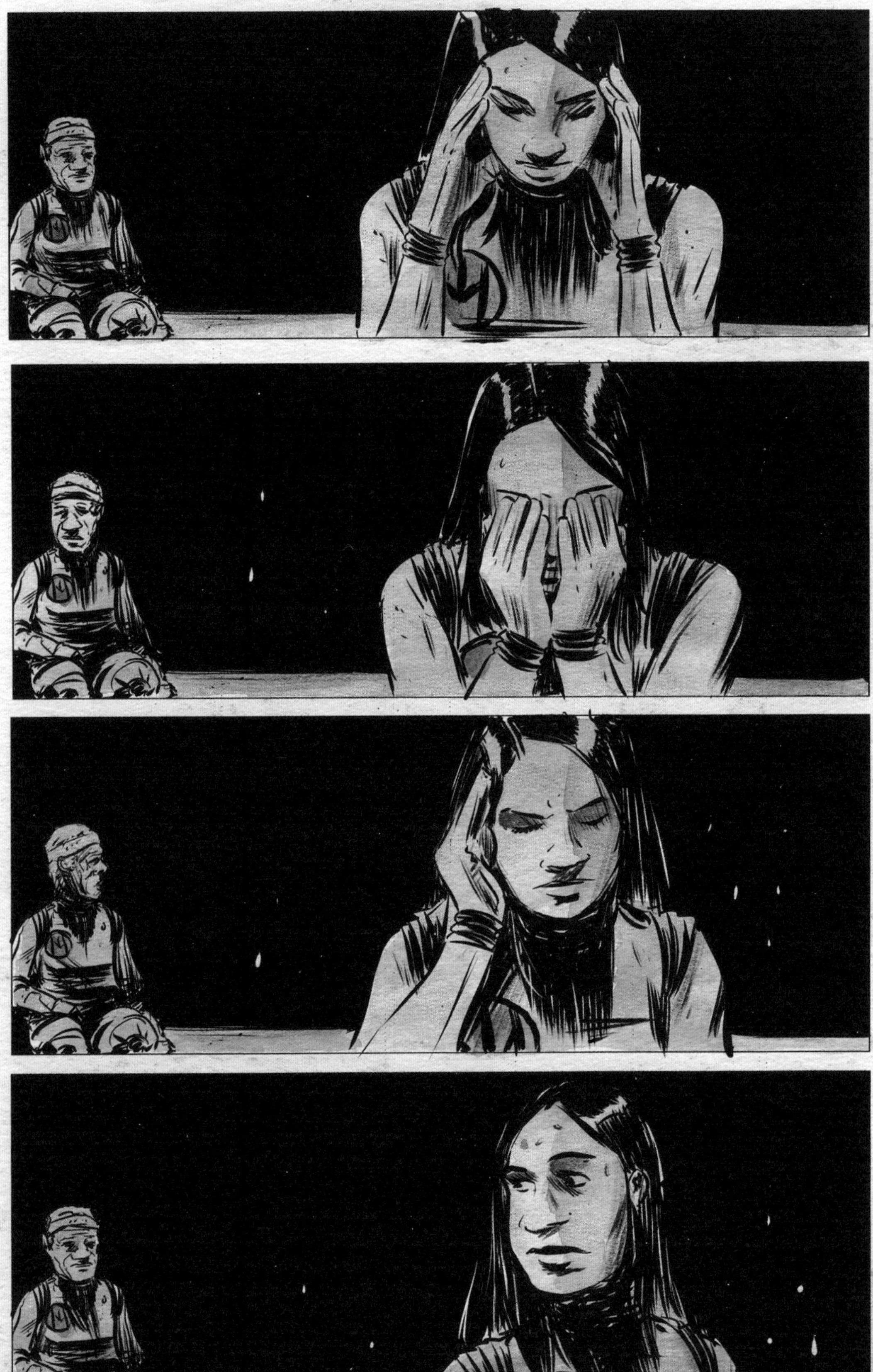

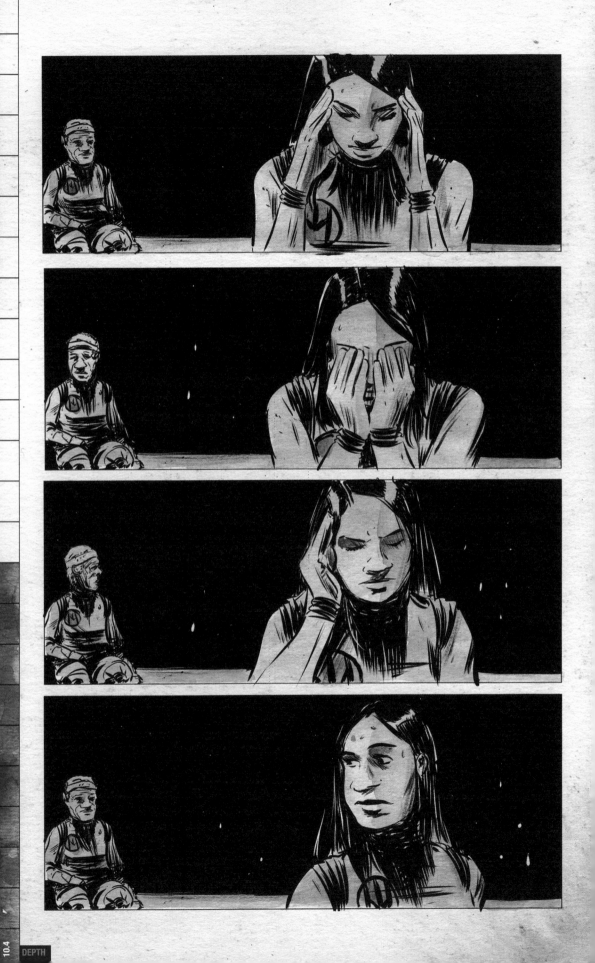

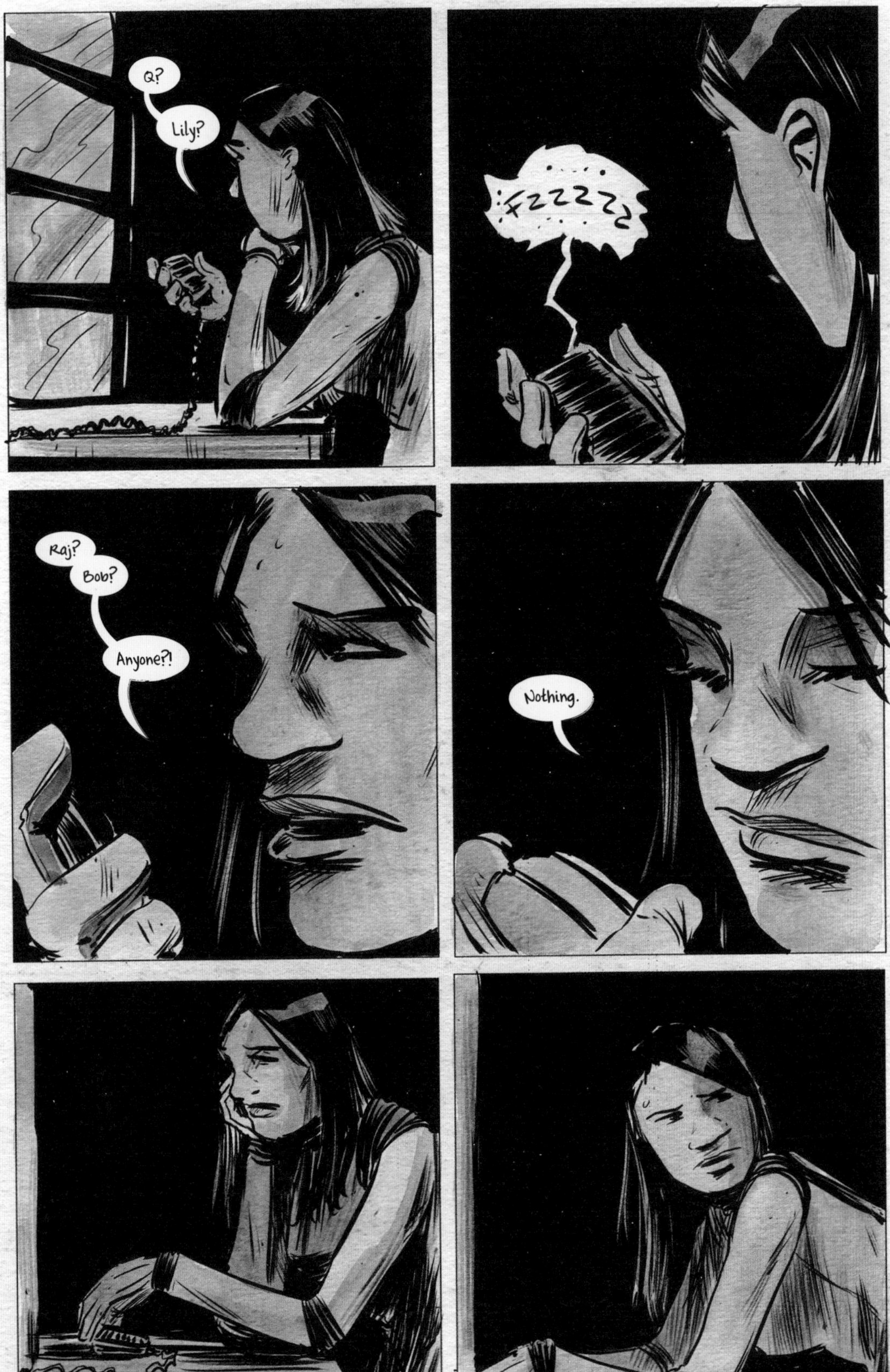
Q?
Lily?
FZZZZZ
Raj?
Bob?
Anyone?!
Nothing.

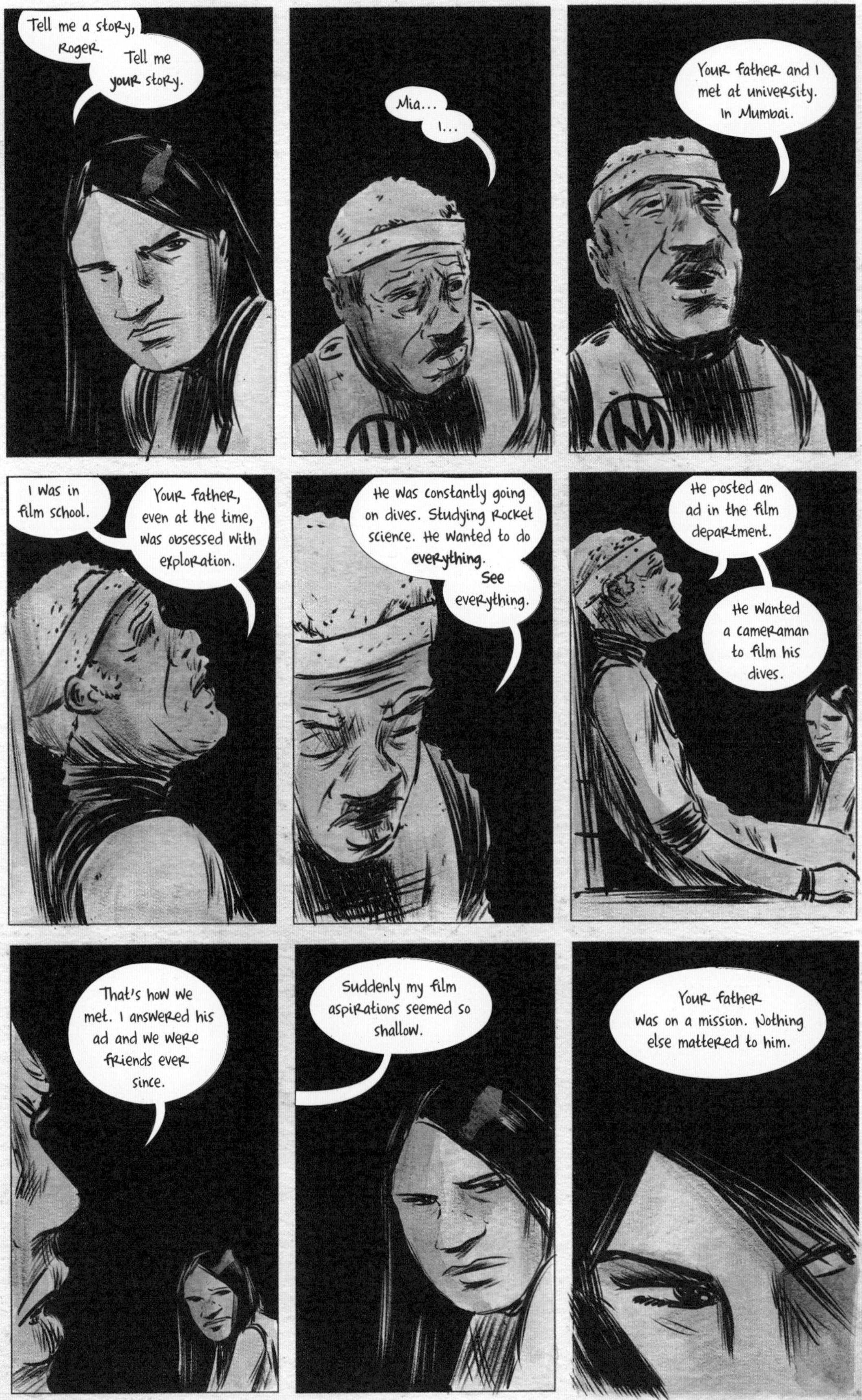
Tell me a story, Roger.
Tell me your story.
Mia... I...
Your father and I met at university. In Mumbai.
I was in film school.
Your father, even at the time, was obsessed with exploration.
He was constantly going on dives. Studying rocket science. He wanted to do everything.
See everything.
He posted an ad in the film department.
He wanted a cameraman to film his dives.
That's how we met. I answered his ad and we were friends ever since.
Suddenly my film aspirations seemed so shallow.
Your father was on a mission. Nothing else mattered to him.

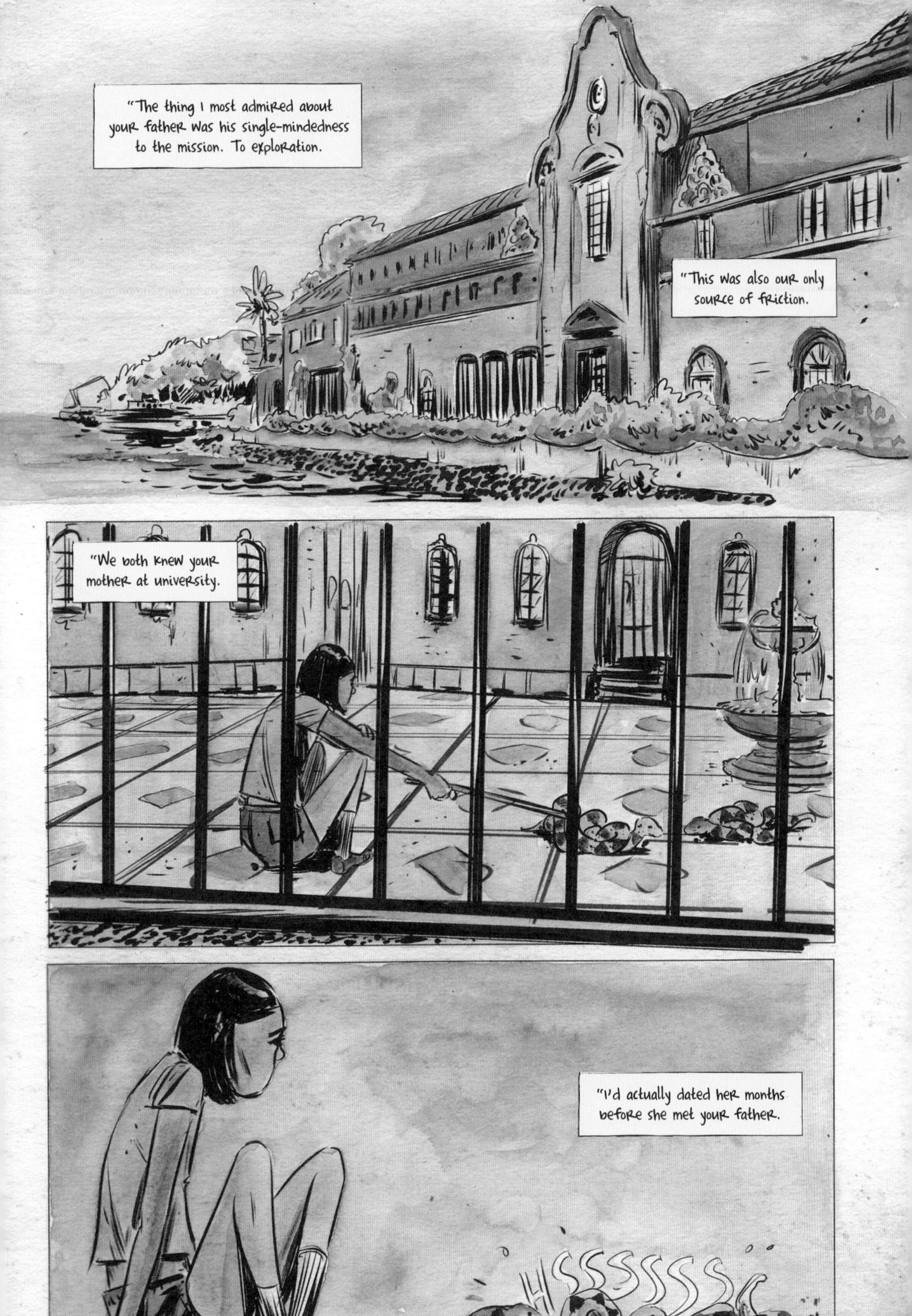
"The thing I most admired about your father was his single-mindedness to the mission. To exploration.
"This was also our only source of friction.
"We both knew your mother at university.
"I'd actually dated her months before she met your father.
HSSSSSSS

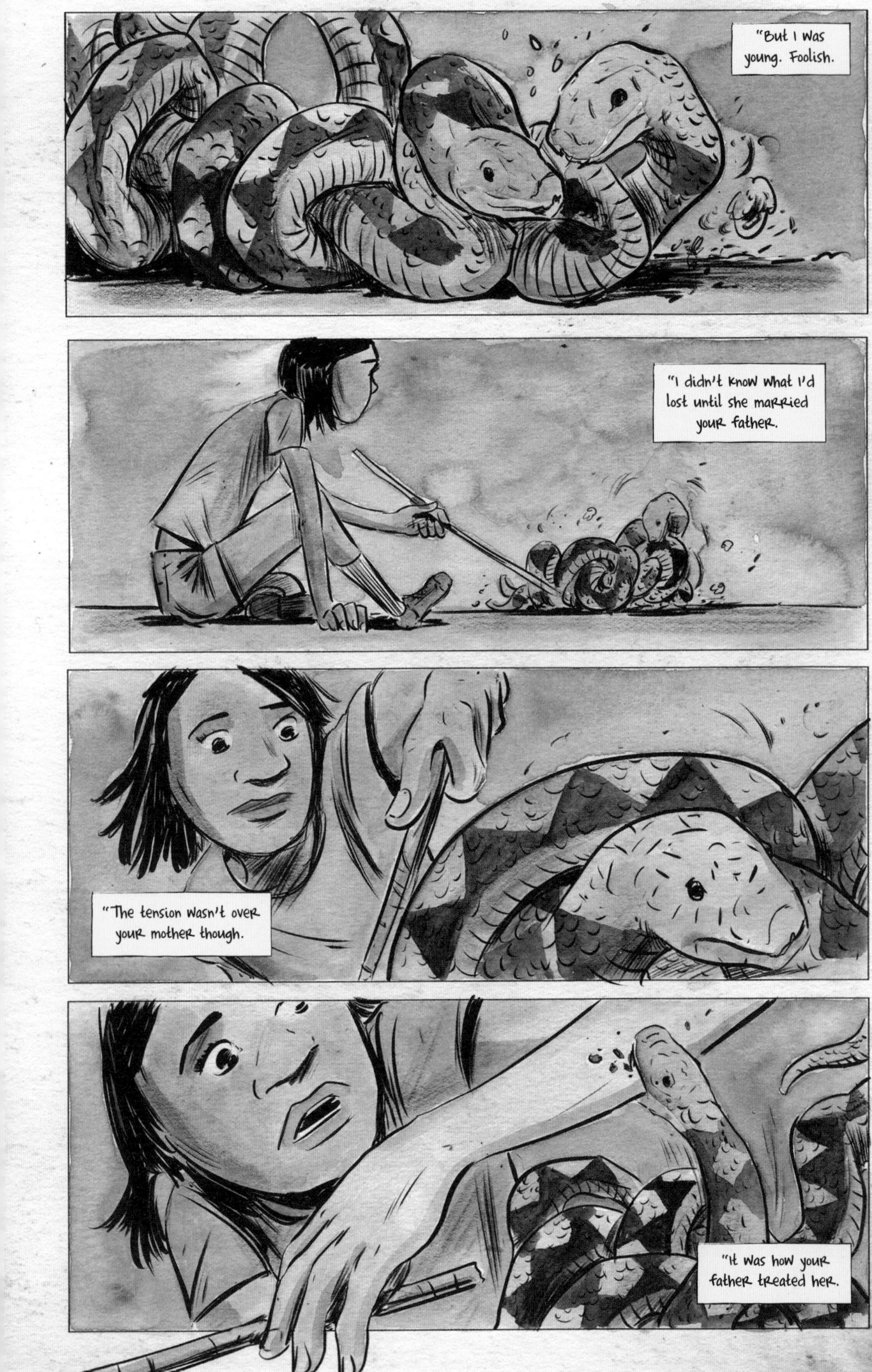
"But I was young. Foolish.
"I didn't know what I'd lost until she married your father.
"The tension wasn't over your mother though.
"It was how your father treated her.

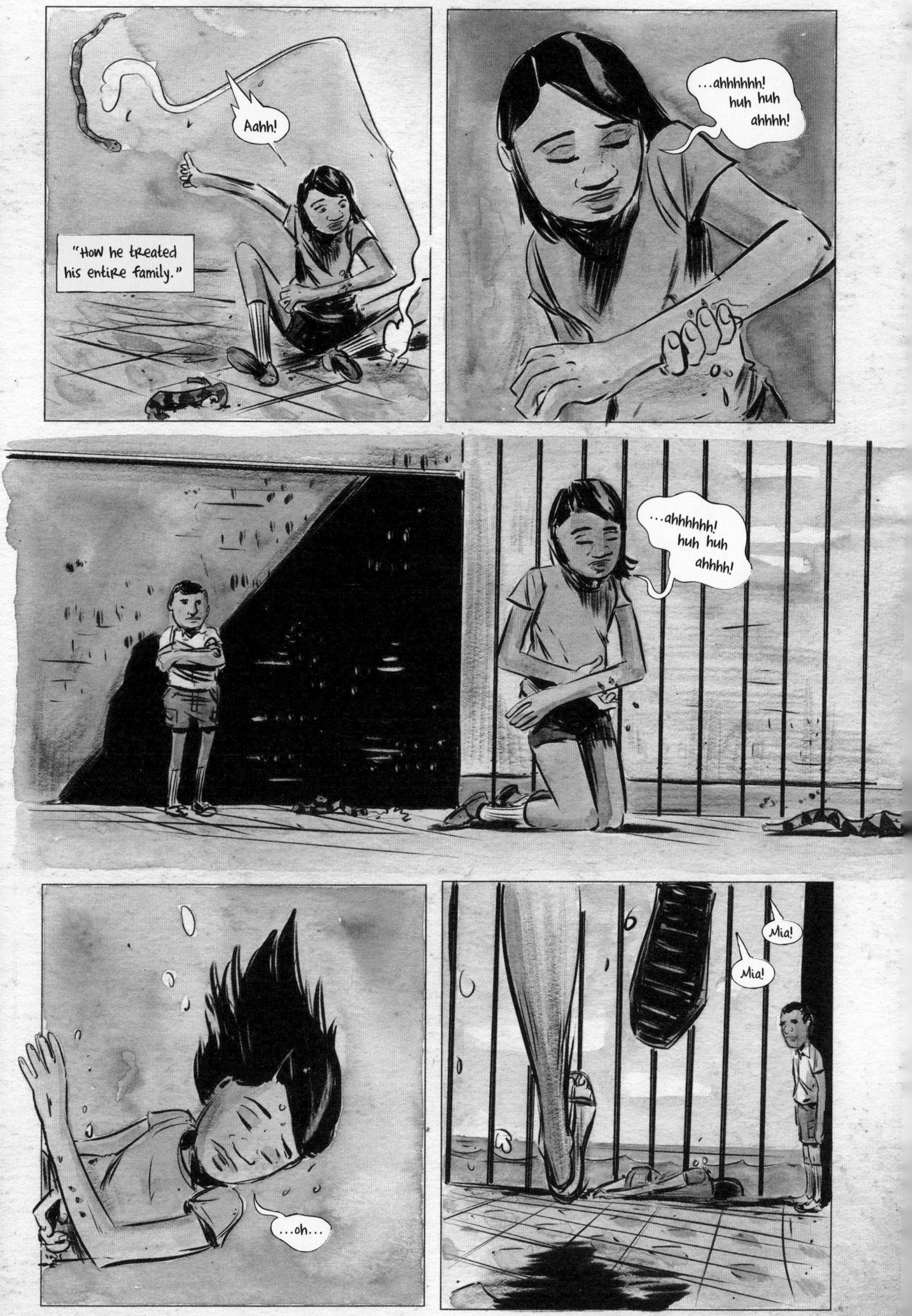
Aahh!
"How he treated his entire family."
...ahhhhhh! huh huh ahhhh!
...ahhhhhh! huh huh ahhhh!
...oh...
Mia!
Mia!

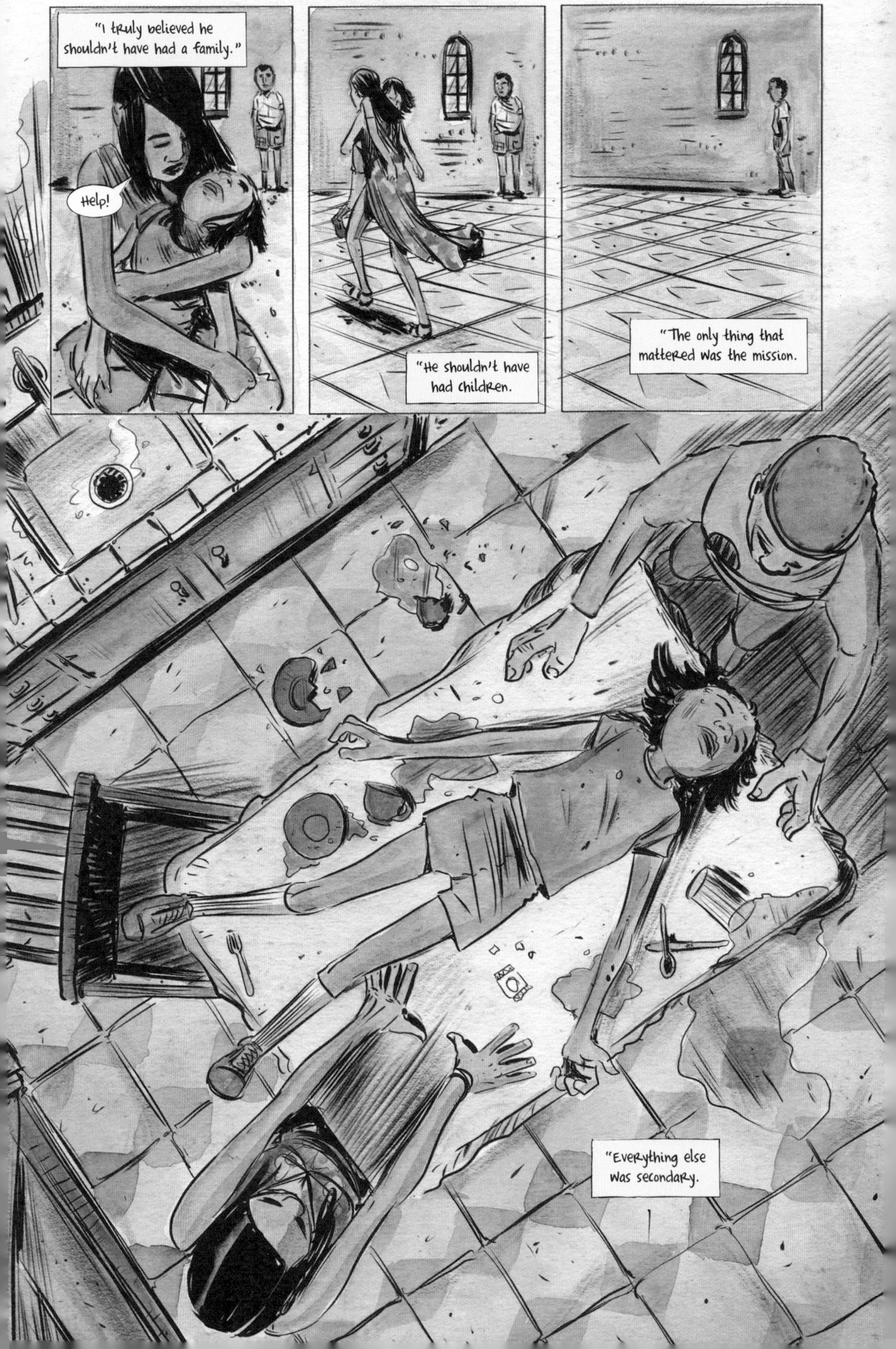

"I truly believed he shouldn't have had a family."
Help!
"He shouldn't have had children.
"The only thing that mattered was the mission.
"Everything else was secondary.

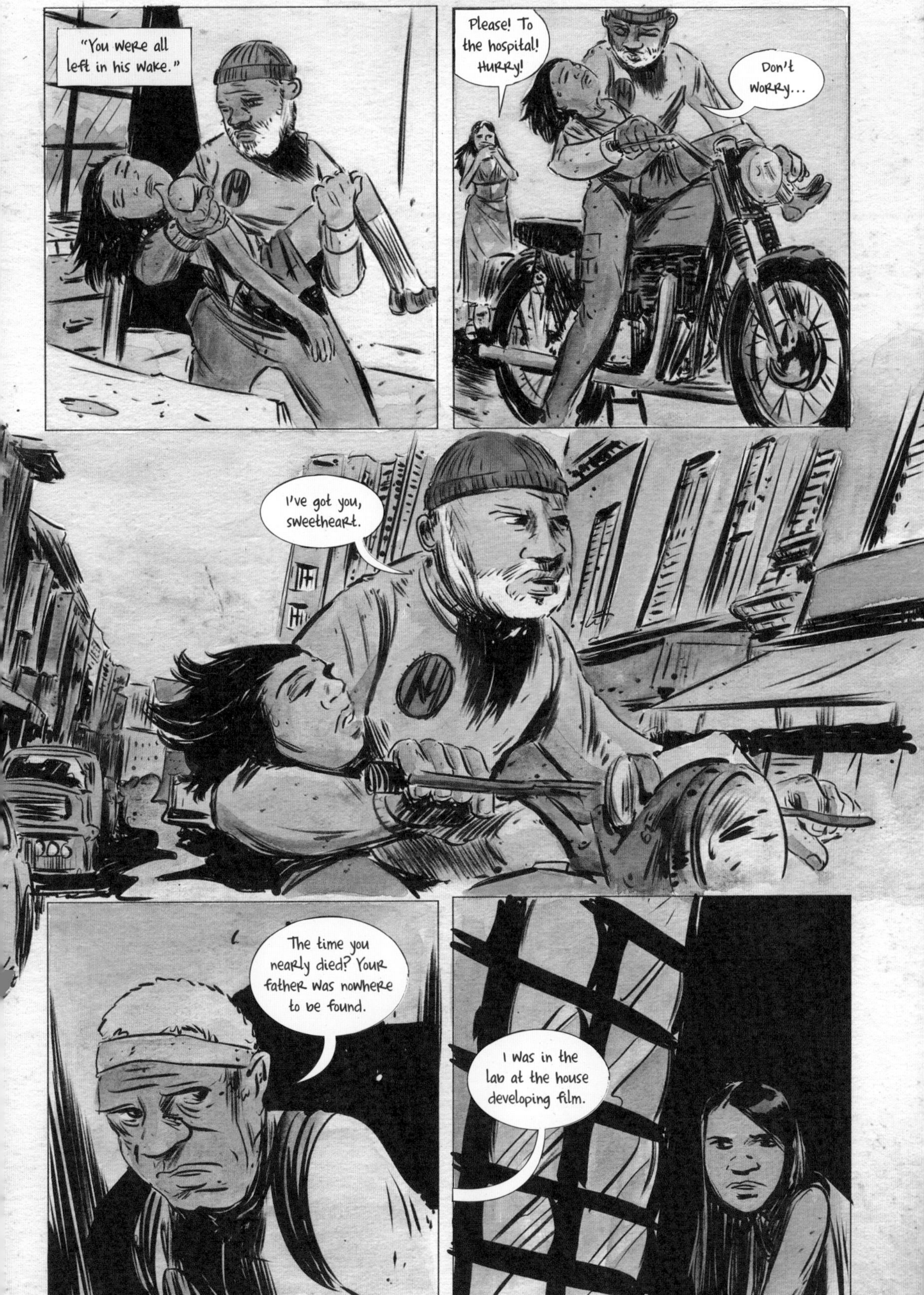
"You were all left in his wake."
Please! To the hospital! Hurry!
Don't worry...
I've got you, sweetheart.
The time you nearly died? Your father was nowhere to be found.
I was in the lab at the house developing film.

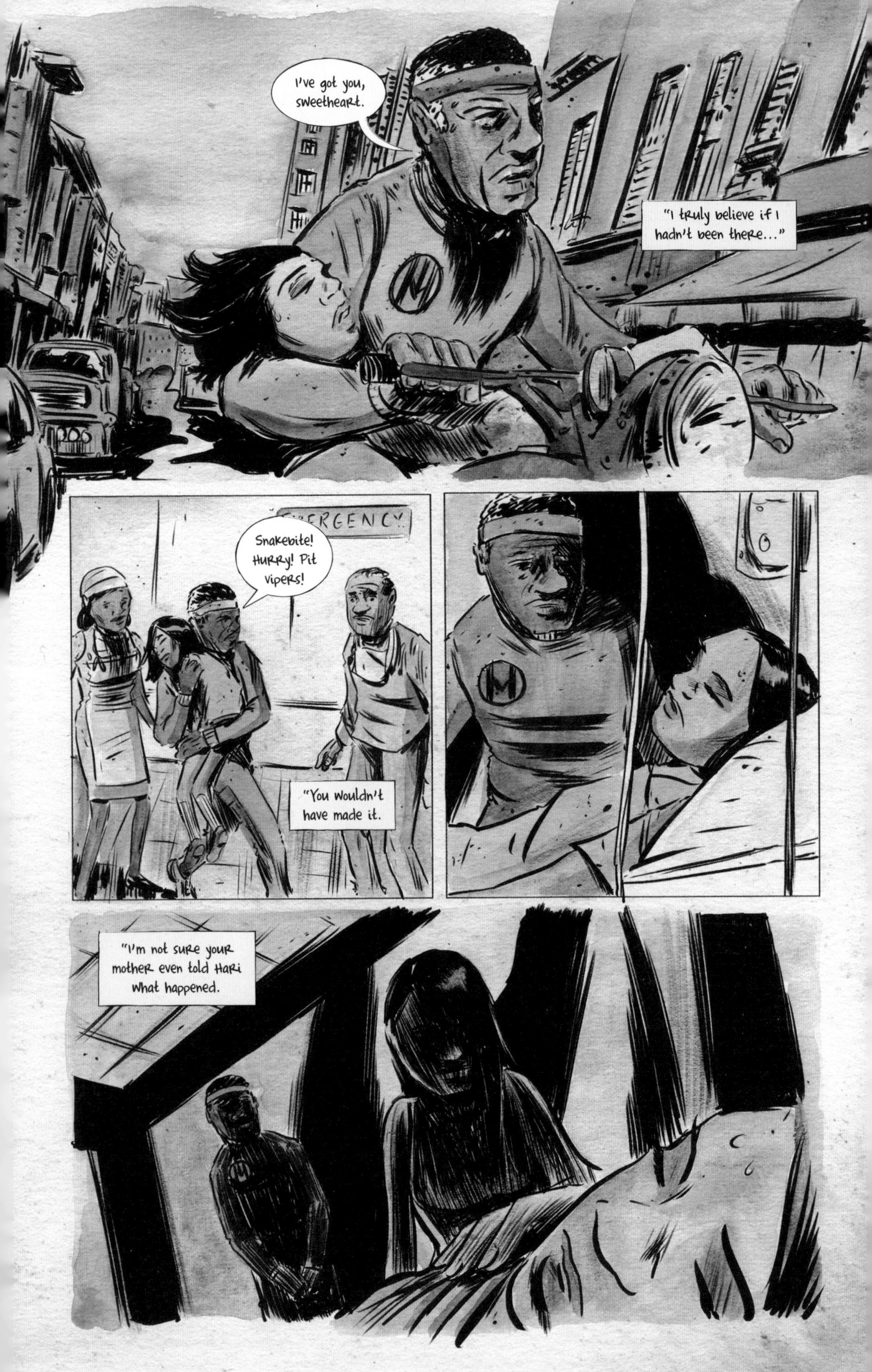
I've got you, sweetheart.
"I truly believe if I hadn't been there..."
Snakebite! Hurry! Pit vipers!
"You wouldn't have made it.
"I'm not sure your mother even told Hari what happened.

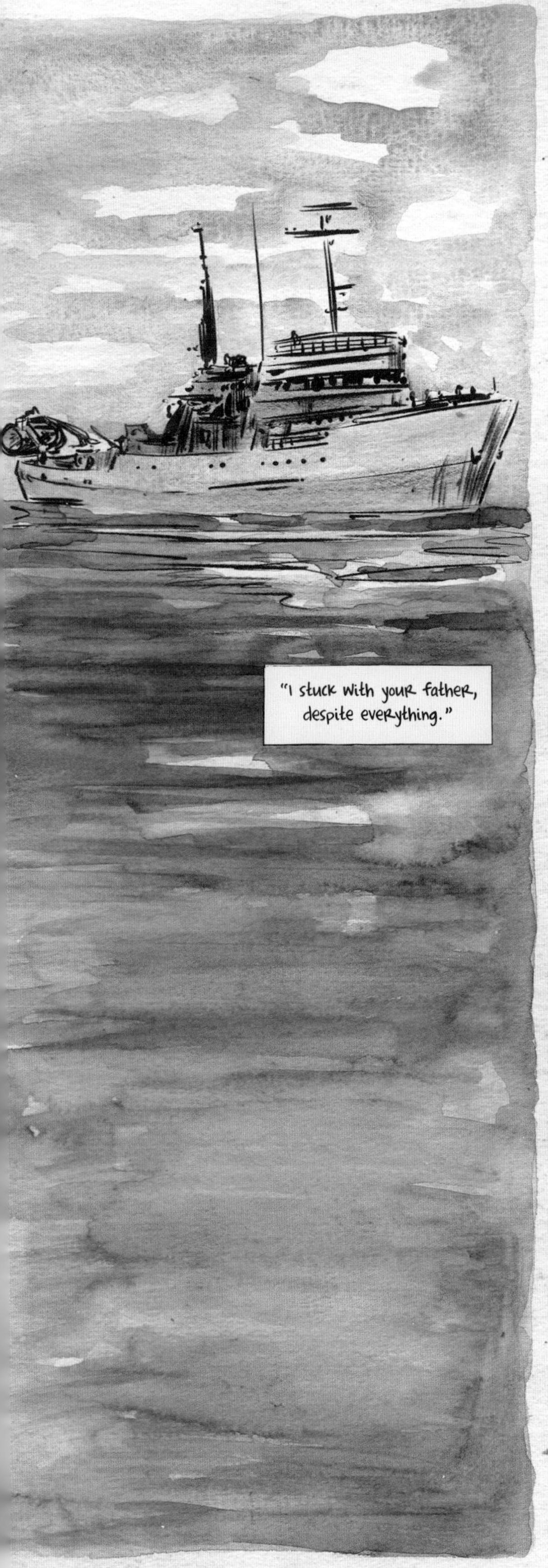
"I stuck with your father, despite everything."

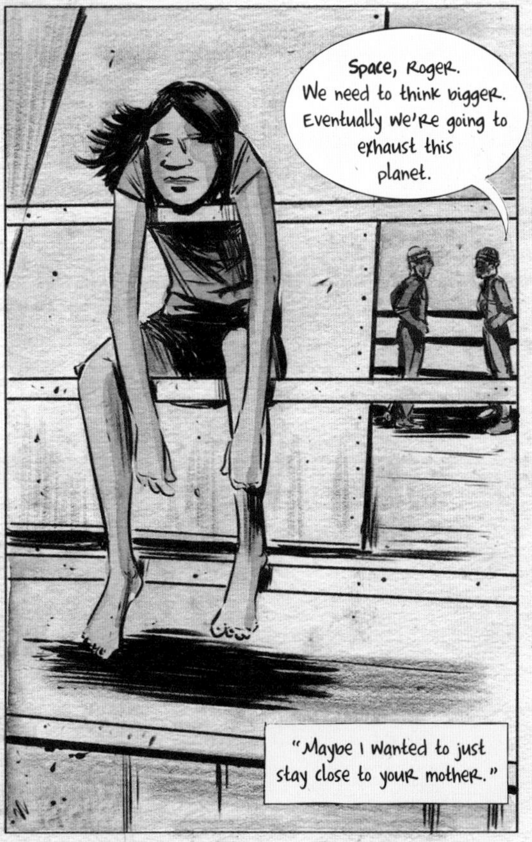
Space, Roger. We need to think bigger. Eventually we're going to exhaust this planet.
"Maybe I wanted to just stay close to your mother."

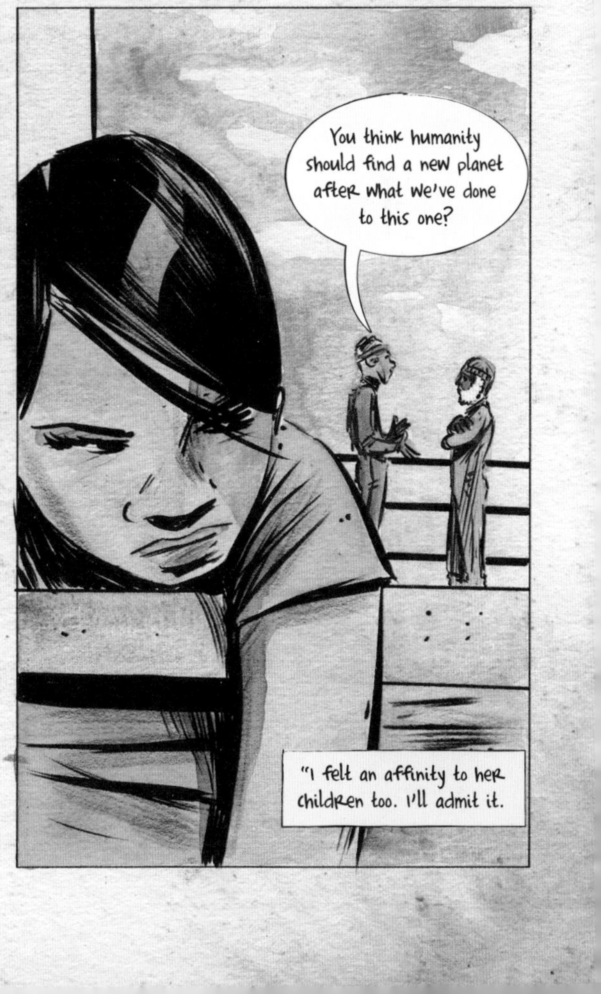
You think humanity should find a new planet after what we've done to this one?
"I felt an affinity to her children too. I'll admit it.

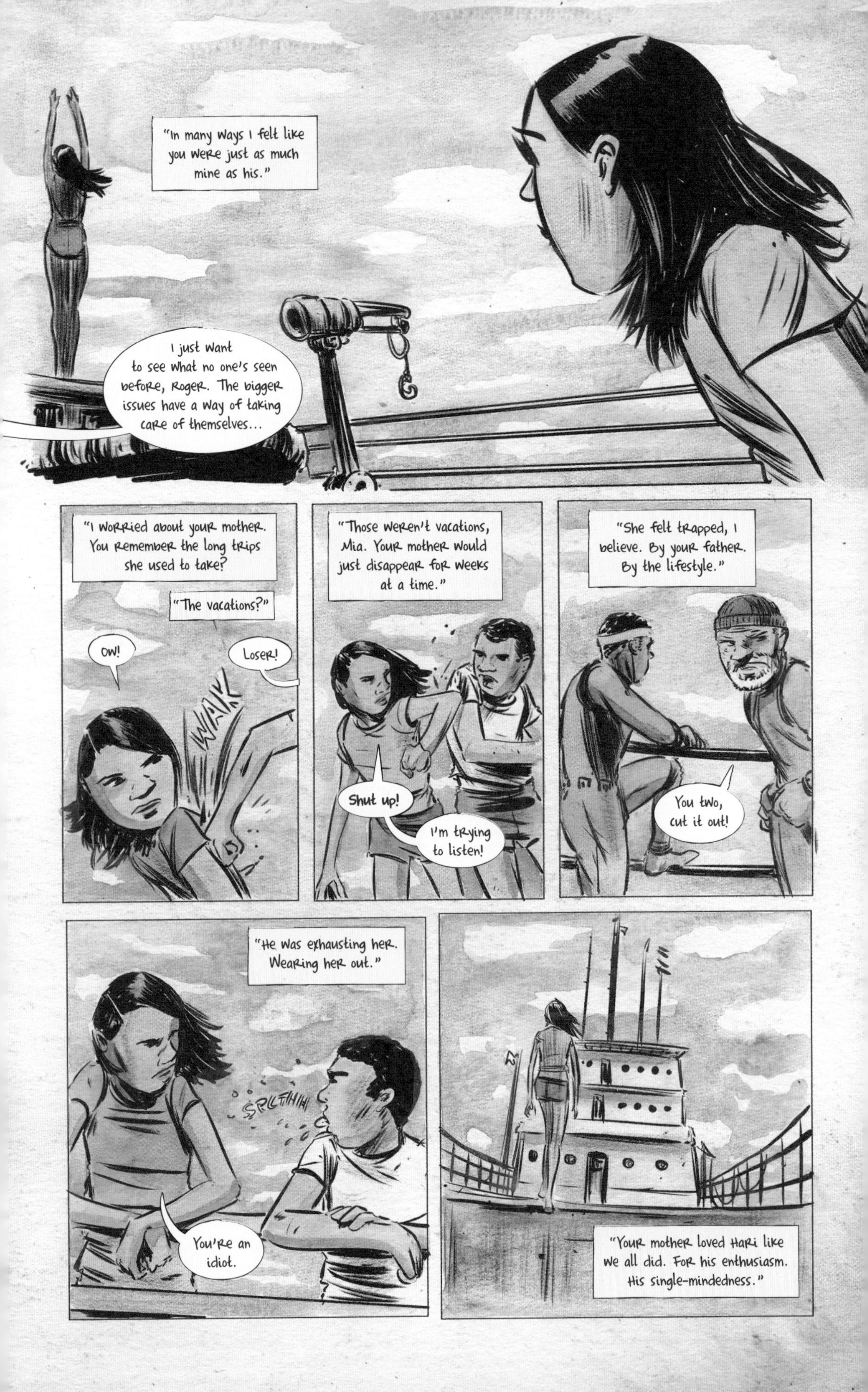
"In many ways I felt like you were just as much mine as his."
I just want to see what no one's seen before, Roger. The bigger issues have a way of taking care of themselves...
"I worried about your mother. You remember the long trips she used to take?
"The vacations?"
OW!
Loser!
WAK
"Those weren't vacations, Mia. Your mother would just disappear for weeks at a time."
Shut up!
I'm trying to listen!
"She felt trapped, I believe. By your father. By the lifestyle."
You two, cut it out!
"He was exhausting her. Wearing her out."
SPLTHH
You're an idiot.
"Your mother loved Hari like we all did. For his enthusiasm. His single-mindedness."

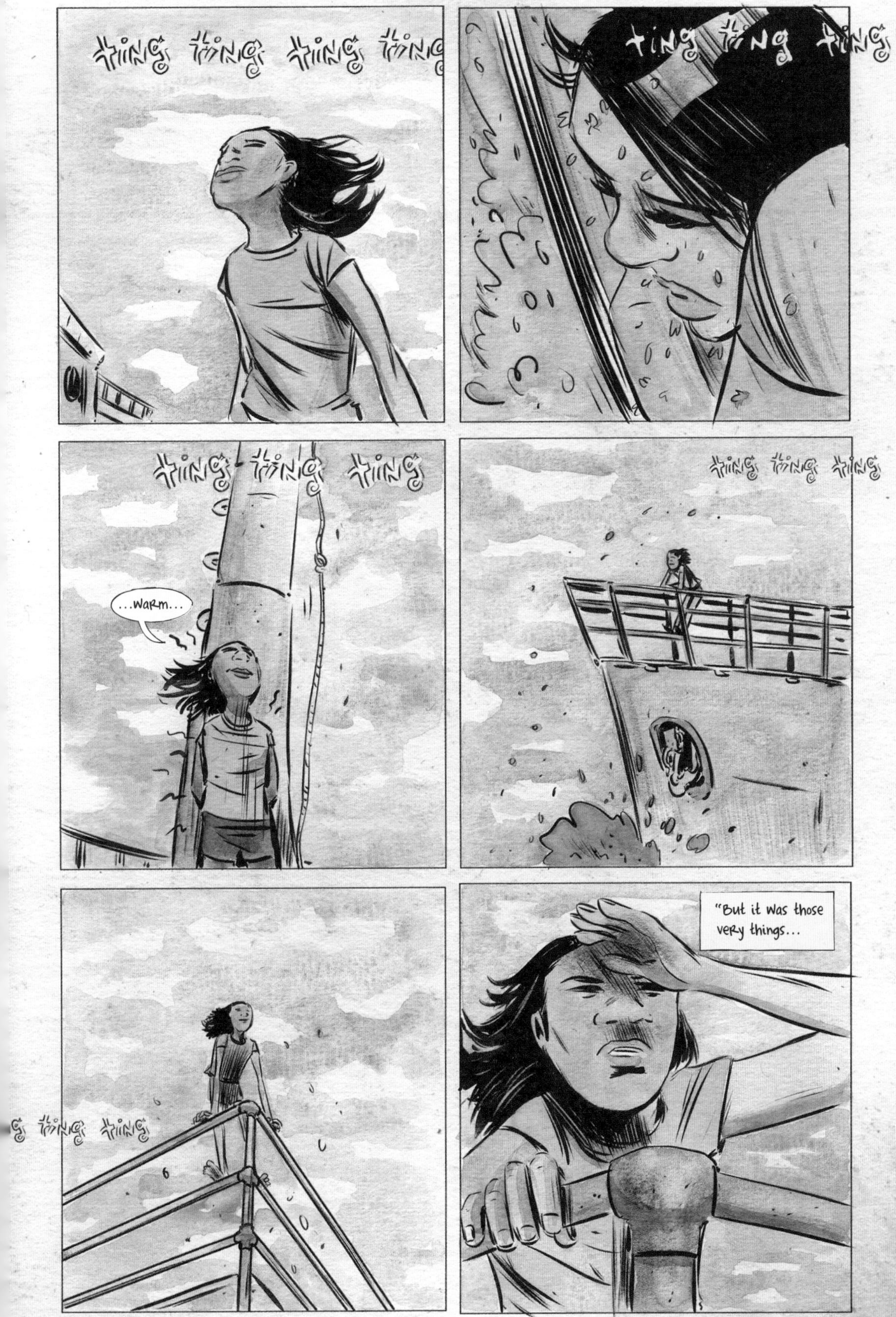
ting ting ting ting
ting ting ting
ting ting ting
...warm...
ting ting ting
g ting ting
"But it was those very things...

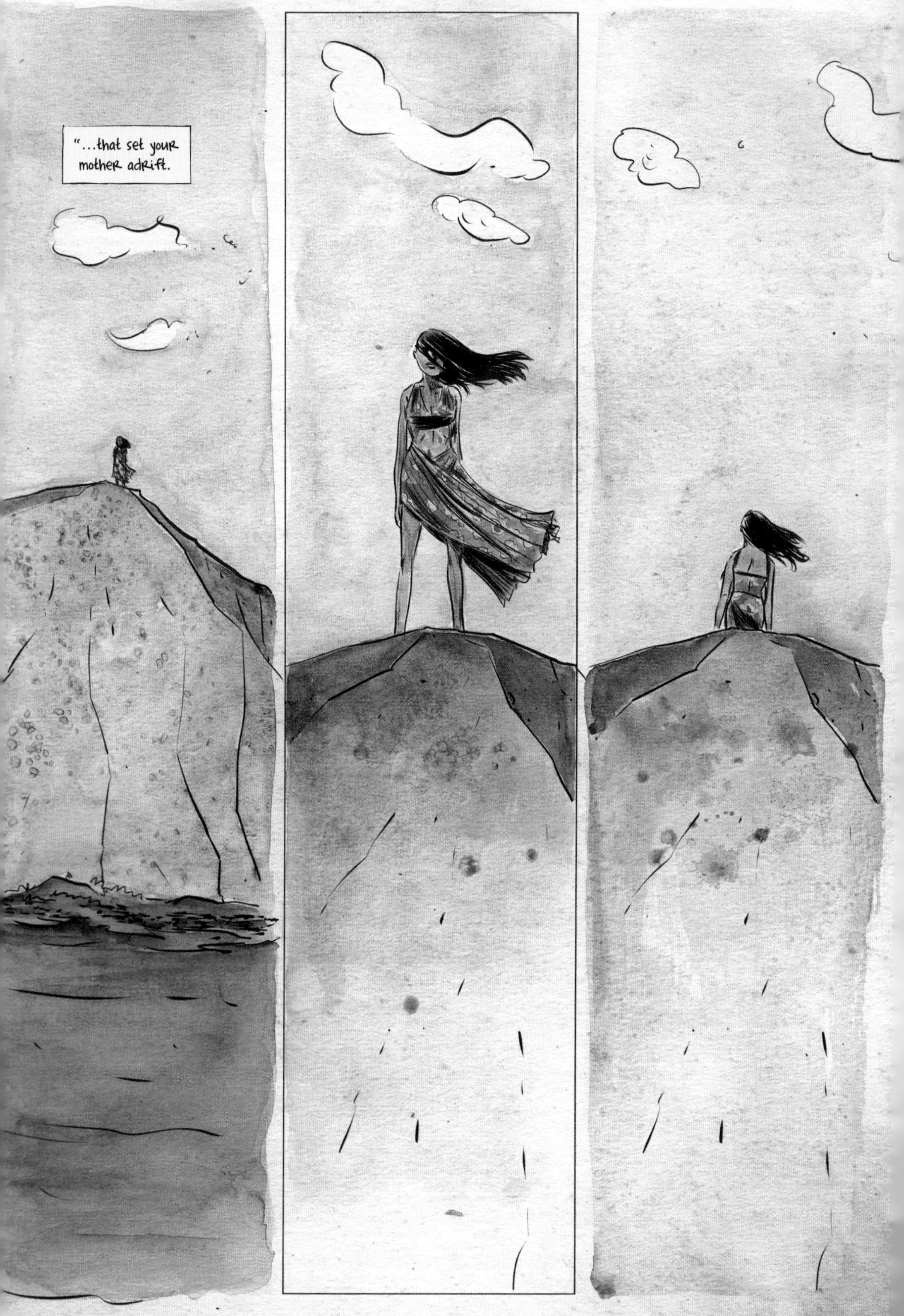
"...that set your mother adrift.

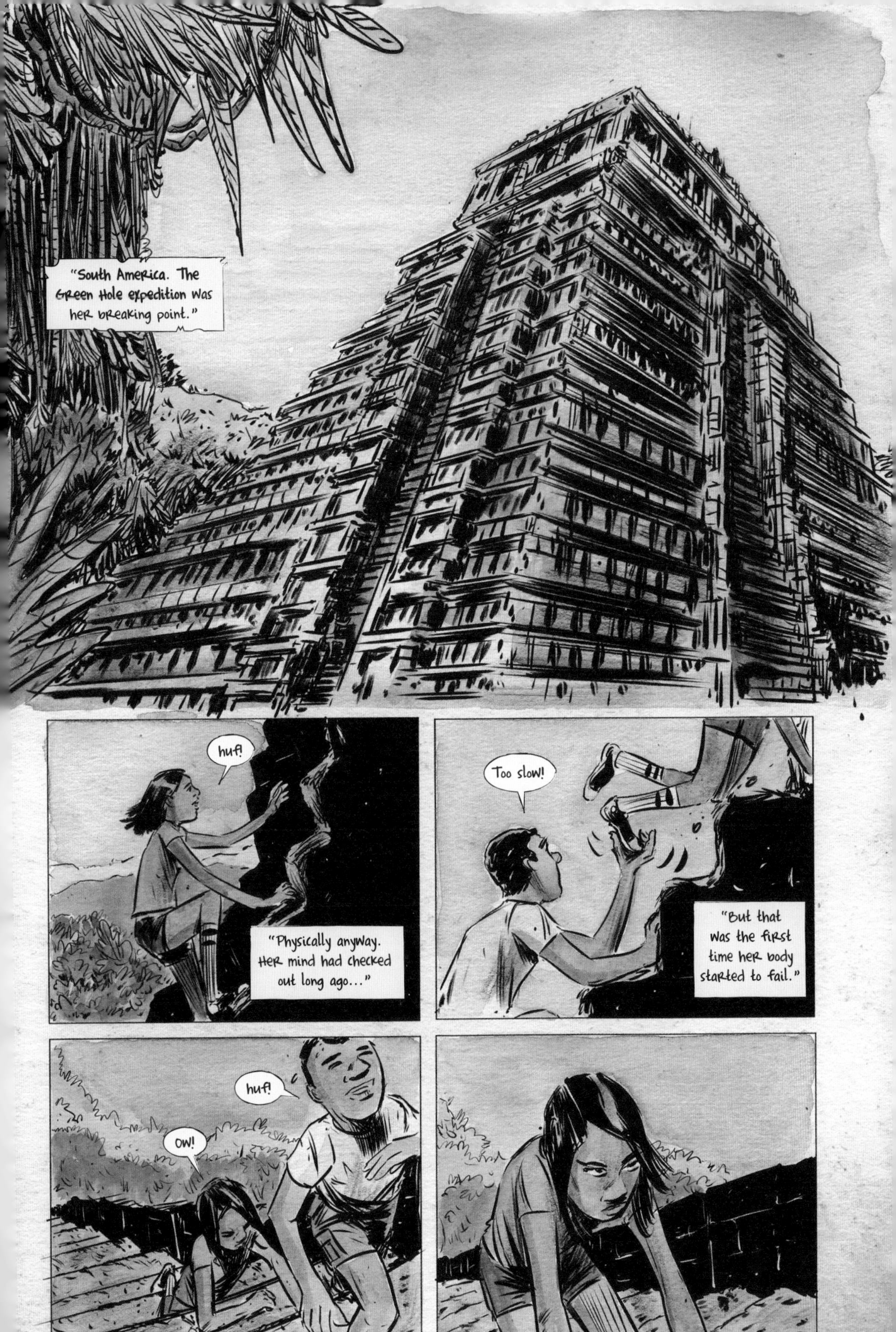
"South America. The Green Hole expedition was her breaking point."
huf!
"Physically anyway. Her mind had checked out long ago..."
Too slow!
"But that was the first time her body started to fail."
huf!
OW!

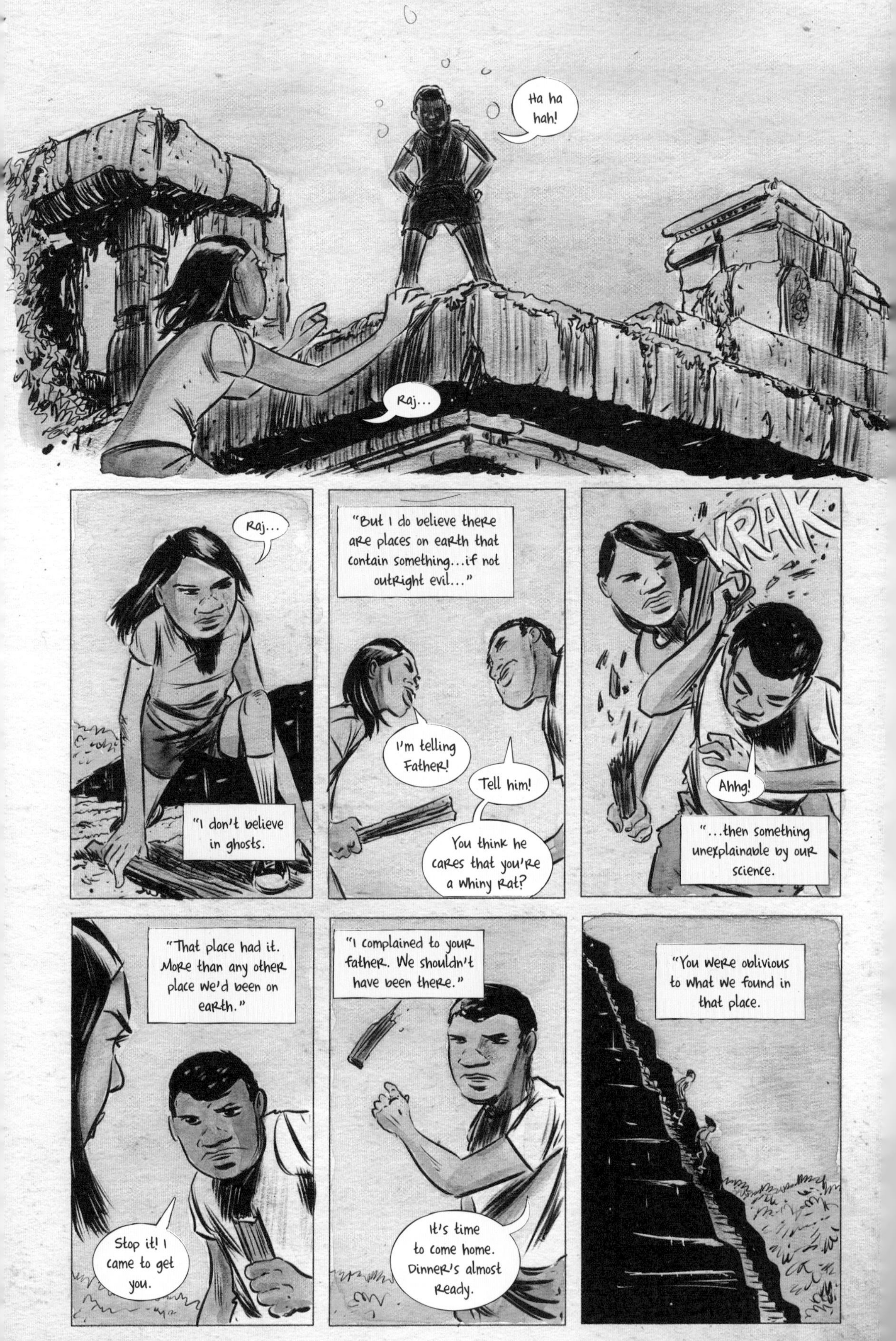
Ha ha hah!
Raj...
Raj...
"I don't believe in ghosts.
"But I do believe there are places on earth that contain something...if not outright evil..."
I'm telling Father!
Tell him!
You think he cares that you're a whiny rat?
KRAK
Ahhg!
"...then something unexplainable by our science.
"That place had it. More than any other place we'd been on earth."
Stop it! I came to get you.
"I complained to your father. We shouldn't have been there."
It's time to come home. Dinner's almost ready.
"You were oblivious to what we found in that place.

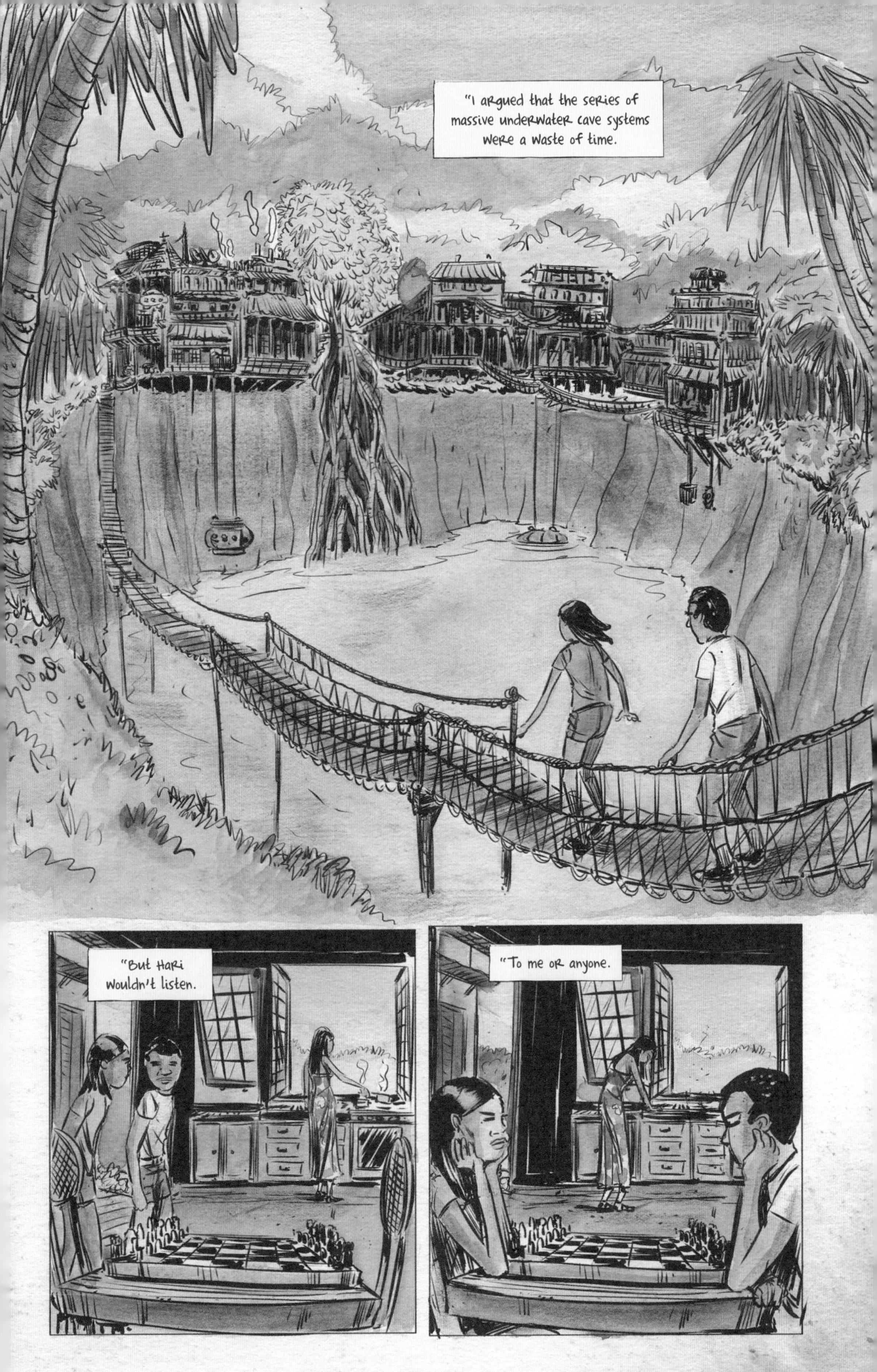
"I argued that the series of massive underwater cave systems were a waste of time.
"But Hari wouldn't listen.
"To me or anyone.

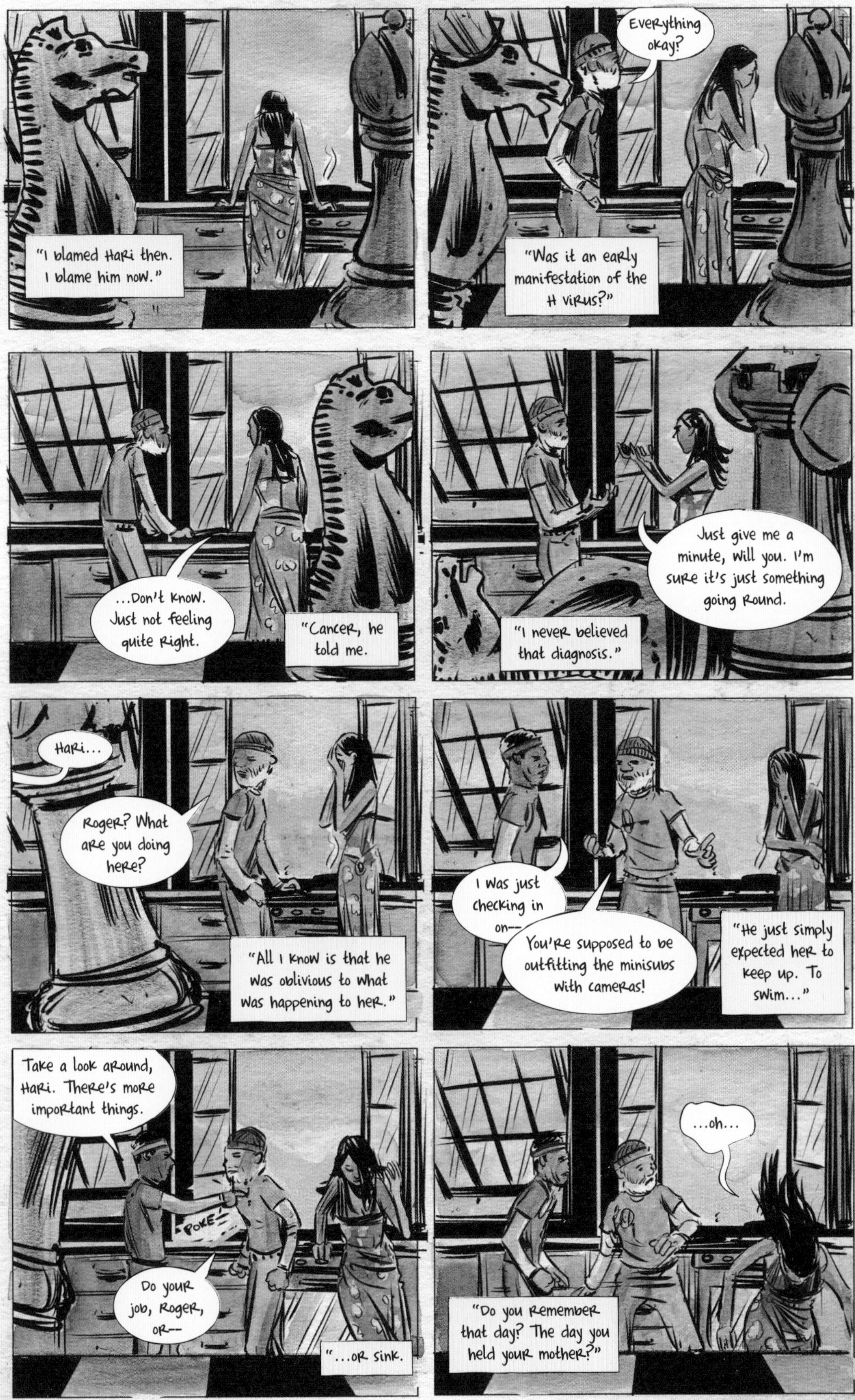
"I blamed Hari then. I blame him now."
Everything okay?
"Was it an early manifestation of the H virus?"
...Don't know. Just not feeling quite right.
"Cancer, he told me.
Just give me a minute, will you. I'm sure it's just something going round.
"I never believed that diagnosis."
Hari...
Roger? What are you doing here?
"All I know is that he was oblivious to what was happening to her."
I was just checking in on--
You're supposed to be outfitting the minisubs with cameras!
"He just simply expected her to keep up. To swim..."
Take a look around, Hari. There's more important things.
POKE
Do your job, Roger, or--
"...or sink.
...oh...
"Do you remember that day? The day you held your mother?"

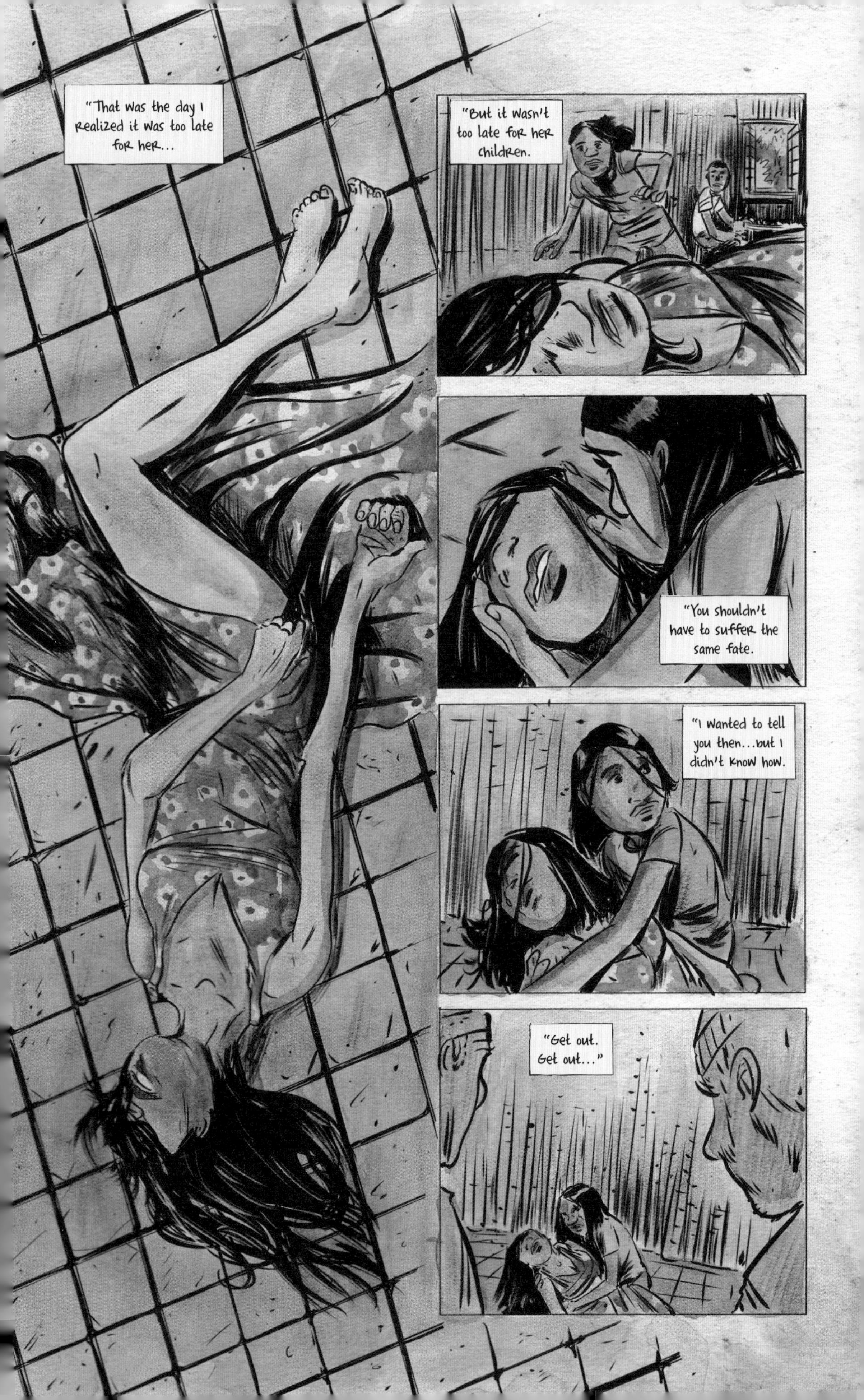
"That was the day I realized it was too late for her...
"But it wasn't too late for her children.
"You shouldn't have to suffer the same fate.
"I wanted to tell you then...but I didn't know how.
"Get out. Get out..."

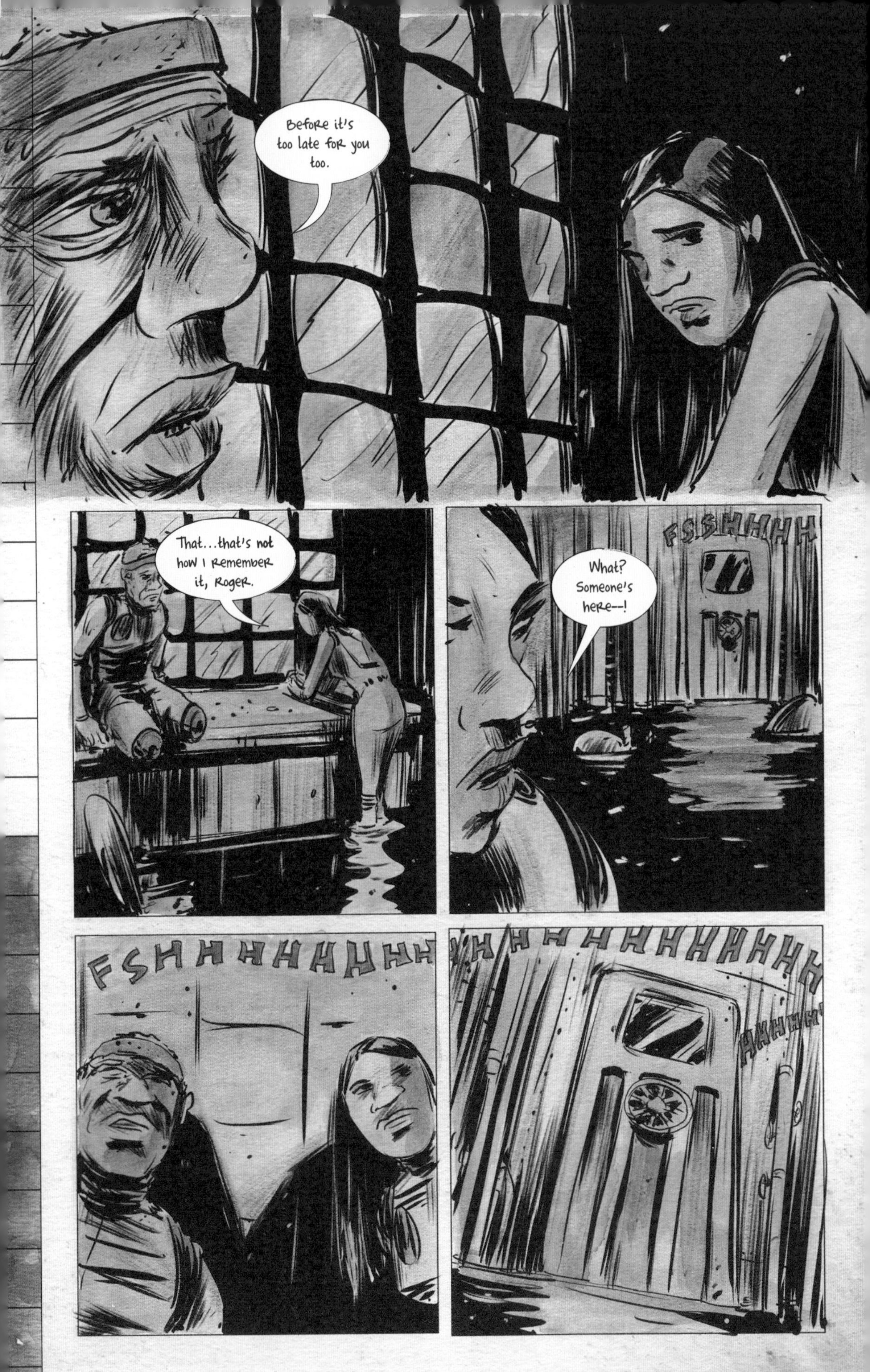
Before it's too late for you too.
That...that's not how I remember it, Roger.
FSSHHHHH
What? Someone's here--!
FSHHHHHHHHHH
HHHHHHHHHHHHH
HHHHH

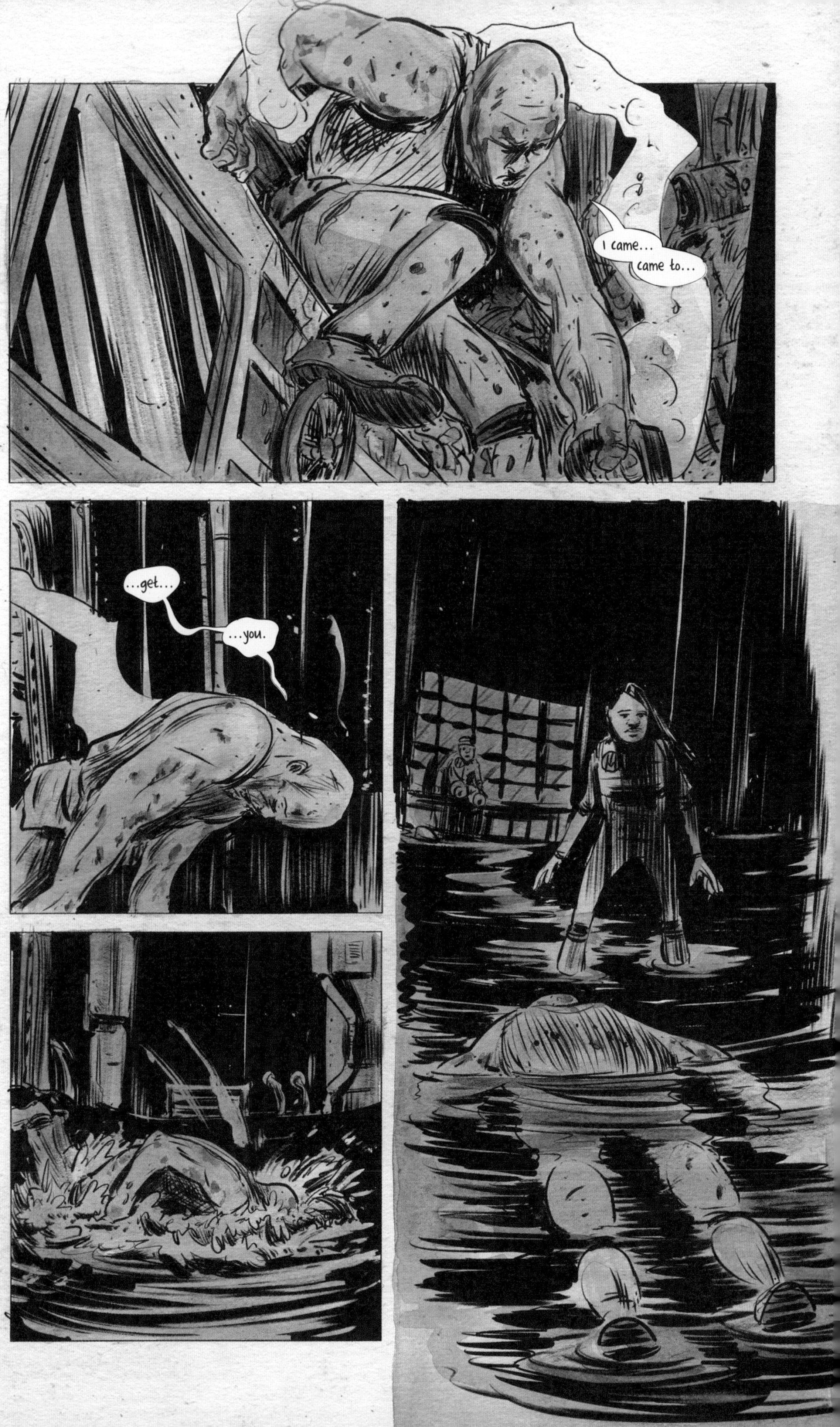
I came... came to...
...get...
...you.

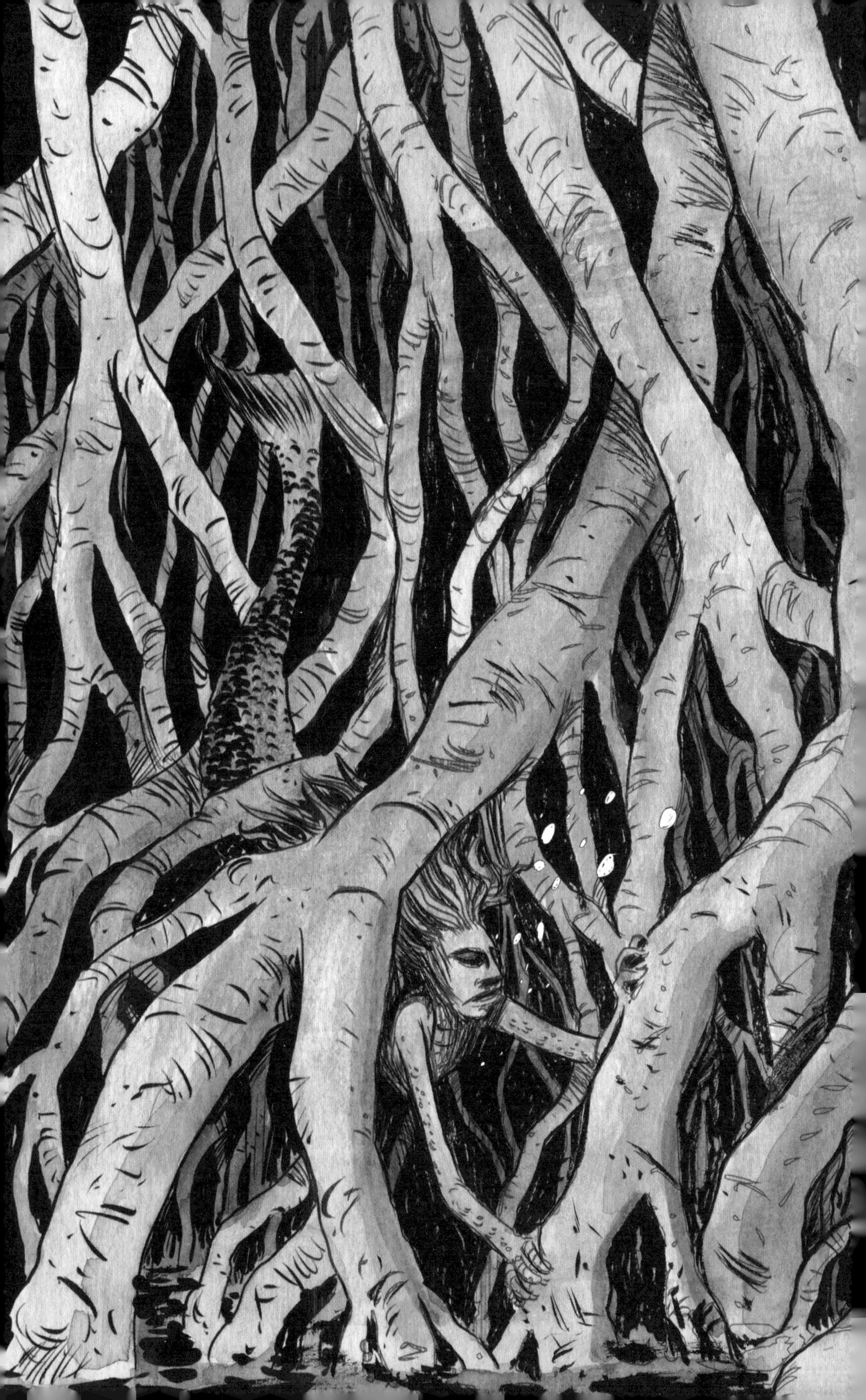

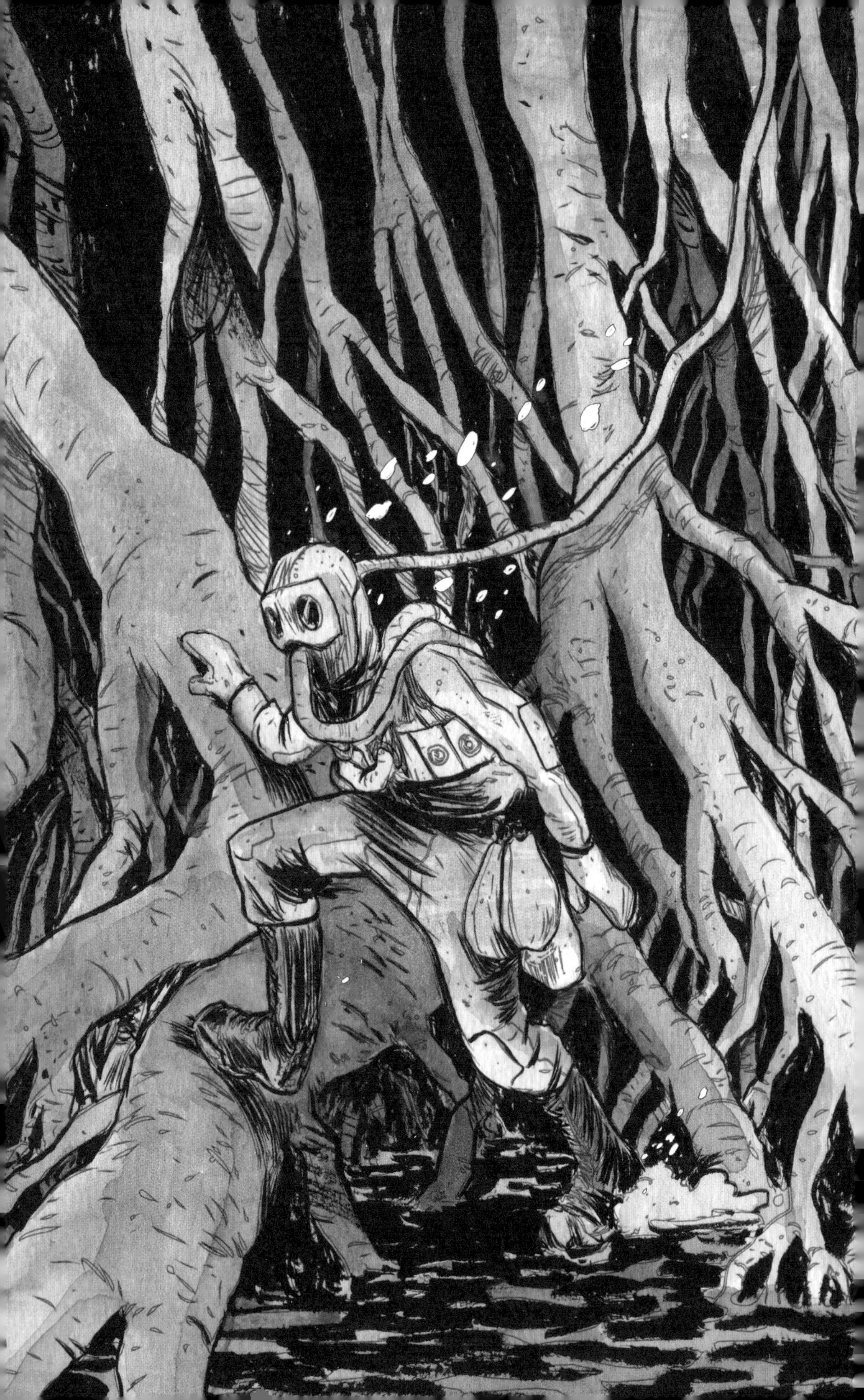

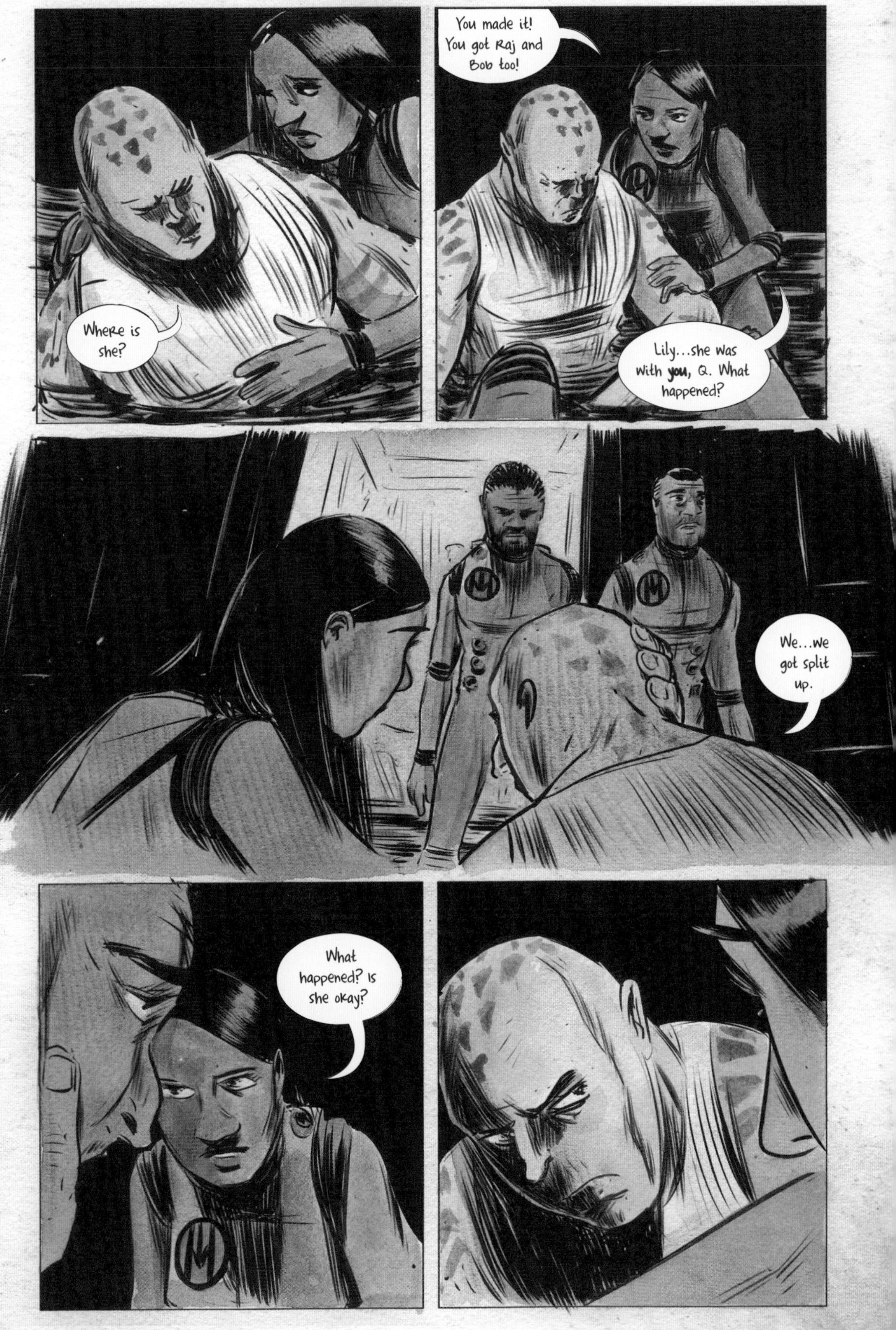
Where is she?
You made it! You got Raj and Bob too!
Lily...she was with **you**, Q. What happened?
We...we got split up.
What happened? Is she okay?

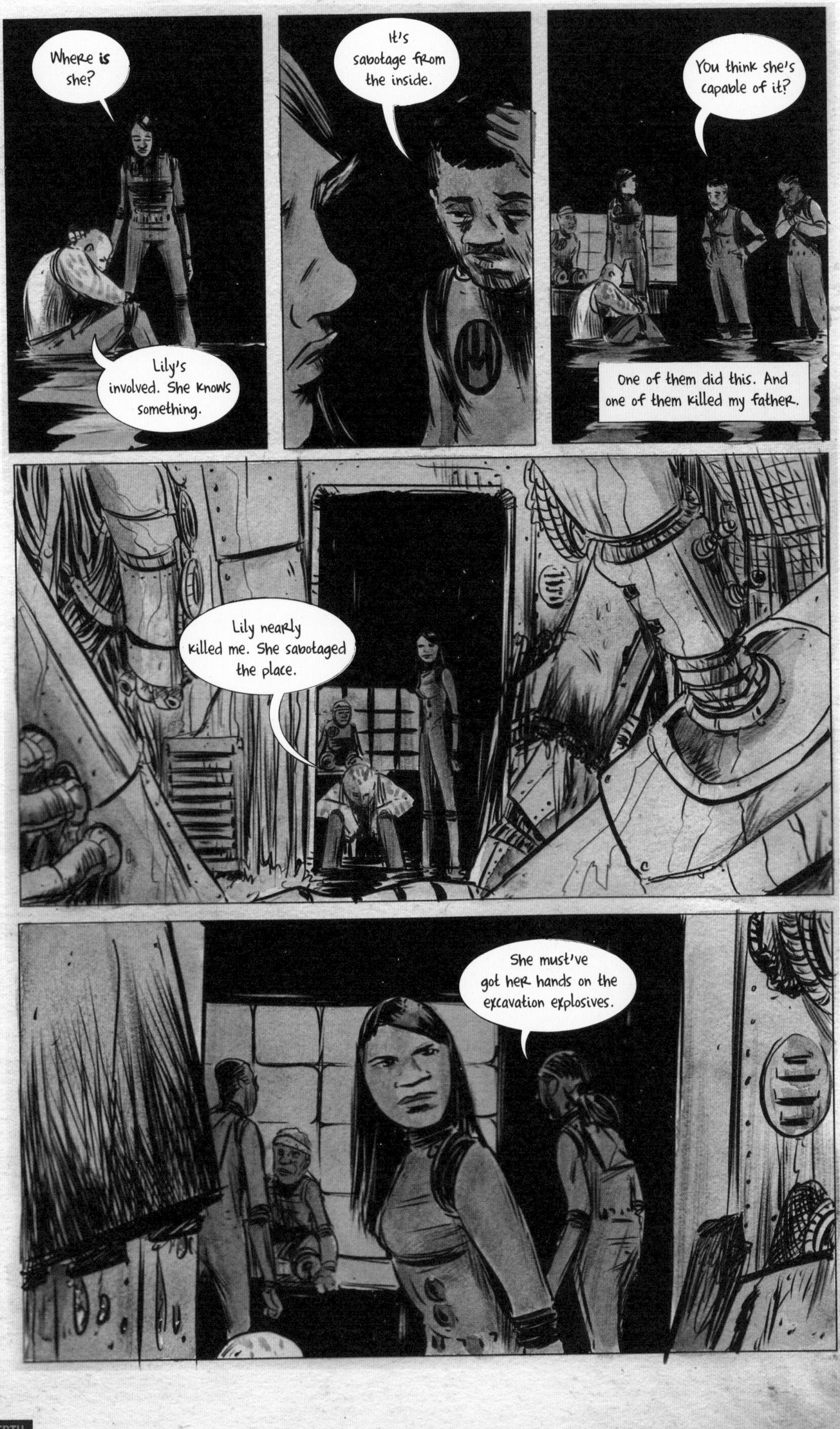
Where is she?
Lily's involved. She knows something.
It's sabotage from the inside.
You think she's capable of it?
One of them did this. And one of them killed my father.
Lily nearly killed me. She sabotaged the place.
She must've got her hands on the excavation explosives.

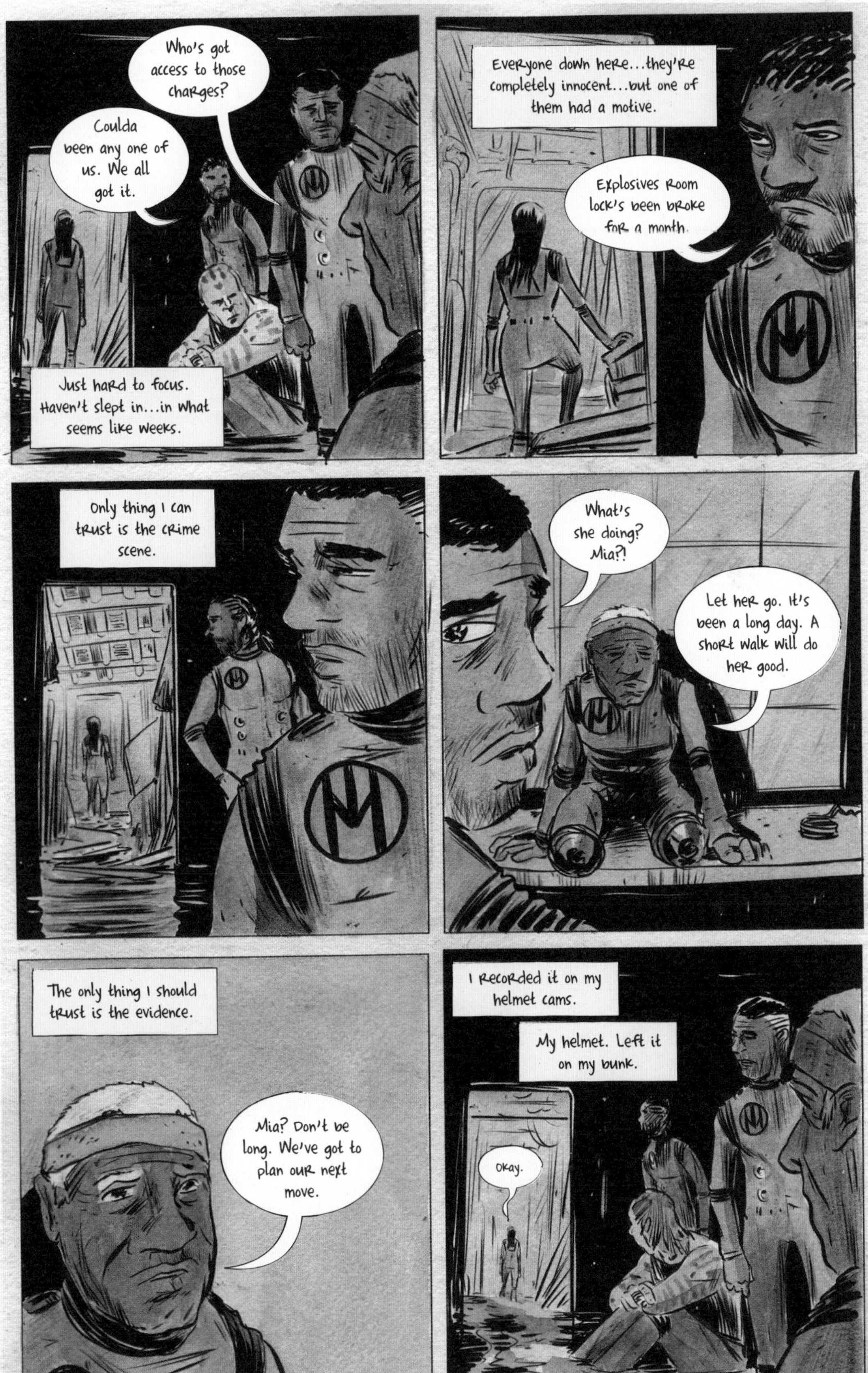
Who's got access to those charges?
Coulda been any one of us. We all got it.
Just hard to focus. Haven't slept in...in what seems like weeks.
Everyone down here...they're completely innocent...but one of them had a motive.
Explosives room lock's been broke for a month.
Only thing I can trust is the crime scene.
What's she doing? Mia?!
Let her go. It's been a long day. A short walk will do her good.
The only thing I should trust is the evidence.
Mia? Don't be long. We've got to plan our next move.
I recorded it on my helmet cams.
My helmet. Left it on my bunk.
Okay.

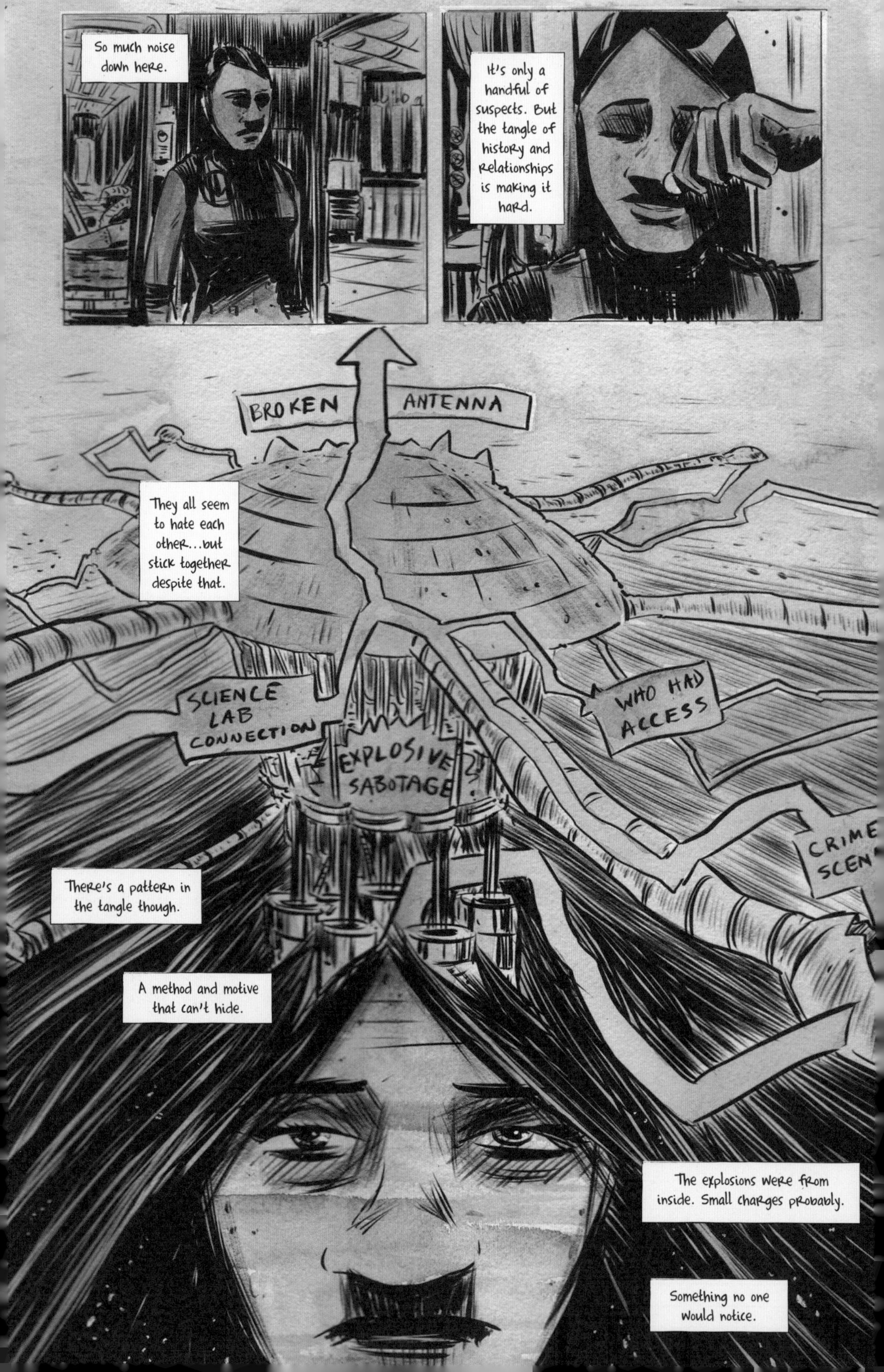
So much noise down here.
It's only a handful of suspects. But the tangle of history and relationships is making it hard.
BROKEN
ANTENNA
They all seem to hate each other...but stick together despite that.
SCIENCE LAB CONNECTION
EXPLOSIVE SABOTAGE
WHO HAD ACCESS
There's a pattern in the tangle though.
A method and motive that can't hide.
The explosions were from inside. Small charges probably.
Something no one would notice.

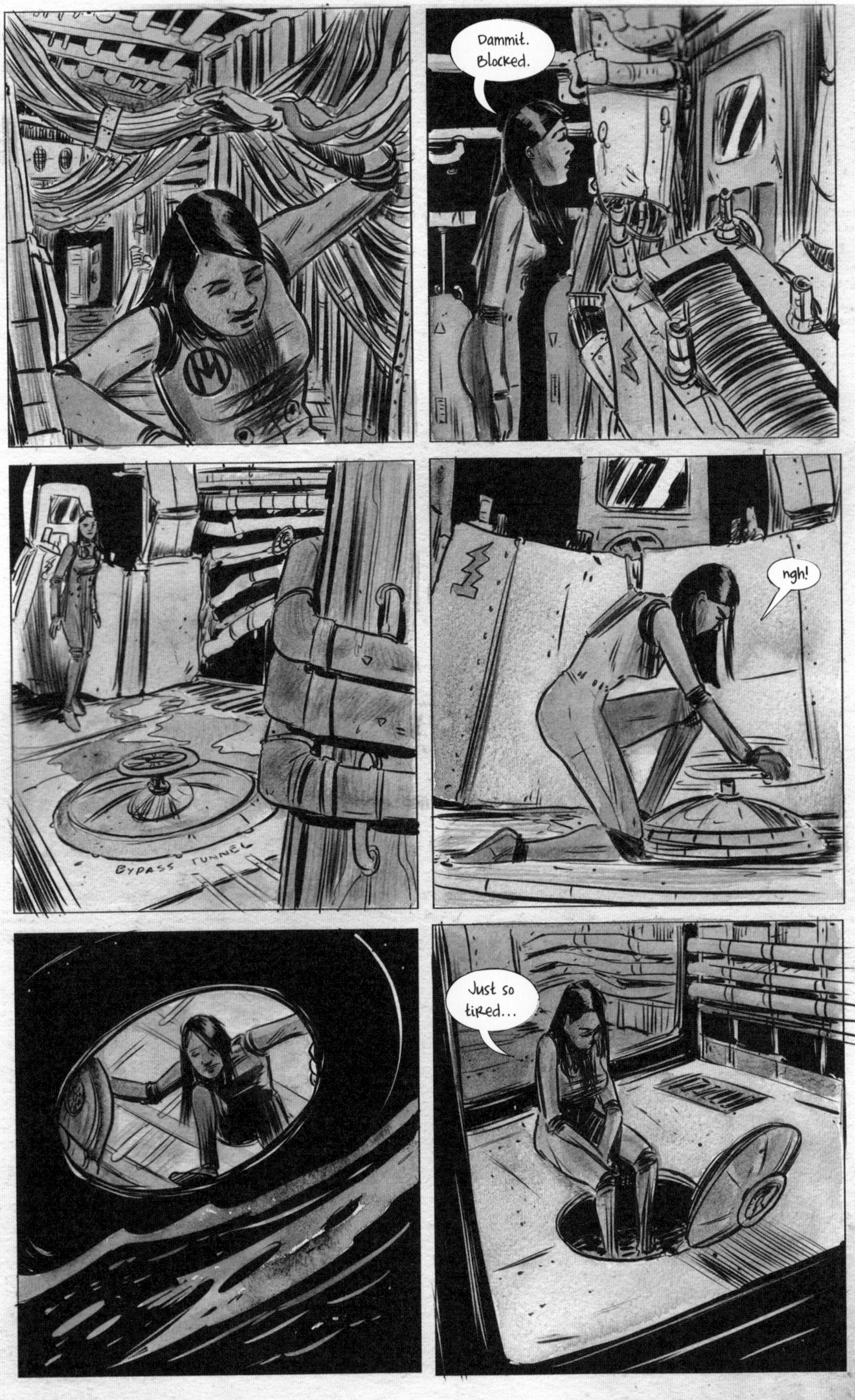
Dammit.
Blocked.
BYPASS TUNNEL
ngh!
Just so
tired...

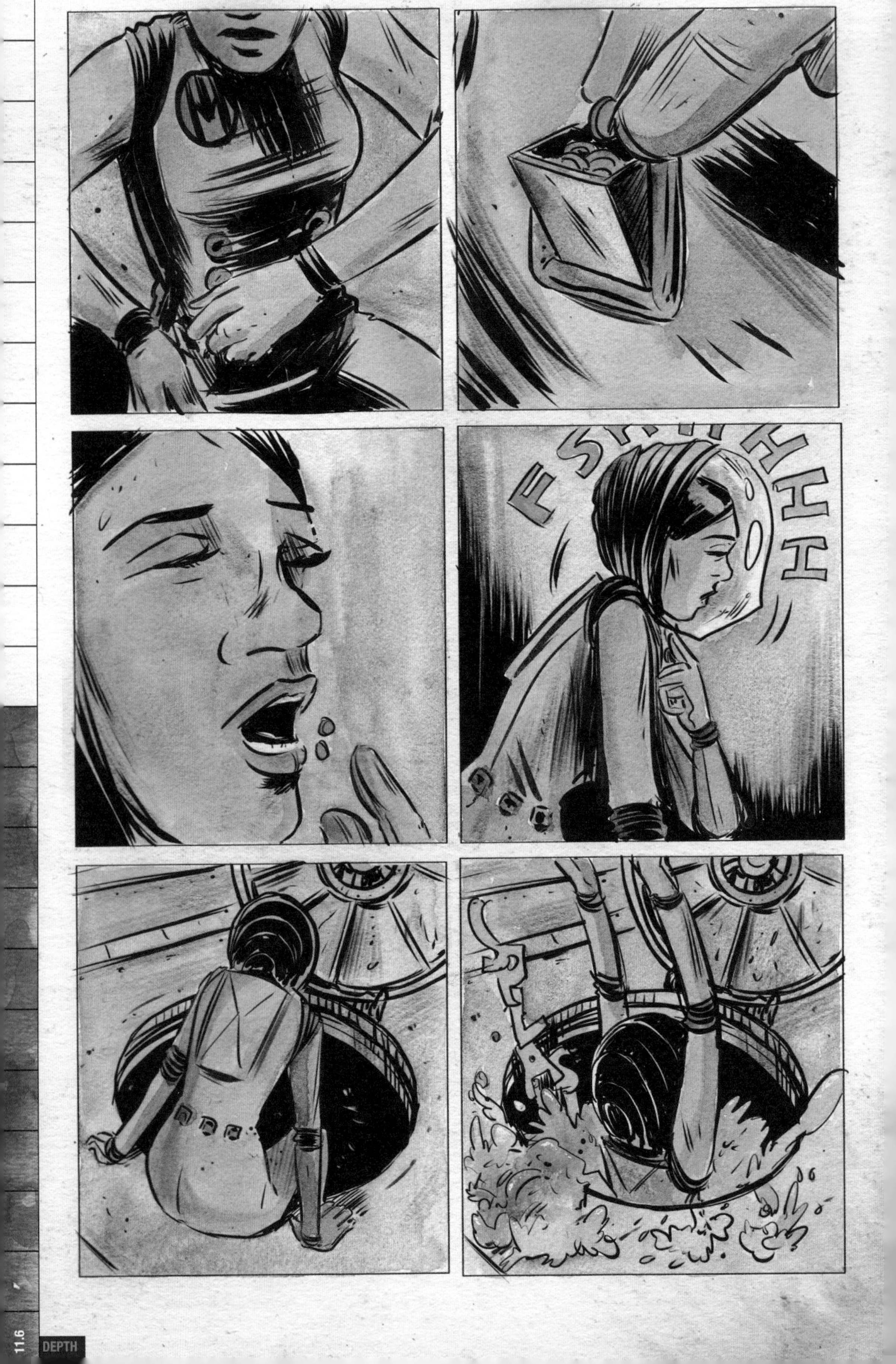
FSHHHHHH

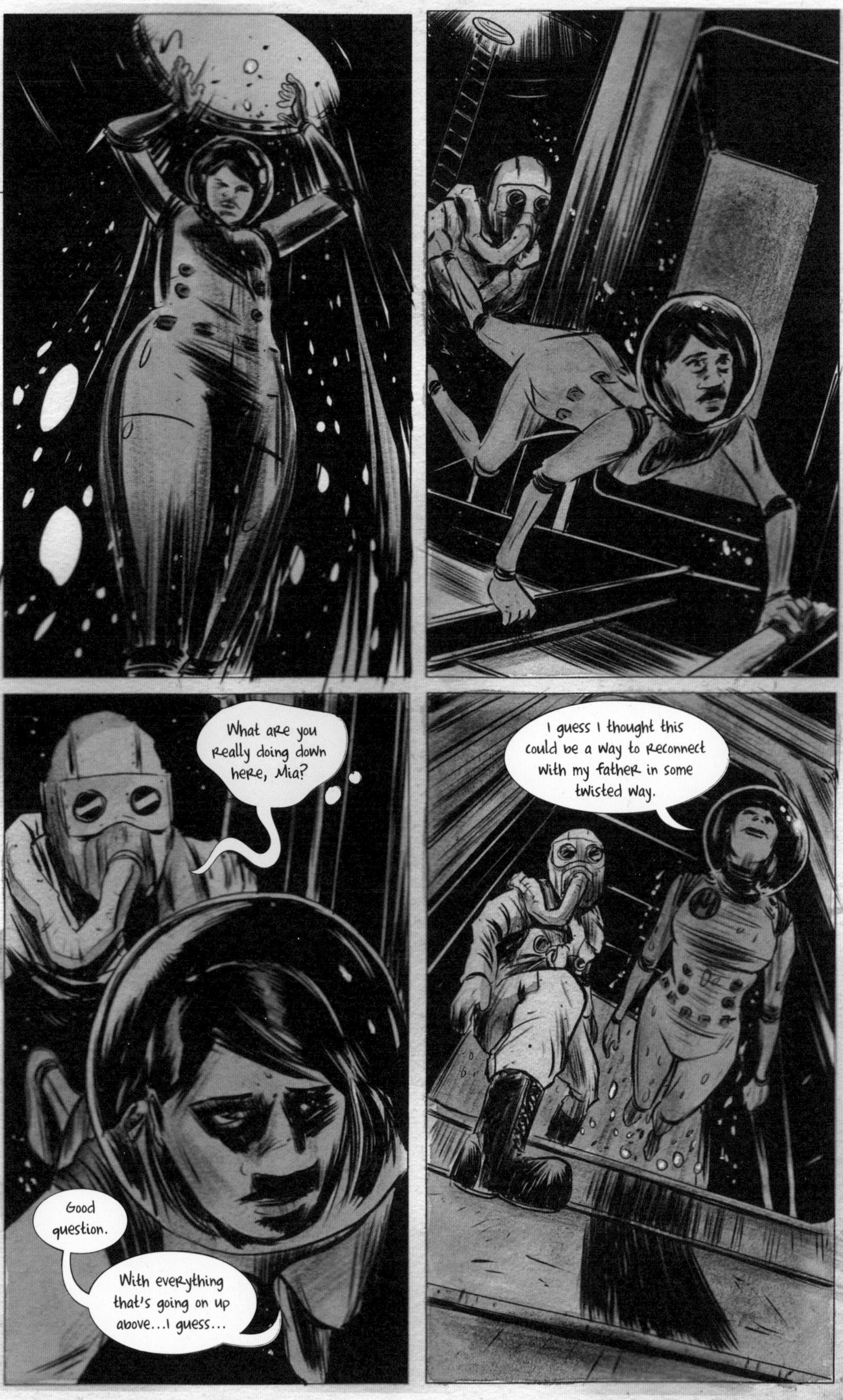
What are you really doing down here, Mia?
Good question.
With everything that's going on up above...I guess...
I guess I thought this could be a way to reconnect with my father in some twisted way.

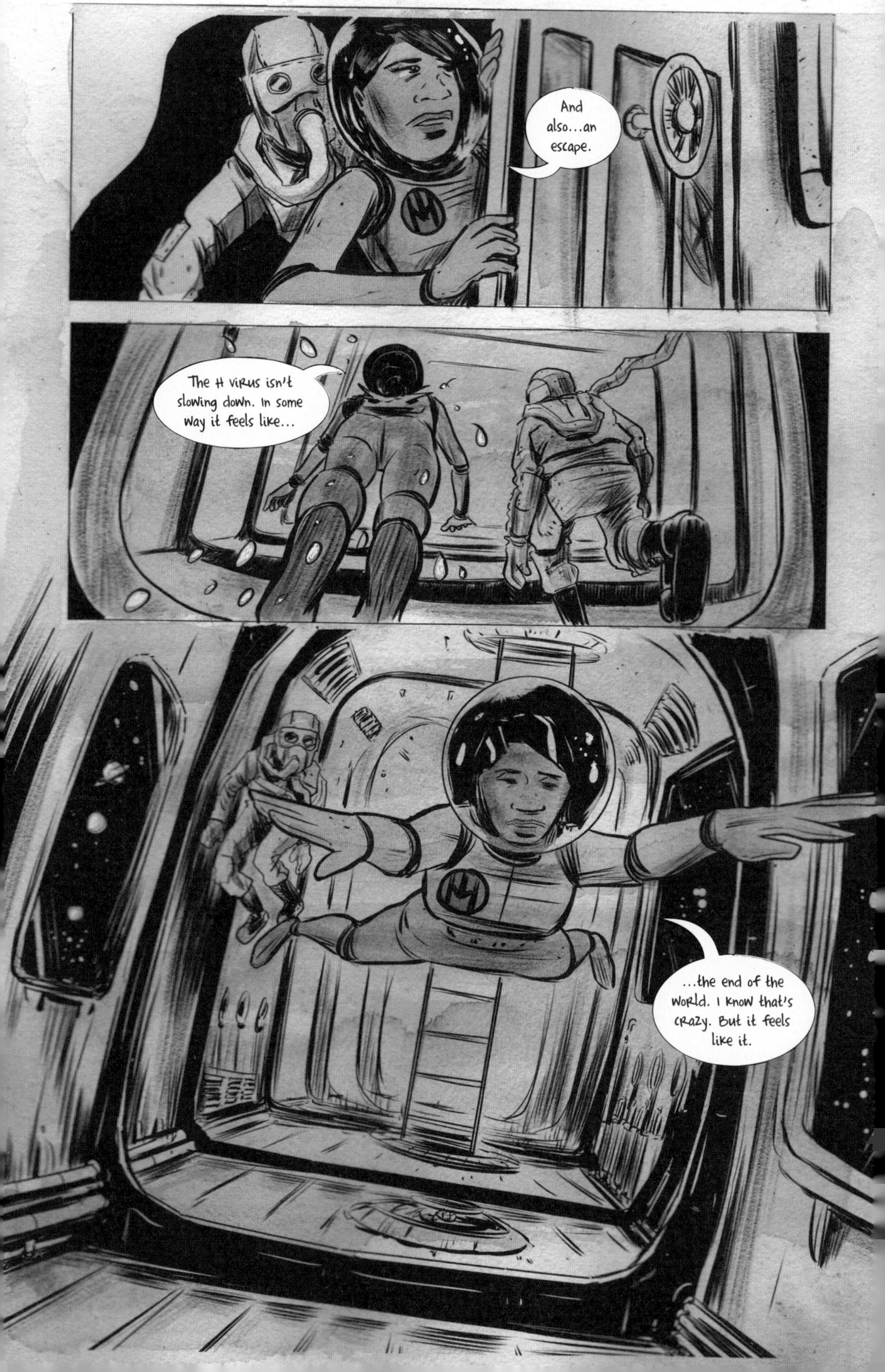
And also...an escape.
The H virus isn't slowing down. In some way it feels like...
...the end of the world. I know that's crazy. But it feels like it.

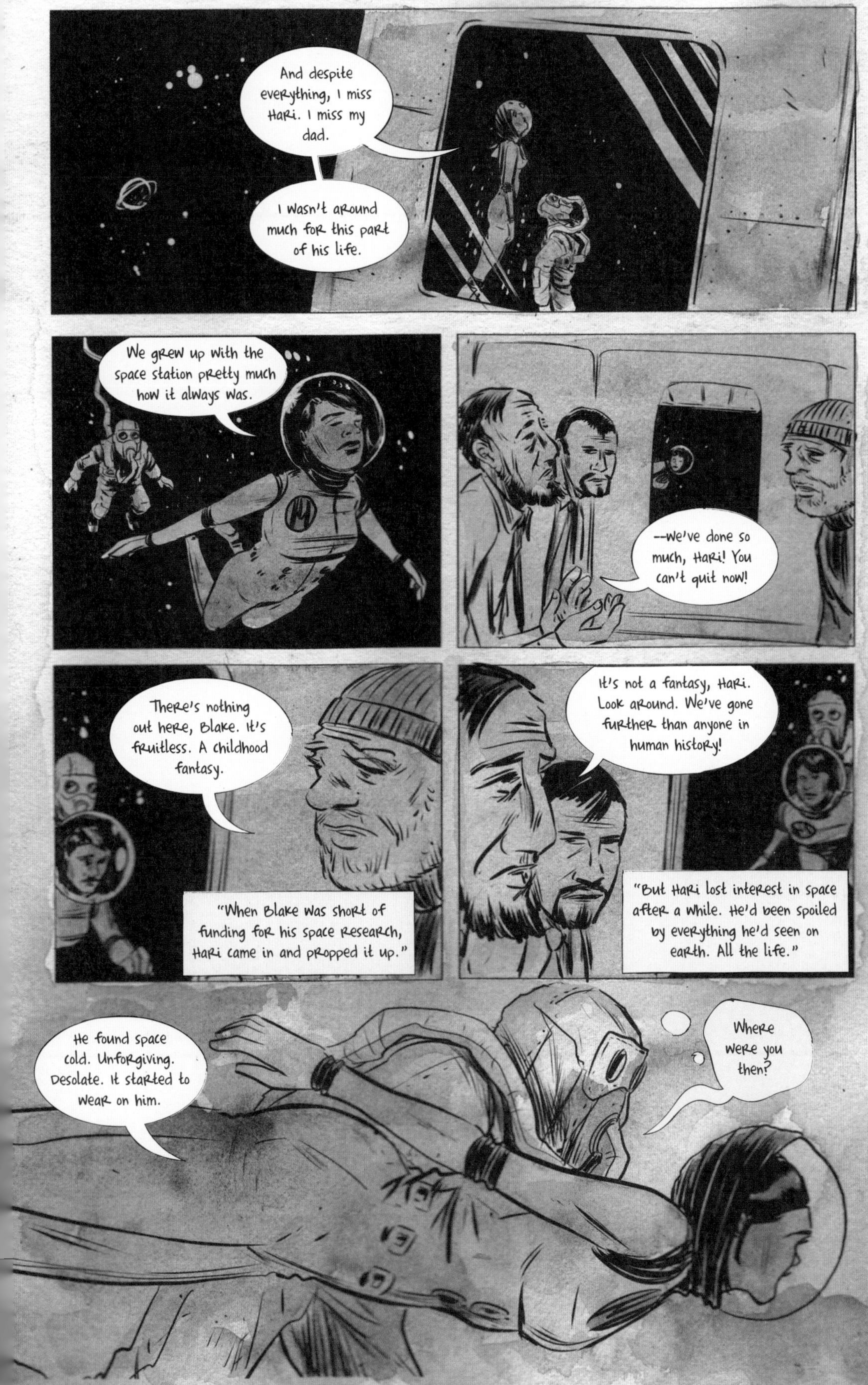
And despite everything, I miss Hari. I miss my dad.
I wasn't around much for this part of his life.
We grew up with the space station pretty much how it always was.
--We've done so much, Hari! You can't quit now!
There's nothing out here, Blake. It's fruitless. A childhood fantasy.
"When Blake was short of funding for his space research, Hari came in and propped it up."
It's not a fantasy, Hari. Look around. We've gone further than anyone in human history!
"But Hari lost interest in space after a while. He'd been spoiled by everything he'd seen on earth. All the life."
He found space cold. Unforgiving. Desolate. It started to wear on him.
Where were you then?

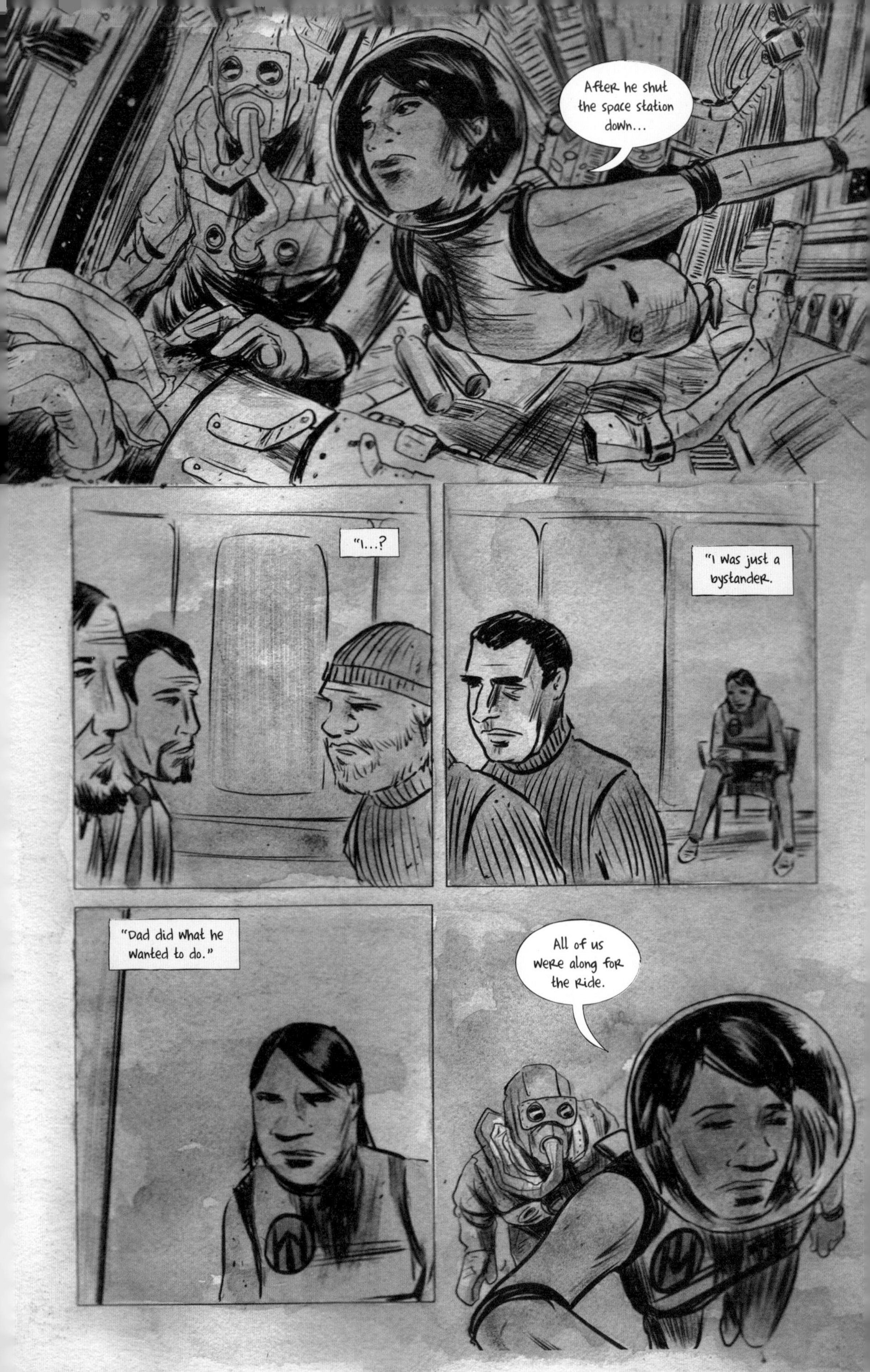
After he shut the space station down...
"I...?
"I was just a bystander.
"Dad did what he wanted to do."
All of us were along for the ride.

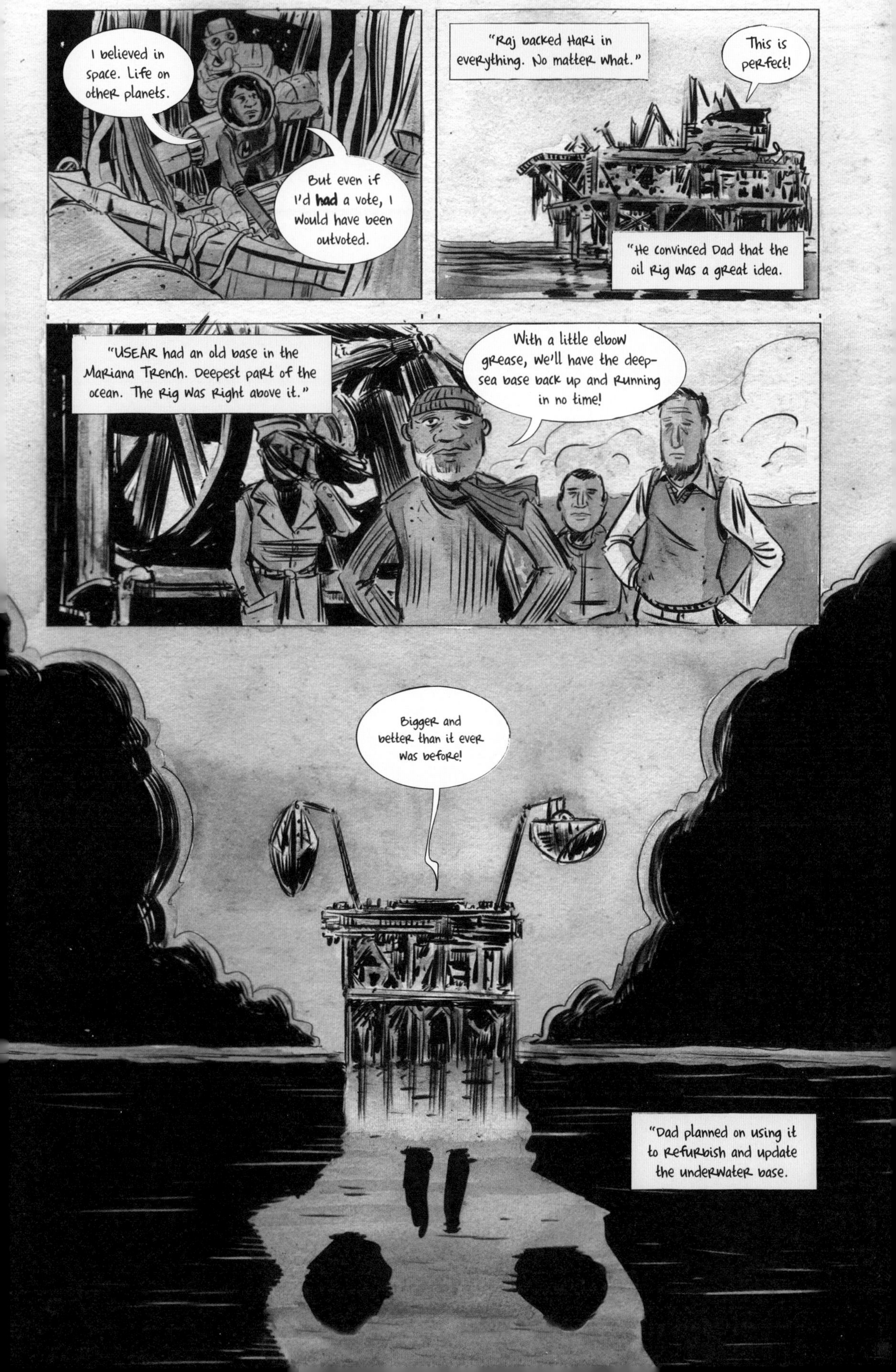
I believed in space. Life on other planets.
But even if I'd **had** a vote, I would have been outvoted.
"Raj backed Hari in everything. No matter what."
This is perfect!
"He convinced Dad that the oil rig was a great idea.
"USEAR had an old base in the Mariana Trench. Deepest part of the ocean. The rig was right above it."
With a little elbow grease, we'll have the deep-sea base back up and running in no time!
Bigger and better than it ever was before!
"Dad planned on using it to refurbish and update the underwater base.

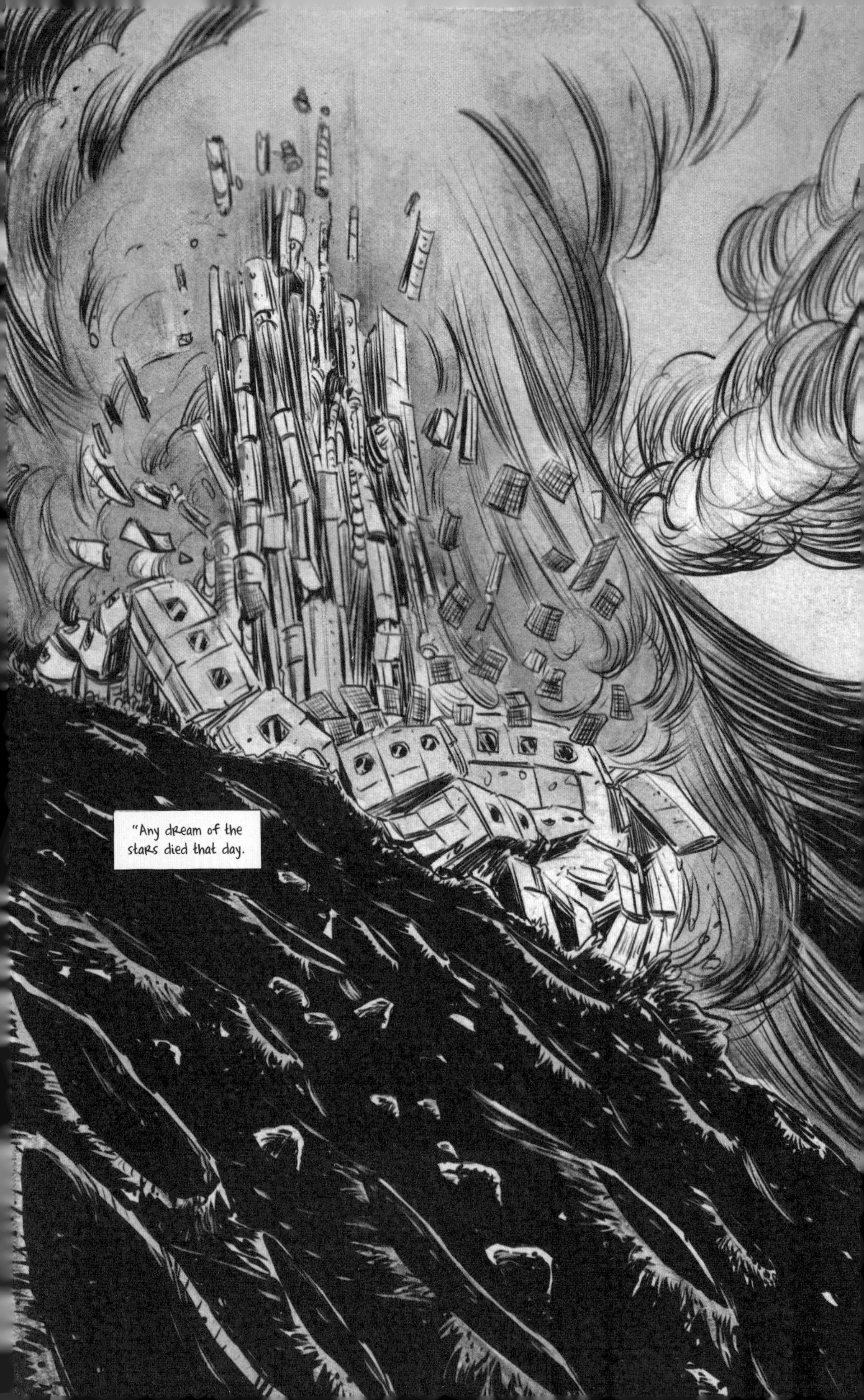
"Any dream of the stars died that day.

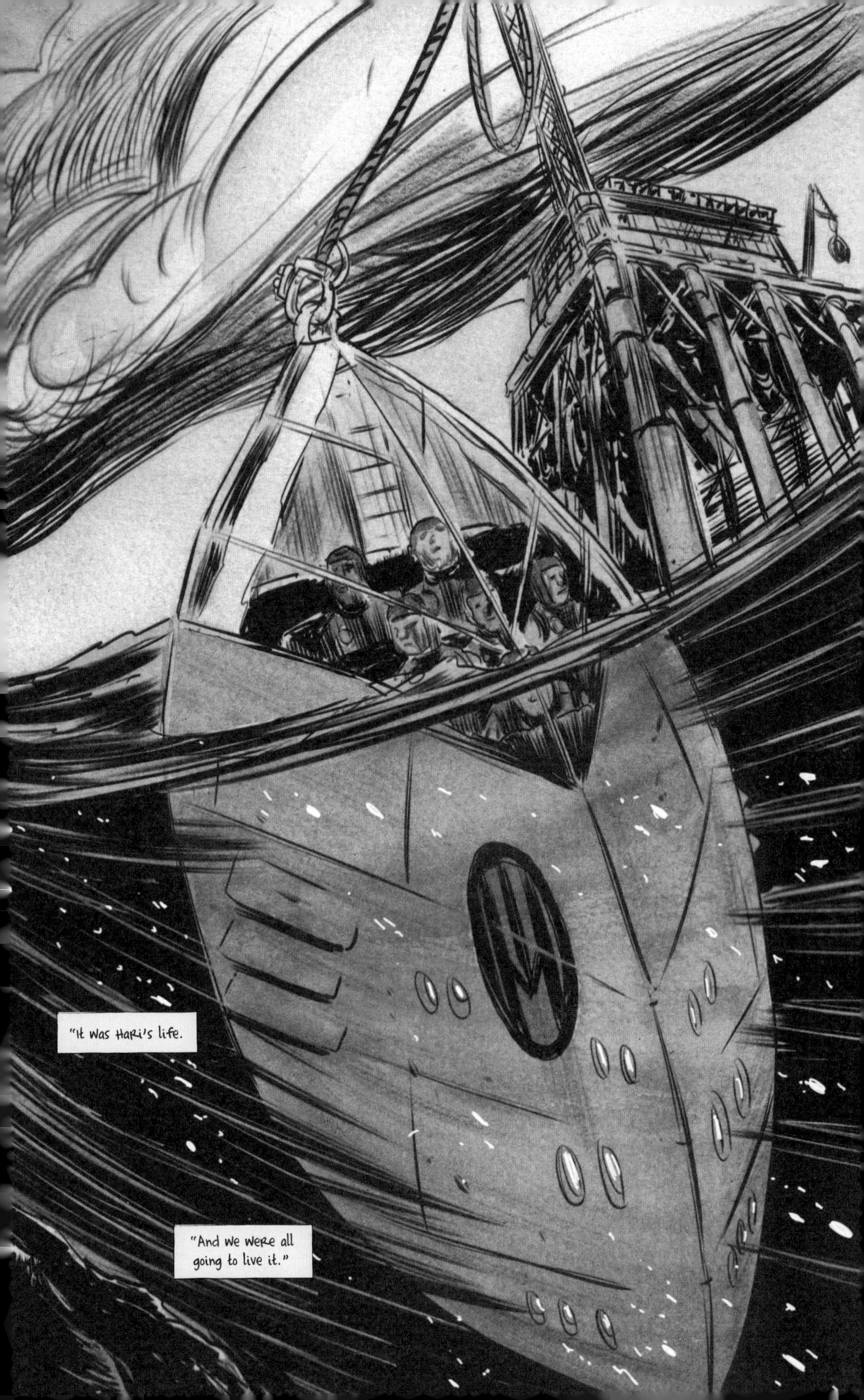
"It was Hari's life.
"And we were all going to live it."

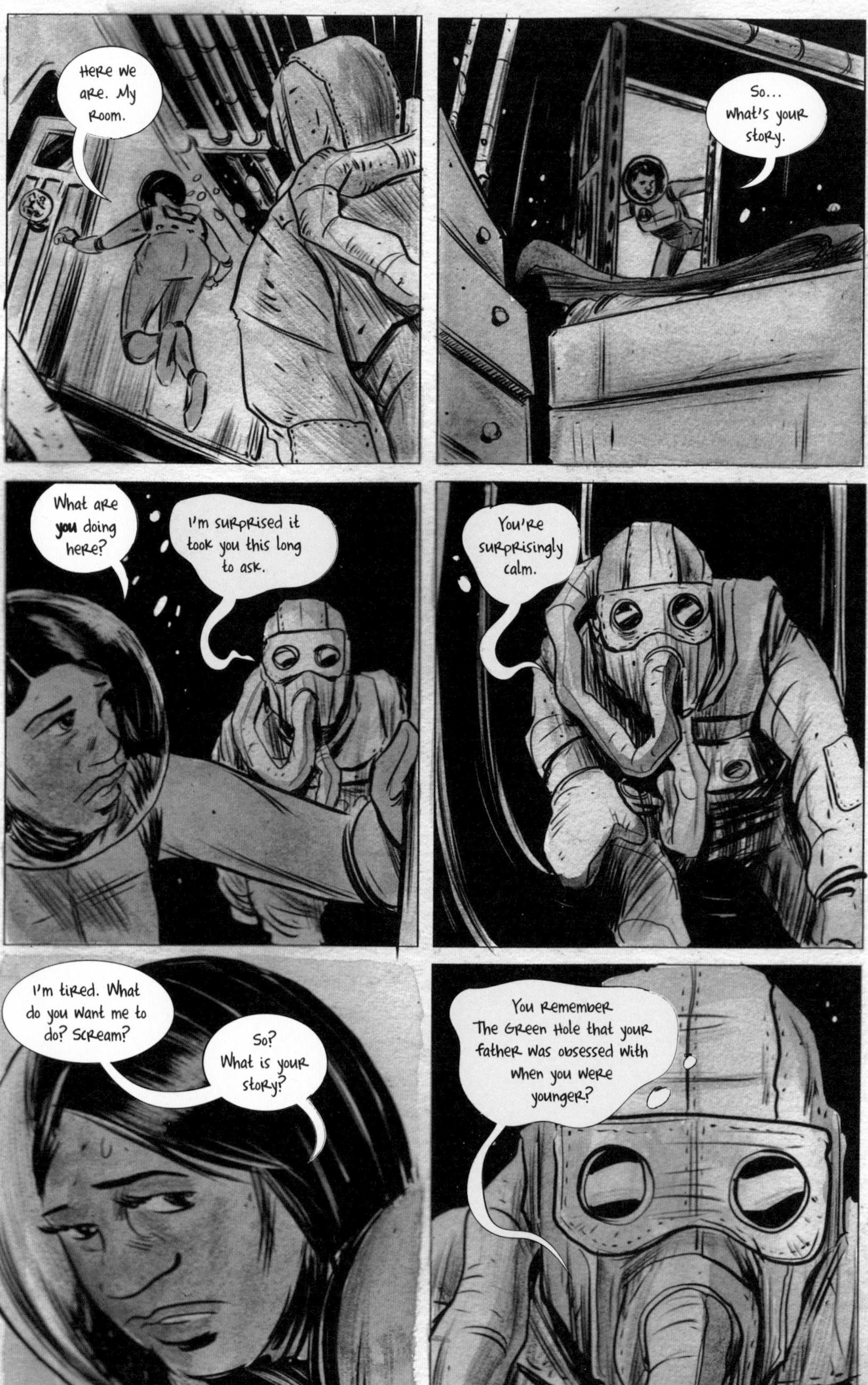
Here we are. My room.
So... What's your story.
What are you doing here?
I'm surprised it took you this long to ask.
You're surprisingly calm.
I'm tired. What do you want me to do? Scream?
So? What is your story?
You remember The Green Hole that your father was obsessed with when you were younger?

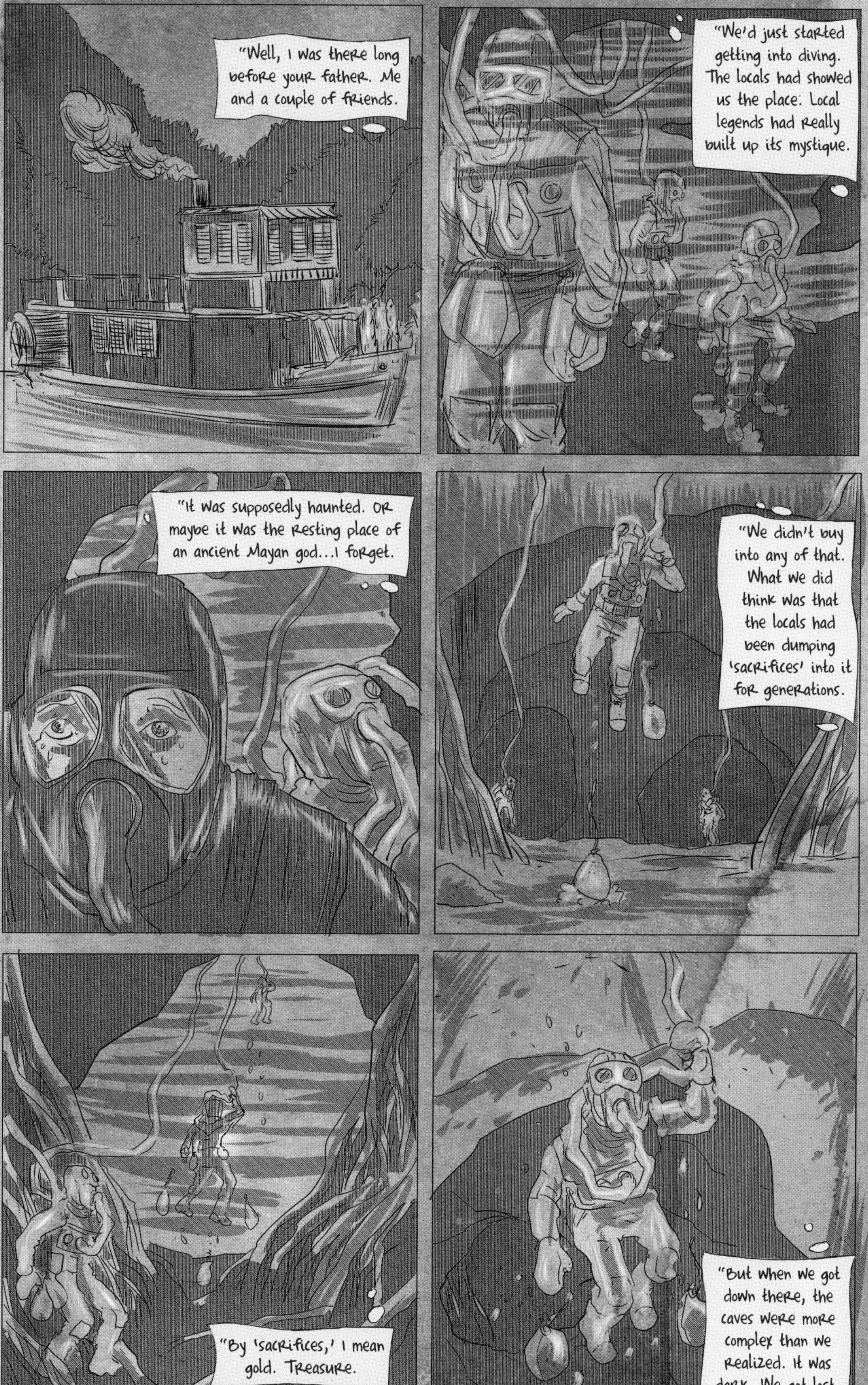
"Well, I was there long before your father. Me and a couple of friends.
"We'd just started getting into diving. The locals had showed us the place. Local legends had really built up its mystique.
"It was supposedly haunted. Or maybe it was the resting place of an ancient Mayan god...I forget.
"We didn't buy into any of that. What we did think was that the locals had been dumping 'sacrifices' into it for generations.
"By 'sacrifices,' I mean gold. Treasure.
"But when we got down there, the caves were more complex than we realized. It was dark. We got lost. We all panicked.

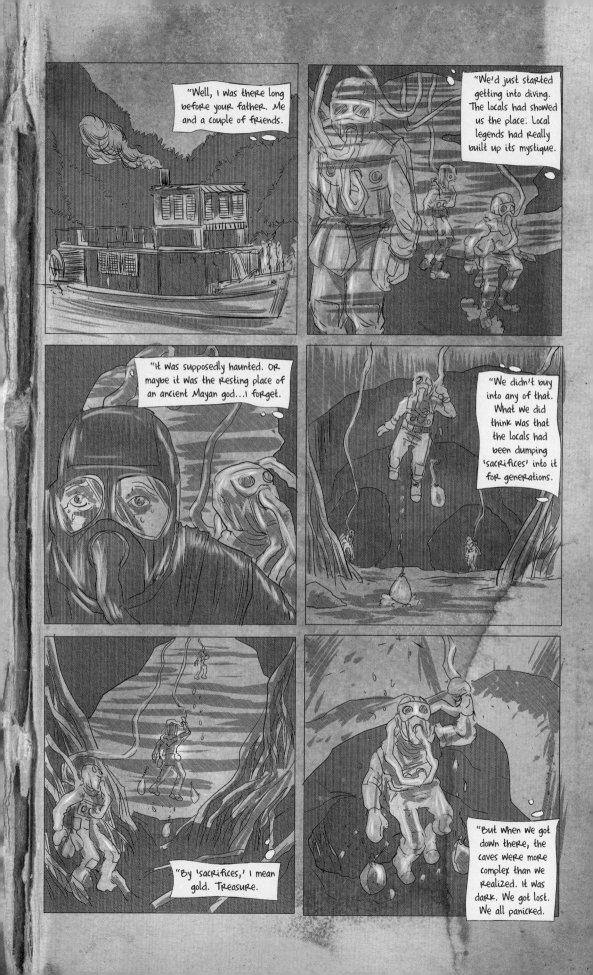

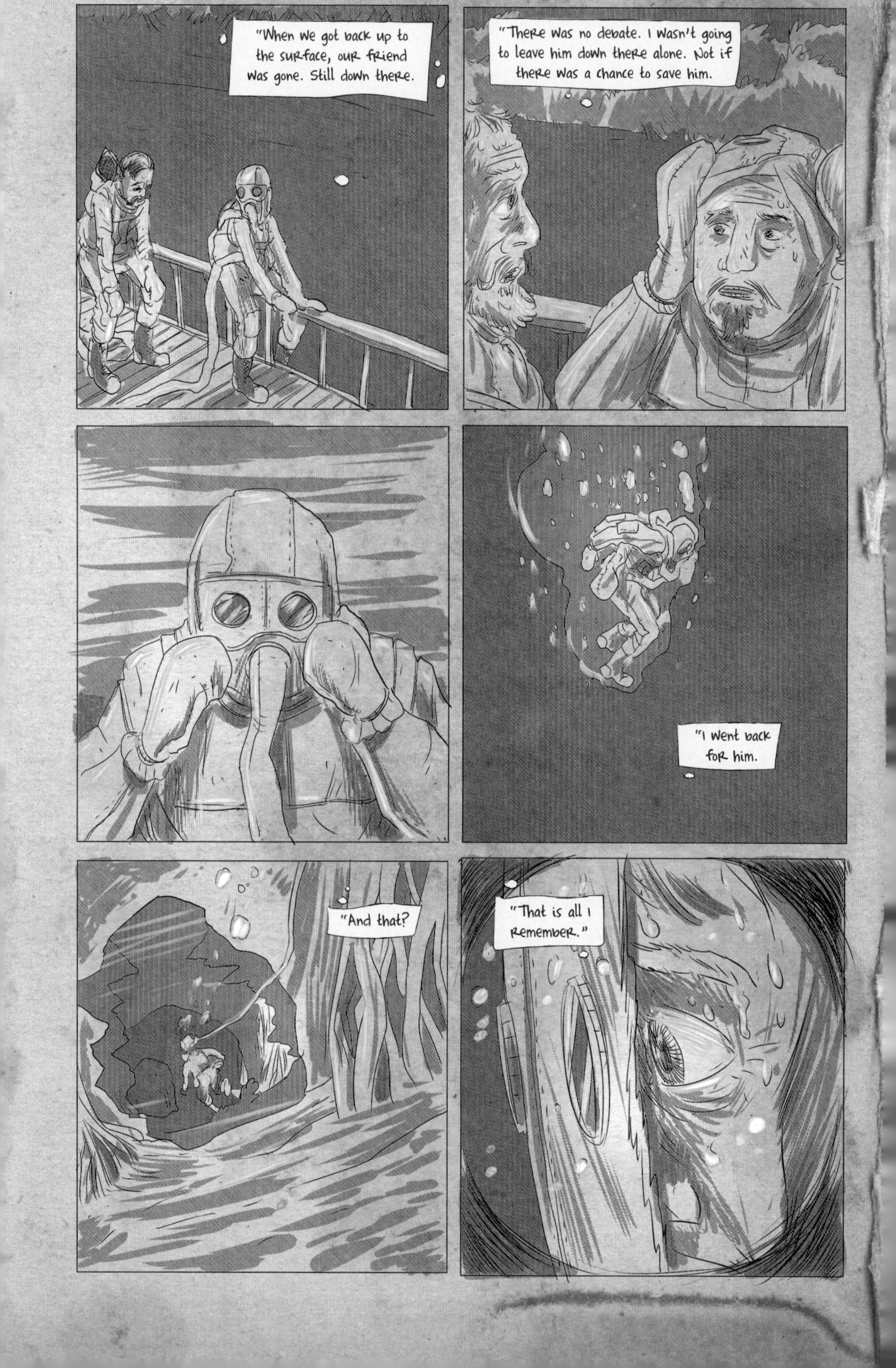
"When we got back up to the surface, our friend was gone. Still down there.
"There was no debate. I wasn't going to leave him down there alone. Not if there was a chance to save him.
"I went back for him.
"And that?
"That is all I remember."

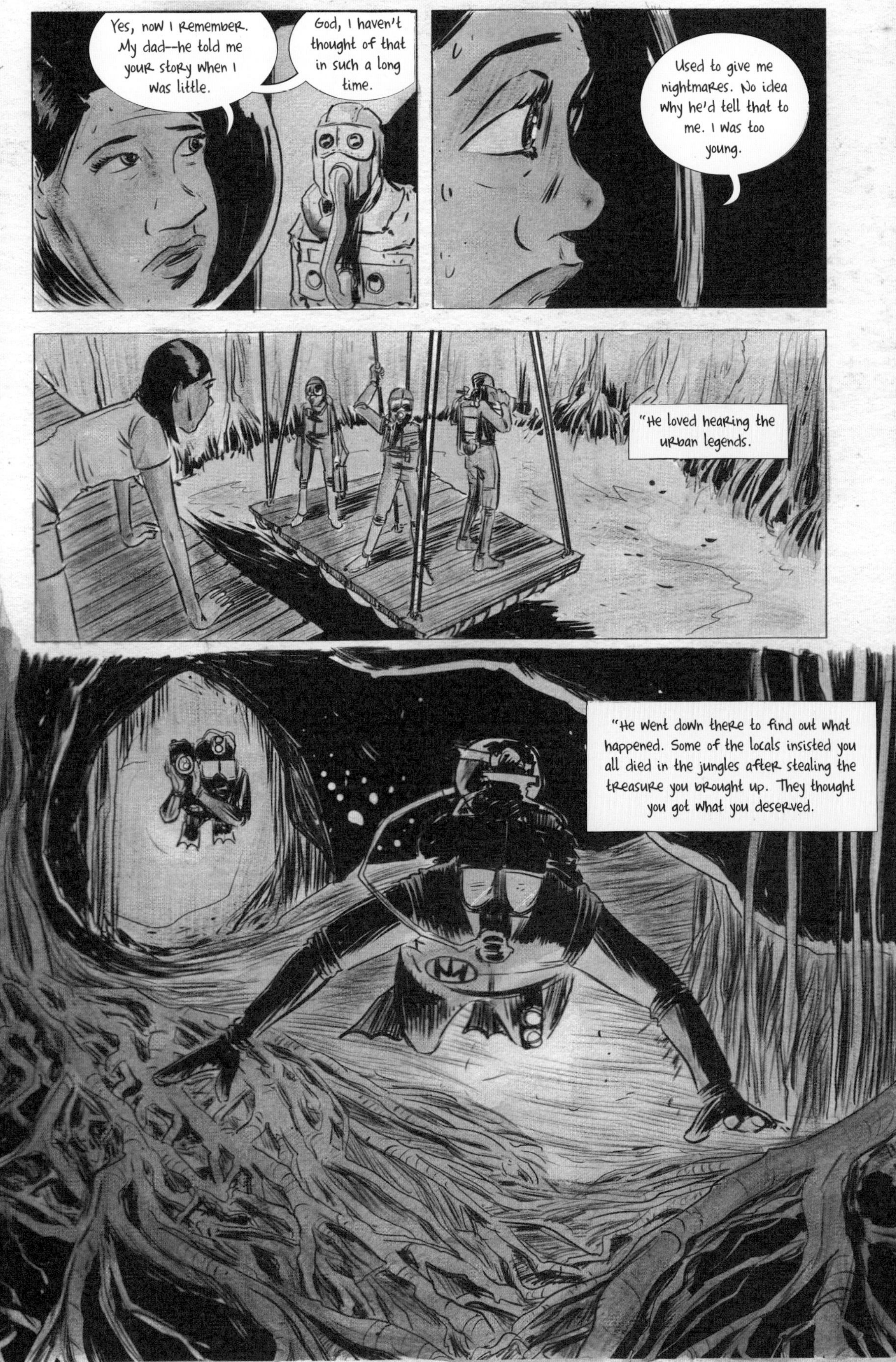
Yes, now I remember. My dad--he told me your story when I was little.
God, I haven't thought of that in such a long time.
Used to give me nightmares. No idea why he'd tell that to me. I was too young.
"He loved hearing the urban legends.
"He went down there to find out what happened. Some of the locals insisted you all died in the jungles after stealing the treasure you brought up. They thought you got what you deserved.

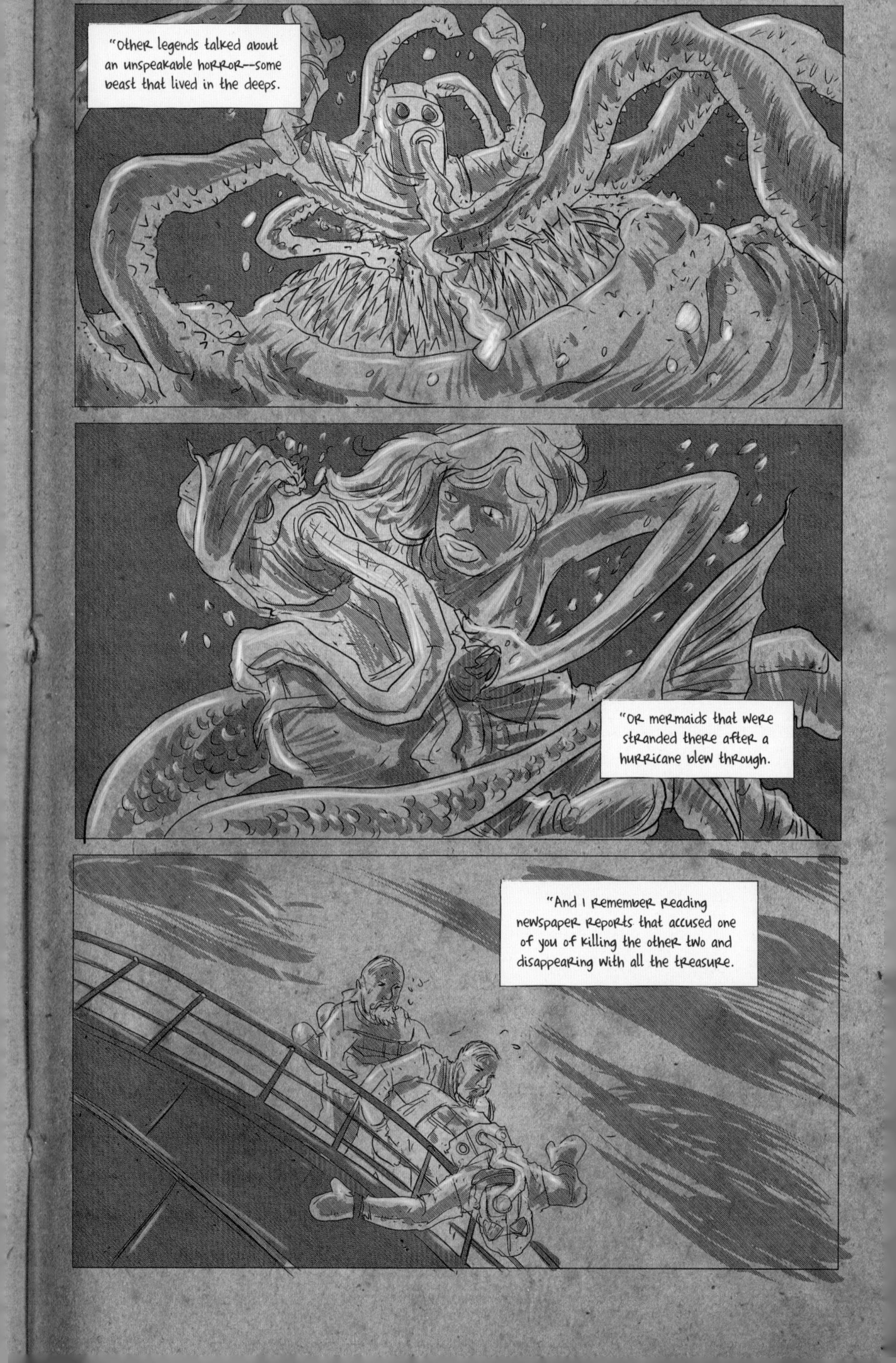
"Other legends talked about an unspeakable horror--some beast that lived in the deeps.
"Or mermaids that were stranded there after a hurricane blew through.
"And I remember reading newspaper reports that accused one of you of killing the other two and disappearing with all the treasure.

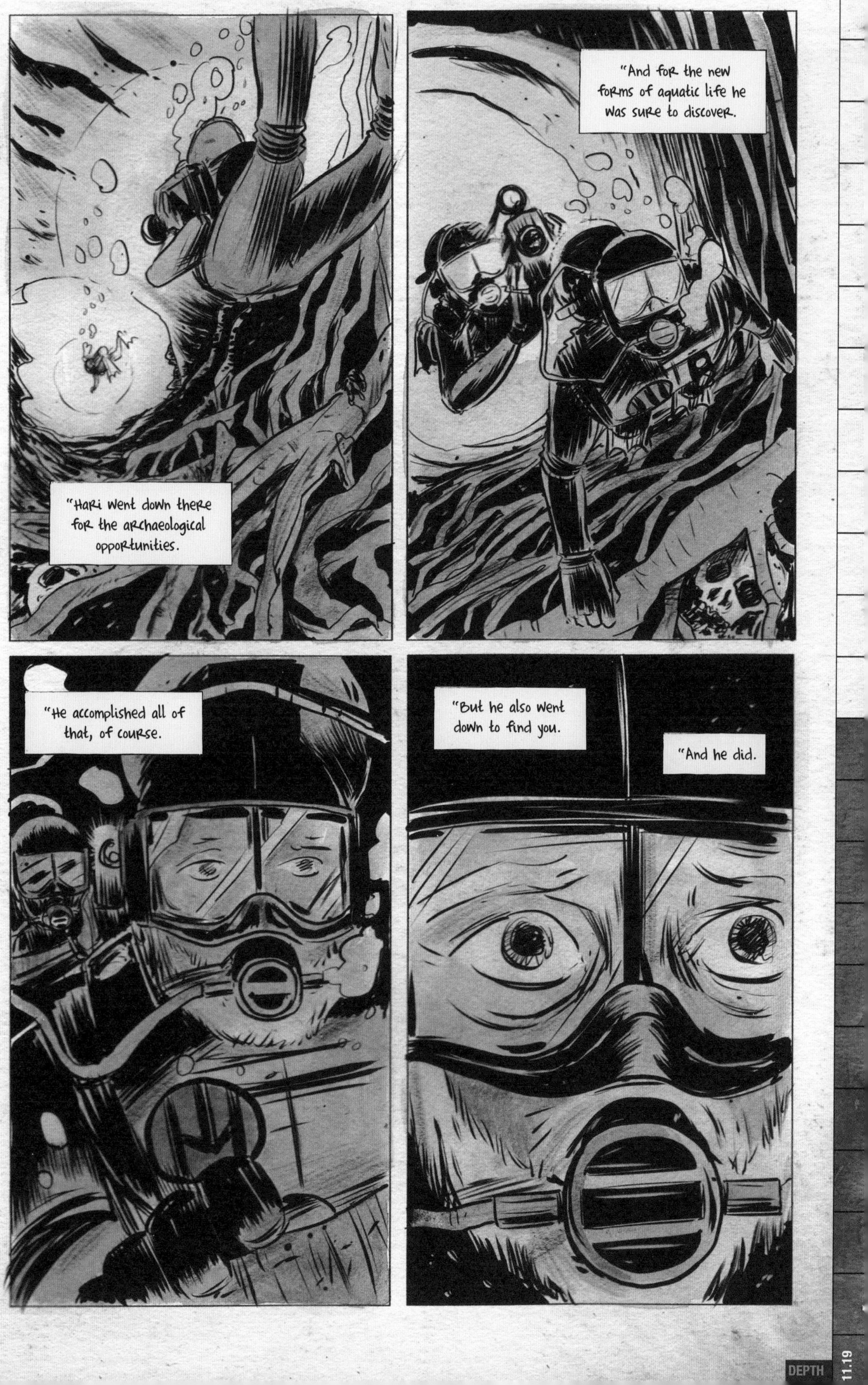
"Hari went down there for the archaeological opportunities.
"And for the new forms of aquatic life he was sure to discover.
"He accomplished all of that, of course.
"But he also went down to find you.
"And he did.

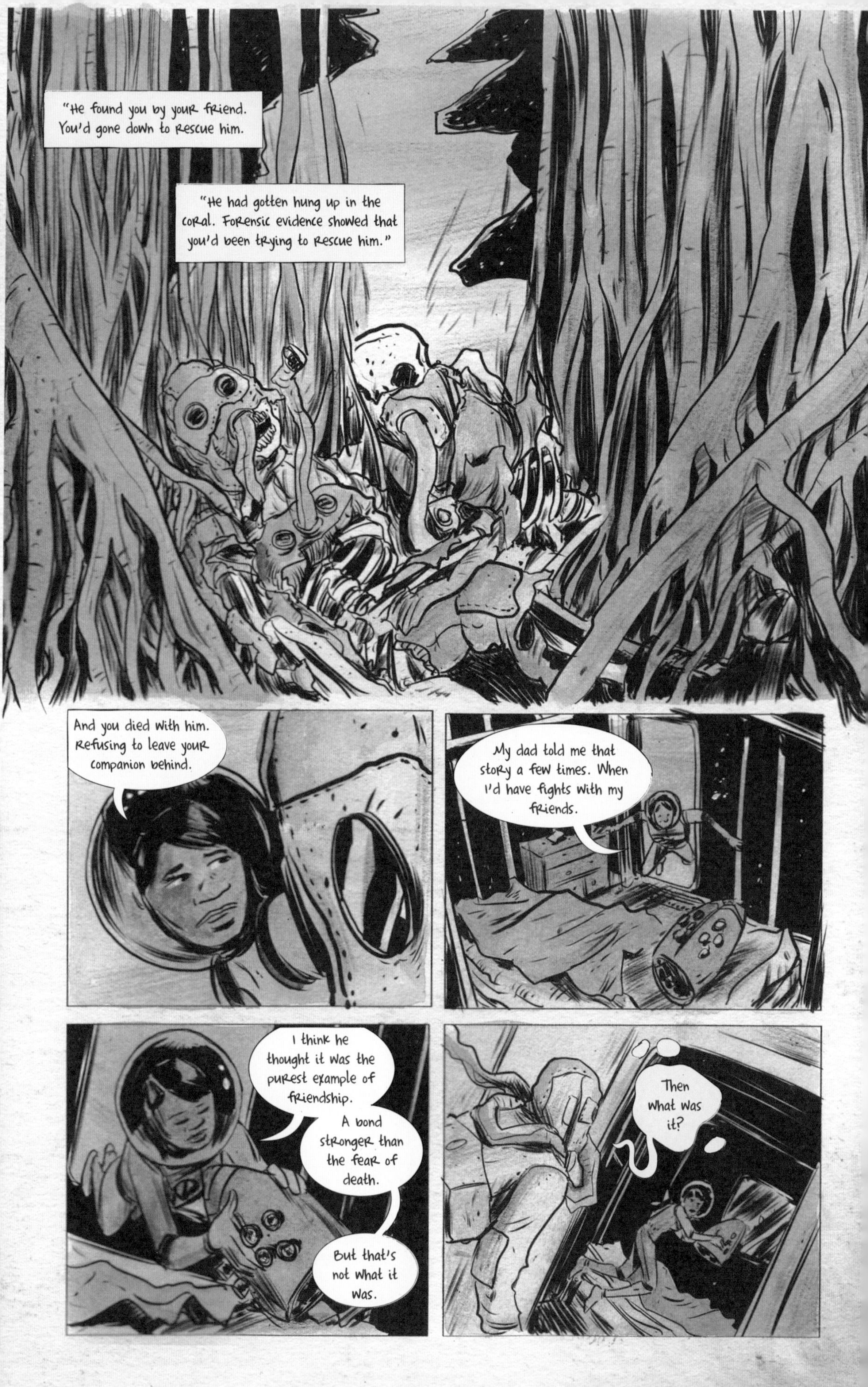
"He found you by your friend. You'd gone down to rescue him.
"He had gotten hung up in the coral. Forensic evidence showed that you'd been trying to rescue him."
And you died with him. Refusing to leave your companion behind.
My dad told me that story a few times. When I'd have fights with my friends.
I think he thought it was the purest example of friendship.
A bond stronger than the fear of death.
But that's not what it was.
Then what was it?

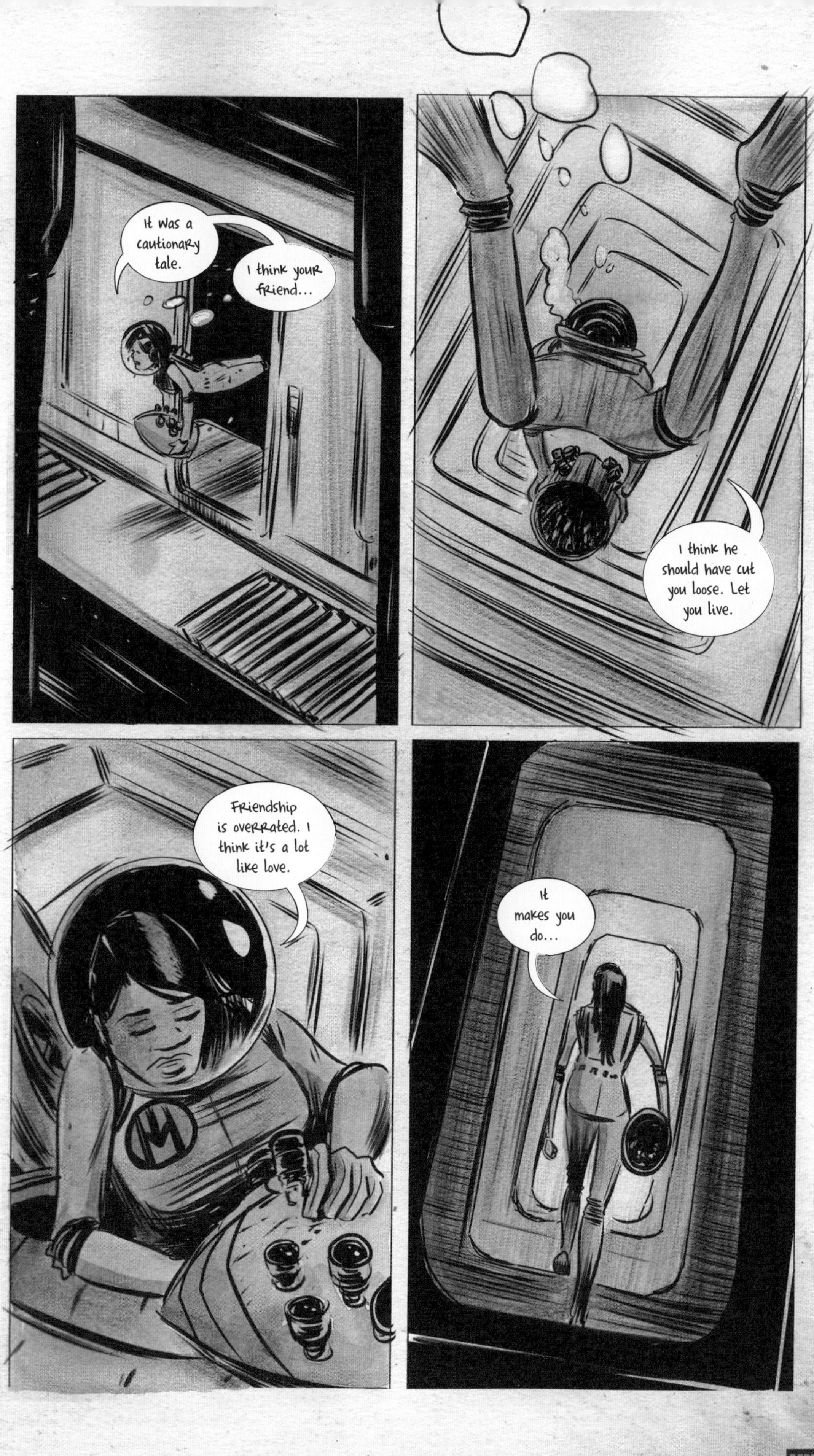
It was a cautionary tale.
I think your friend...
I think he should have cut you loose. Let you live.
Friendship is overrated. I think it's a lot like love.
It makes you do...

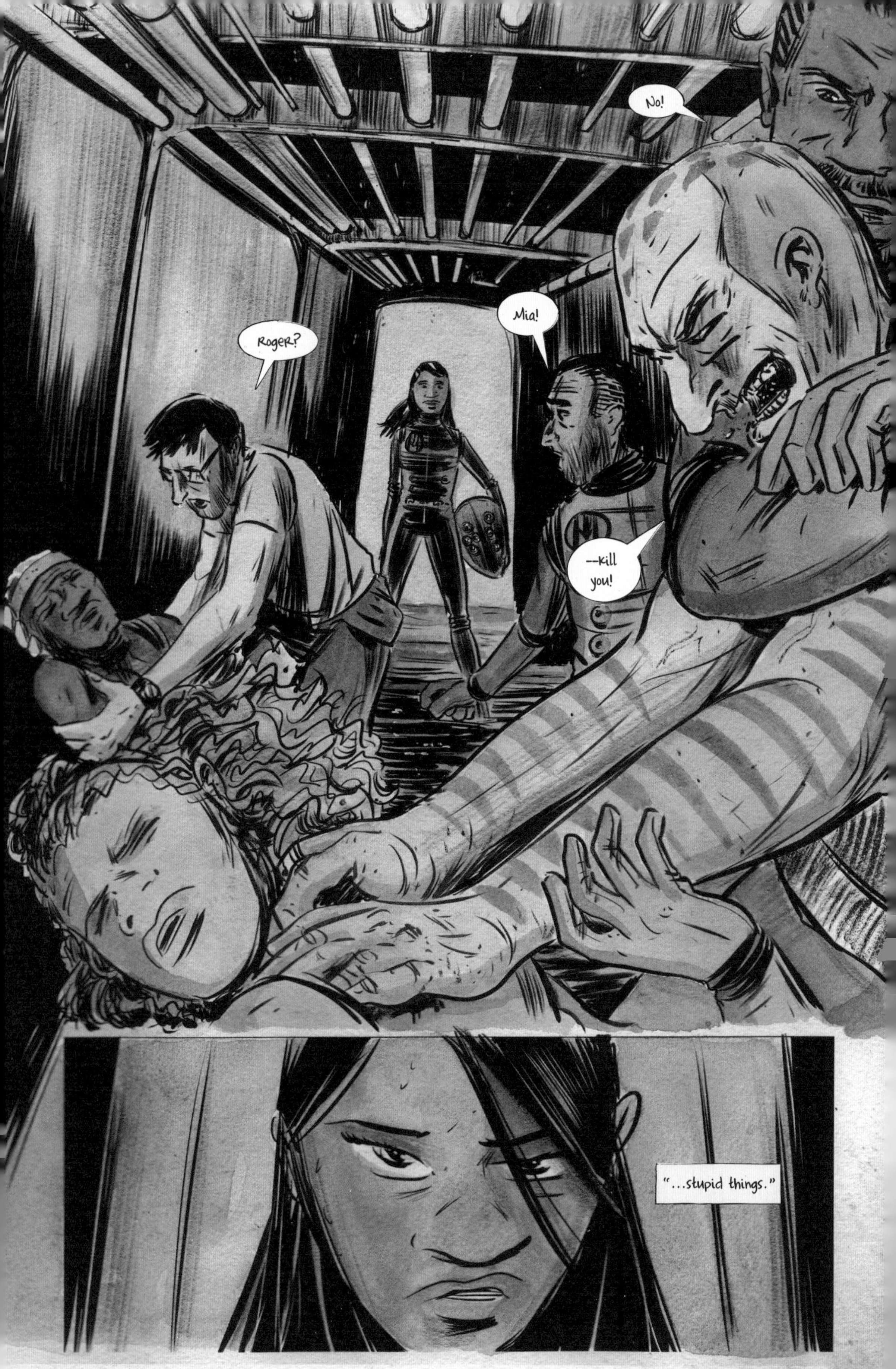
No!
Roger?
Mia!
--kill you!
"...stupid things."

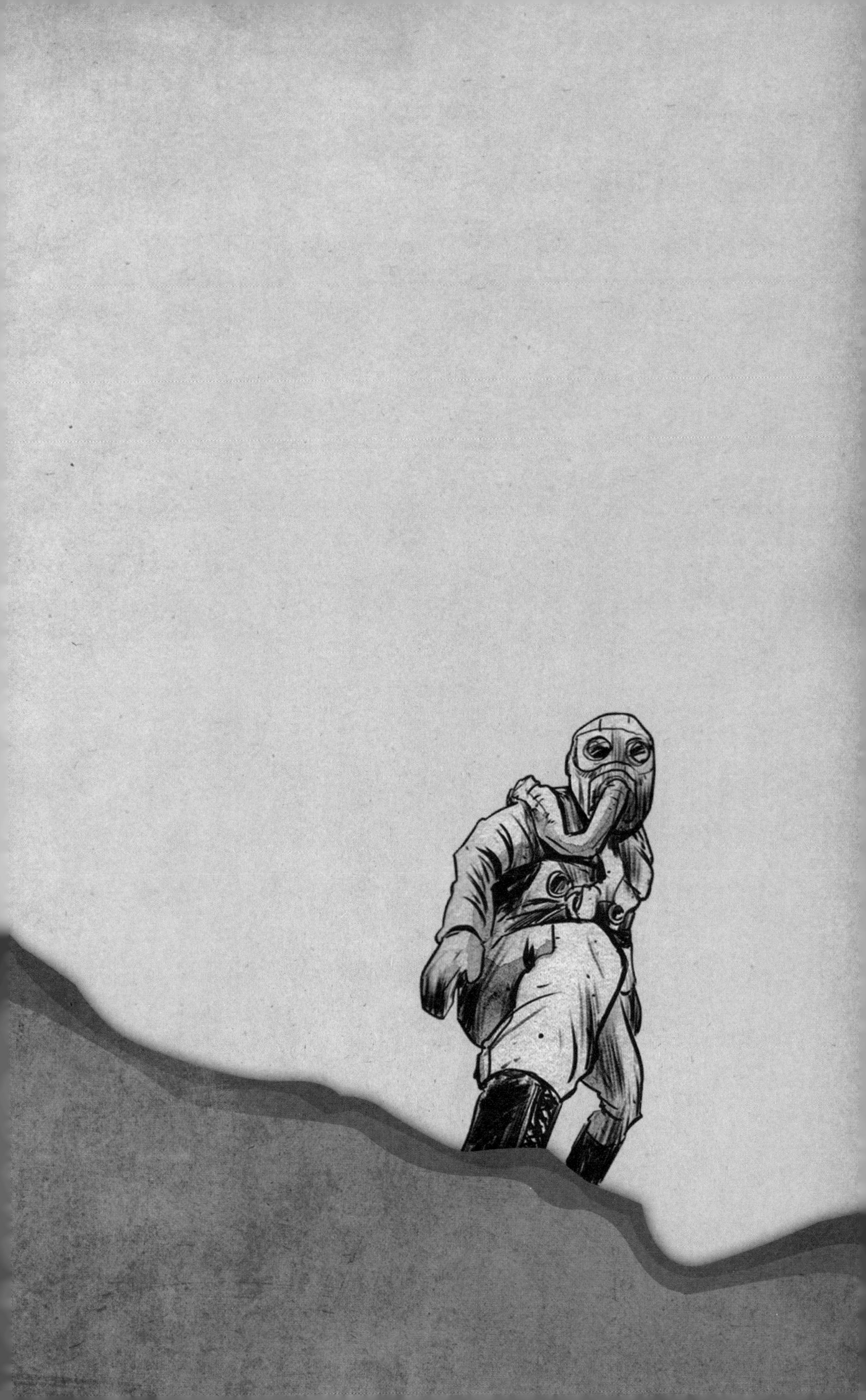

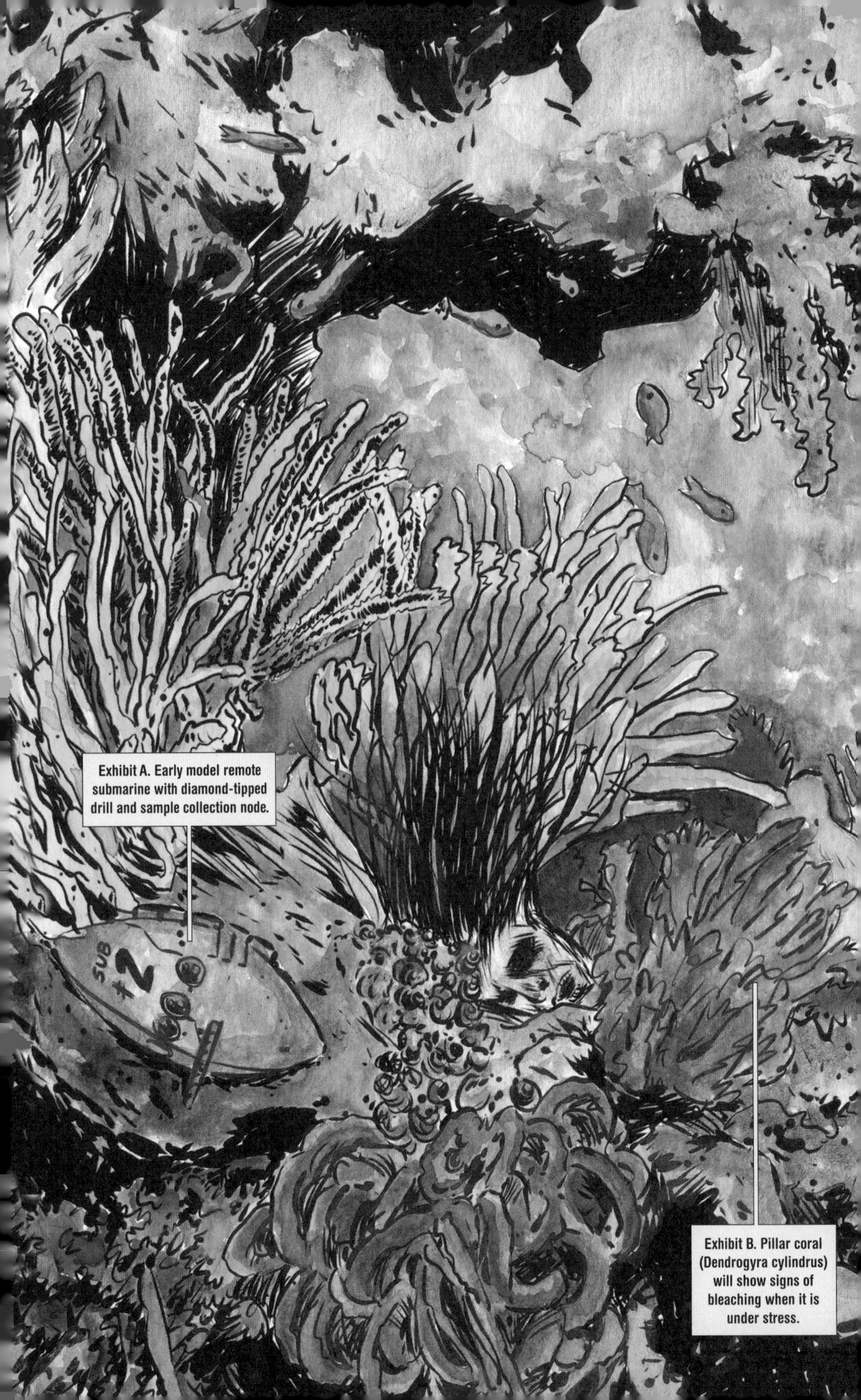
Exhibit A. Early model remote submarine with diamond-tipped drill and sample collection node.
SUB #2
Exhibit B. Pillar coral (Dendrogyra cylindrus) will show signs of bleaching when it is under stress.

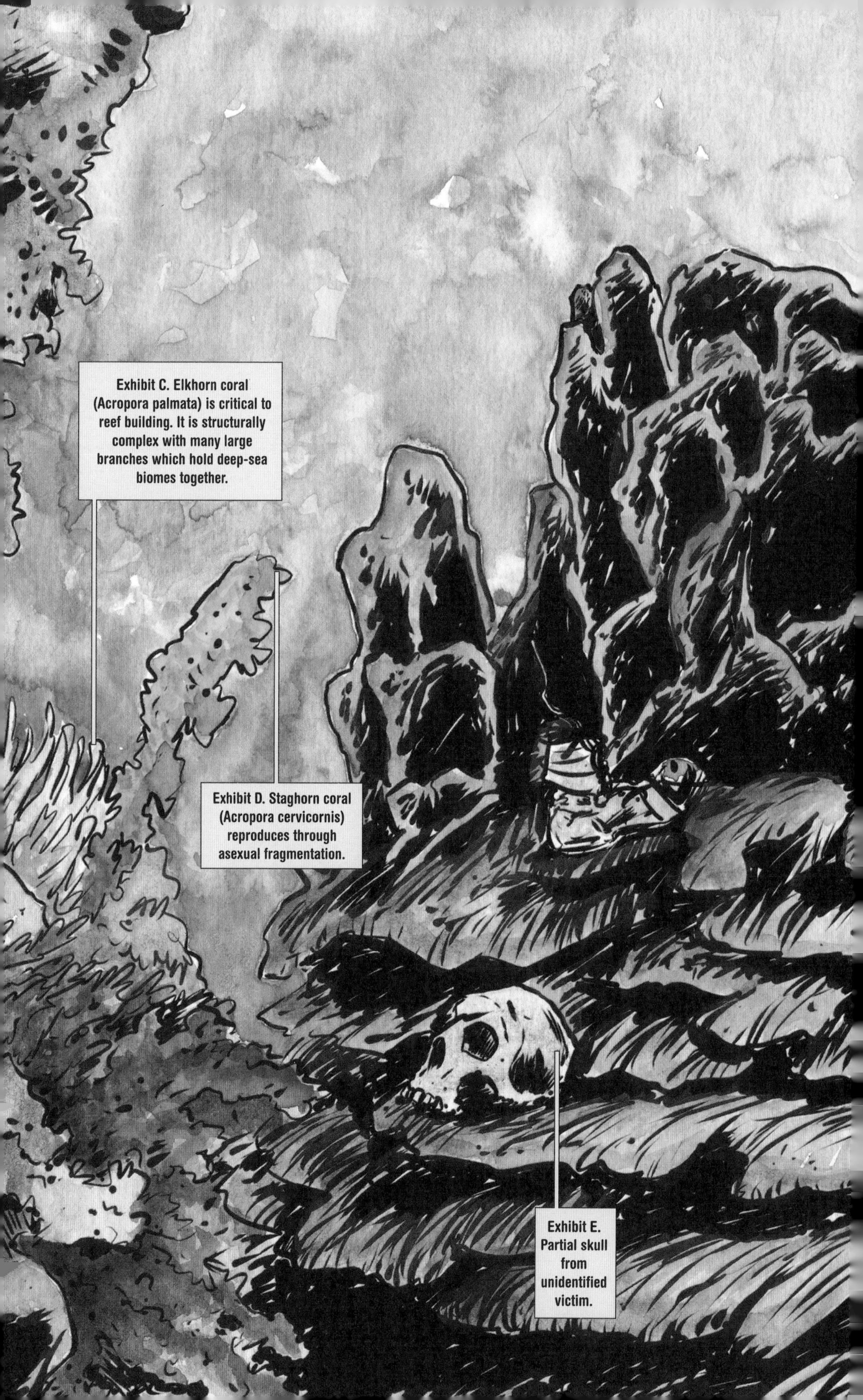
Exhibit C. Elkhorn coral (Acropora palmata) is critical to reef building. It is structurally complex with many large branches which hold deep-sea biomes together.
Exhibit D. Staghorn coral (Acropora cervicornis) reproduces through asexual fragmentation.
Exhibit E. Partial skull from unidentified victim.

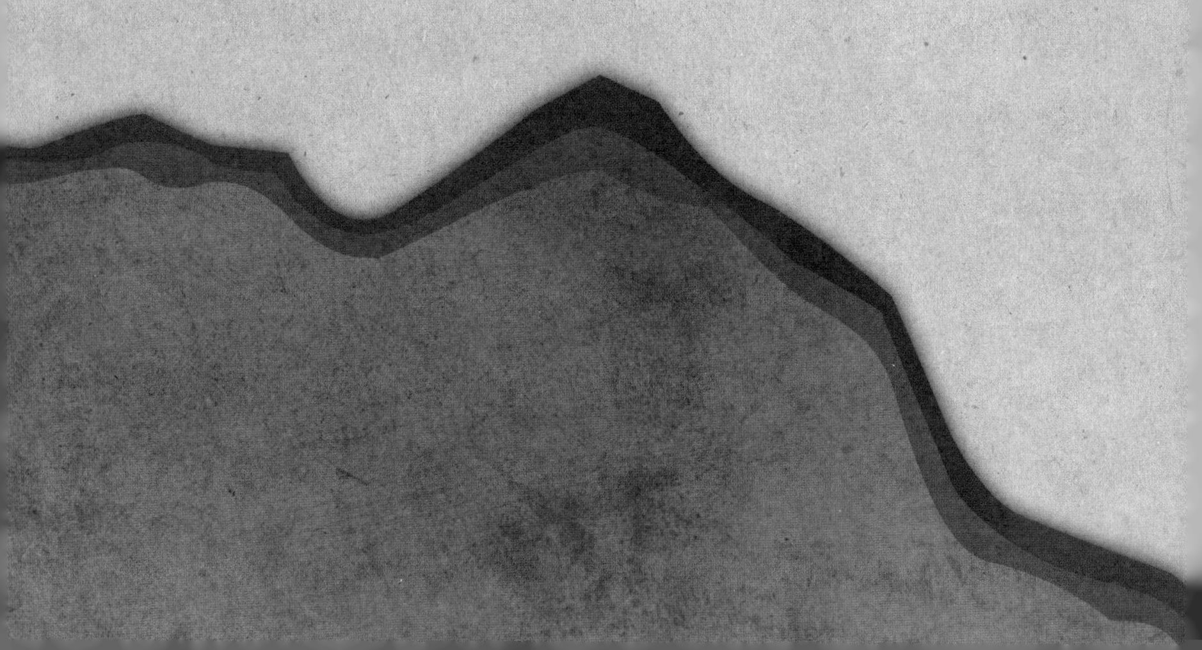

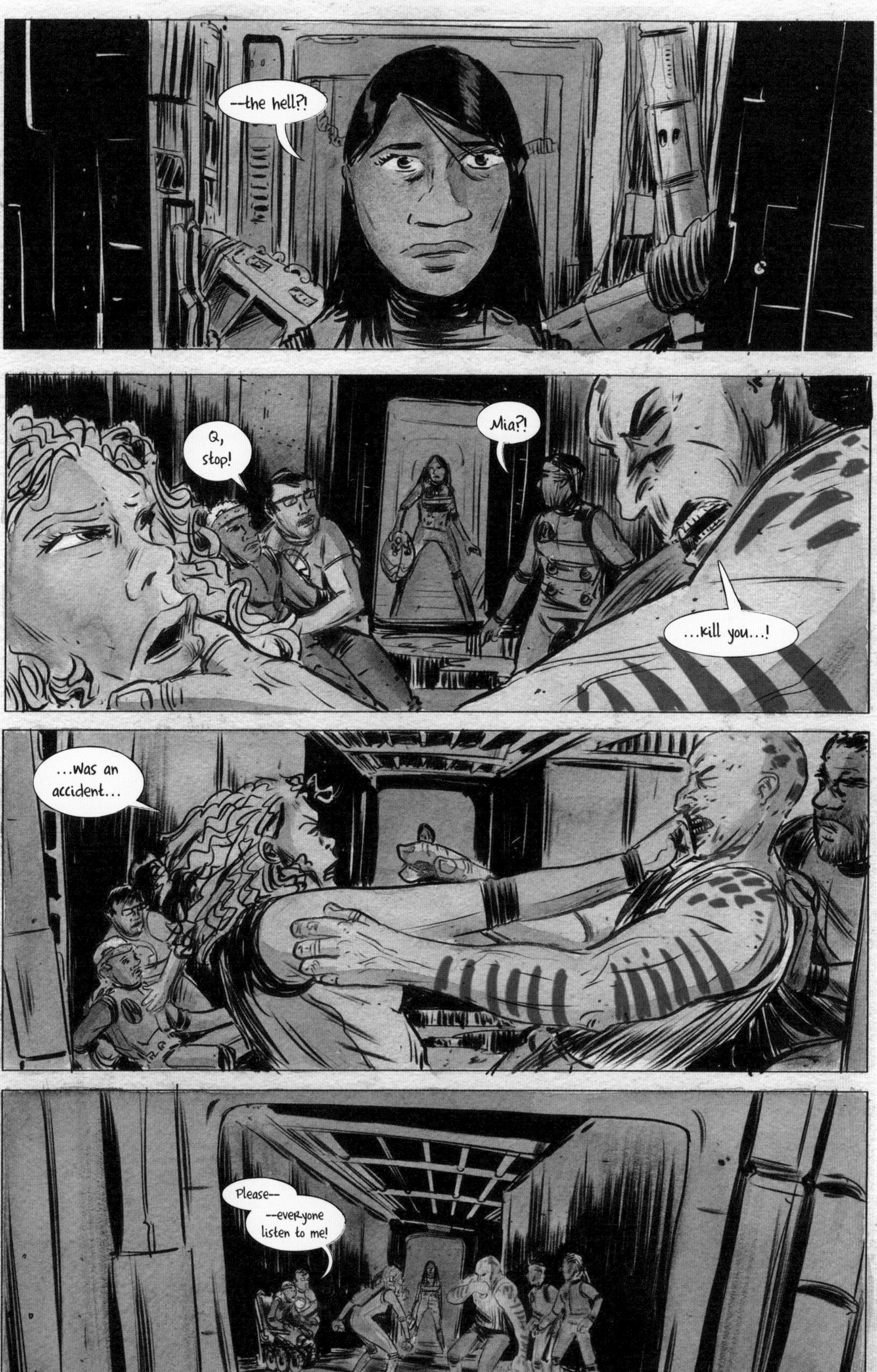
--the hell?!
Q, stop!
Mia?!
...kill you...!
...Was an accident...
Please--
--everyone listen to me!

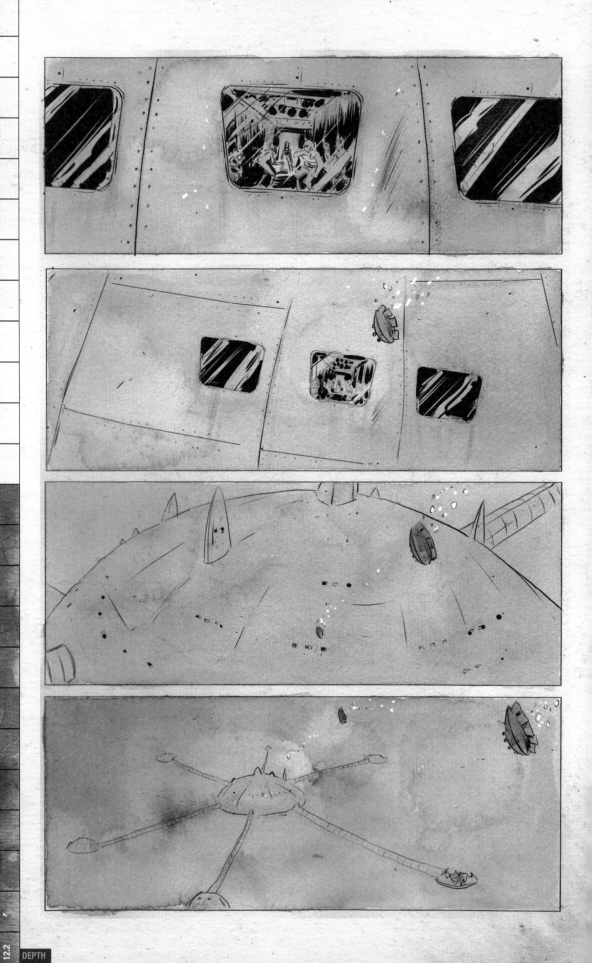

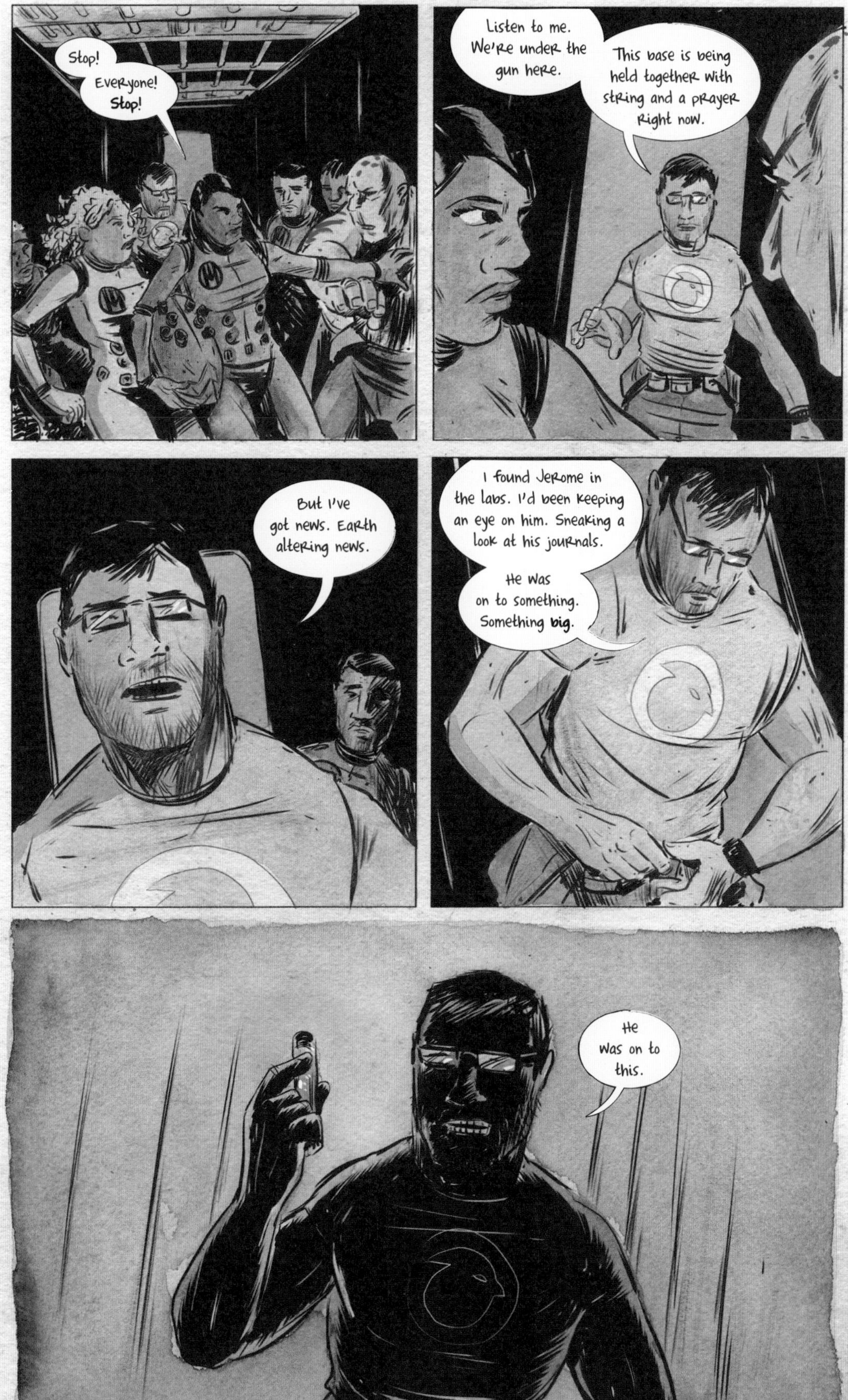
Stop!
Everyone! Stop!
Listen to me. We're under the gun here.
This base is being held together with string and a prayer right now.
But I've got news. Earth altering news.
I found Jerome in the labs. I'd been keeping an eye on him. Sneaking a look at his journals.
He was on to something. Something **big**.
He was on to this.

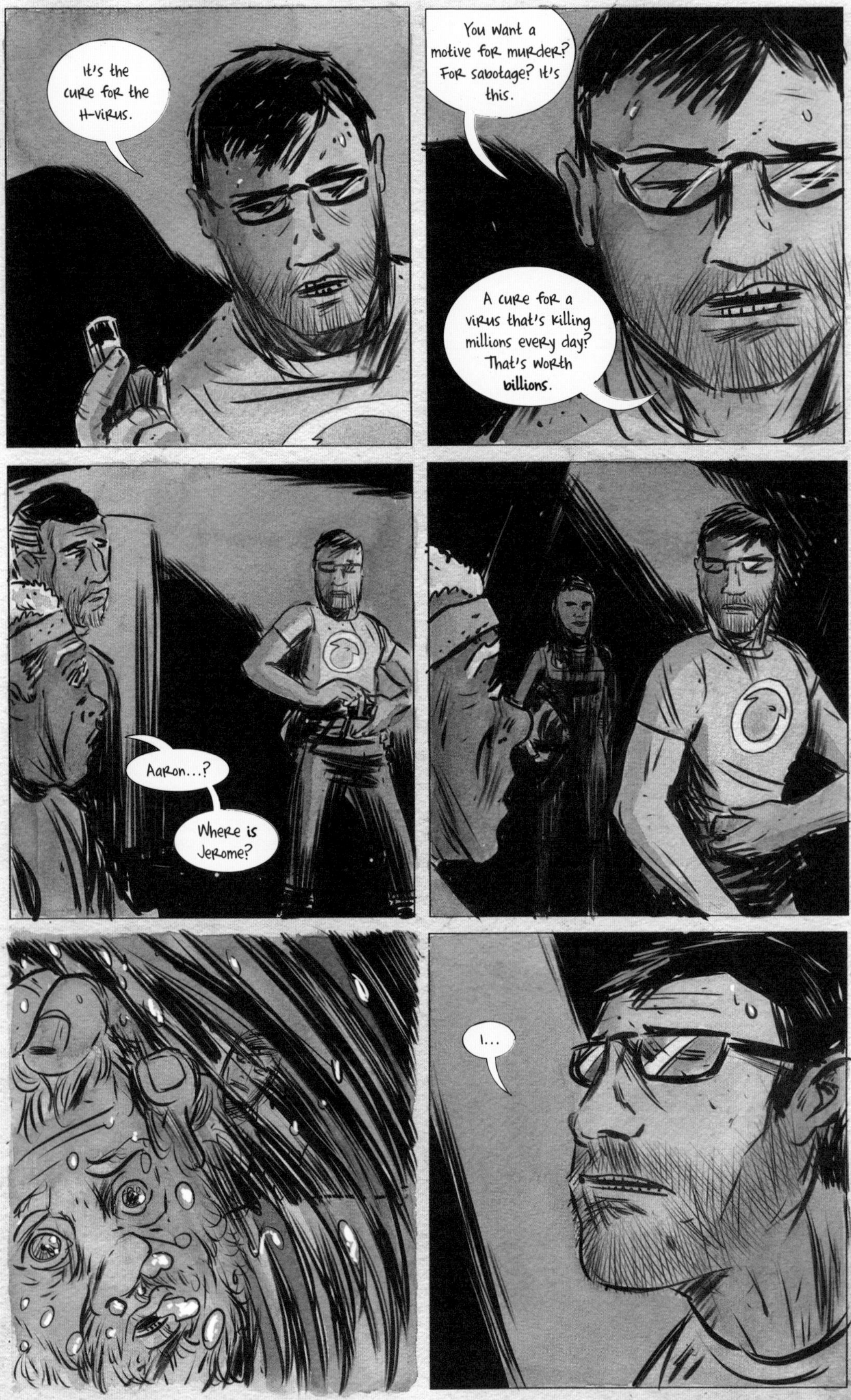
It's the cure for the H-virus.
You want a motive for murder? For sabotage? It's this.
A cure for a virus that's killing millions every day? That's worth billions.
Aaron...?
Where is Jerome?
I...

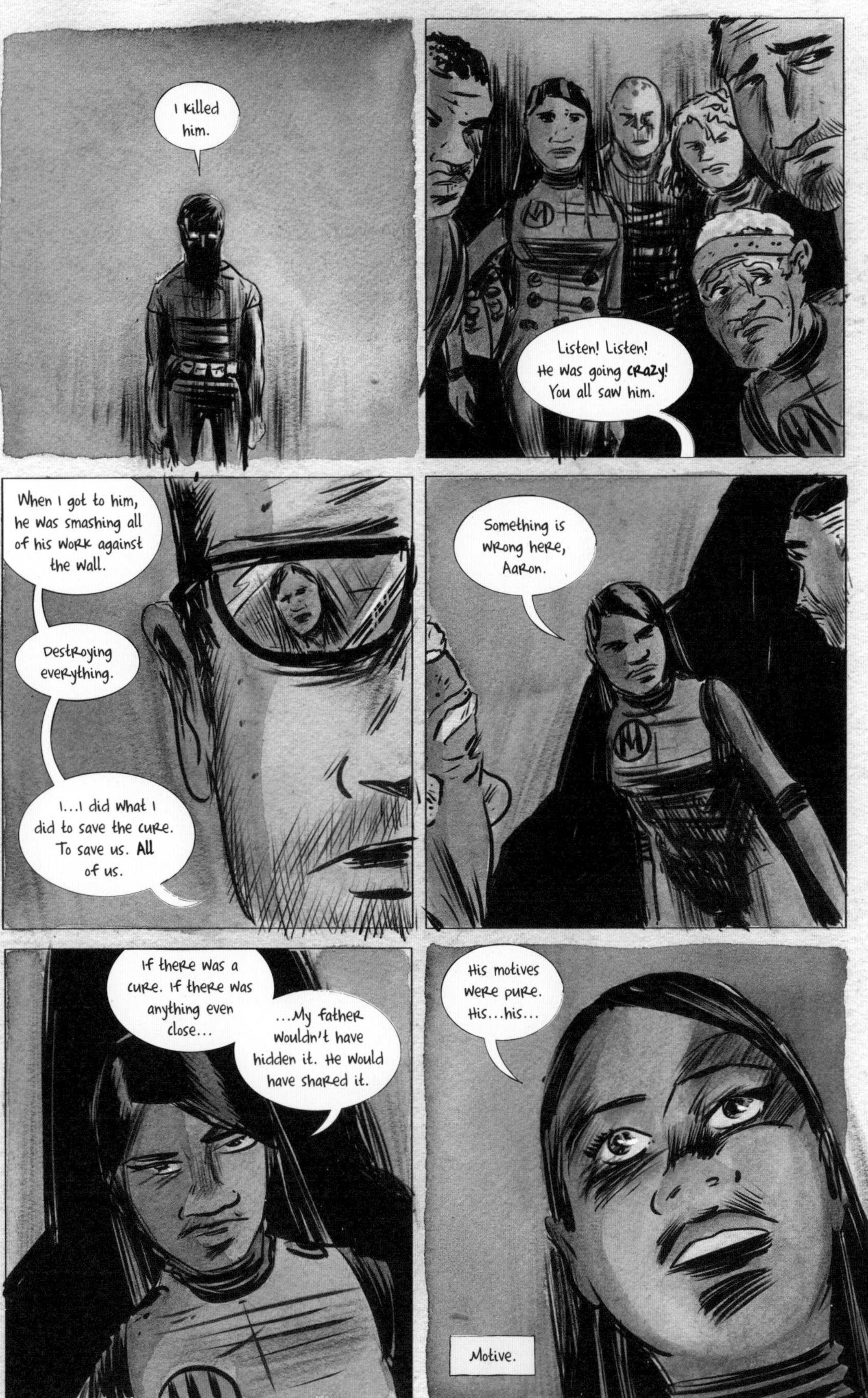
I killed him.
Listen! Listen! He was going CRAZY! You all saw him.
When I got to him, he was smashing all of his WORK against the wall.
Destroying everything.
I...I did what I did to save the cure. To save us. ALL of us.
Something is wrong here, Aaron.
If there was a cure. If there was anything even close...
...My father wouldn't have hidden it. He would have shared it.
His motives were pure. His...his...
Motive.

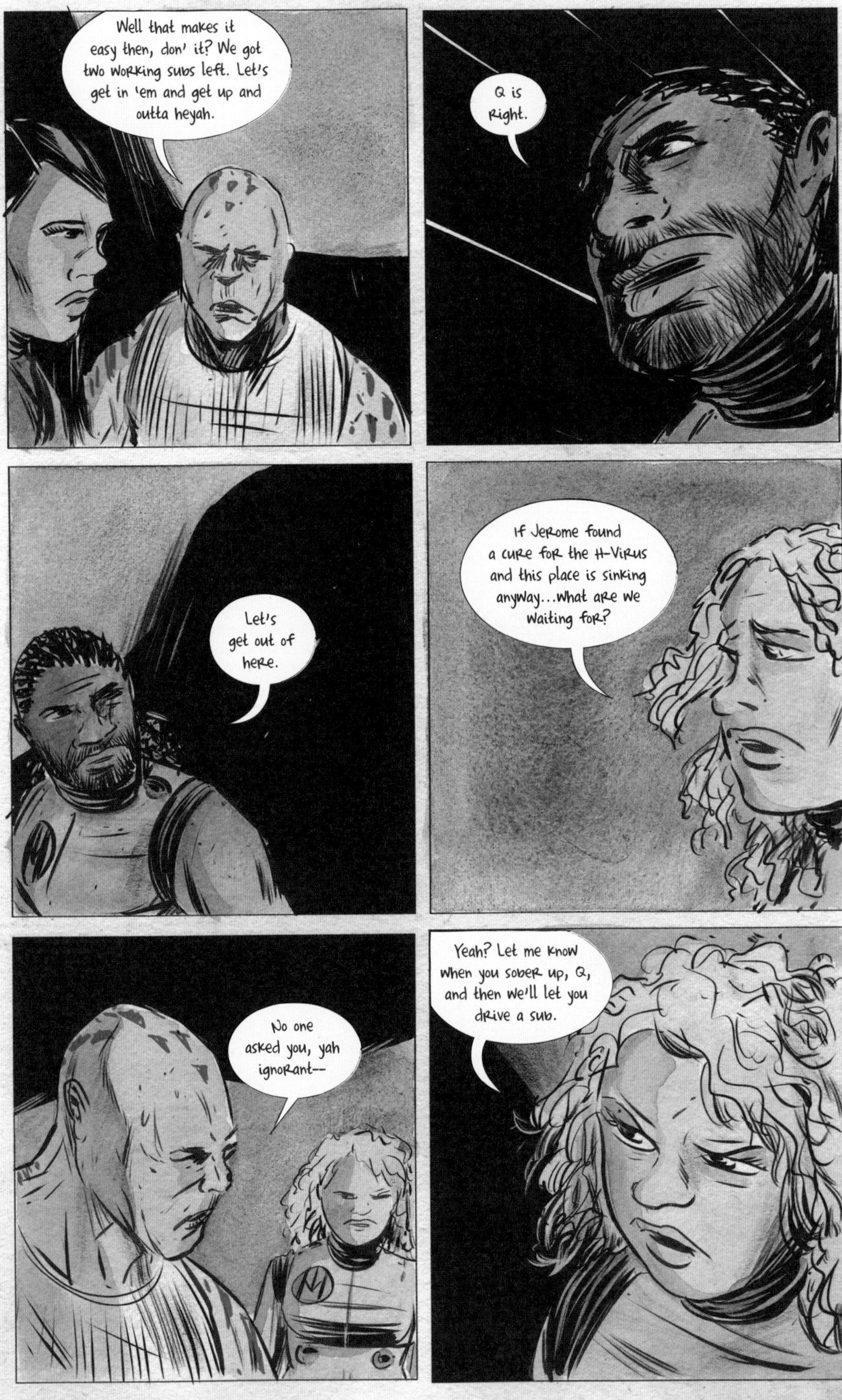
Well that makes it easy then, don' it? We got two working subs left. Let's get in 'em and get up and outta heyah.
Q is Right.
Let's get out of here.
If Jerome found a cure for the H-Virus and this place is sinking anyway...What are we waiting for?
No one asked you, yah ignorant--
Yeah? Let me know when you sober up, Q, and then we'll let you drive a sub.

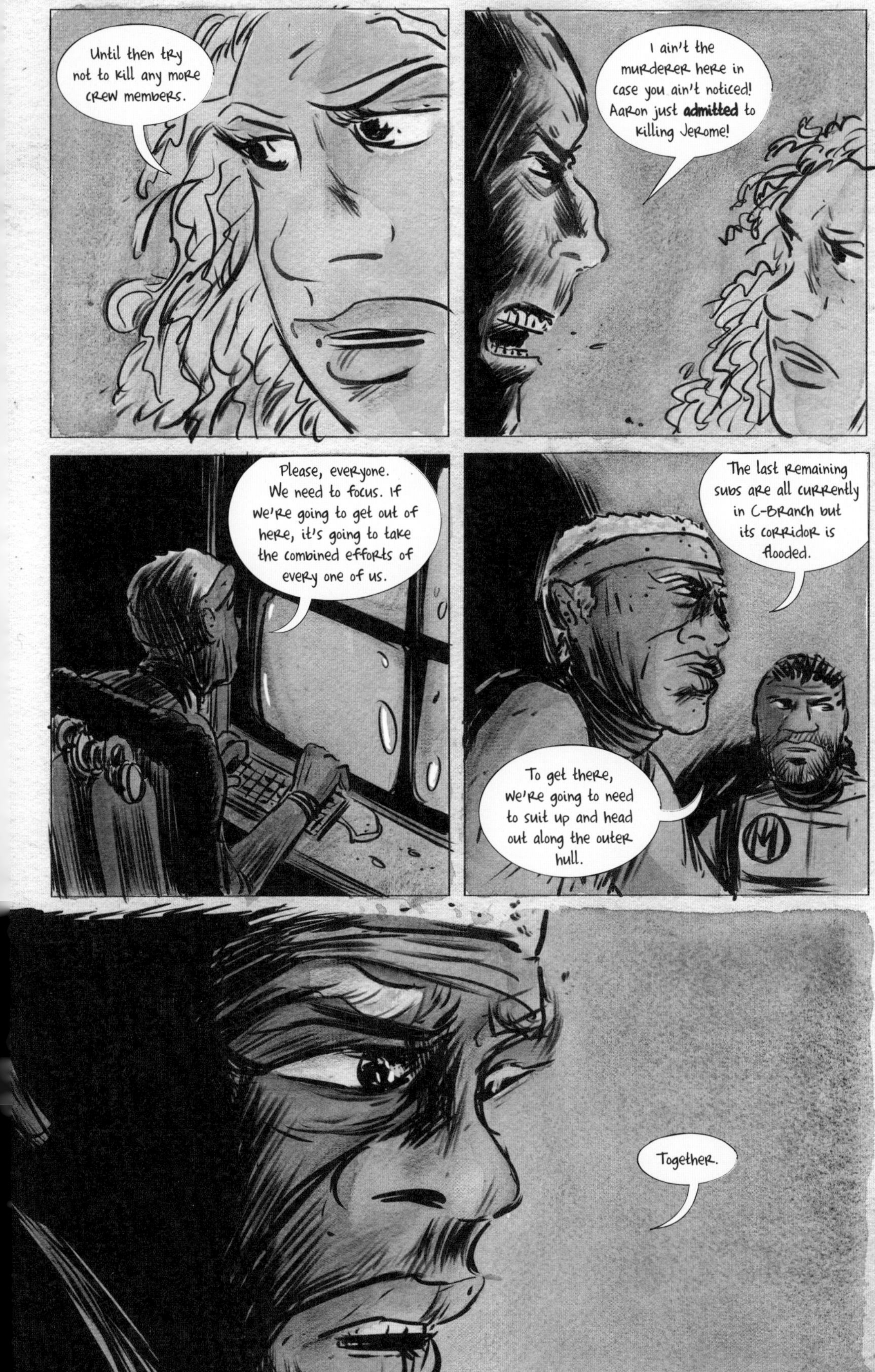
Until then try not to kill any more crew members.
I ain't the murderer here in case you ain't noticed! Aaron just **admitted** to killing Jerome!
Please, everyone. We need to focus. If we're going to get out of here, it's going to take the combined efforts of every one of us.
The last remaining subs are all currently in C-Branch but its corridor is flooded.
To get there, we're going to need to suit up and head out along the outer hull.
Together.

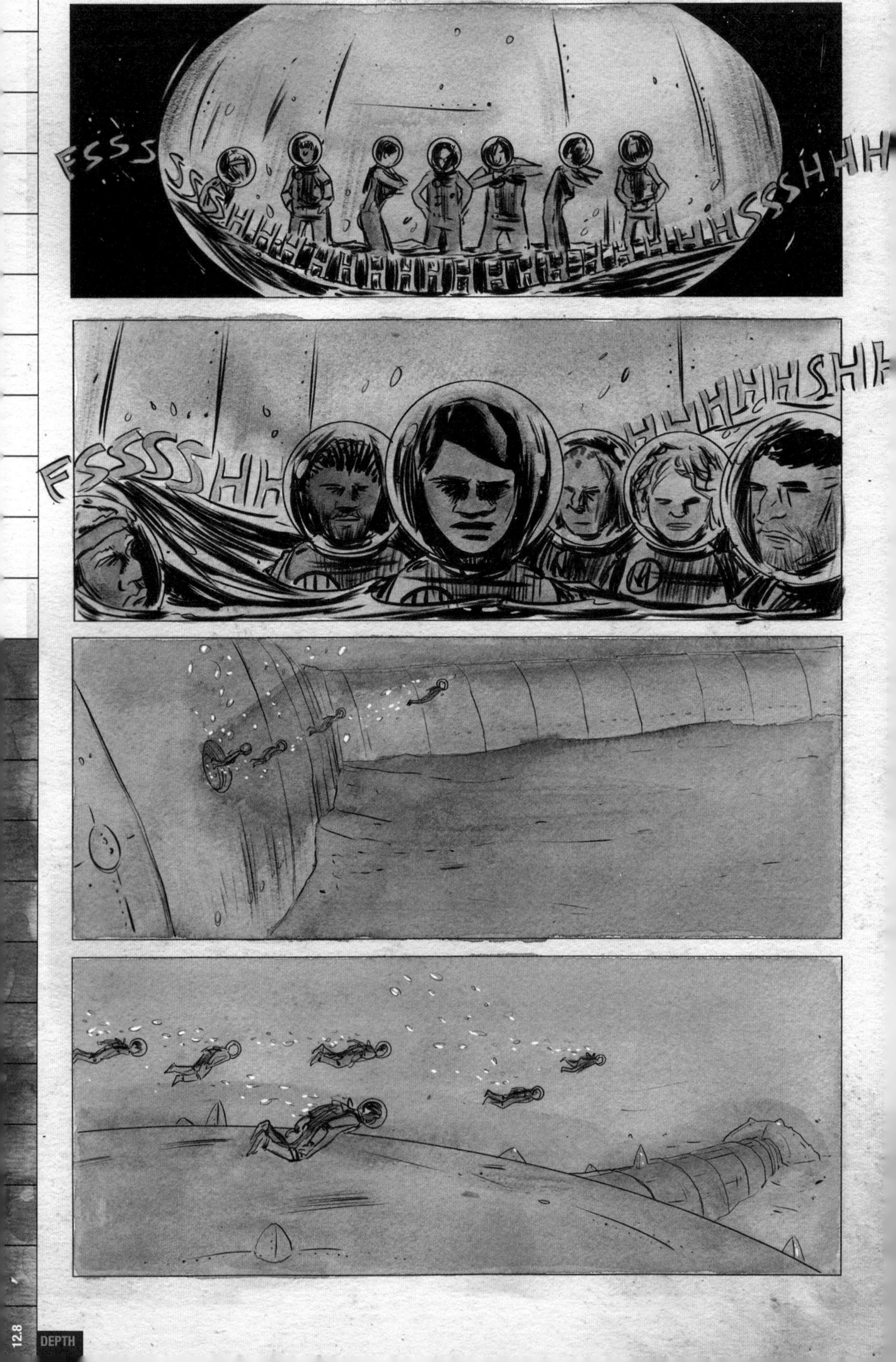
FSSSSSHHHHHHHHHHHHHHHHHHHHHHHSSSHHH
FSSSSSHHHHHHHHHHSHH

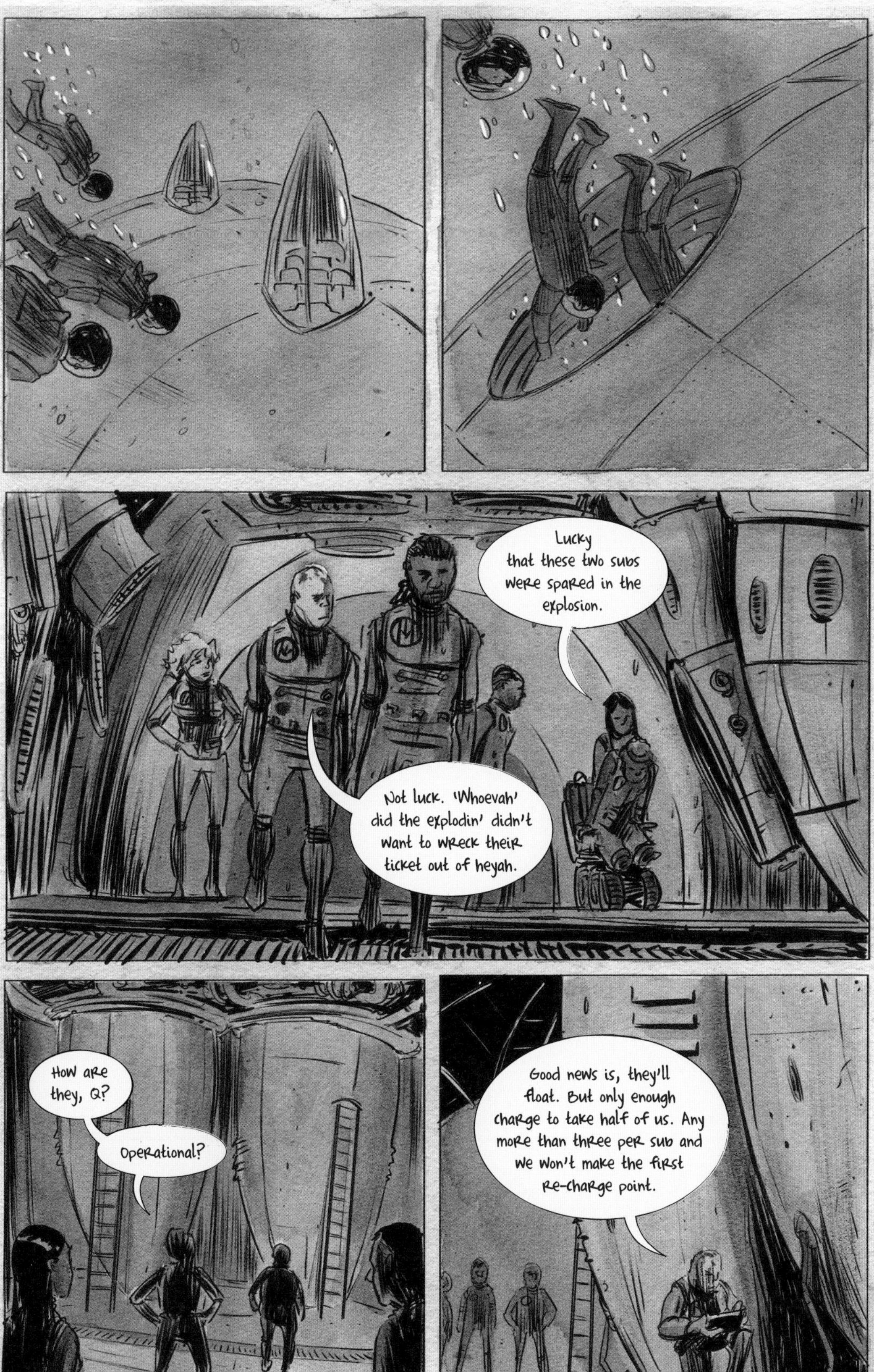
Lucky that these two subs were spared in the explosion.
Not luck. 'Whoevah' did the explodin' didn't want to wreck their ticket out of heyah.
How are they, Q?
Operational?
Good news is, they'll float. But only enough charge to take half of us. Any more than three per sub and we won't make the first re-charge point.

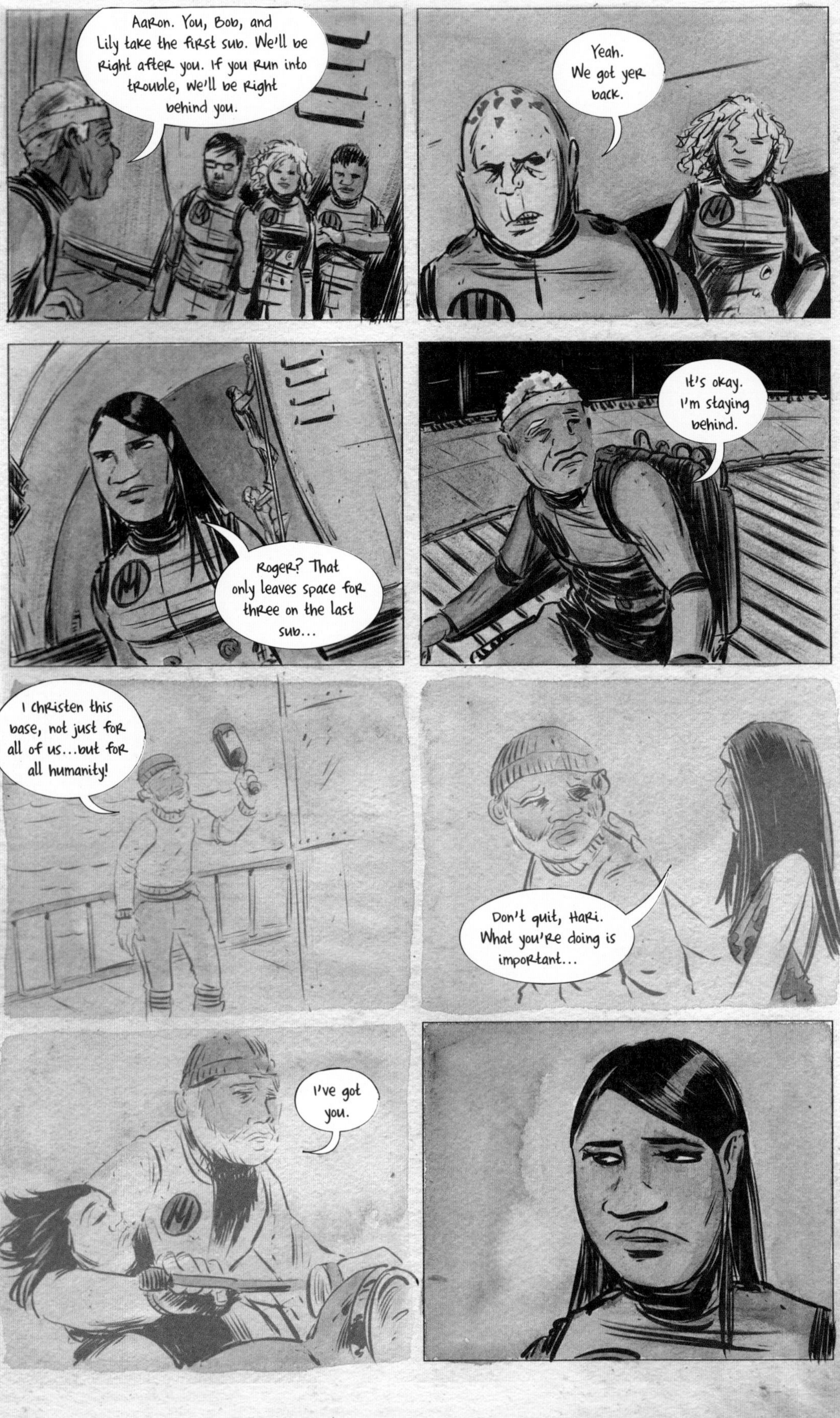
Aaron. You, Bob, and Lily take the first sub. We'll be right after you. If you run into trouble, we'll be right behind you.
Yeah. We got yer back.
Roger? That only leaves space for three on the last sub...
It's okay. I'm staying behind.
I christen this base, not just for all of us...but for all humanity!
Don't quit, Hari. What you're doing is important...
I've got you.

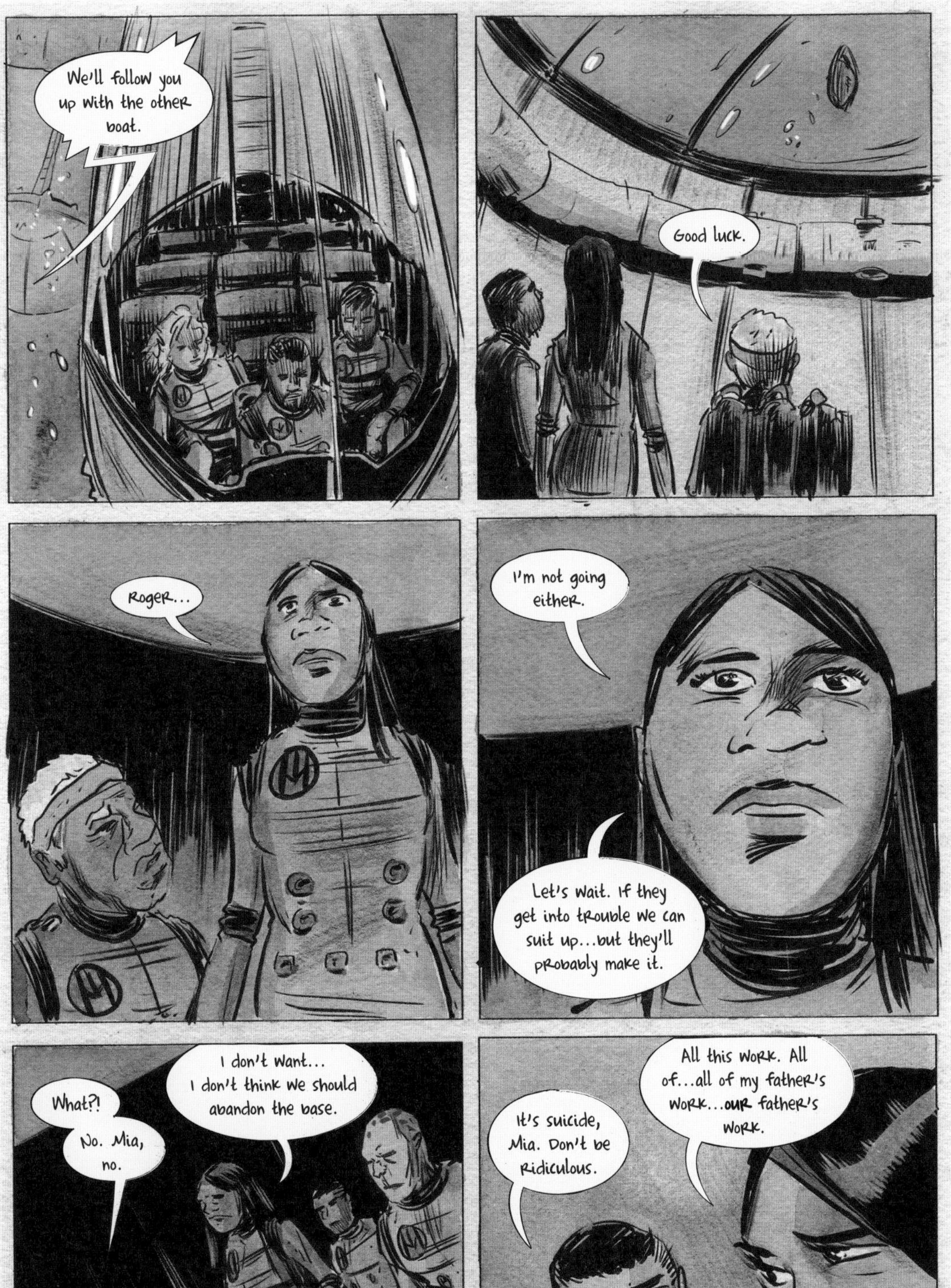
We'll follow you up with the other boat.
Good luck.
Roger...
I'm not going either.
Let's wait. If they get into trouble we can suit up...but they'll probably make it.
What?!
No. Mia, no.
I don't want... I don't think we should abandon the base.
It's suicide, Mia. Don't be ridiculous.
All this work. All of...all of my father's work...our father's work.
We can't just leave it to sink...we can't let it be lost.

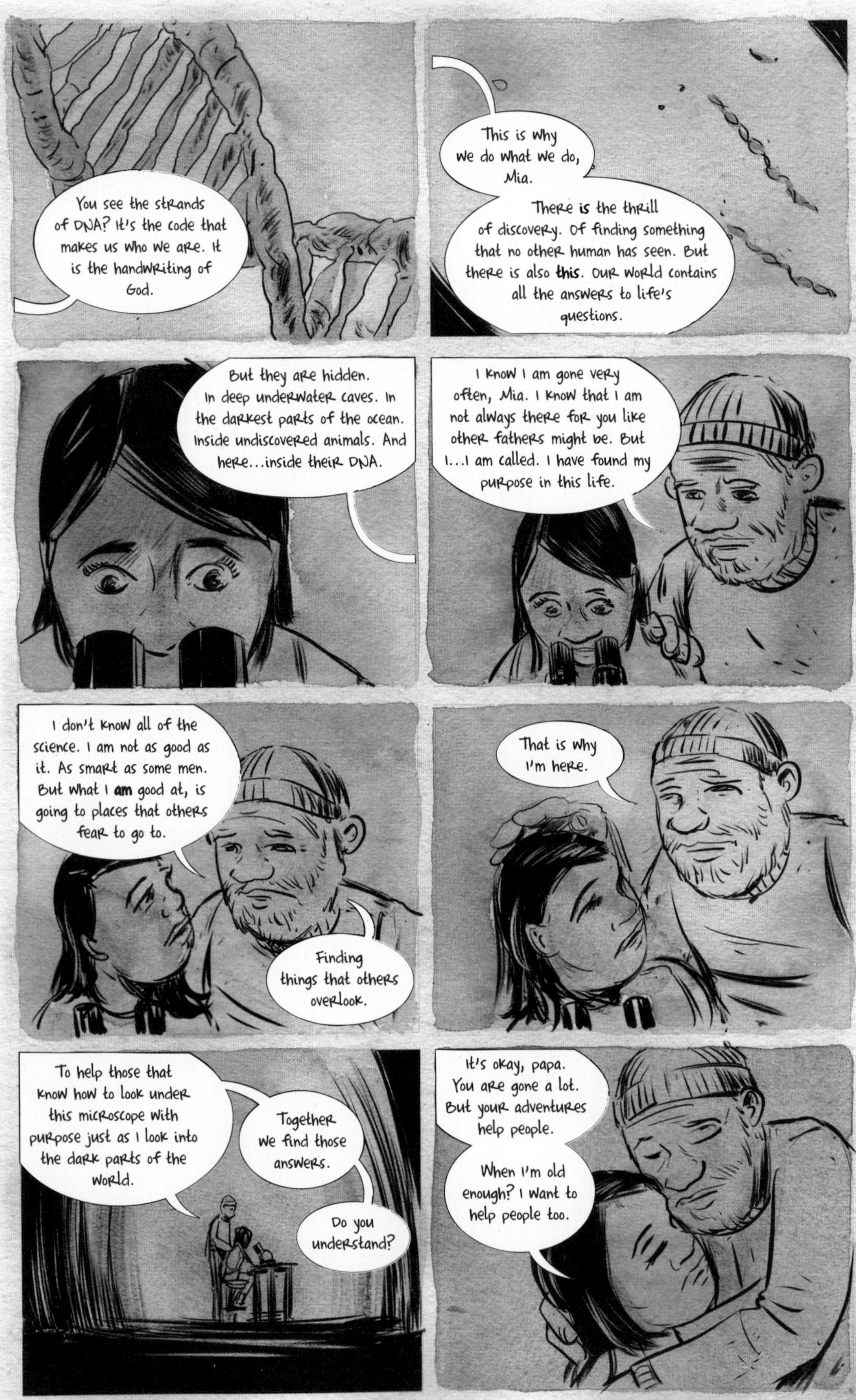
You see the strands of DNA? It's the code that makes us who we are. It is the handwriting of God.
This is why we do what we do, Mia.
There **is** the thrill of discovery. Of finding something that no other human has seen. But there is also **this**. Our world contains all the answers to life's questions.
But they are hidden. In deep underwater caves. In the darkest parts of the ocean. Inside undiscovered animals. And here...inside their DNA.
I know I am gone very often, Mia. I know that I am not always there for you like other fathers might be. But I...I am called. I have found my purpose in this life.
I don't know all of the science. I am not as good as it. As smart as some men. But what I **am** good at, is going to places that others fear to go to.
Finding things that others overlook.
That is why I'm here.
To help those that know how to look under this microscope with purpose just as I look into the dark parts of the world.
Together we find those answers.
Do you understand?
It's okay, papa. You are gone a lot. But your adventures help people.
When I'm old enough? I want to help people too.

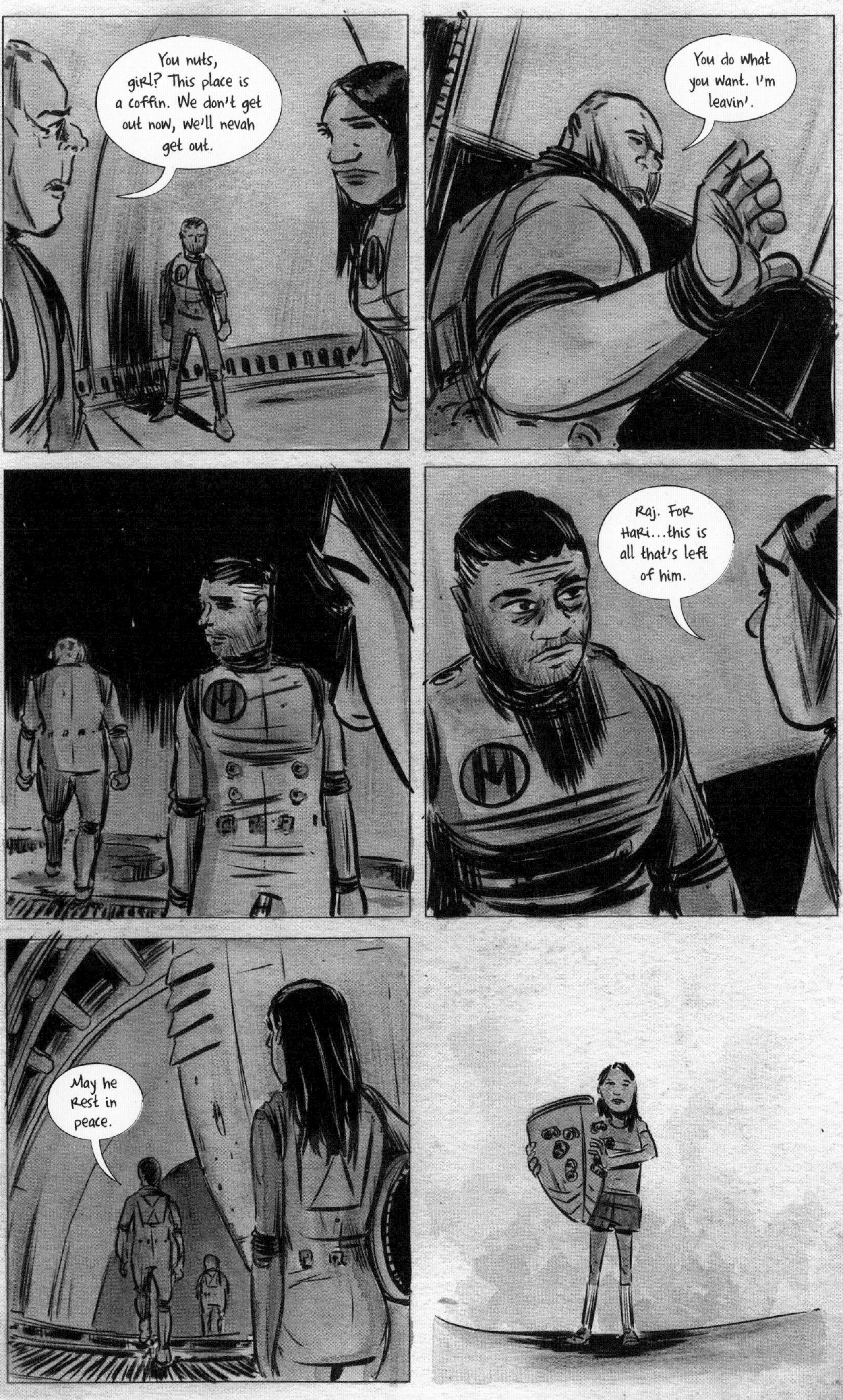
You nuts, girl? This place is a coffin. We don't get out now, we'll nevah get out.
You do what you want. I'm leavin'.
Raj. For Hari...this is all that's left of him.
May he rest in peace.

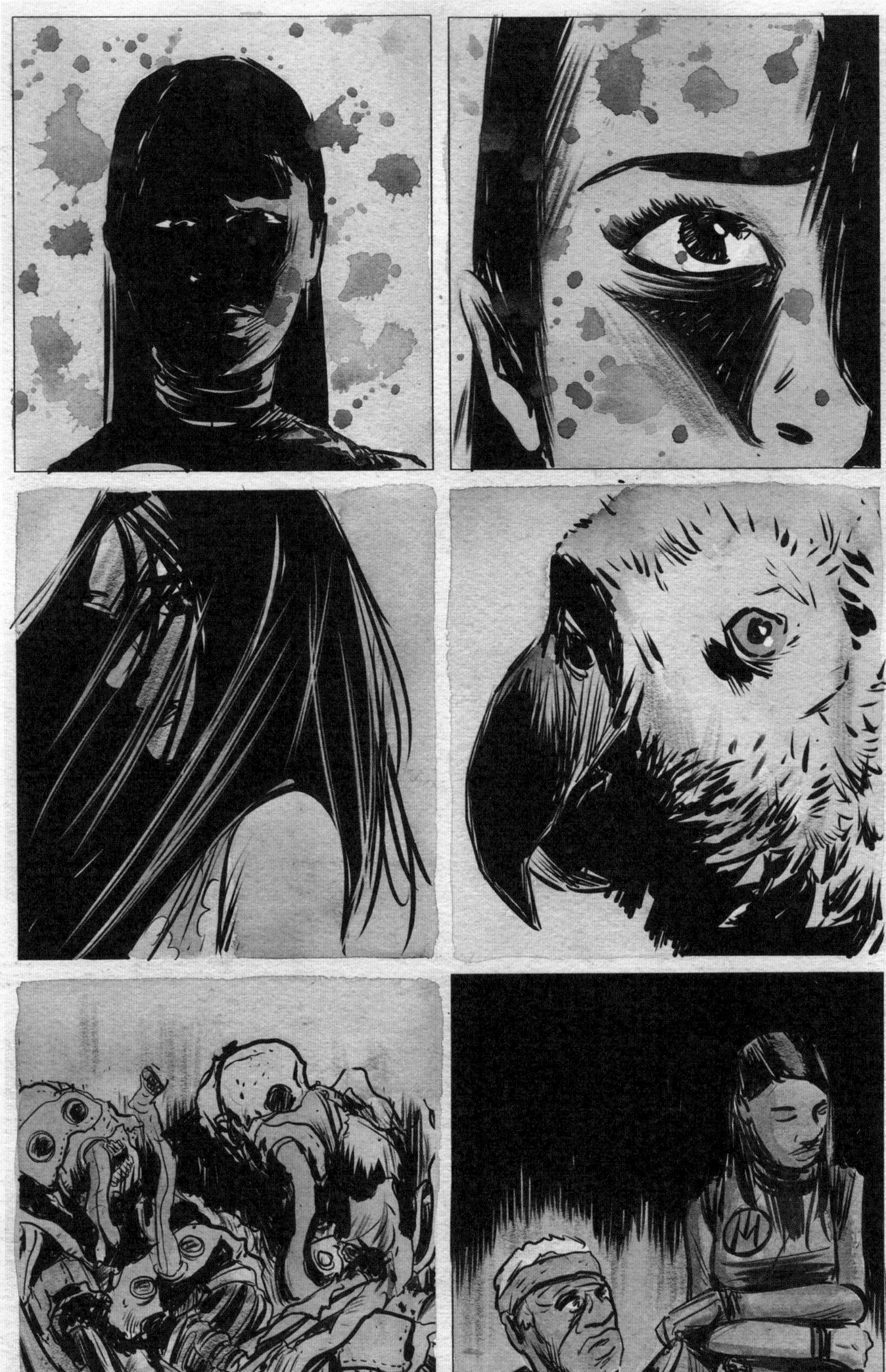

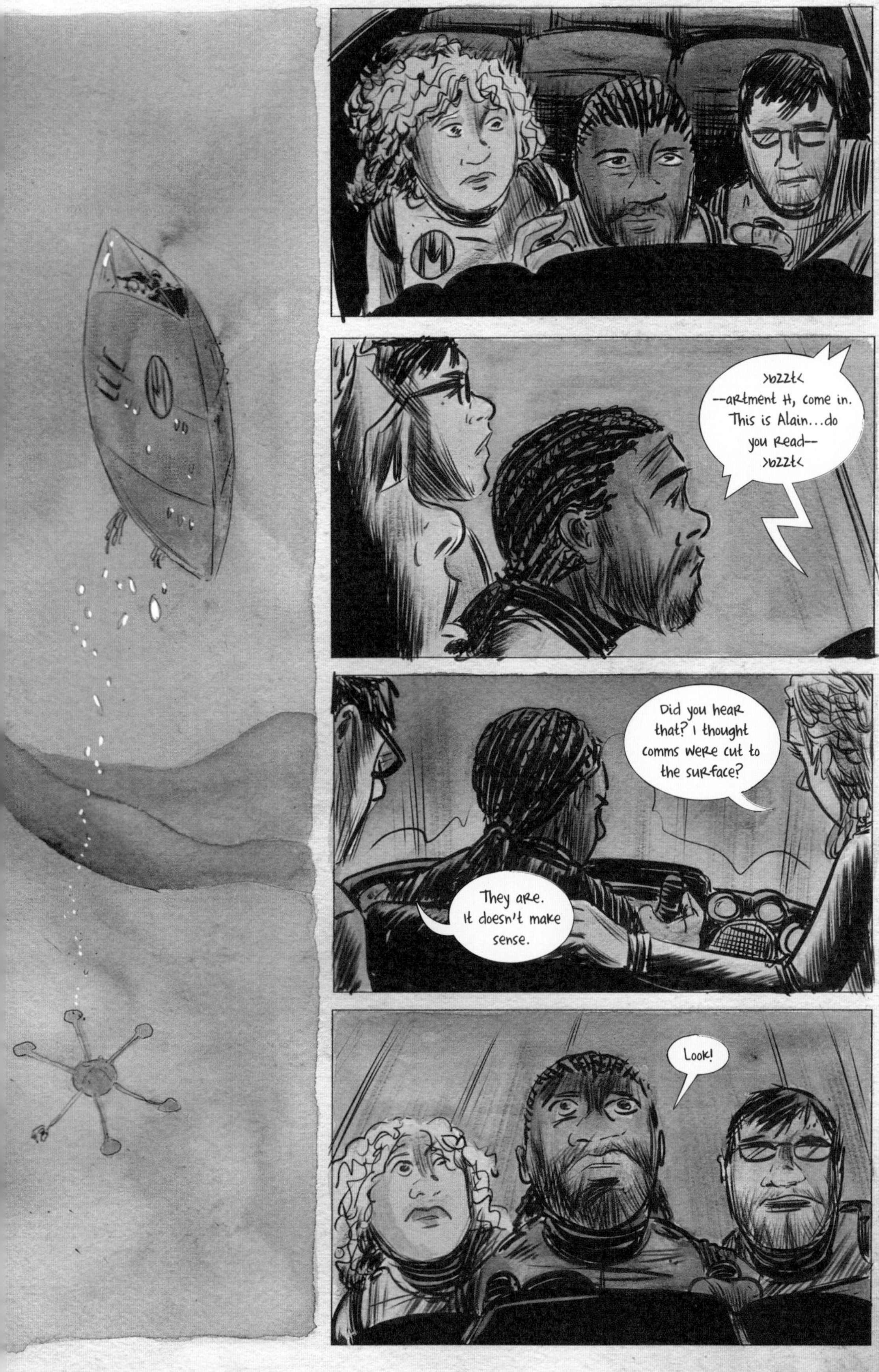
>bzzt< --artment H, come in. This is Alain...do you read-- >bzzt<
Did you hear that? I thought comms were cut to the surface?
They are. It doesn't make sense.
Look!

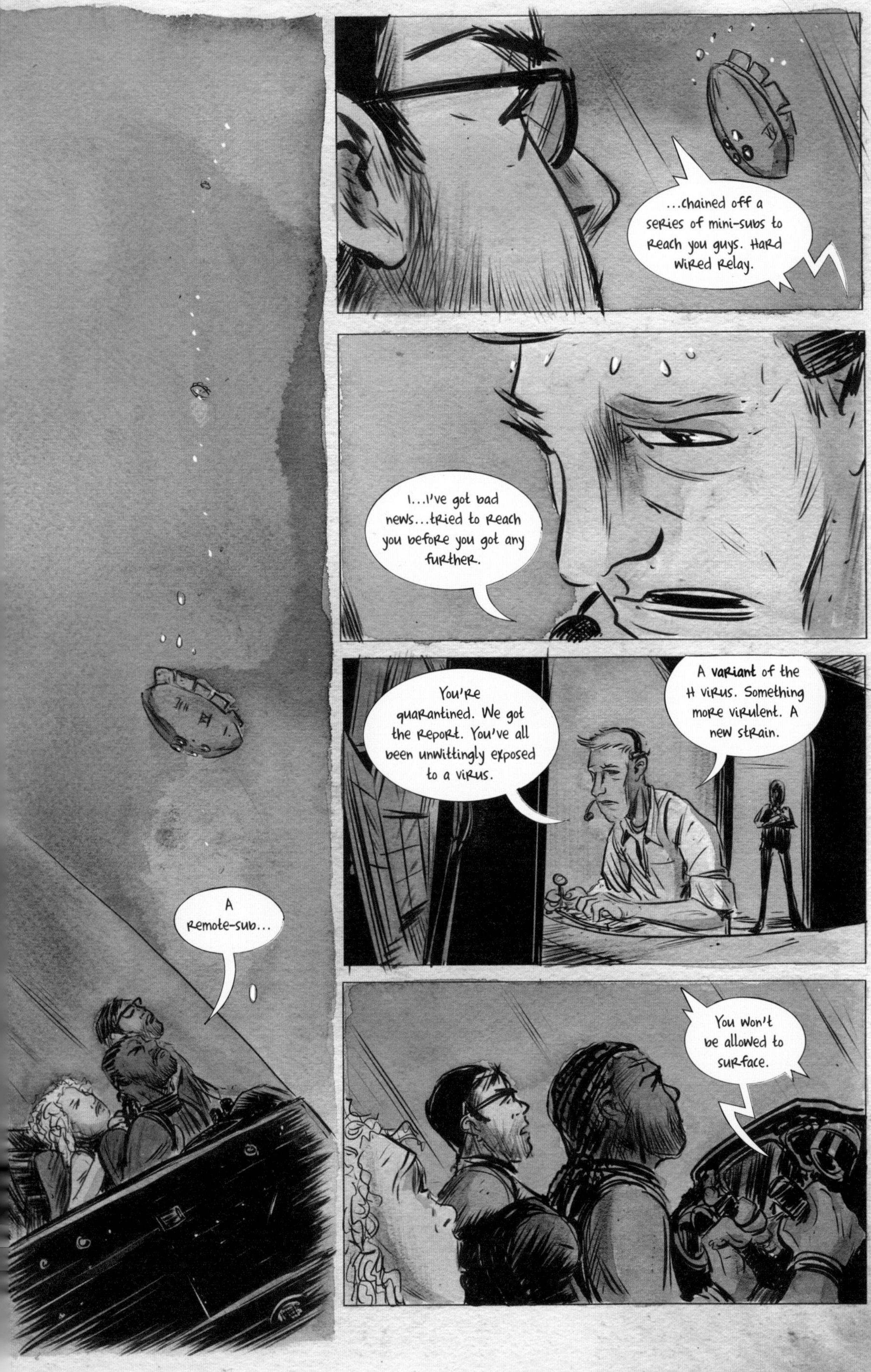
A Remote-sub...
...chained off a series of mini-subs to Reach you guys. Hard Wired Relay.
I...I've got bad news...tried to Reach you before you got any further.
You're quarantined. We got the Report. You've all been unwittingly exposed to a virus.
A **variant** of the H virus. Something more virulent. A new strain.
You won't be allowed to surface.

What?!
No! How?!?
You crazy?!?!
You don't understand, Alain. We have the cure. For the H-virus. Right now. We can deliver it. Jerome discovered it. We've got it.
I'm...I'm afraid it's irrelevant. I'm just following orders. We can't risk it. We can't risk another outbreak up here. Not until we know you guys aren't carrying something even worse that we can't fix.

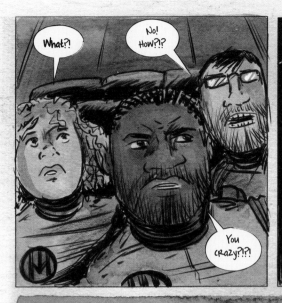

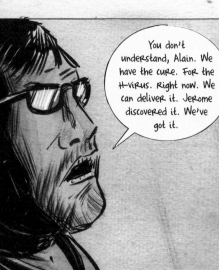

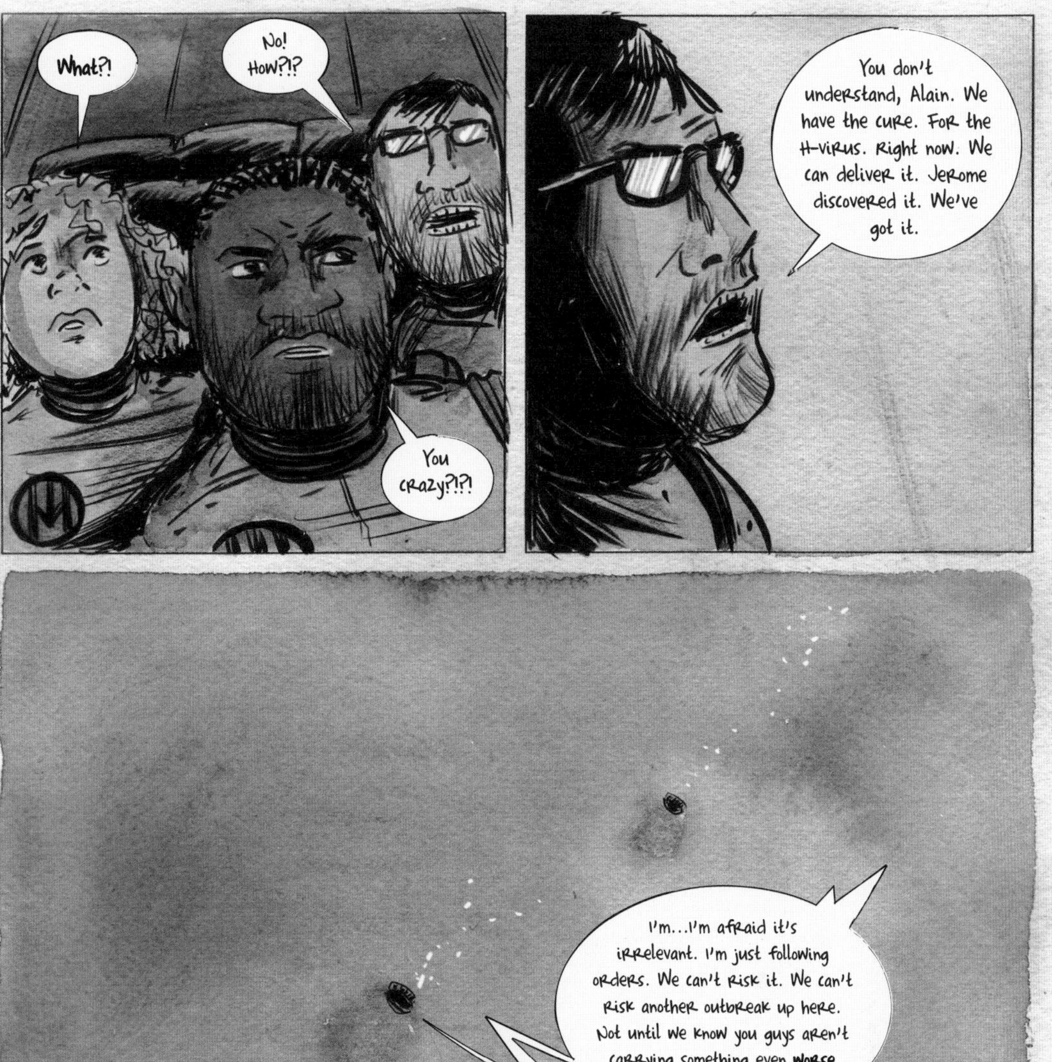

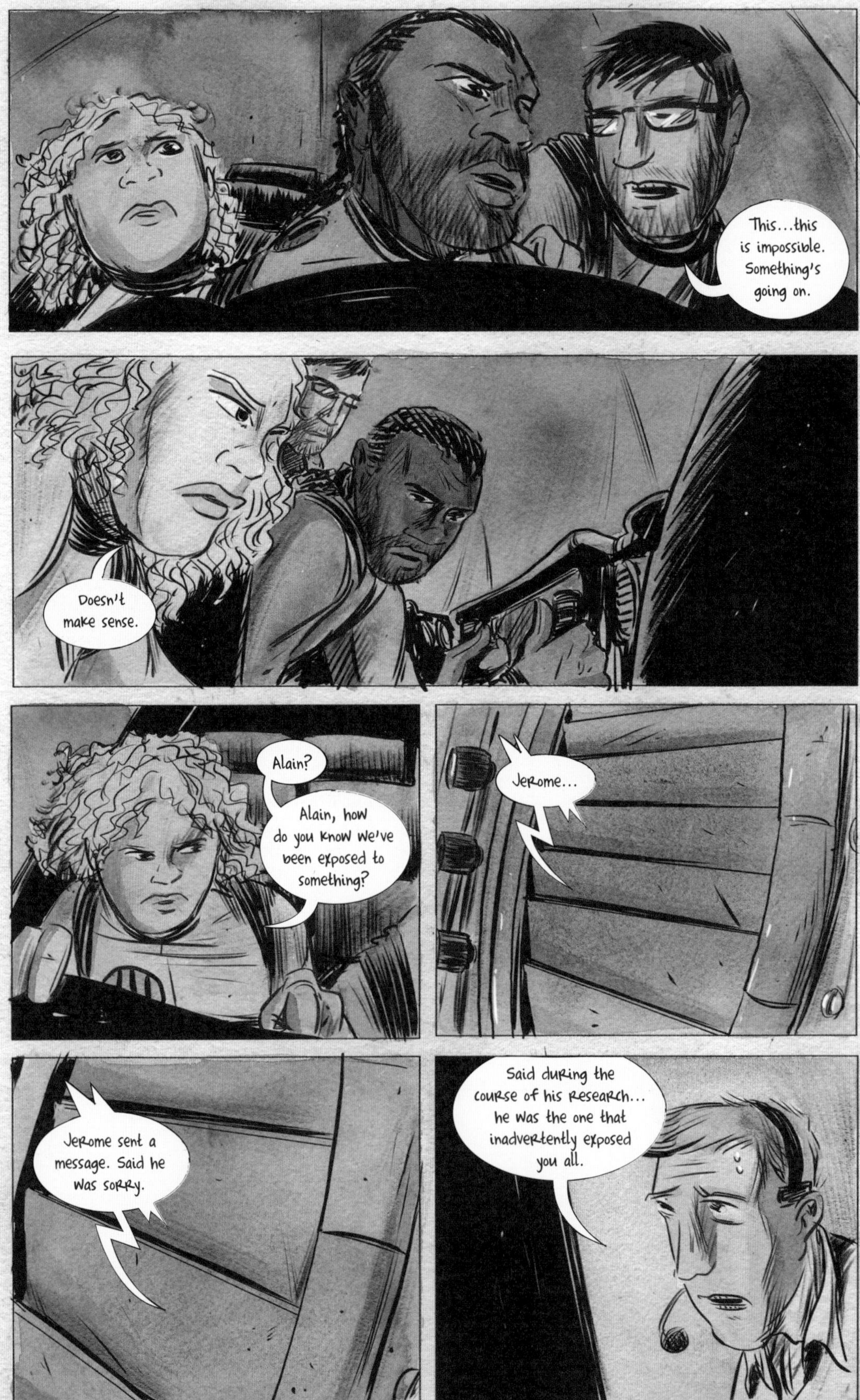
This...this is impossible. Something's going on.
Doesn't make sense.
Alain?
Alain, how do you know we've been exposed to something?
Jerome...
Jerome sent a message. Said he was sorry.
Said during the course of his research... he was the one that inadvertently exposed you all.

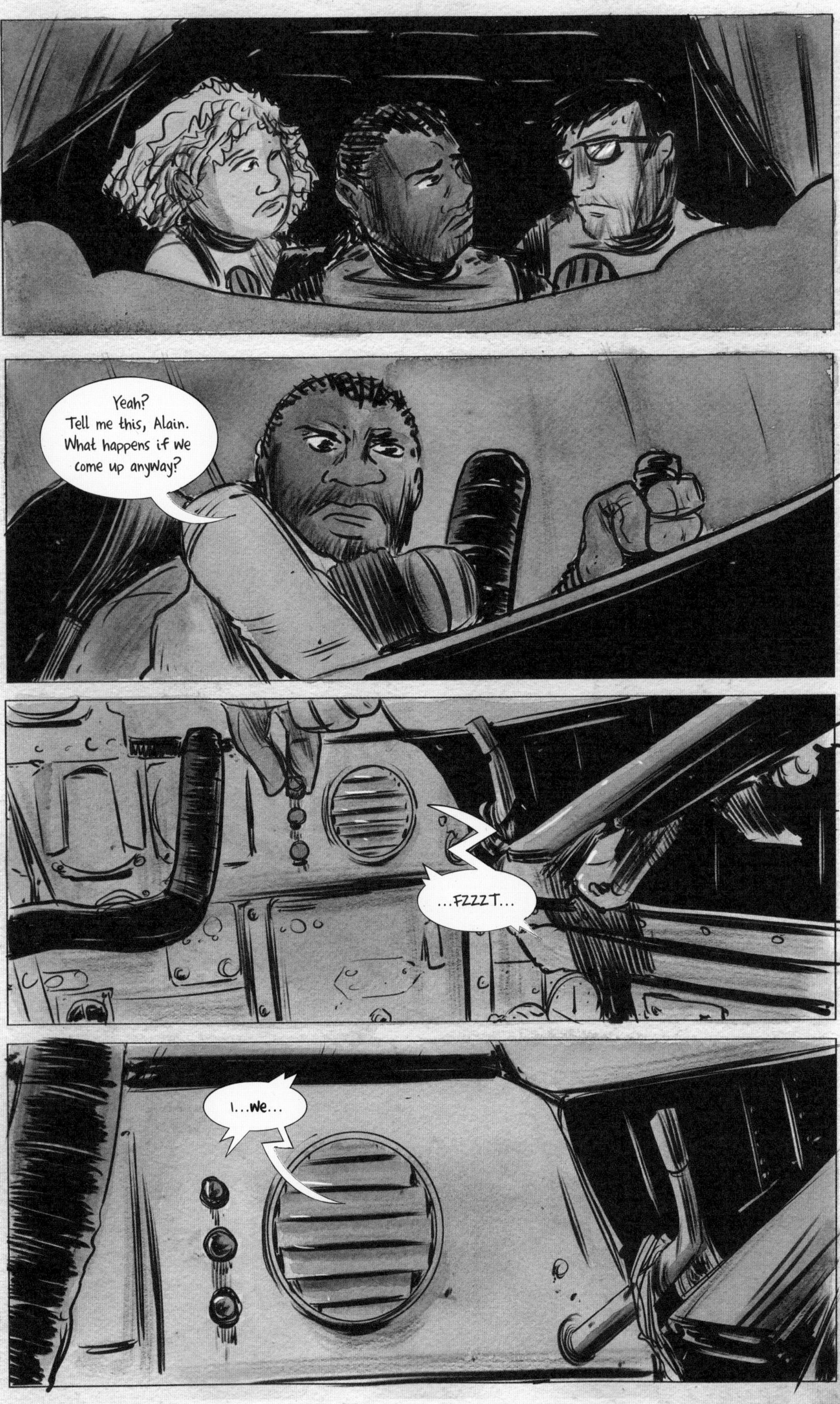
Yeah? Tell me this, Alain. What happens if we come up anyway?
...FZZZT...
I...we...

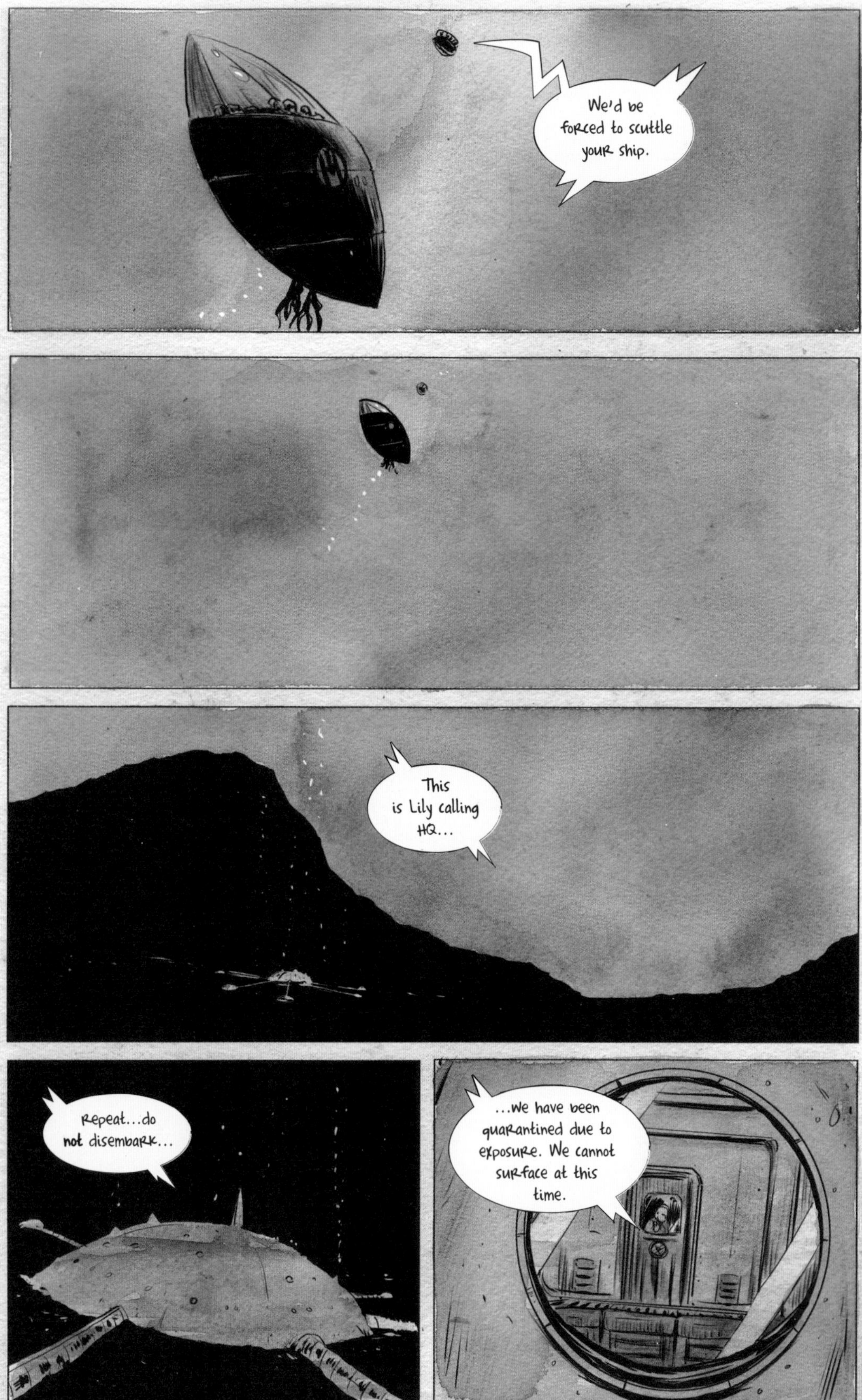
We'd be forced to scuttle your ship.
This is Lily calling HQ...
Repeat...do **not** disembark...
...we have been quarantined due to exposure. We cannot surface at this time.

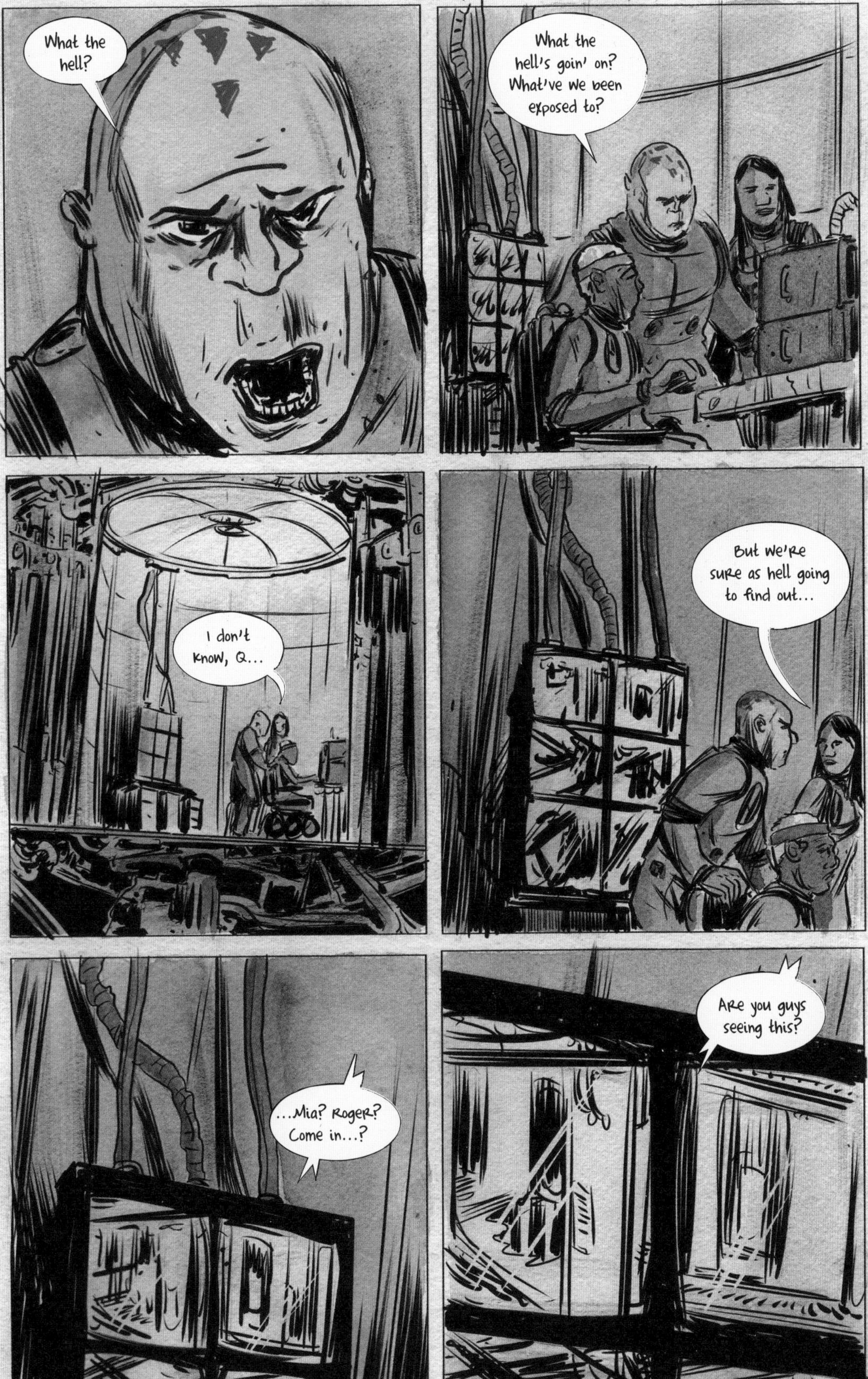
What the hell?
What the hell's goin' on? What've we been exposed to?
I don't know, Q...
But we're sure as hell going to find out...
...Mia? Roger? Come in...?
Are you guys seeing this?

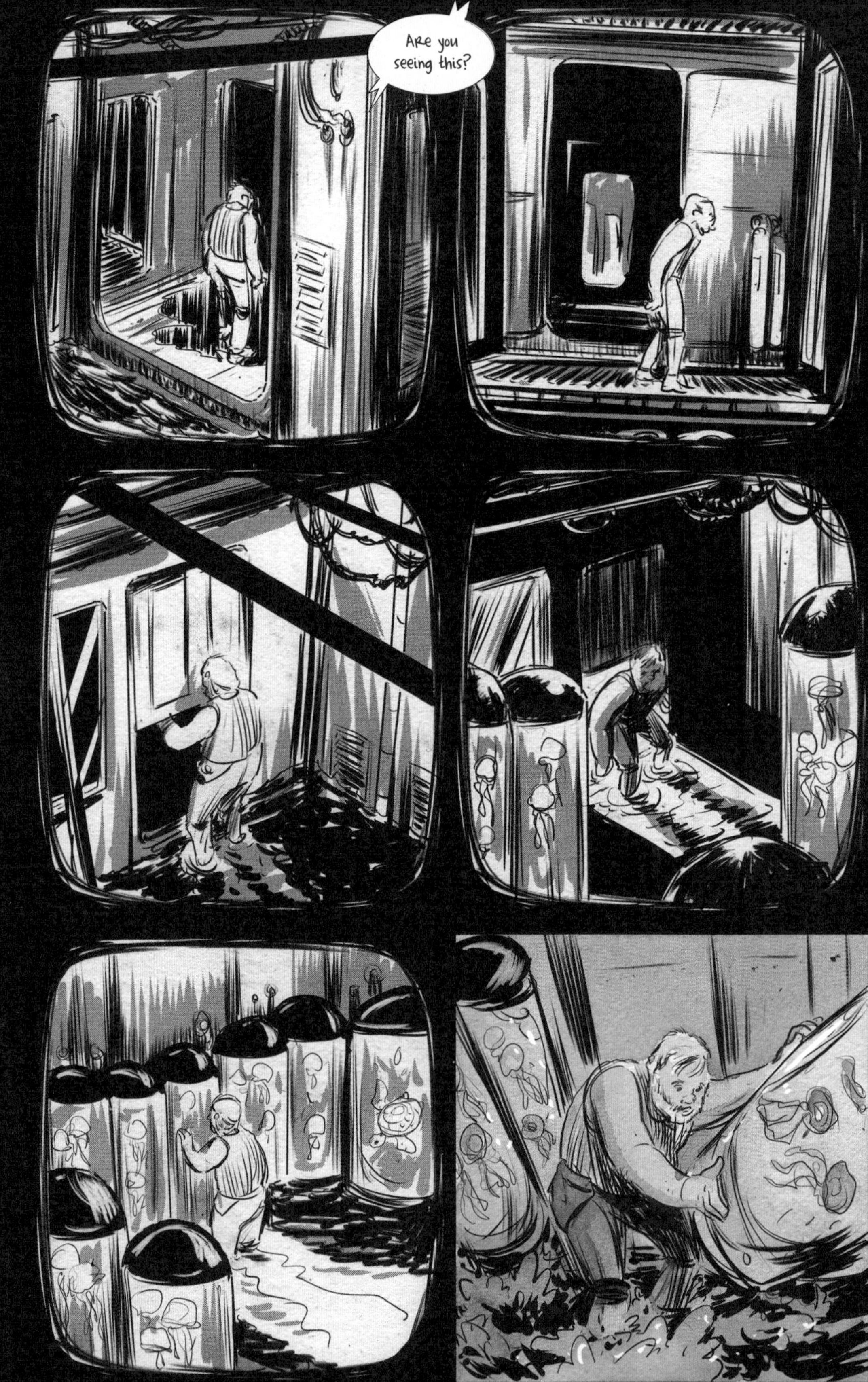
Are you seeing this?

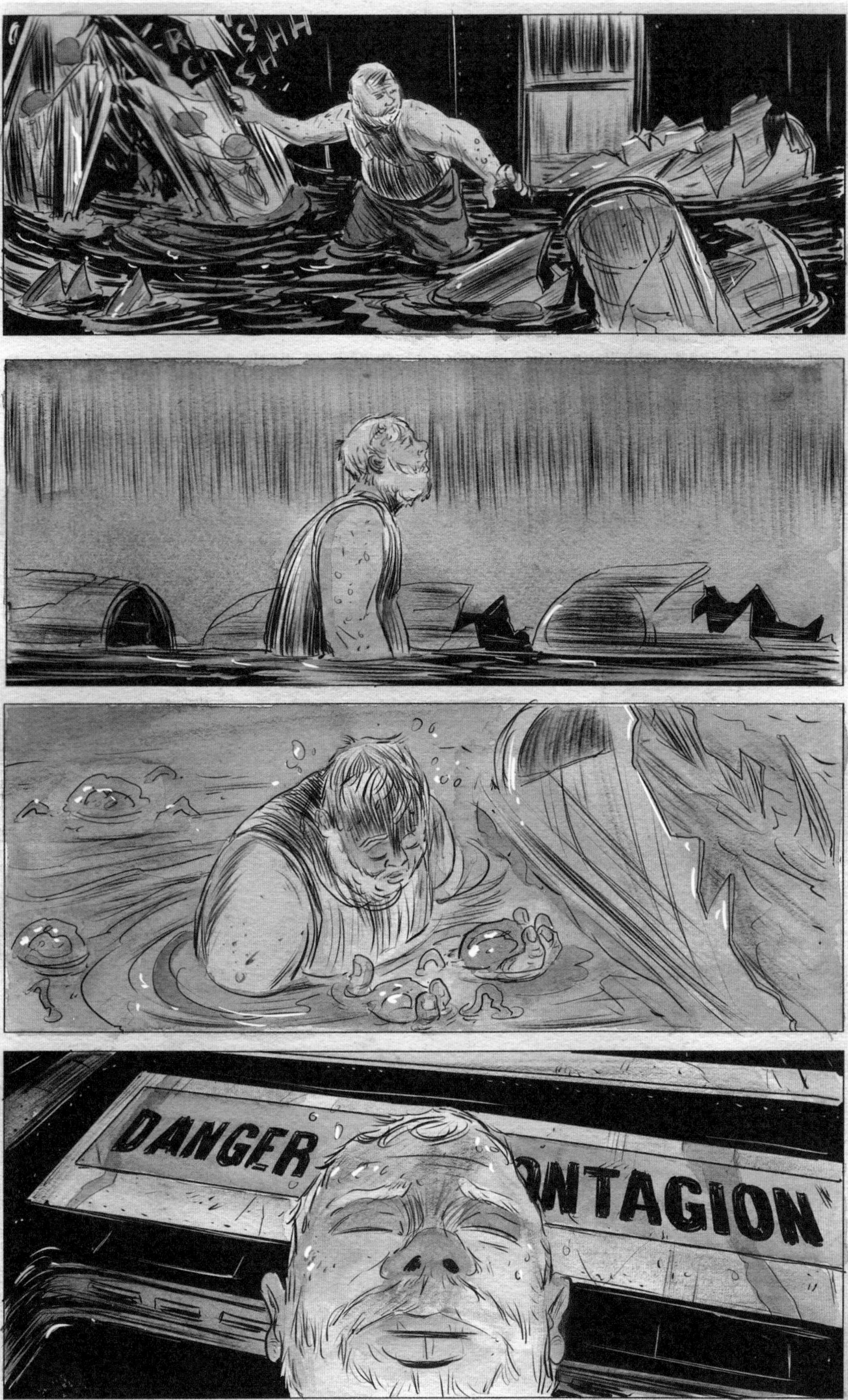
DANGER
ONTAGION

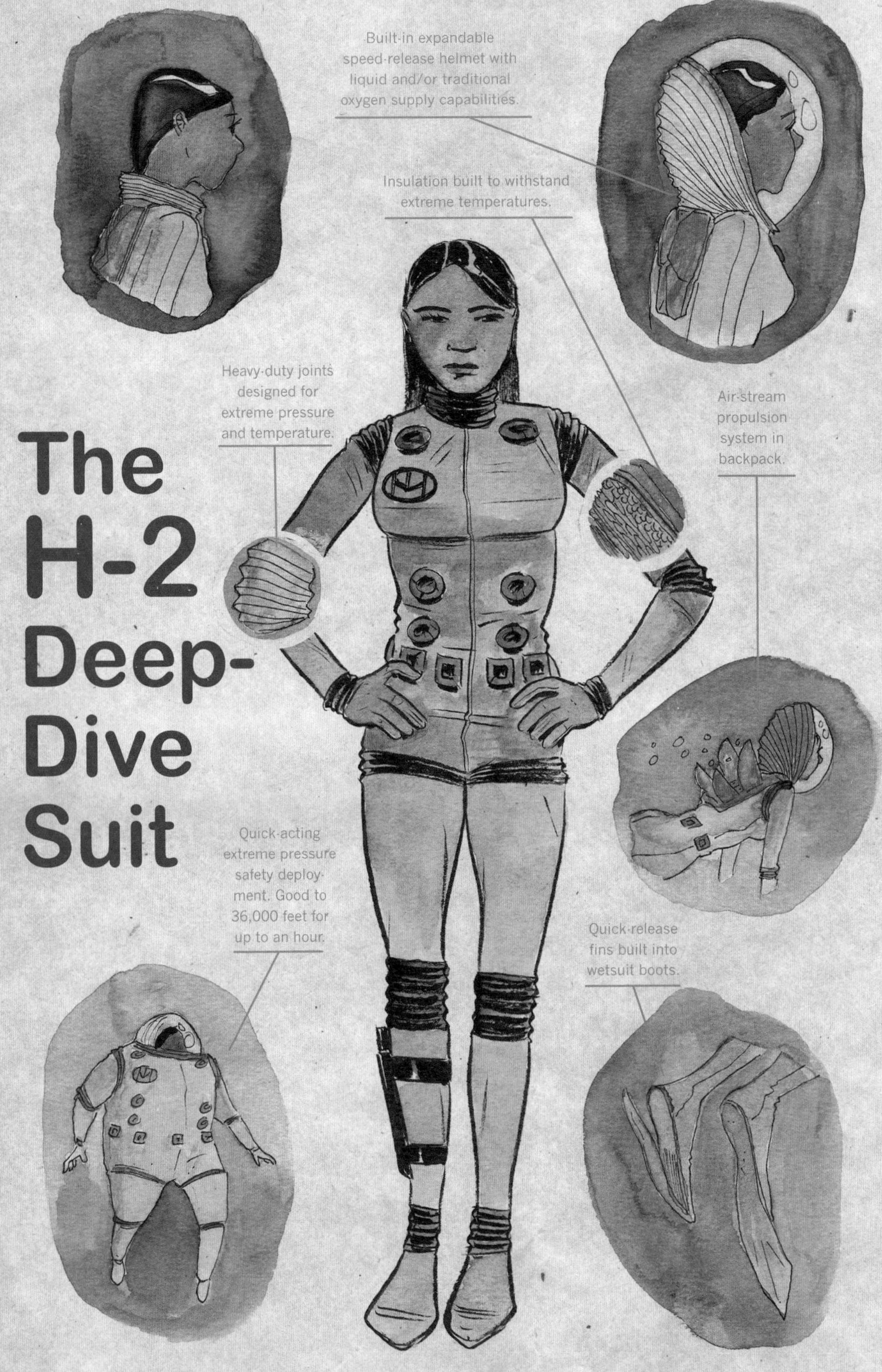
The H-2 Deep-Dive Suit
Built-in expandable speed-release helmet with liquid and/or traditional oxygen supply capabilities.
Insulation built to withstand extreme temperatures.
Heavy-duty joints designed for extreme pressure and temperature.
Air-stream propulsion system in backpack.
Quick-acting extreme pressure safety deployment. Good to 36,000 feet for up to an hour.
Quick-release fins built into wetsuit boots.

Colossal Squid

Mesonychoteuthis hamiltoni

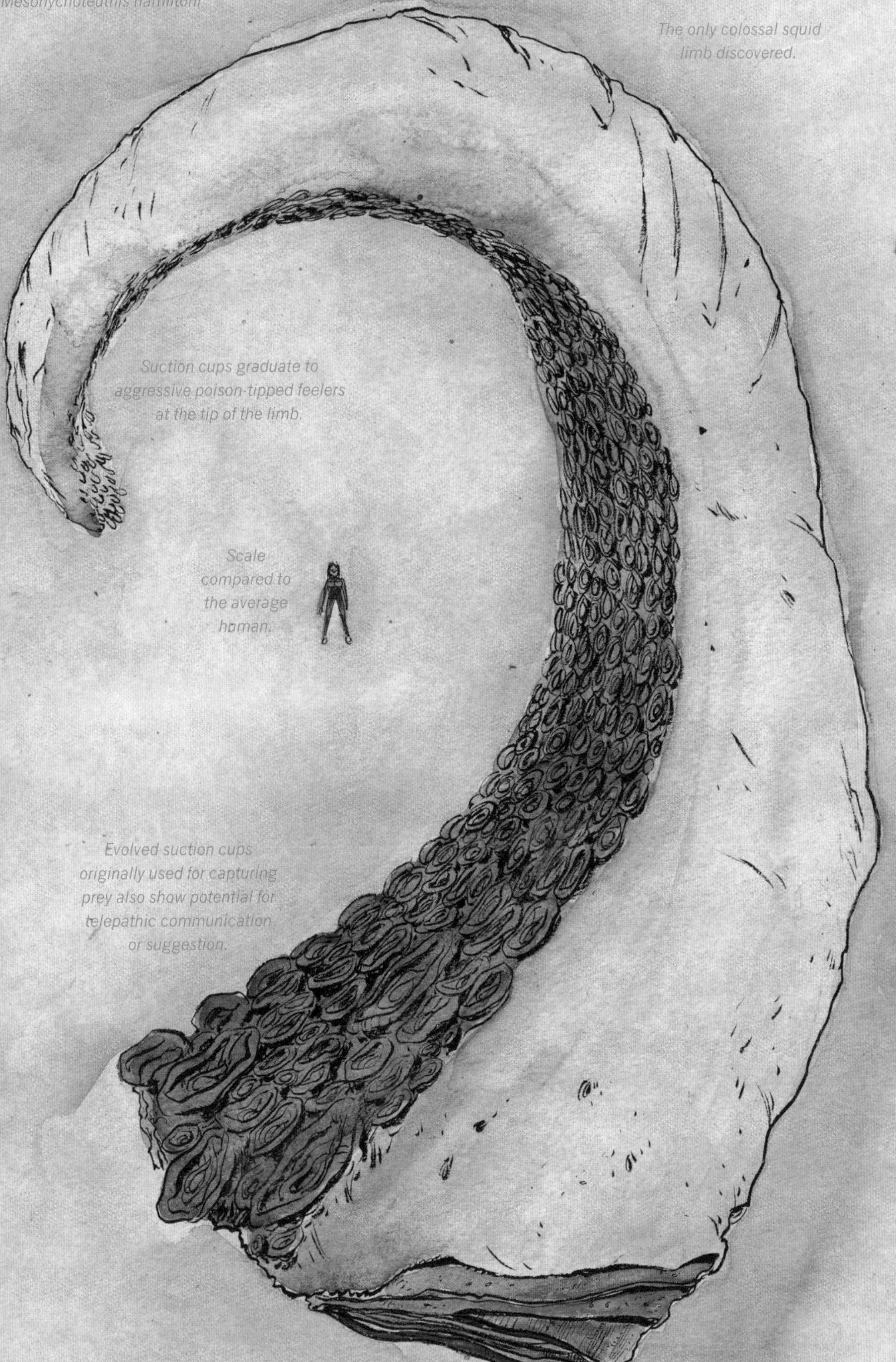
The only colossal squid limb discovered.
Suction cups graduate to aggressive poison-tipped feelers at the tip of the limb.
Scale compared to the average human.
Evolved suction cups originally used for capturing prey also show potential for telepathic communication or suggestion.

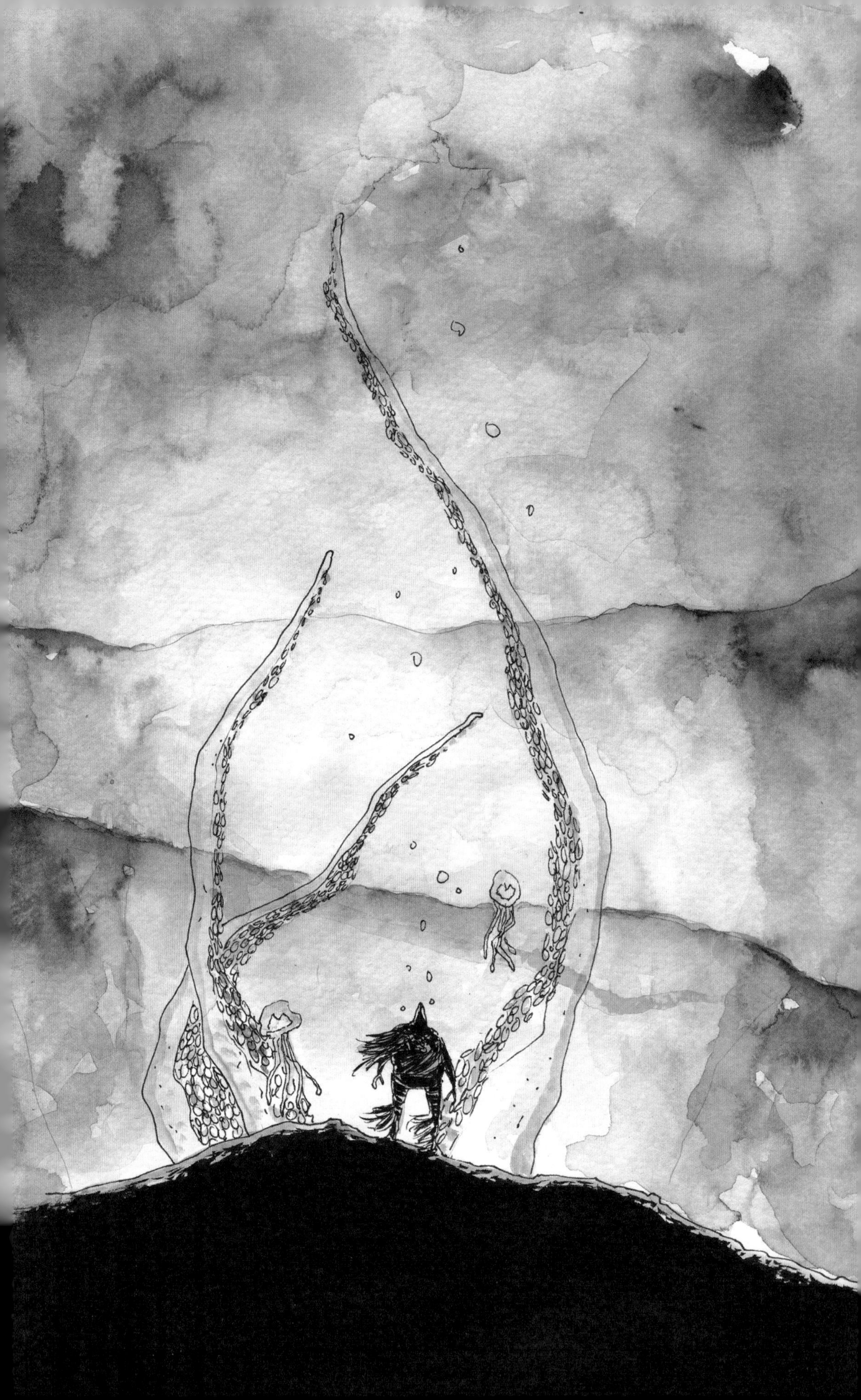

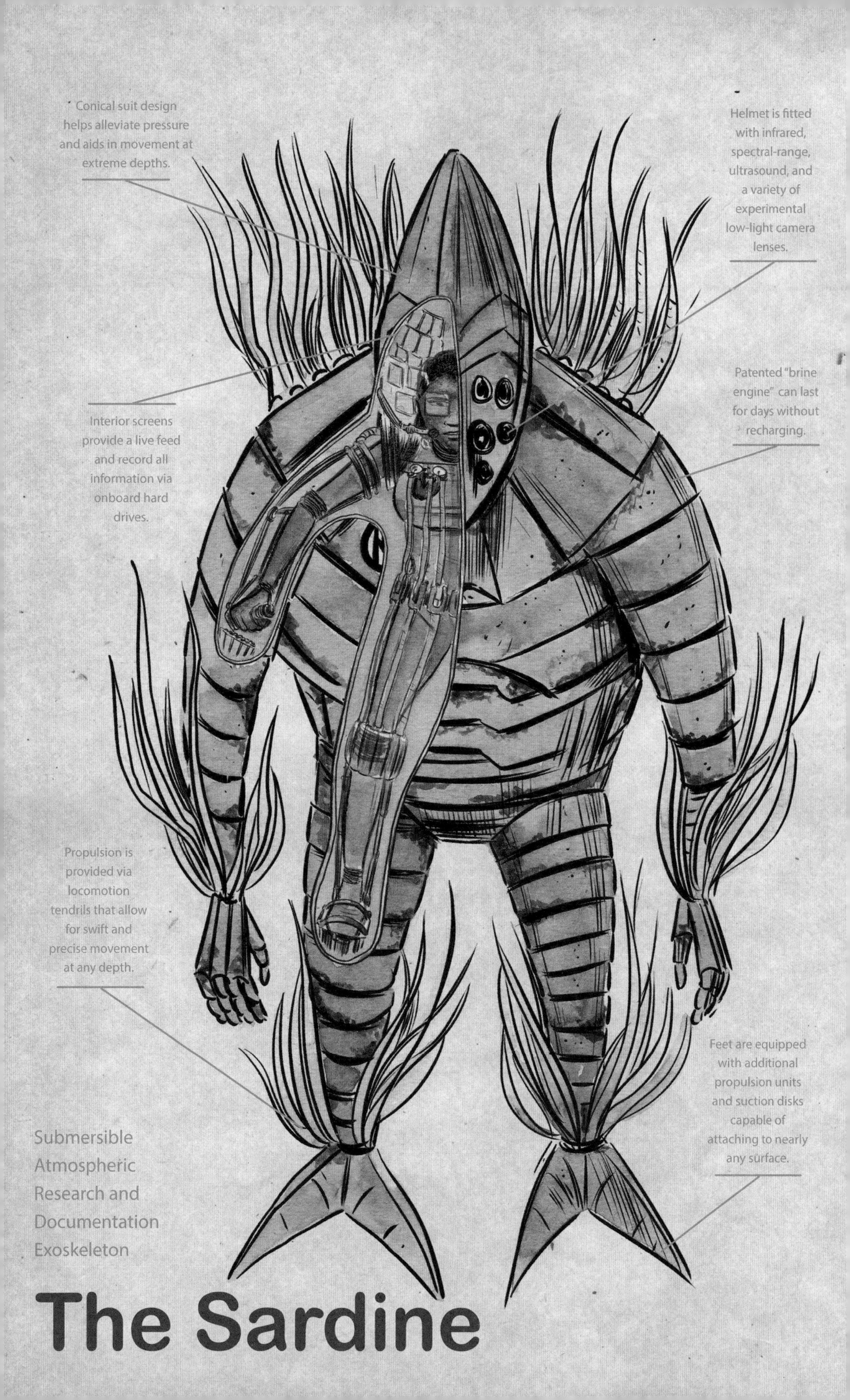
Conical suit design helps alleviate pressure and aids in movement at extreme depths.
Helmet is fitted with infrared, spectral-range, ultrasound, and a variety of experimental low-light camera lenses.
Patented "brine engine" can last for days without recharging.
Interior screens provide a live feed and record all information via onboard hard drives.
Propulsion is provided via locomotion tendrils that allow for swift and precise movement at any depth.
Feet are equipped with additional propulsion units and suction disks capable of attaching to nearly any surface.
Submersible Atmospheric Research and Documentation Exoskeleton
The Sardine

Sea Mime *(mare parrot)*

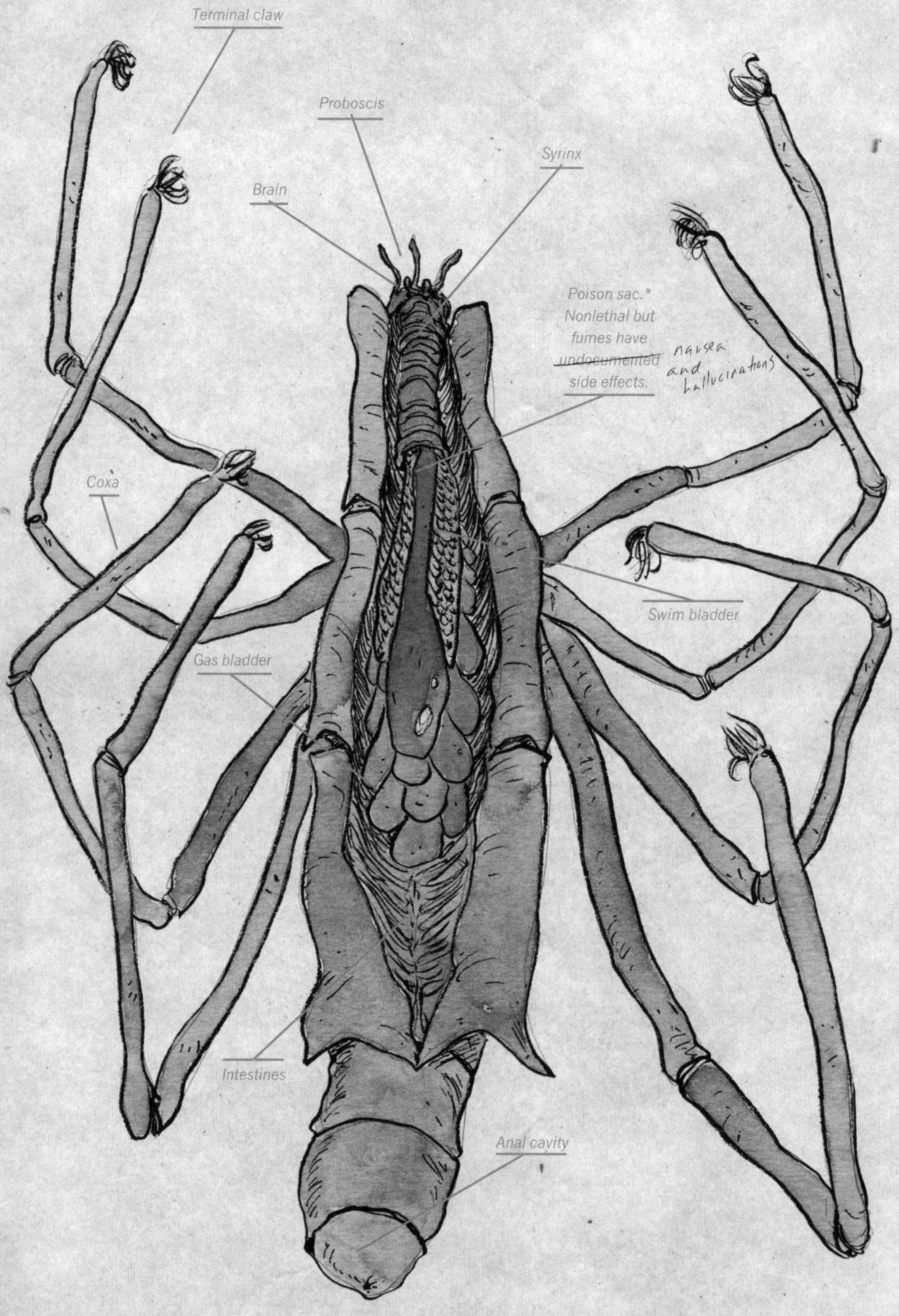

Terminal claw
Proboscis
Syrinx
Brain
Poison sac.*
Nonlethal but
fumes have
~~undocumented~~ nausea and hallucinations
side effects.
Coxa
Swim bladder
Gas bladder
Intestines
Anal cavity

*Trait not shared by any similar species

The HELM

Human Emergency Life Mask

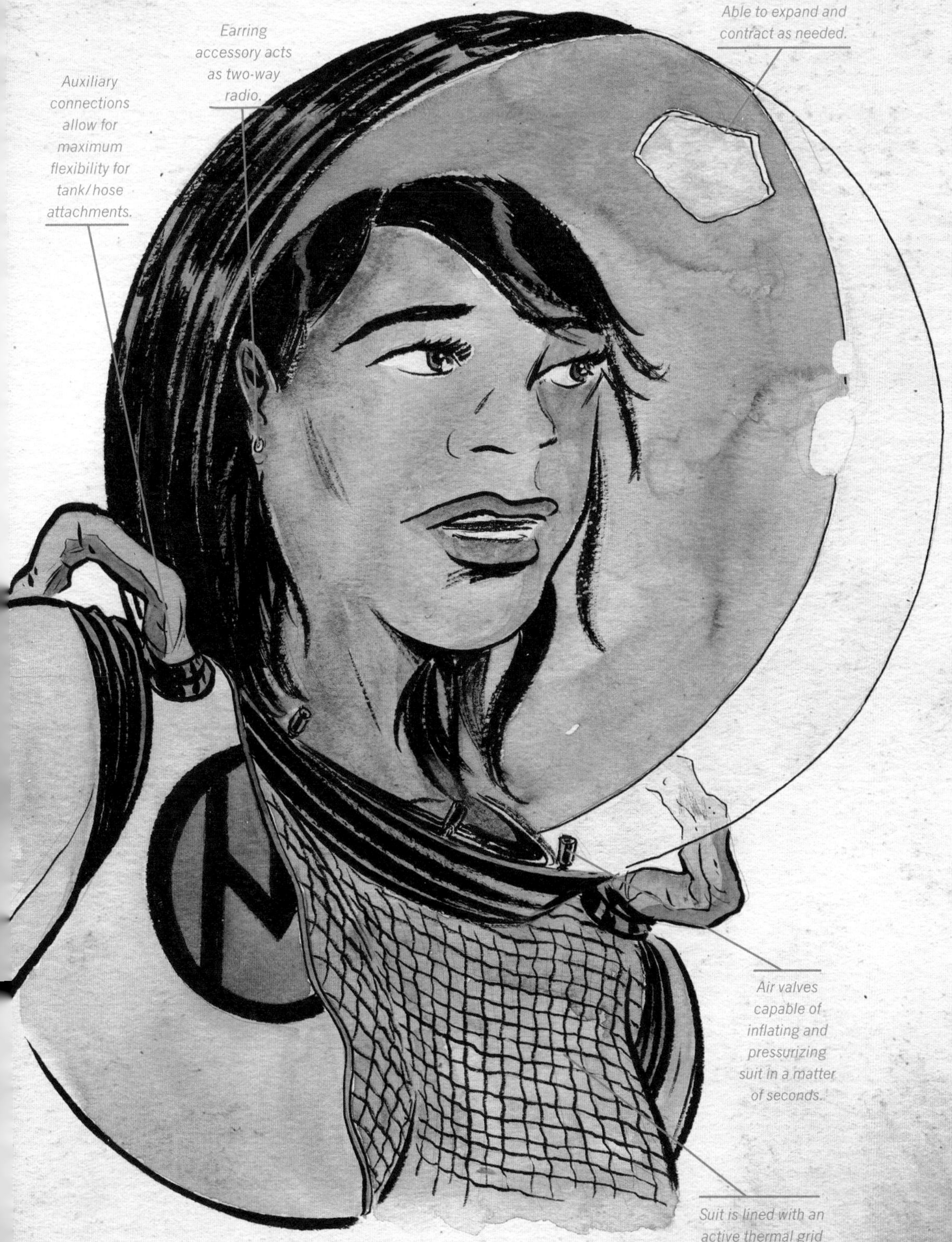
High-stress polymer is flexible and nearly unbreakable. Able to expand and contract as needed.
Earring accessory acts as two-way radio.
Auxiliary connections allow for maximum flexibility for tank/hose attachments.
Air valves capable of inflating and pressurizing suit in a matter of seconds.
Suit is lined with an active thermal grid capable of heating and cooling as needed.

Psychic Jellyfish

(Aurelia psychicae)

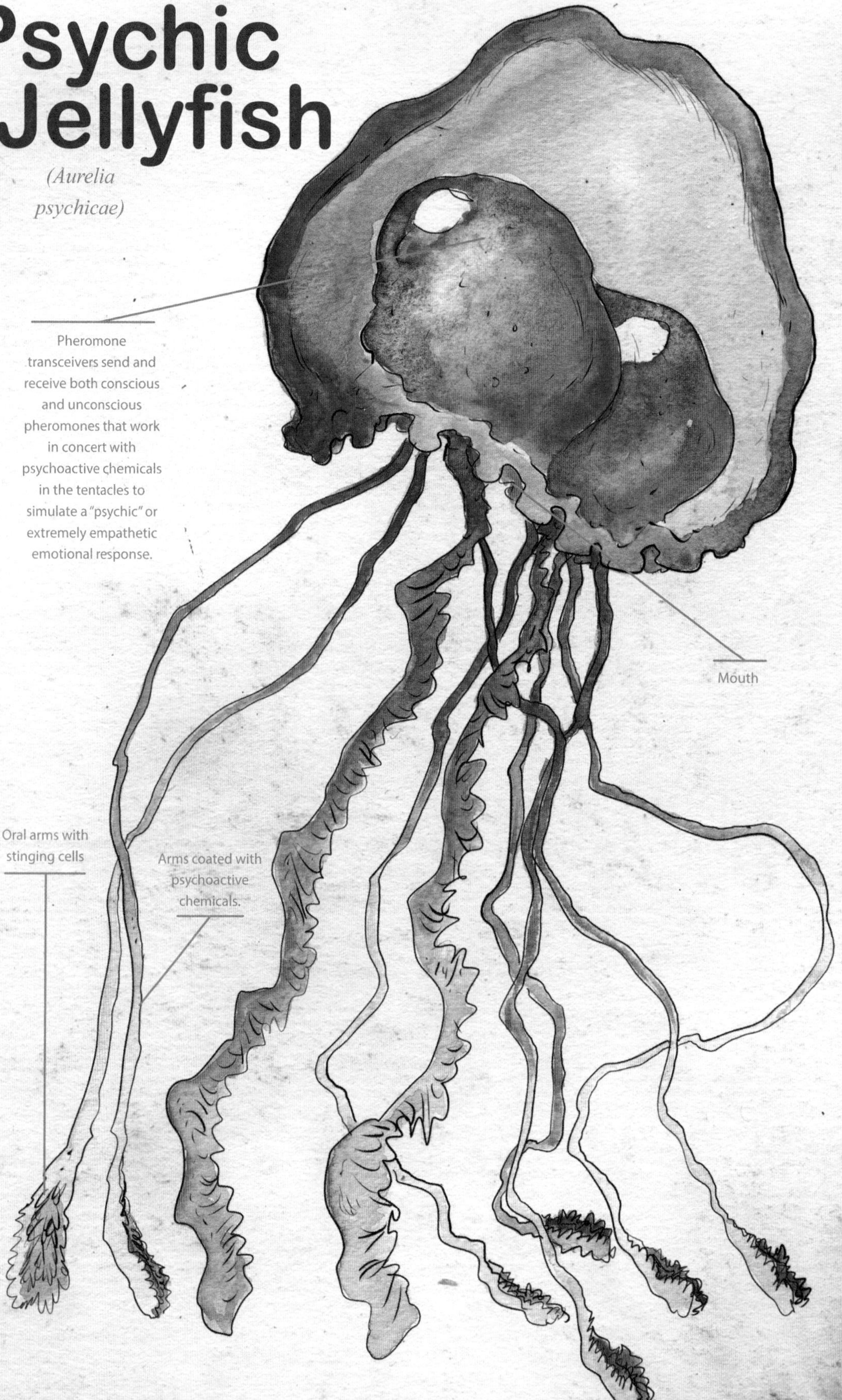
Pheromone transceivers send and receive both conscious and unconscious pheromones that work in concert with psychoactive chemicals in the tentacles to simulate a "psychic" or extremely empathetic emotional response.
Mouth
Oral arms with stinging cells
Arms coated with psychoactive chemicals.

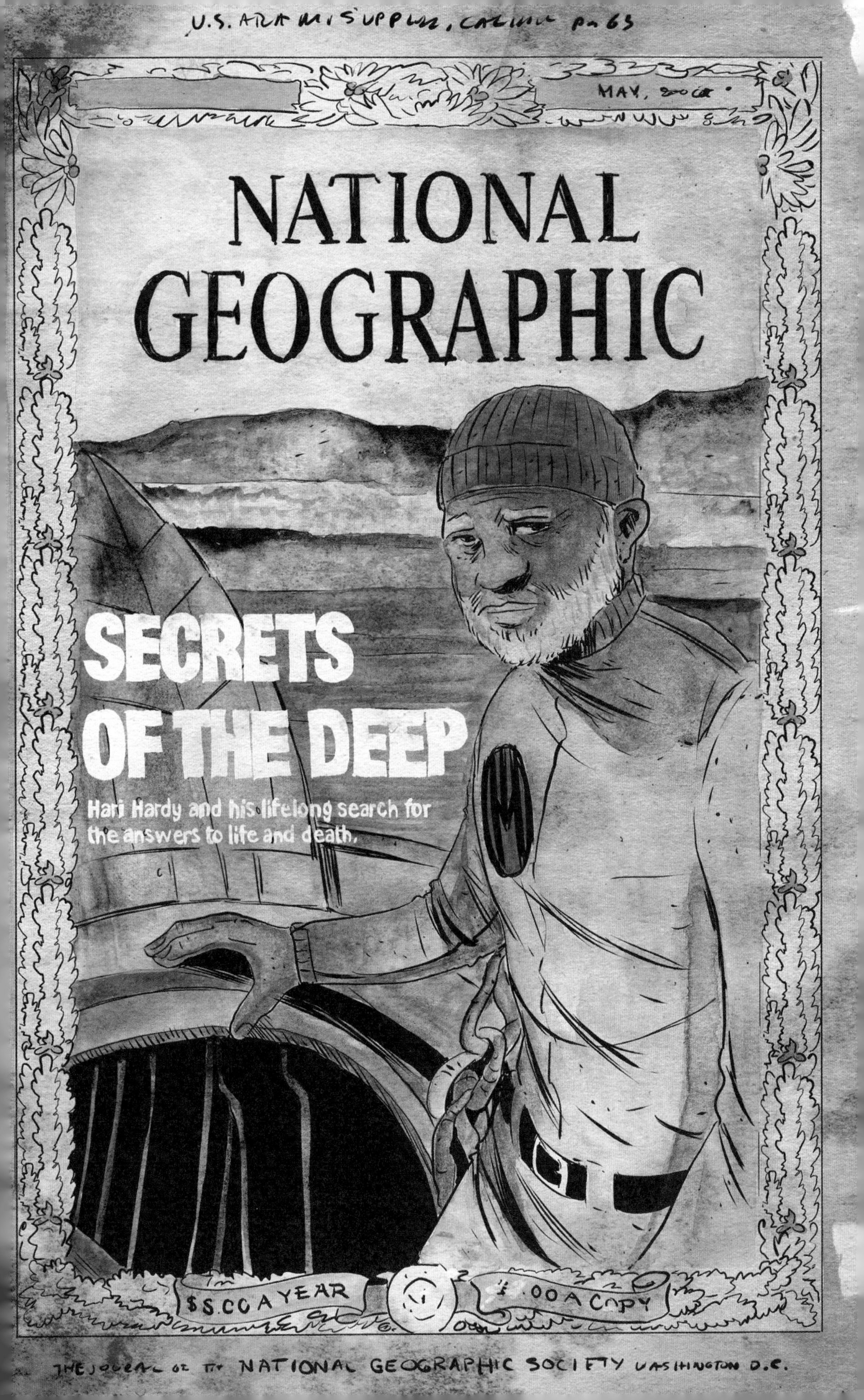
MAY,
NATIONAL GEOGRAPHIC
SECRETS OF THE DEEP
Hari Hardy and his lifelong search for the answers to life and death.
A YEAR
.00 A COPY
NATIONAL GEOGRAPHIC SOCIETY

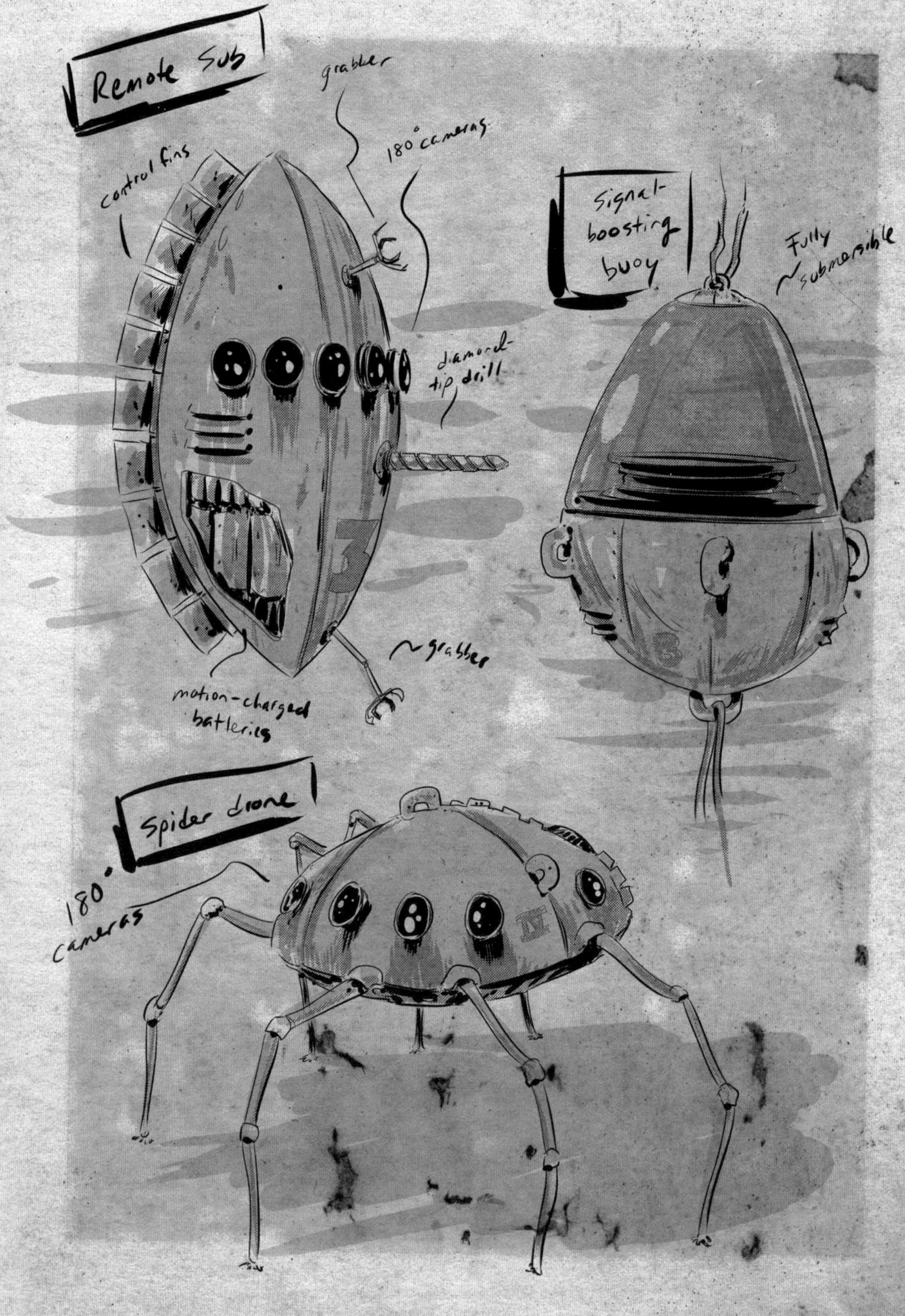

Remote Sub
grabber
180° cameras
control fins
diamond-tip drill
grabber
motion-charged batteries
Signal-boosting buoy
Fully submersible
Spider drone
180° cameras

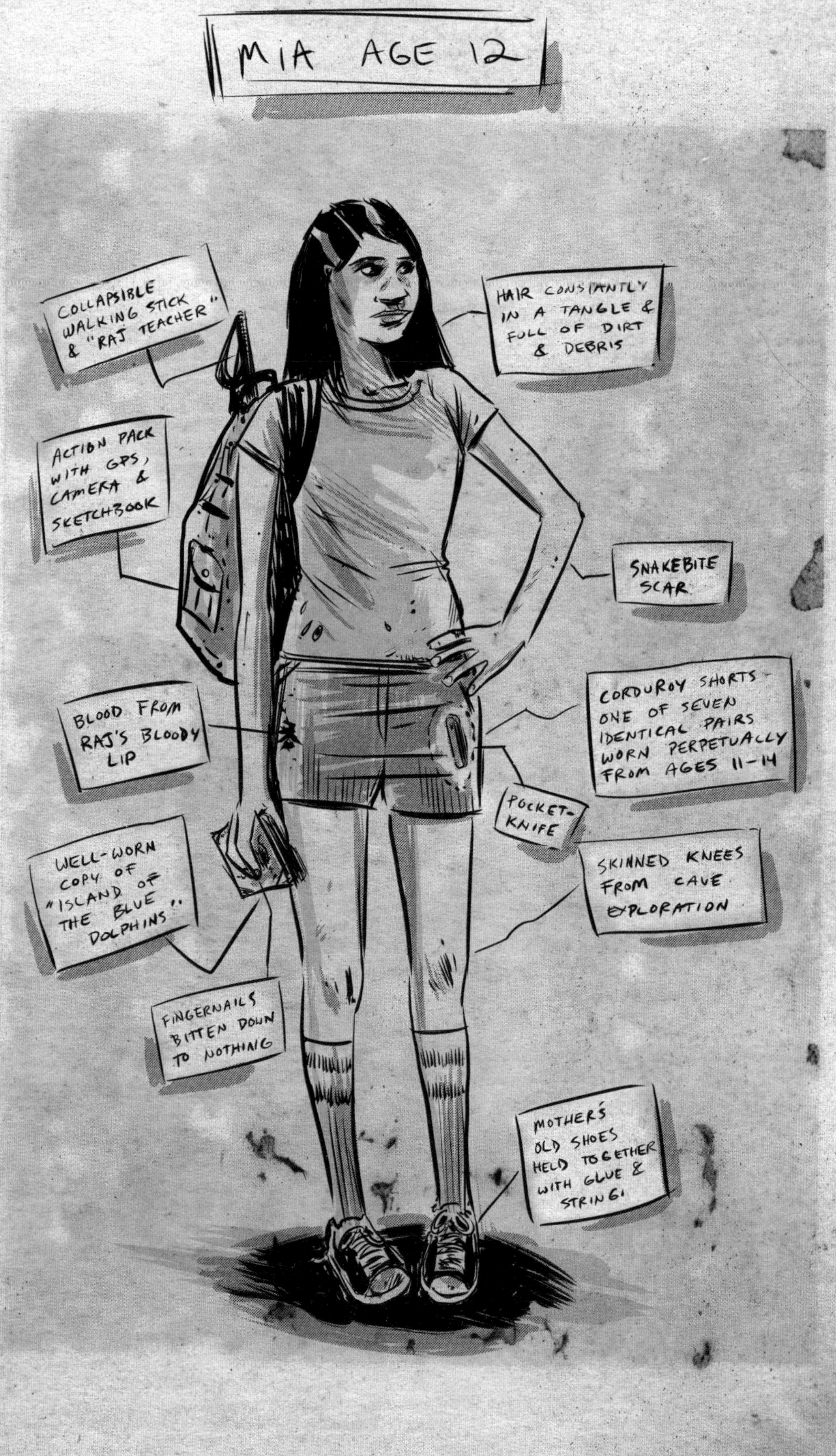
MIA AGE 12
COLLAPSIBLE WALKING STICK & "RAJ TEACHER"
HAIR CONSTANTLY IN A TANGLE & FULL OF DIRT & DEBRIS
ACTION PACK WITH GPS, CAMERA & SKETCHBOOK
SNAKEBITE SCAR
CORDUROY SHORTS - ONE OF SEVEN IDENTICAL PAIRS WORN PERPETUALLY FROM AGES 11-14
BLOOD FROM RAJ'S BLOODY LIP
POCKET-KNIFE
WELL-WORN COPY OF "ISLAND OF THE BLUE DOLPHINS".
SKINNED KNEES FROM CAVE EXPLORATION
FINGERNAILS BITTEN DOWN TO NOTHING
MOTHER'S OLD SHOES HELD TOGETHER WITH GLUE & STRING.

(No Model.)

Diving Apparatus.

No. 236,858.

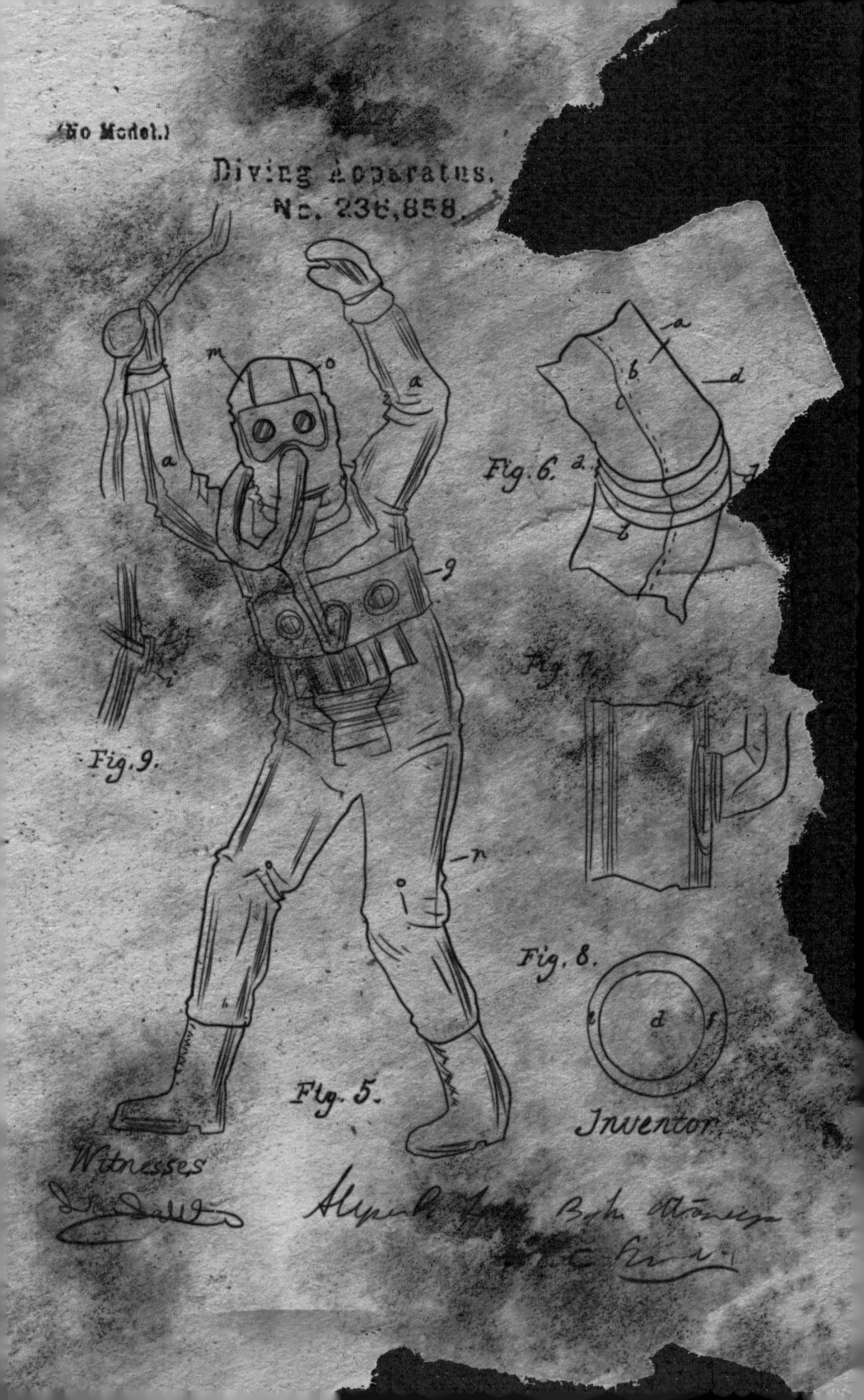

Fig. 5.
Fig. 6.
Fig. 7.
Fig. 8.
Fig. 9.

Witnesses

Inventor

The Activist Philanthropist

Blake Mortimer

Very few people have ever seen your office. I imagine it's pretty immaculate.

On the contrary. My place is a mess. Piles of paper and prototypes everywhere. I will admit to being a little fastidious when it comes to germs. I have airlocks and a decontamination station. For obvious reasons. The H virus that's ravaging our cities won't be the last epidemic of its kind.

For being one of the richest men in the world, you're relatively unknown to most people. Why do you think that is?

I'd be lying if I told you it was unintentional. I believe in living life with focus and purpose. Anything that gets in the way of what I'm trying to do is something I avoid. Fame and the press isn't something I enjoy or seek.

I hope we're not wasting your time.

On the contrary. Sometimes exposure is a necessary evil. I'm trying to raise awareness for our new initiative to not only explore the farthest reaches of space, but to establish a viable living alternative to our current planet.

As a lifelong friend and financier of the adventurer/ explorer Hari Hardy, what caused your split?

I love Hari to death but as we get older, we find that our outlooks on what is important have begun to differ.

In what way?

I won't speak for Hari, but I can say my core belief is that our planet is dying. Our population is obviously becoming unsustainable. With the technology at our disposal, no one should be starving. The H virus should not be ravaging our population. But you can't argue with what you see all around you. Hari views Earth as a ship that just needs repairing. I see it as a life raft heading toward a new frontier of possibilities.

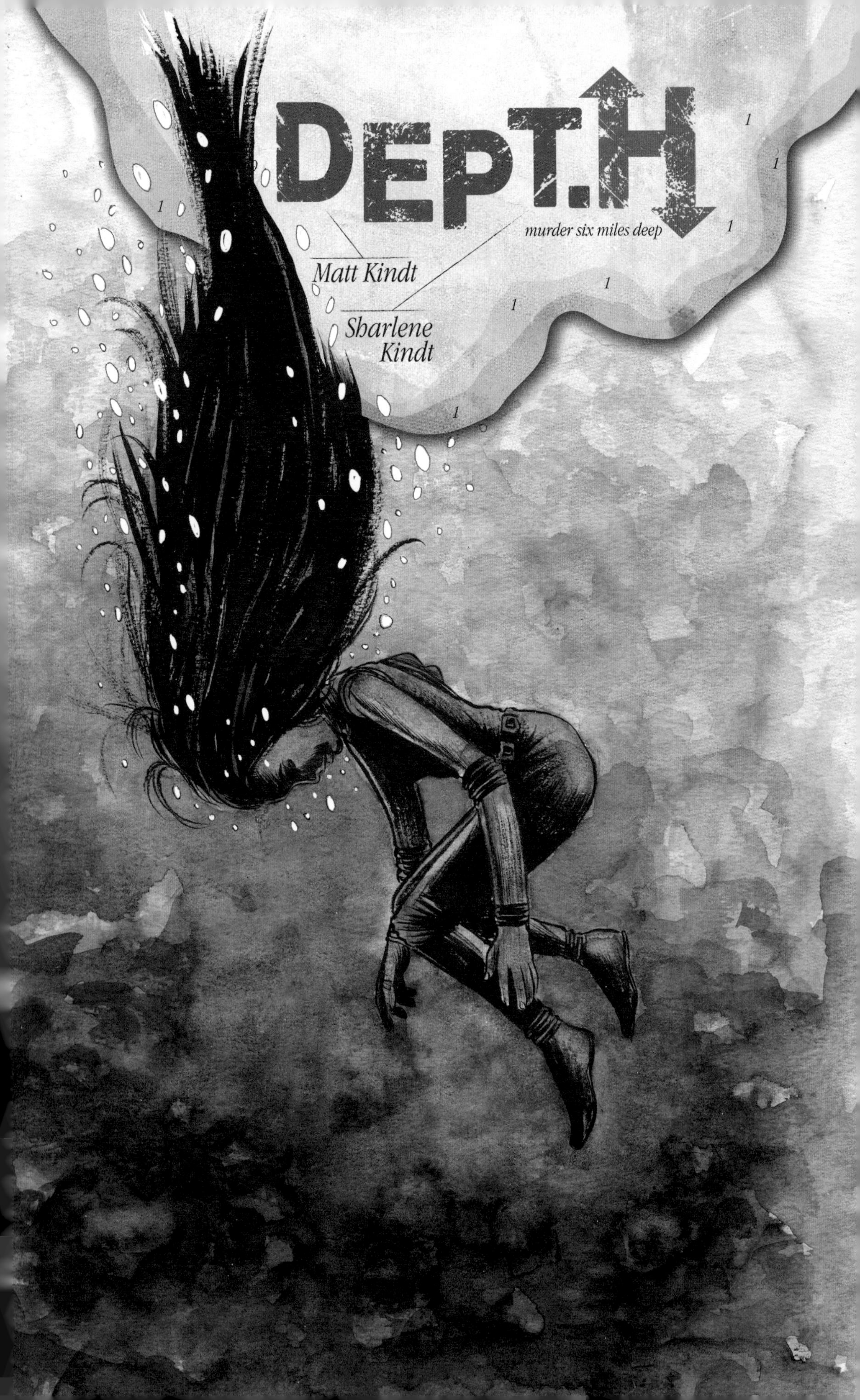
DEPT.H
murder six miles deep
Matt Kindt
Sharlene Kindt

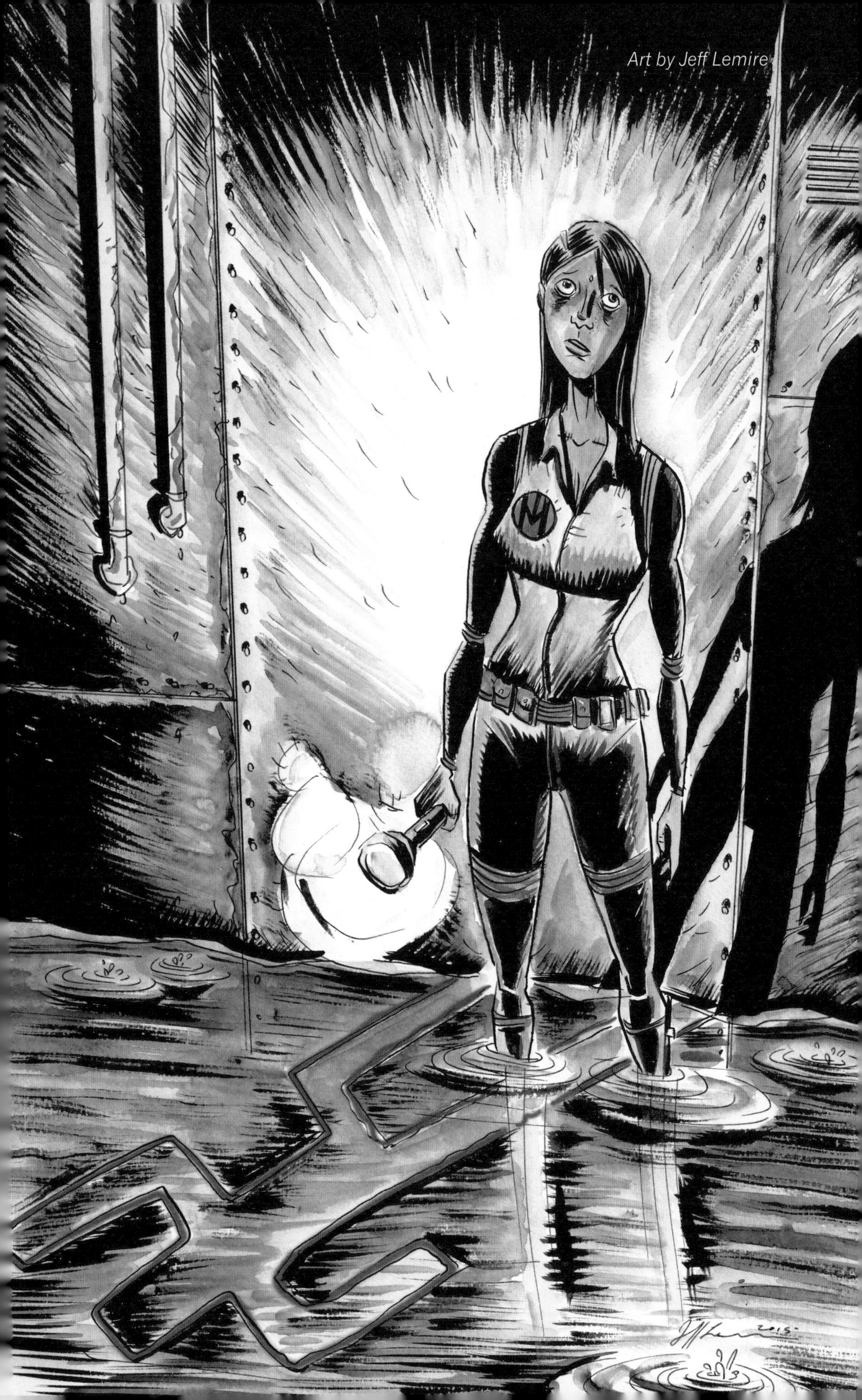

Art by Jeff Lemire

matt kindt

"I'll read anything Kindt does." —Douglas Wolk, author of *Reading Comics*

MIND MGMT
VOLUME 1: THE MANAGER
ISBN 978-1-59582-797-5
$19.99
VOLUME 2: THE FUTURIST
ISBN 978-1-61655-198-8
$19.99
VOLUME 3: THE HOME MAKER
ISBN 978-1-61655-390-6
$19.99
VOLUME 4: THE MAGICIAN
ISBN 978-1-61655-391-3
$19.99
VOLUME 5: THE ERASER
ISBN 978-1-61655-696-9
$19.99
VOLUME 6: THE IMMORTALS
ISBN 978-1-61655-798-0
$19.99

**POPPY! AND THE
LOST LAGOON**
With Brian Hurtt
ISBN 978-1-61655-943-4
$14.99

PAST AWAYS
With Scott Kolins
ISBN 978-1-61655-792-8
$12.99

**THE COMPLETE
PISTOLWHIP**
With Jason Hall
ISBN 978-1-61655-720-1
$27.99

**3 STORY: THE
SECRET HISTORY
OF THE GIANT MAN**
ISBN 978-1-59582-356-4
$19.99

2 SISTERS
ISBN 978-1-61655-721-8
$27.99

**DEPT. H VOLUME 1:
PRESSURE**
ISBN 978-1-61655-989-2
$19.99